Spanish Colonial Silver Coins in the Florida Collection

A FLORIDA HERITAGE PUBLICATION

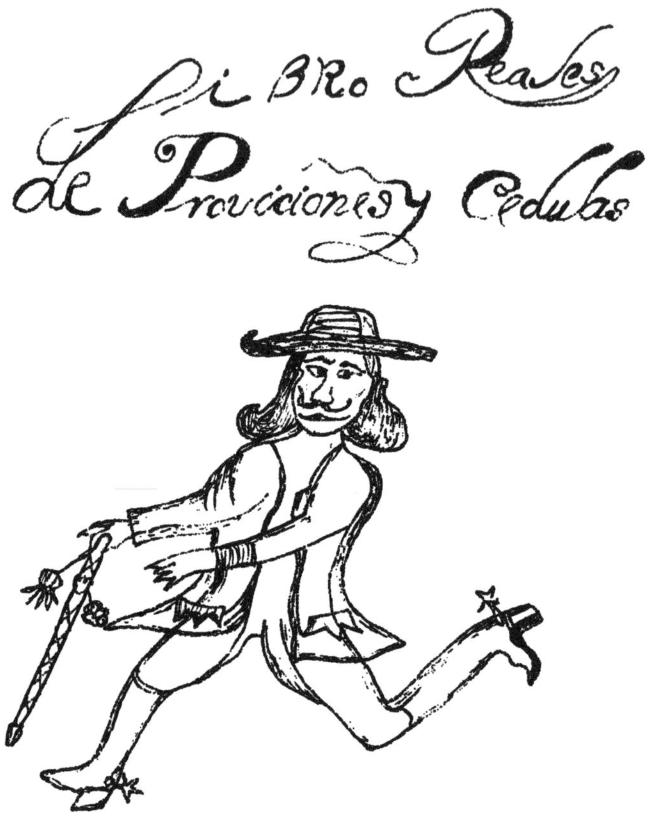

The *Corregidor* of Potosí in 1643. This remarkable graffito, no doubt drawn by a bored bookkeeper, was found inside the front cover of an archival register listing regulations and royal decrees in force at Potosí for the year 1643. The sketch represents a Spanish dandy, probably Blas Robles de Salzedo, the *corregidor* of Potosí, carrying his badge of office in the form of a *vara de mando* (the silver-headed and tasseled wooden staff seen in his right hand). There is a wealth of cultural information in this doodle: we see that influential men in this mining town wore broad-rimmed hats, affected dramatic mustachios, kept their hair shoulder length, dressed in jackets having large cargo pockets, were shod in knee-length spurred boots, and wore extreme stacked heels. The *corregidor's* energetic demeanor suggests he is very confident and no doubt feels he will not be caught by the special investigator sent by the viceroy to ferret out the corruption and counterfeiting rampant at that time in Potosí.

Spanish Colonial Silver Coins in the Florida Collection

Alan K. Craig

Florida Bureau of Archaeological Research
Division of Historical Resources

University Press of Florida
GAINESVILLE · TALLAHASSEE · TAMPA · BOCA RATON
PENSACOLA · ORLANDO · MIAMI · JACKSONVILLE · FT. MYERS

05 04 03 02 01 00 6 5 4 3 2

Library of Congress Cataloging-in-Publication Data
Craig, Alan K.
Spanish colonial silver coins in the Florida Collection
p. cm. — (A Florida heritage publication)
ISBN 0-8130-1748-3 (alk. paper)
1. Coins, Spanish—Florida—History. 2. Silver coins—Florida—History. 3. Florida—History—Spanish colony, 1565–1763. 4. Florida. Division of Historical Resources—Numismatic collection. I. Title. II. Series.
CJ189.C73 2000
737.4946—dc 00-024588

A Florida Heritage Publication

The University Press of Florida is the scholarly publishing agency for the State University System of Florida, comprising Florida A&M University, Florida Atlantic University, Florida Gulf Coast University, Florida International University, Florida State University, University of Central Florida, University of Florida, University of North Florida, University of South Florida, and University of West Florida.

University Press of Florida
15 Northwest 15th Street
Gainesville, FL 32611
http://www.upf.com

Contents

Maps

Illustrations

Figures (coins)

Tables

Foreword

This book on Spanish colonial silver coins is a product of events that began centuries ago. Somewhat by historical and geographic accident, Florida waters became the final resting place of many ships and of many more men engaged in the transport of vast amounts of silver and gold from the New World to Europe. From the time of Columbus through the early nineteenth century, the European crowns, principally of Spain, oversaw a complex system of exploration, conquest, settlement, and exploitation of native people and lands. At the root of the enterprise lay an insatiable desire for precious metals and minerals that could support the expansionist colonial economies of Spain, Portugal, Britain, and a few other countries. So important was the regular infusion of mineral wealth into the royal houses, and thence to the bankers and creditors, that the loss of a treasure shipment, or worse, an entire fleet, reverberated throughout the European economic system.

By the early eighteenth century, the time of the two major fleet losses in Florida waters, most of the value of a treasure shipment was already promised to creditors and mortgagers in Italy and Germany. Spain's attempt to strictly control the fabulous windfall of silver from the mines of Potosí, Bolivia, and of Mexico eventually failed to support either the growth of its own economy or the self-sufficiency of its colonies. By the mid-nineteenth century little remained to show for the vast Spanish treasure system; the part that lay at the bottom of the sea off the Florida coast was forgotten for another one hundred years.

The two major fleet losses in Florida, in 1715 and 1733, both occurred as a result of hurricanes. The earlier tragedy left a string of broken hulls and scattered wreckage along a stretch of the east coast of the Peninsula running roughly 50 miles from Sebastian Inlet to Ft. Pierce Inlet. More than 1,000 people perished and eleven vessels were lost. On board was the accumulated treasure of four annual shipments that had been delayed, amounting to almost seven million pieces of eight. Eighteen years later a larger fleet of four armed galleons, eighteen merchant ships, and a few smaller vessels was wrecked on the treacherous coral reefs of the Florida Keys. This section of the Caribbean shipping routes had been well known to pilots as an area to be avoided, as it is so designated today by the Florida Keys National Marine Sanctuary. In comparison with the 1715 Fleet, the 1733 Fleet contained substantially less silver and gold; being in shallow, calm water, the 1733 Fleet was also easier for Spanish salvage crews to access.

Records in the files of the Division of Historical Resources show that cannons from one of the 1715 ships off Ft. Pierce were salvaged for scrap metal even before 1930. During World War II the war effort encouraged additional salvage of scrap cannon and anchors, but it was not until the late 1950s and early 1960s that the source and true identity of coins and artifacts on the beach began to be realized. The early days of east coast treasure hunting have been the subject of several books recounting personal adventures of salvors (Wagner and Taylor 1967; Burgess 1977), while others have focused more on the archaeological and historical context of the shipwrecks (Clausen 1965; Burgess and Clausen 1982). Treasure hunting in the Keys has been documented by Meylach and Whited (1971) and Weller (1993).

It is interesting to follow the changes in treasure hunting over the last several decades. The early days of the individual and independent treasure hunter are past, as are the easy finds. Treasure-hunting operations now are organized undertakings by modern corporations and occur in the context of government cooperation and control. The law of diminishing returns has had its way with the increasingly expensive search for the finite remains of the treasure fleets. Each year more people try a little harder to recover that which is more difficult to find.

The accumulation of the Florida Collection of silver coins reflects in a dramatic way the statistics of a recovery effort by private salvors lasting some forty years. In the Florida Keys, where the water surrounding the reefs is usually clear and shallow and where remains of ballast-laden wrecks once were visible as great, unnatural piles of stones, the ships of the 1733 Fleet were first identified from the air and on the water in the 1950s. With the aid of documents and maps from the Spanish archives, Art McKee and others found most of the 1733 ships one after the other. Each new discovery that could be correlated with a shipwreck on the eighteenth-century maps revealed a little more about the locations of the remaining undiscovered wrecks. By the late 1960s, most of the wrecks had been thoroughly dug through, and the 1733 Fleet was of little interest to salvors. The coins, which could be sold, were always rarer than the artifacts, which brought in little money to finance the continuing search.

The dramatic recoveries of gold and silver that caused the gold rush of the east coast and led to its name, the Treasure Coast, began in the early 1960s by the Real Eight Company, headed by Kip Wagner. Just like a new mine, the unexplored wrecks yielded hundreds of coins at once on some days and in some locations. In one day, using the newly invented blower, Mel Fisher's crew recovered more than 1,000 gold coins at one location. In the first major divisions of the 1715 recoveries, silver coins were so plentiful that they were accounted for by weight rather than by count. The 25 percent retained by the state of Florida under terms of the very early leases were selected by choosing one of four equal-sized piles of coins. In those days little note was made of individual coins, either numismatically or monetarily. In fact, little numismatic information was available to guide selection of rare or unusual pieces, even if they were considered individually.

Although thousands of coins were owned by the state of Florida, and while considerable effort was expended to inventory and identify the state's gold coins, it was not until the early 1980s that a comprehensive approach to the collection was begun. Frances Keith, then employed by the Division of Historical Resources, began to separate and classify both gold and silver coins, and, more important, to construct a computerized database. The division's files contain many examples of painstaking inventories conducted on paper ledger sheets of coins available for division and coins added to the collection, as well as various partial inventories and analyses. But not until the advent of personal computers some fifteen years ago did the huge task of recording, maintaining, and analyzing the vast amounts of numismatic data available in the collection become feasible. Thus, it was with great interest that I received a proposal around 1985 from Dr. Alan Craig to prepare a complete study of the Florida gold coin collection. Unknown to me at the time, Dr. Craig was a man of many talents especially suited to this undertaking. Professionally, he was a geographer and geologist specializing in Latin American studies and was an avid student of New World Spanish numismatics. For almost fifteen years, Dr. Craig has served as a dedicated and trustworthy expert to the Florida Collection. During that time he published a popular book on the state's holdings in gold coins (Craig 1988; revised 2nd ed. 2000 by University Press of Florida), has advised on many coins available to the state for division, and recently completed the comprehensive documentation and analysis of the silver coin collection, which is the basis for this book.

When the database of gold coins was completed, it became possible to make informed decisions about what coins available for division would make a numismatic contribution to the collection. Since then, it has been our policy to represent each example of mint, denomination, assayer, and significant numismatic variation by several specimens. At the same time that we could be selective about what we wanted, we could also feel confident in not selecting the many coins potentially available to us that were already well represented in the collection. As a result, the gold coin collection has become more focused and more encompassing as more of the gaps in series are gradually filled in. For salvors whose material was being divided, this new knowledge ensured that coins not important for the collection would be divided among them instead of the state. Finally, under this arrangement, it was possible to enhance the state's selection of nonnumismatic material as well.

Once the gold coin collection was cataloged, studied, and published, we turned our attention to the vastly larger silver coin collection. Over the years since the bulk of the collection accumulated in the 1960s, a few attempts had been undertaken to inventory and manage the collection in a modern fashion, but its sheer size made this difficult at best. Bear in mind that the collection was assembled at a time when salvaged coins were inventoried and divided by the pound instead of the coin. It was common knowledge that there would be many duplicates in the collection, but the actual task of inventorying, cataloging, recording, and analyzing the numismatic data available for silver coins was not approached until it was clear that the job would be competently done and completed within a reasonable time.

Once again the Division of Historical Resources contracted with Dr. Craig to undertake the documentation and presentation of the whole collection, and once again the Florida Bureau of Archaeological Research staff provided considerable support. For this project, each coin was individually recorded and assigned a unique catalog number in the computer database. The analysis and resulting tables and totals in this book represent the Florida Collection as it existed in 1997. Of course, the collection continues to change, and specimens acquired after that date will be reported in future publications. Interesting coins were photographed by the hundreds, and all coins throughout this book are enlarged 150 percent for greater visability. Many months were devoted to compiling descriptive statistics of the many varieties and types of coins represented in the Florida Collection. Preparation of a manuscript catalog involved further refinement of the analysis, as well as construction of dozens of analytical tables by computer. Literally thousands of person-hours were necessary to bring our level of understanding of the silver coin collection up to modern standards.

Knowledge of the collection affects the way that a division of salvaged material is approached. With no effective understanding of what was already in the Florida Collection, the Florida Bureau of Archaeological Research did not select silver coins available for division from those sites that had already contributed thousands of coins to the collection. As a result, very few silver coins have been added to the collection from the 1715 Fleet recoveries since 1983. However, salvage of wrecks previously unrepresented in the collection, especially the Jupiter Wreck and a wreck of the 1810 period, has resulted in the informed selection of scores of new coins. The most numismatically important specimens are transitional dates from the Potosí mints, not well represented in any collection, and the rare Lima Star coins of 1659. Finally, now that cataloging of silver coins is complete, we can select specific silver coins available through divisions that will fill gaps in the collection as it now stands.

It is a pleasure to be able to recognize the salvors who recovered the silver coins that make up the Florida Collection. By far the greatest number of coins was collected under Lease 1329, held for many years by the Real Eight Company. Between 1964 and 1974 Real Eight made substantial recoveries from all of the known 1715 wrecks as well as the 1618 site now known as San Martín, but the nature of the records kept during this early period make it impossible to determine which coins came from which wreck. More than 95 percent of the silver coins in the Florida Collection, some 21,962 coins, were recovered by the Real Eight Company before 1974. Also in this early period of leases, some fifty coins were obtained from Armada Research Inc., under the terms of Lease A6/2044.

Following the reorganization of the state's salvage program in 1975, new contract numbers began to be assigned, designated with an initial "S" for salvage and "E" for exploration. Between 1975 and 1982, ten separate salvage contracts resulted in a little more than five hundred coins being added to the collection. Only four of these contracts added more than five coins to the collection; Peninsular Exploration and Salvage Corporation under Contract S-21 contributed just over two hundred fifty coins, while S-11, Undersea Mining, and S-15, the Real Eight Company, added nearly one hundred coins each. The other six contracts of this period added a total of fourteen coins (S-1, American Power Spraying, two coins; S-6, Marine-Tech Salvage Inc., two coins; S-8, Armada Research Inc., five coins; S-14, Peninsular Exploration and Salvage Corp., one coin; S-20, Doubloon Salvage, three coins; and S-22, Rex Stocker, one coin). By 1982 the principal holdings in silver had been well established, accounting for 98 percent of the silver shipwreck coins now in the Florida Collection.

In 1983 the state of Florida entered into an out-of-court settlement agreement that resolved a three-year dispute in federal court over ownership and jurisdiction of shipwreck sites on state-owned sovereignty submerged lands. The salvage program, which had been discontinued for lack of clear state jurisdiction, was begun again. Since that time the principal salvage activity in Florida waters has been conducted by Cobb Coin Company Inc., now reorganized as Salvors Inc. In this most recent period of the evolving salvage program, the federal admiralty court granted custodianship and title to Salvors Inc. for all of the 1715 sites and the 1618 site. As specified in the out-of-court settlement agreement, Salvors Inc. and the state of Florida entered into salvage contracts for these sites; under the terms of the contracts and the agreement, the state receives a representative one-fifth cross section of each shipwreck site. Under six separate salvage contracts (S-23, S-25, S-26, S-27 [a three-party contract with Circle Bar Salvage Inc.], S-32 [originally held by The Quest, An Exploration Corporation], and S-36 [Salvors Inc.], recoveries resulted in the addition of eighty-nine silver coins from the 1618 and 1715 sites. Although more than 35,000 silver coins were recovered under these contracts, it was not possible to know which would be unrepresented in the Florida Collection, and very few were chosen. Many of these recoveries were made by subcontractors to Salvors Inc.

Since 1990 two sites have produced coins not previously represented in the collection. These are a 1659 ship known as the Jupiter Wreck being recovered by Jupiter Wreck Inc. and an unidentified 1810 wreck called the Holden Wreck, salvaged under Contract S-36 with Salvors Inc. These two salvage operations contributed approximately 200 and 100 coins, respectively, to the Florida Collection. Also during the period 1983 to the present, several other companies and individuals recovered silver coins that were added to the collection. These were Quest Exploration Corp. (Contract S-19, one coin), Frank Allen (Contract S-24, two coins), Island Treasures Inc. (Contract S-28, seven coins), and Old World Treasure Quest Inc. (beach finds, thirteen coins).

The accumulation and care of the Florida Collection of silver coins have involved scores of people over many decades. Some rough calculations suggest that more than 125,000 silver coins have been recovered and made available for division between the state and salvors in the past thirty-five years. More than 175 separate leases, exploration contracts, salvage contracts, and agreements have granted permission to companies and individuals to search for and, more rarely, to recover material from historic shipwreck sites in Florida waters. Some fifty admiralty cases filed in federal courts prior to the passage of the Abandoned Shipwreck Act provided additional federal jurisdiction over salvage activities. Hundreds of individuals have played some role in recovering the coins that make up the Florida Collection.

In an effort so long lasting and so complex, it has not always been possible to collect and maintain records that meet modern expectations of accuracy, reliability, and completeness. In the past fifteen years we have organized and reviewed many file cabinets of old salvage records and accumulated many more file cabinets of new records. Now, with the aid of computers, management of such large data sets is easier and more reliable than in the past, and the quality of data is better. There is much opportunity for error in using old records and making assumptions about incomplete data.

Given this risk, we have been conservative in using data only to the extent warranted and have avoided making what would seem to be safe assumptions about the source of coins as to shipwreck site or year when this is not clearly recorded. For the most part, the information that makes up the catalog of silver coins has been recovered from coins themselves, rather than from records about the recovery of the coins. Over the years, considerable effort has been expended by the Division of Historical Resources to manage the various contracts, to select from the material available for division, to maintain records on the state's collections, to conserve coins so they will not deteriorate, and to analyze the numismatic data that are presented in this catalog. The state's salvage program is always subject to criticism by salvors who believe controls are too stringent and the share that the state retains too large, and by archaeologists and preservationists who believe controls are too lax and artifacts should remain in public ownership.

Finally, it is a privilege to acknowledge the employees of the Research and Conservation Laboratory of the Division of Historical Resources who have worked diligently to establish and care for the Florida Collection and to increase public knowledge of its wonderful contents, especially Dr. David Dickel, James Levy, Roy Lett, Frank Gilson, and Michelene Lucas.

James J. Miller, Ph.D.
State Archaeologist
Chief of Archaeological Research

Preface

Interest in my earlier book on Spanish gold coins of the Florida Collection (Craig 1988) proved to be greater than anyone anticipated. This encouraged the Florida Bureau of Archaeological Research to commission the writing of a second volume dealing with the much larger number of silver coins comprising the bulk of the Florida Collection. I feel privileged to have been asked to prepare a detailed analysis and assess the historical significance of these many thousands of artifacts, most of them salvaged from shipwrecks in Florida's territorial waters.

At the time this project was conceived, neither the bureau nor I fully understood the enormous extent of the state's holdings in silver. Unlike the meticulously recorded gold coins, thousands of unclassified silver coins were formerly accepted, sometimes in large clusters, by the state as part of its legal 25 percent (before 1981) and later, 20 percent division of all salvaged artifacts. The vast majority of these coins, more than 95 percent, were received by the state before 1975 in the early period of the 1715 Fleet recoveries. Many of these coins, stored in canvas bank bags, were often covered with sand, sea growth, and the chemical products of corrosion from their long submergence in saltwater. Many important numismatic details of these coins could not be seen until they had been treated by electrolysis and carefully cleaned.

The task seemed straightforward: examine the coins for their numismatic significance, describe for the owners (in other words, the citizens of the state of Florida) what was there and why it was important, and, finally, prepare a scholarly description that also could be enjoyed by the nonspecialist. This last requirement is the basis for the considerable background information offered in this book on the culture and political economy of Spain's New World empire. The Florida Collection represents a unique and historically significant body of evidence about New World colonialism by European powers. Its study is of more than numismatic significance alone.

The first requirement, to examine the coins, was physically exhausting; everyone knows there are "two sides to a coin." So, to make a thorough numismatic study of the roughly 23,000 silver coins stored in bags, boxes, cases, trays, and sacks, each one was handed to me inside the security vault in the presence of a capitol security guard. Each coin was assigned a unique catalog or accession number, and relevant data were entered into a computer file. This was done by Dr. David Dickel, Conservation Laboratory supervisor and curator of the collection. My identification and comments were recorded, and certain specimens were selected for photography and inclusion in this book. Therefore, we were committed to more than 45,000 observations on which to base the descriptive statistics. To complicate matters, several thousand newly recovered coins were examined in Tallahassee for division purposes while this study was in progress. Fortunately from a work standpoint, only a few of these new coins were added to the Florida Collection.

On a typical day, working five to six hours, we were able to process about 750 coins until hunger, eyestrain, or other imperatives required a shuffling of personnel within the vault (obviously, no one is allowed to remain there alone—not even the guards). At the close of each day, we all left together following a strict sign-out ritual.

Although most coins examined turned out to be of Mexican origin, I emphasize the famous Bolivian mining town of Potosí because of my lifelong interest in this subject. I have researched the mint located there using data I found in the archives at Sevilla, Madrid, Potosí, Sucre, La Paz, Santiago, and Arequipa. My own recent research (Craig and West 1994, Craig and Simmons 1995) and that of others (Bakewell 1975, 1984, 1988; Brown 1986) make it clear that silver deposits extracted from Potosí's Cerro Rico over the past 450 years have made this mountain the single most prolific silver producer on earth.

Indeed, the same can be said for Potosí's coinage in terms of production figures, even though the Florida Collection is largely composed of Mexican 8-reales coins. This preponderance of Mexican coins is a result of large amounts of treasure salvaged from the 1715 Plate Fleet, which received a cargo of several million silver coins at Vera Cruz, Mexico. Of course future wrecks may radically change this distribution; the Florida Collection is not static. It is quite possible the collection will receive additional specimens of considerable numismatic importance. With luck, some of these future additions will fill in gaps we now see in the collection's framework outlined in this study.

I am indebted to the following individuals who have contributed in various ways to this book. Of course they are not to be blamed for any errors or lapses that may have occurred; these remain entirely my responsibility. Thanks, then, are due: Hans Eric Carlsson, Lyn Chin, William Collins, James Dunbar, Dan Dombrosky, Frank Gilson, Julius Grigore, Jr., Harold Holden, Gene Hynds, Jonathan Lammers, Chip Kreis, James Levy, Peter Leo, Eugene Lyon, Edgar Balta Martínez, Lawrie Nester, Mable Revell, Ernie Richards, Dave Simmons, Jack Aiken Soux, Kenneth Springer, Gene Turner, Robert Weller, and especially Kendall W. Brown, David Dickel, and James J. Miller.

Alan K. Craig, Ph.D.
A.N.A. 10211
Boca Raton
September 1999

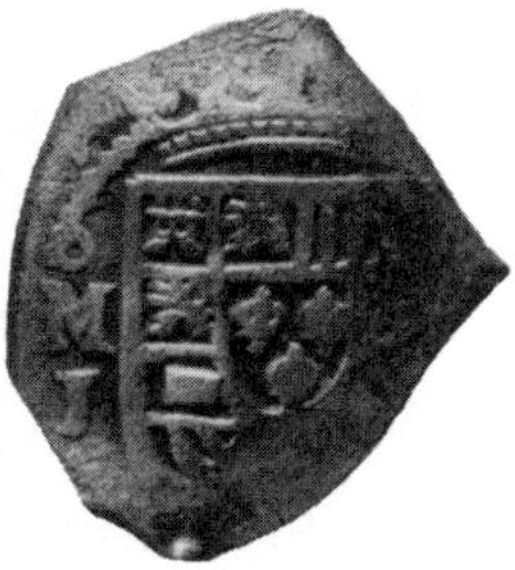

PART I

Spanish Colonial Political Economy

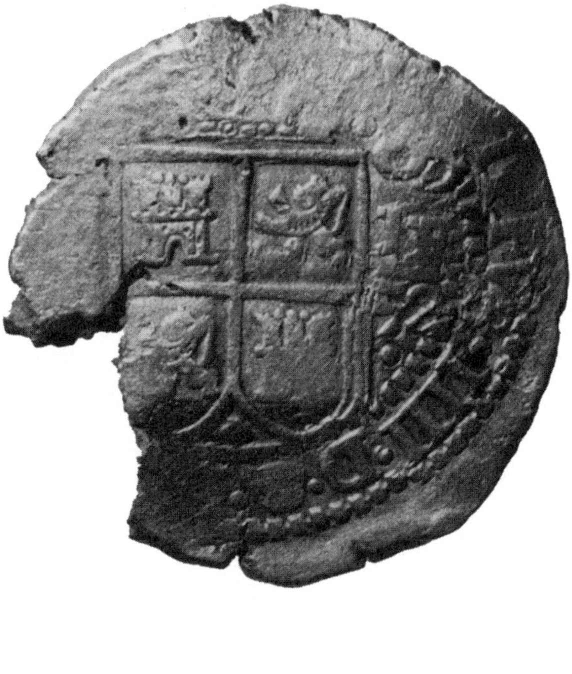

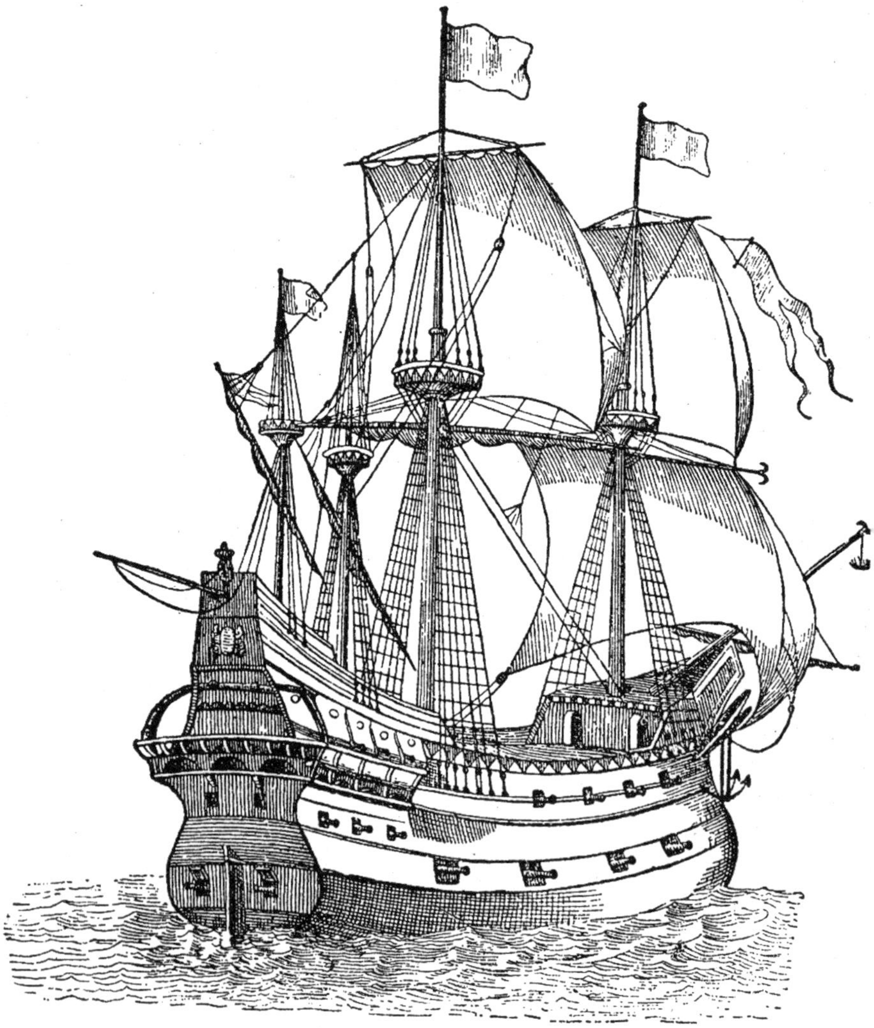

Illus. 1.1. A small Spanish galleon, lightly armed but designed for carrying cargo in the transatlantic trade.

CHAPTER I

Introduction and Historical Background

The Florida Collection of artifacts recovered from shipwrecks inside territorial waters reflects many interesting aspects of Spanish colonial political economy. This book focuses on Spanish silver coins of the collection, emphasizing details that are not necessarily self-evident. We can say with assurance this remarkable collection is unique, both in the United States and in the world, because it consists almost entirely of specimens salvaged from sunken Spanish wrecks found inside the boundaries of Florida territorial waters. These limits were established in 1821 when the Territory of Florida was acquired from Spain. The result is an unusual arrangement: the east coast boundary extends seaward three nautical miles, while the west coast of the Peninsula has a boundary set at three Spanish leagues.

Just where the east coast of Florida ends and the west coast begins and from where these measurements start might seem only matters of academic interest. But in fact they have been exceedingly difficult to determine and critical in terms of what is (and is not) represented in the Florida Collection. Spanish galleons often sailed across from Vera Cruz in Mexico to Havana, Cuba, and several sunken treasure ships have been located in the Gulf of Mexico in recent years. However, none so far has been found inside the territorial limits of Florida's west coast, which would require salvaged artifacts to be divided with the state.

As a consequence, no longer are there any coins from the famous *Atocha* site held by the state in Tallahassee.[1] Representation of important numismatic specimens known to have been salvaged from wrecks of the 1733 Fleet in the Florida Keys is another disappointment in terms of additions to the collection, because many of these wrecks were situated beyond Florida's boundary to the south.[2]

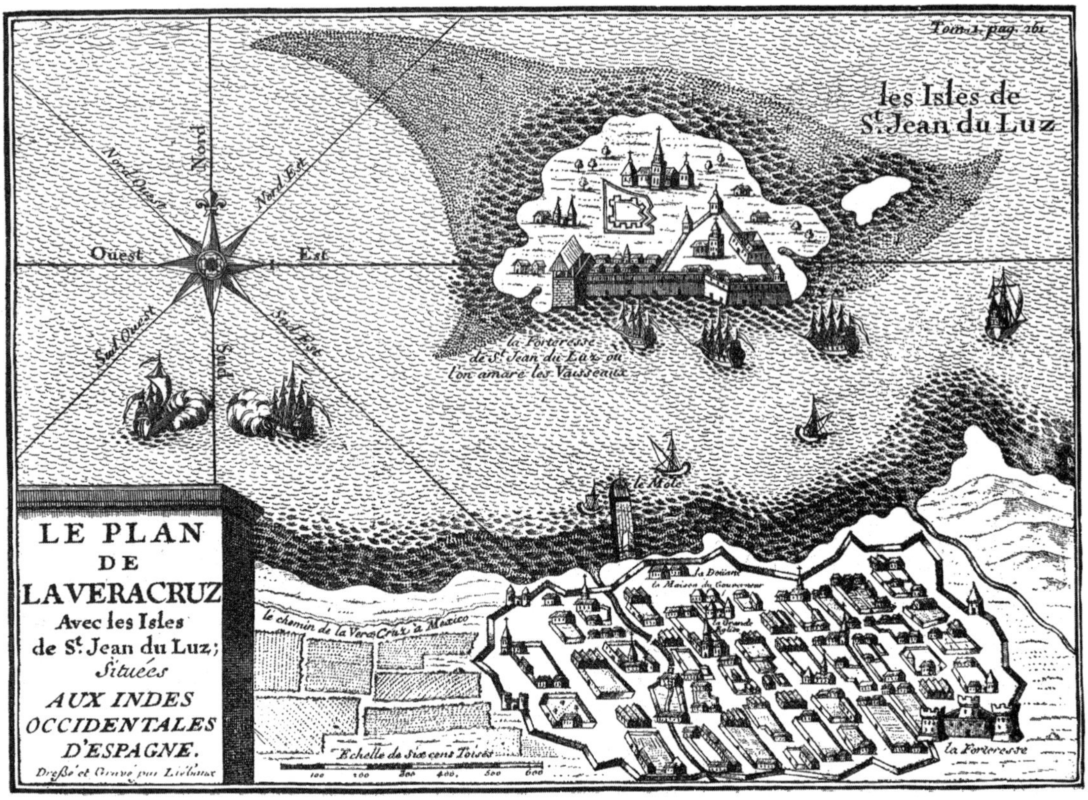

Map 1.1. Plan of Vera Cruz (1744).

On the other hand, the Florida Collection has impressive holdings in some 25,000 Spanish silver and gold coins presently in a computerized collection inventory. More than 95 percent are specimens recovered from the remains of eleven ships driven aground along a 35-mile stretch of the southeastern coast during the infamous hurricane of 1715. The remainder of the collection comes from Spanish shipwrecks of other years, also known to have been sunk by severe storms and hurricanes.

The east coast origin of shipwreck coins is not difficult to understand when we consider relationships existing between sailing ports, the Florida Peninsula, and a north-flowing Gulf Stream. It was this powerful oceanic current sweeping through the Straits of Florida and hugging the east coast that acted like a giant slingshot, propelling the otherwise slow-moving galleons northward along the Florida coast toward South Carolina, then across the northern Atlantic to Cádiz in Spain. Even in calm weather this great river of tropical water at times swings within a mile of Florida beaches. Ships sailing along the east coast were often blown ashore by the fiercest hurricane winds, those of the northeast quadrant.

Obviously there were many accidents that could befall treasure shipments. Land robbers, sea pirates, and hurricanes took a heavy toll. Most of the silver coins and associated artifacts in the Florida Collection came from shipwrecks caused by the hurricanes of 1715 and 1733, in which together more than a thousand sailors lost their lives. Another hurricane or severe storm in late 1659 or early 1660 was probably responsible for the wreck of a Spanish ship at Jupiter Inlet. It contained important numismatic specimens from Cartagena, Santa Fé de Bogotá, and the new designs produced in Lima and transitional coins from Potosí resulting from reforms of 1652.

No doubt there are other Spanish ships sunk off the Florida coasts whose cargoes of crudely made silver and gold cob coins never made the long trip up the Guadalquivir River of Spain to the customs dock at Sevilla. And it remains to be seen if the Florida Collection will someday have a representative assortment of the well-known Spanish-milled portrait dollars for public display and scholarly study.

To explain why so many gold and silver coins were being shipped in the first place is a more complicated matter. We need to consider briefly some early events in the discovery of the New World and the effect they had on the political economy of Spain.[3]

We remember Columbus promised King Ferdinand and Queen Isabella of Spain great riches if they would fund his explorations to seek

Map 1.2. Ports and sailing routes of the Spanish treasure fleets.

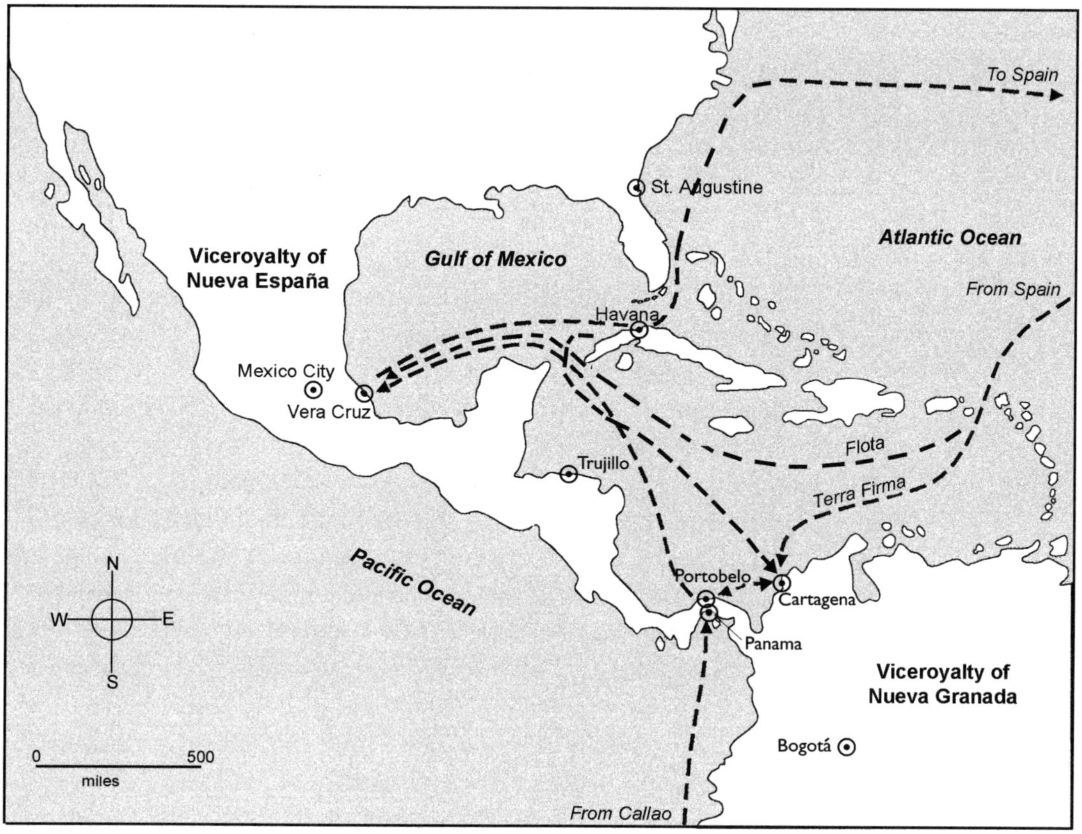

a new route to the Far East. Indeed, on his first voyage he discovered gold in streams flowing down to the north coast of Hispaniola.[4] This precipitated a mad rush to explore the Caribbean and shortly thereafter the mainland of Central and South America, seeking out sources of gold and silver worn by Indians as ornaments.

The first large trove sent back to Spain came from Mexico, where Hernán Cortéz and his lieutenants had seized the accumulated treasures of the Tarascan chiefs. Even at this early date (ca. 1522) not all loot arrived safely at the Torre de Oro customs house in Sevilla; at least one ship barely made it past Florida before it sank.[5]

Even greater amounts of specie began to flow back to Spain after the conquests of other parts of the Americas, particularly Colombia and Peru, where Giménez de Quesada and Francisco Pizarro plundered and laid to waste the high civilizations of the Andes.

After 1532 there was an astonishing flood of precious metals, gems, and pearls sent back by conquistadors, pioneer entrepreneurs, and official tax collectors of the treasury. These latter men were charged with the responsibility of collecting a series of taxes imposed by the king, who graciously allowed his vassals in the New World to risk their lives in search of mineral wealth, all of which legally belonged to him alone.

As tax monies from Mexico began to swell the king's coffers, they excited his expansionist plans and related religious ambitions. Charles V now could strengthen the Church and suppress heretical tendencies. The year 1545 is pivotal; it marks the discovery of the world's richest silver deposits at Potosí in the viceroyalty of Peru. There on the slopes of Cerro Rico more than 5,000 mining claims were staked in the next three years. By the time the king died in 1556, an avalanche of silver was pouring out of Spain's New World empire into the Royal Treasury.

The king's son who inherited the throne was none other than Felipe II, the epitome of conservatism and a religious fanatic. Ultimately, he used New World silver to pay mercenary soldiers to fight his battles in northern Europe and to build the Great Armada. His attempt to invade England and the loss of this fleet in 1588 virtually bankrupted the treasury and threw his country into economic chaos.

Felipe II and his son Felipe III, together with their successors, continued to mortgage royal estates to private bankers, using the anticipated arrival of more American treasure as collateral. With a series of such loans, they launched wars and embroiled themselves in various ill-fated European adventures. These decisions were made on the assumption that sooner or later the treasure fleets would arrive. When a ship laden with precious metals did not arrive, either through storm or piracy, impact on the Spanish economy was immediate and severe. However, so many did manage the trip safely over the years that the cumulative

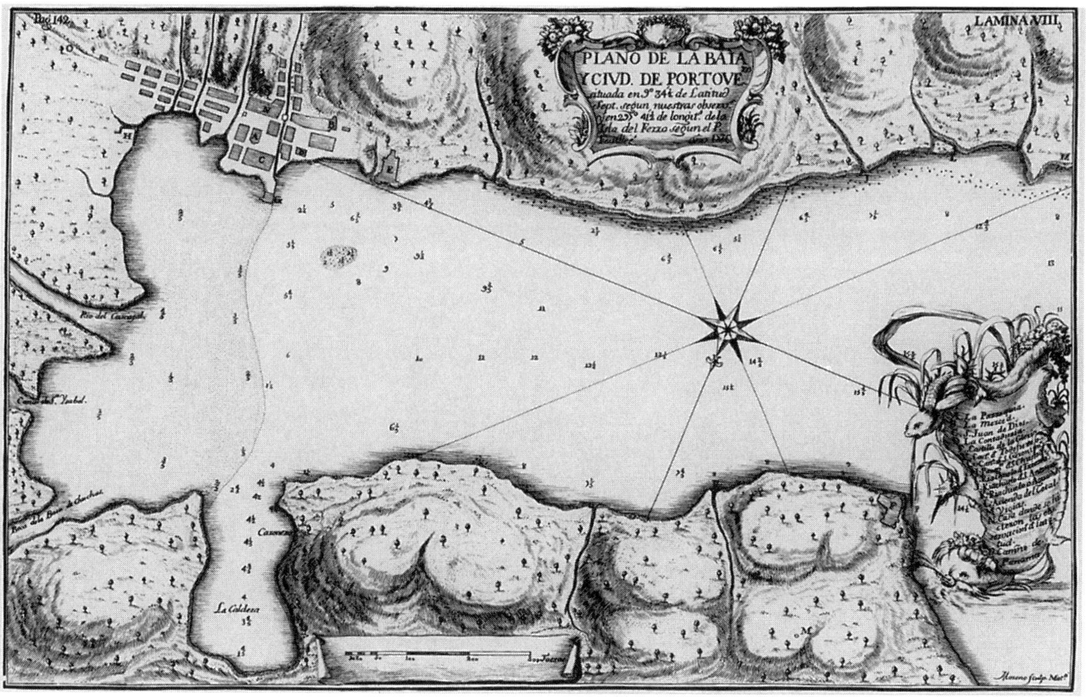

Map 1.3. "Plan of the Bay and City of Porto Bello," 1736.

influx of New World silver destabilized many European economies, causing widespread inflation and abrupt rises in commodity prices, especially in Spain.[6]

Safe land routes for transportation of treasure were just as essential for its successful delivery to Spain as were carefully chosen sea routes. From the mid-1530s onward, Mexican coins were easily moved "downhill" from the mint at what is now Mexico City to the adjacent port of Vera Cruz with only modest precautions being taken along the way. The entire trip by mules could be accomplished in ten days or less, and there were no great costs involved. Much the same can be said for the trickle of gold and silver minted at Santa Fé de Bogotá, although this pathway required a more laborious trip out of the mountains and downstream on the Magdalena River to the port of Cartagena. While a few misadventures may be recorded for these two routes, at least they were free of pirate raids that plagued Panama and the Peruvian coast.

Potosí and Lima were an entirely different matter. To begin with, we should remember all mining activities at Potosí were shut down for the four winter months of June through September, when water supply for hydraulic stamp mills was frozen and ore could not be processed. Therefore, mint operations were scheduled to begin with a flurry of activity in spring (September–November), culminating in the year's-end dispatch of accumulated coins and ingots down to the port of Arica in what is now northernmost Chile.

Illus. 1.2. View of the port of Callao (1620) serving Lima. This artist's conception of the period bears little resemblance to the actual surroundings.

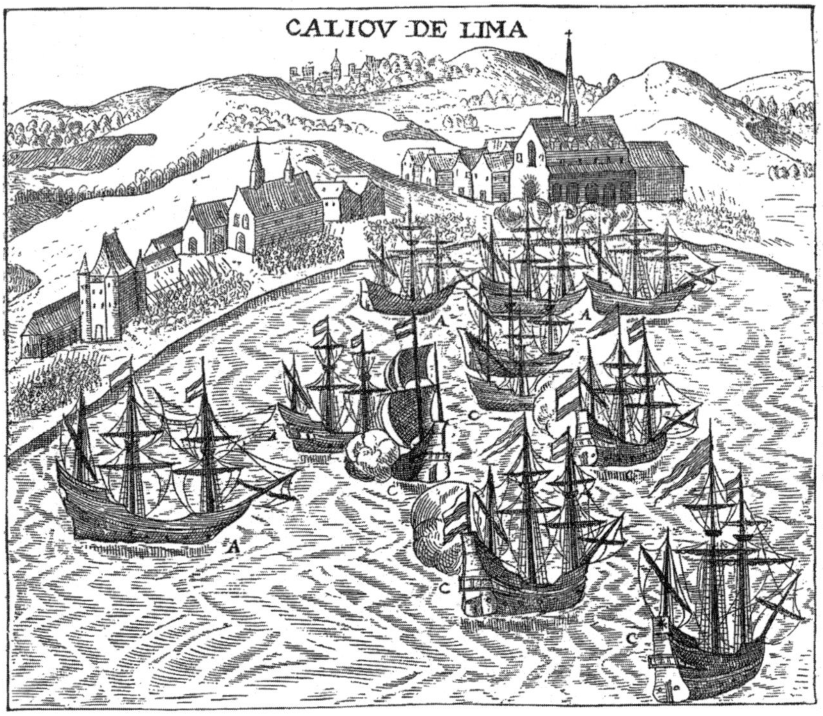

This trip, which seems such a short map distance, could not be made in less than two months across the more than 200 leagues (more than 500 miles) involved. The animals used were llamas, more adaptable than mules to crossing the extreme high-altitude wasteland of the Lípes district. But there were neither fortifications at Arica nor even a real harbor; valuables were rafted out to small coastal sailing ships anchored beyond the surf and heavy swells. These precarious arrangements allowed shipments to reach Lima's port of Callao promptly compared with the arduous overland route requiring four months through the Andes. However, it did not take long for foreign pirates to enter the southeastern Pacific and to sniff out and plunder this undefended transfer by sea.[7]

Consequently the Arica–Callao leg eventually was abandoned and everything began to come down the "silver road" between Potosí and Lima even though transportation costs for king and commoners alike were much higher. Armed galleons, alone or in small convoys, carried treasure northward to Panama where it was unloaded and carried across the Isthmus by mules to the Caribbean side at Portobelo.

The Portobelo Trade Fair

One of the most unusual commercial arrangements to evolve in Spanish America was located on the north coast of Panama at a well-protected anchorage known as Portobelo (map 1.3). Here Spanish galleons arrived laden with cargoes of European luxuries, Spanish wines, and foodstuffs, in addition to every kind of clothing, hardware, houseware, and firearms, to mention some of the more common items. These goods were landed from ships anchored close inshore under protection of forts (G and E in map 1.4). Numerous sailcloth pavilions were erected in the plaza behind the customhouse to protect newly arrived merchandise from tropical showers. These tents also offered some shade for merchants who impatiently awaited the arrival of treasure-laden mule trains sent across the Isthmus from Panama City when there was news the fleet had arrived.[8]

Over the years, these humble mules carried hundreds of millions of pesos in heavy silver ingots and pieces of eight (Walton 1994: 221), specie that Lima merchants sent to pay for items to replenish their stores.[9] In addition, very large amounts of specie belonging to the king of Spain were often delivered to Portobelo for transshipment by a plate fleet on its way back to Spain. Other large amounts of cash were dispatched from all over South America to be sent back to business partners, relatives, or religious orders in Spain. At the time it was the safest

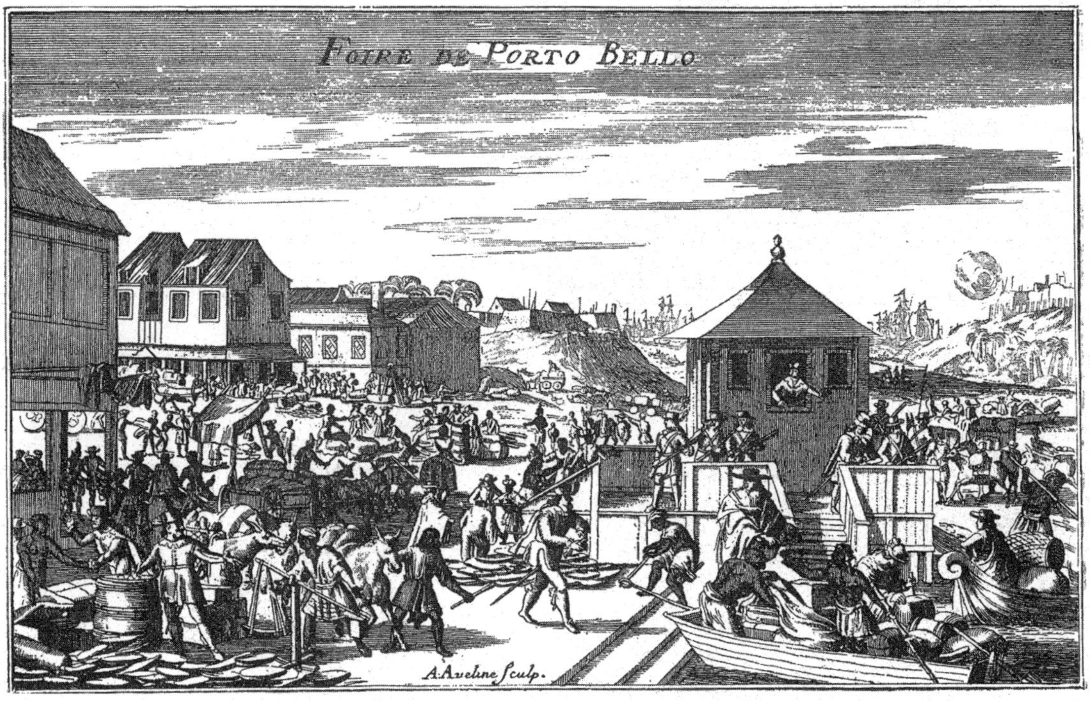

Illus. 1.3. This scene of the Porto Bello (Portobelo) Fair is an accurate and realistic rendition of the activities that took place there, including European goods being sold for gold and silver from the South American mints.

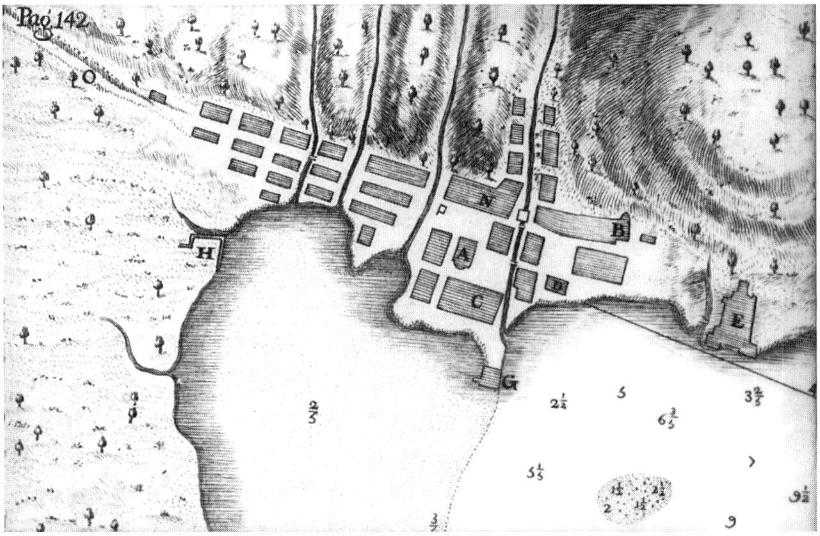

Map 1.4. Close-up of portion of "Plan of the Bay and City of Porto Bello," 1736.

and fastest but not always a reliable means. Any losses by misadventure of the king's tax monies were traditionally reimbursed by the fleet owners, but commoners took their chances.

Gleaming piles of heavy silver ingots, many worth thousands of pesos each, were casually stacked on the ground while waiting for sales to be consummated. Ingots and sacks of coins in payment of the king's *quinto* (20 percent excise) tax were carefully packed six ingots to a custom-made heavy wooden case painted, as always for the Royal Treasury, a bright red. More care must have been taken of the strong linen bags of newly minted silver coins that could easily be stolen if left unguarded. These too were placed on board galleons in wooden chests of various sizes. Whoever the owner, and whatever the amount, the fleet's silvermaster was obliged to count and register this specie and mark ingots with his own initial.[10]

In fact everything had been counted and registered when first placed on board at Arica or Callao, counted again when offloaded in Panama, counted once more when turned over to muleteers, and counted yet again on arrival at Portobelo. In spite of these official attempts at control, we know considerable amounts of untaxed silver and gold, plus other valuables, were constantly being smuggled through the fair system and sent back to Spain. Although some researchers believe the clandestine quantity equaled or exceeded what was properly registered, no case has been reported in which Royal Treasury funds were stolen or lost in transit between checkpoints.

Since many coins struck in the viceroyalty of Peru became debased and suspect after 1630, they were seldom received willingly by Mexican business firms. Therefore, it is probably accurate to say virtually all Lima and Potosí cobs now in the Florida Collection were once carried down a trail that enters the village of Portobelo (O), shown in the extreme upper-left-hand corner of map 1.4. By the same reasoning we can say few, if any, Mexican coins ever came down this mule trail. The Florida Collection's numerous gold coins from the mint at Santa Fé de Bogotá, and the very few silver cobs struck at Bogotá and Cartagena, also never made this transisthmian trip. Instead, they were loaded on board at Cartagena before (or in a few cases, after) the fleet arrived at Portobelo.[11]

There were many ways in which a shipment of silver could be delayed within this system. When large amounts were expected, but did not appear, ships were made to wait late into the summer hurricane season, sometimes with terrible results. Added to risks of nature, chronic wars between Spain and its neighbors might cause years to go by with no heavily armed guard galleons available for dispatch to the Americas.

By 1740 the importance of the trade fair at Portobelo had virtually ended. Ship design was vastly improved and navigation around Cape Horn was increasing, eliminating the need for cumbersome transshipment across the Isthmus of Panama and speeding up correspondence and deliveries to the west coast of South America.[12]

The vicissitudes of transporting treasure and its slow passage through the Portobelo trade fair were factors Spanish authorities could not control. Instead they exercised their talents for bureaucratic administration by tightly regulating every aspect of colonial mint operations. The authority to do so came down to them in a series of royal proclamations, some signed with a full-page flourish: "*YO . . . El Rey.*"

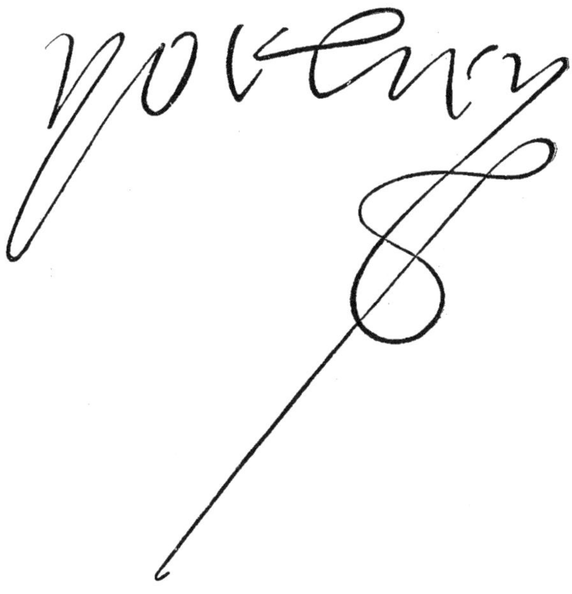

Illus. 1.4. Yo El Rey. A typical signature of the Spanish king Felipe II, who signed his decrees simply: "Yo El Rey" (I, the King).

CHAPTER 2

Organization of the Spanish Colonial Mints

According to Pradeau (1938) the first mainland mint of the Americas was actually located in the house of Hernán Cortés, conqueror of Mexico. To compensate himself for any possible inconvenience, Cortés decided he should be paid 500 pesos per year in rent. It was a *Cédula Real* dated May 11, 1535, that authorized this mint to begin striking silver coins in denominations of 3, 2, 1, and ½ reales. Copper was authorized for 8 and 4 *maravedís* coins if Viceroy Mendoza, who had previously been treasurer at the Granada mint in Spain, deemed it necessary. After Mendoza arrived in Mexico City on October 15, 1535, the mint was given 1,000 marks (500 lb.) of silver to begin coinage. This amount was supplied by the Royal Hacienda from the king's own tax receipts. No doubt it had to be reimbursed eventually in some way.

Expenses of coining were defrayed by charging 3 reales per mark of silver converted to coin, but from this amount 1 real was deducted and returned to the king as his royalty. Since 68 reales were required to be made from a mark of silver, the total possible in reales from the first 1,000 marks was 68,000. However, we do not know the distribution by denomination, although the extreme scarcity of 3-reales coins in today's collections suggests that very few, if any, of these were made from this particular allotment of silver. It is likely most coins were 2's and 1's, but certainly some ½-real coins were included because examples are known in collections.

Assay charges by the Mexico City mint were 2 pesos for every gold assay and an additional 4 reales for each mark of gold assayed. Stamping in the circular *quinto* tax seal on a gold ingot was done at the cost of a mere ½-real. Silver was assayed at 3 pesos for every 10 marks and from each 100-mark lot, an ounce of silver was extracted (proportionately less for smaller lots). No silver was to be received by the mint for conversion into coins unless it bore the official tax stamp proving the king's fifth had been paid. Mendoza later suggested this tax be collected at the mint and the death penalty for possession of untaxed silver be rescinded.

Mint officials (not the actual coiners) were to be appointed by the viceroy every two years, but in 1537 some Spaniards arrived in Mexico to claim these honorific positions. In no case were mint officials authorized to buy or sell bullion, a situation which soon encouraged private individuals to become silver brokers. They were known as *mercaderes de plata*.

Pradeau (1938:25) believes that work on the first dies began by March 10, 1536, and he indicates Axiquipilco Indians were required to work in the mint and pay tribute (amount unspecified) to mint officials for a two-year period. Mendoza appointed Francisco del Rincón as the first assayer and Antón de Vides as the die engraver (*tallador*). Archival records indicate the first coins were struck in April 1536. By 1549 these beautifully made coins were still produced but Viceroy Mendoza was peeved at the slackness of mint officials. He ordered all employees to be at the mint from 9 to 11 in the morning and 3 to 5 in the afternoon; furthermore, the total number of employees was not to exceed thirty and they must all be Spaniards of good repute.

The house of Cortés continued to be used as the mint until a building specifically designed for that purpose was decreed in 1569. By 1729 this building was deemed too small and another was begun in 1731 and completed in 1734 at a cost of some half-million pesos. Later additions and improvements continued until 1782, by which time total cost exceeded 1 million pesos.

Pradeau makes an important contribution to our understanding of mint officials by pointing out their appointments by either viceroy or king made them royal employees. The *Cédula Real* of August 21, 1565, signed by the king at Bosque de Segovia, decreed mint offices of treasurer, assayer, engraver, smelter, and weigher were open for sale to the highest bidders. For example, in 1607 the title of treasurer sold for 150,000 pesos, and in 1612 it sold for 260,000 pesos. The combined bid for smelter, assayer, and engraver went for 160,000 pesos. Since no one paid these men a salary, their bids and expected profits were based on the volume of silver and gold they anticipated would be processed at the mint (presumably calculated on projected mine production) and their various rights and privileges for converting the same into coins. Thus mine operators, or any other owners of raw silver, paid their salaries from fees for their services in converting crude silver into assayed ingots and coins.

In most instances the holder of a franchise to perform various functions in the mint was not the actual person doing the work. The high bidder often proved to be a wealthy absentee courtier or merchant in Spain who then hired skilled specialists to perform these functions. Since bids were in effect direct gifts to the king (who was always strapped for money), favors in court and even noble titles were sometimes arranged for the winner to offset the possibility that the anticipated level of income would not soon materialize.

From the mid-sixteenth century onward, a performance bond (*fianza*) was required of holders of the more important positions and by the eighteenth century everyone was required to pay in advance to the treasury a *media annata,* which was nothing less than one-half of their first year's salary. This draconian tax must have been very difficult for many appointees to pay in a declining mining economy. Nevertheless, there always seemed to be wealthy merchants and silver brokers ready and eager to make loans to these mint workers, no doubt at special interest rates or, as we shall see in chapter 3, in exchange for clandestine access to the Potosí mint and its equipment. While there is very little archival record of the effect these practices may have had in Mexico, a convincing argument can be made that chronic corruption found at the Potosí mint was caused in large part by pressure from these loan sharks for access to, and special privileges within, the mint itself until such loans were repaid. The opportunities for blackmail must have been endless.

Originally, these mint positions were purchased for life and on death of the holder his heirs received one-third of the new sale price. However, an officeholder could resign or sell the office to anyone who met legal requirements. Everything was operated as a profit-making business; only the treasurer was required to document the amount of seigniorage (Spanish *señorage,* a specific tax paid to the king) collected and transferred to the Crown.[1]

During mint reforms of 1652, the chief smelter and the chief assayer at the Mexico City mint were made royal employees, paid by the Crown. Finally, all mint activities were incorporated into the Royal Treasury by the *Cédulas Reales* issued in 1728, 1730, and finally on July 14, 1732. Yet in spite of these edicts, contractors continued to buy positions through competitive bidding until everything in Mexico became fully under government control on August 3, 1762.

Coin design changes, sometimes accompanied by reduced silver content, caused widespread concern and had to be announced clearly and firmly to prevent confusion in business dealings. In the viceroyalty of Nueva España (Mexico) this occurred when the pillar and waves design begun in 1732 was replaced in 1772 by coins bearing a portrait of King

Carlos III. According to Pradeau (1938: 61) special arrangements were made at the Mexico mint to ensure a smooth transition.[2] This mint from its inception was considered the model for other, younger mints to emulate. Working conditions there were generally favorable and my research suggests the personnel were treated with consideration.[3]

All Spanish-milled silver coins were widely accepted in commerce and in fact remained legal tender in the United States until the mid-nineteenth century. During the eighteenth century ½-real coins from the Mexico mint were sent in quantity to Spanish Florida where they circulated freely. When the Florida Parishes of Louisiana became incorporated into the United States, these small coins were viewed somewhat contemptuously and were referred to as *picayunes*. The Creole expression "not worth a picayune" is still heard in Louisiana today.

An effort to establish a branch mint in Guatemala at the old capital of Antigua began in 1714 with a letter to the king. He finally responded in 1731 authorizing construction to begin. This building was completed in 1739 but partially milled coins of transitional design on handmade planchets probably began to appear in 1733 with the mint mark G. The fully milled coins (on round, machine-cut planchets) were not produced until 1754. In 1773 an earthquake destroyed this building and the mint was moved to what is now Guatemala City. Since 1776 Guatemalan coins have borne the new mint mark NG, for Nueva Guatemala.

Weights, Measures, and Fees

The exact legal weights for Spanish colonial coins changed through time, as seen in table 2.1, based on early *Cédulas Reales* including the one announcing mint reforms of June 9, 1728. The weights shown in grams are equivalent metric weights converted from Spanish units described in these documents. The weights shown in table 2.1 were entirely theoretical and none of the colonial mints was able to meet these precise standards in every coin produced.

Hence the concept of *fuerte* and *feble* arose. These words meaning "strong" and "weak" applied to coins that fell to either side of the established standards for weight. Of course the tendency was to produce slightly underweight coins, since in a large *partida* (production run) everyone except the king would benefit if slightly underweight coins were produced in moderation. As might be expected, there were numerous attempts by the king's advisors in Spain to micromanage this process, but with little or no observable success.

Underweight coins also benefited owners of silver if they required only small-denomination coins because they might receive a few extra

Table 2.1. Official Spanish Silver Colonial Coin Weights According to Royal Proclamations

Denomination	1535–1728 Weight in Grams	1728–1825 Weight in Grams
8 reales	27.4680	27.0642
4	13.7340	13.5321
2	6.8670	6.7660
1	3.4335	3.3830
½	1.7167	1.6915
¼	0.8584	0.8457

Source: Burzio (1958: vol. 2, 171).

reales from a large amount of silver turned in (assuming the coiners did not skim off the excess coins).[4] Overweight coins cheated both owners of silver and the Royal Hacienda, and, if too numerous, their presence in a production run was easily detected. This could cause the whole batch to be remelted at considerable expense to the mint and the assayers involved.

Señorage and *Braceage*

Before the mint reforms of 1728, all Spanish colonial mints were operated by franchisees who purchased the right to operate a mint by direct negotiation with the king. Bids of these powerful individuals were based on their perception of how much gold and silver would be available from the mines for conversion into coinage. What they were allowed to charge for their services was based on a number of taxes and fees that evolved through time and, to some extent, not all were uniformly applied by all mints. Potosí was viewed by everyone as a complicated but productive machine or "cash cow," capable of producing great benefits to all concerned if managed properly.[5]

Señorage was a tax charged by the king to owners of precious metal in exchange for the privilege of using his name, or portrait, on a coin. This in turn was his guarantee that the coin was genuine and of correct weight and alloy. In 1576 Juan Ignacio de Torres de Vera reported to the Council of the Indies that next to the *quintos,* the most important royal income was derived from 1 real of *señorage* charged per *marco* of assayed silver because six new furnaces operating at Potosí processed 300,000 *marcos* per year.[6] Theoretically, this tax would generate about 37,500 pesos per year; in reality both local officials and the viceroy commonly appropriated these monies because their administrative expenses were so great.

The assayer's fee for smelting, assaying, and stamping a silver ingot was decreed at 1.5 percent of its value (*Cédula Real,* August 24, 1619).[7] Obviously when news of this finally reached the mints (probably not until one or two years later) it did not take long for assayers to figure out their profits would increase, and workloads decrease, by processing larger and larger ingots, limited only by a size that could be conveniently handled by owners. As a result over the next few years thousands of silver bars were cast at Potosí and a nearby foundry at Oruro, with an average weight of 83.5 lb. (Craig, forthcoming). But there were other local charges also affecting the way in which raw silver was converted into coin.

For example, in 1579 assayer Alonso López Barriales was permitted by the *Audiencia* (High Court) at La Plata (now known as Sucre, the de jure capital of Bolivia) to charge 2 reales per *piña* (lump of very pure sponge silver) for the cost of charcoal necessary to smelt it prior to assay.[8] Under these circumstances, assayers may have encouraged mine and mill owners to bring them raw silver in small lots since it very well might take more than 2 reales' worth of charcoal to smelt a really large mass of sponge silver. Of course, these were the early years during the development of a new refining process introduced at Potosí from Mexico where it was known as patio amalgamation (ca. 1576), when "fine-tuning" was still in progress. Soon *piñas* of uniform shape were brought to the mint after they had been formed by pounding them into more or less standardized triangular wooden molds.[9]

Arguments between assayers and owners of raw silver over details of cost were always in favor of the assayer since he was not legally bound to accept an unprofitable consignment, while owners were legally obligated to have their sponge silver processed and taxed within thirty days. Having untaxed silver on hand in any form other than ore was theoretically a serious legal matter; but records show that for several centuries people in the viceroyalties of South America commonly used such silver as barter in their petty business transactions.

Salaries of Public Officials

In the notoriously litigious culture of Spain, and especially in its empire in America, it was necessary to have a strong judicial system staffed by highly trained and well-educated *licenciados* who were lawyers. High courts were established as soon as practical after conquest and for the viceroyalty of Peru the court was located deep in the interior of what is now Bolivia. The location at La Plata was chosen as a compromise between pleasant living conditions and a need to guard the king's taxation interests at the nearby high-altitude silver mines at Potosí. These

Table 2.2. Salaries of Functionaries of the *Audiencia* of Charcas, ca. 1580

Lic. Ramírez de Quiñones, president	5,000 *ducados*
Lic. Matienzo, judge	4,000 *ducados*
Lic. Recalde, judge	4,000 *ducados*
Lic. Antonio López de Haro, judge	4,000 *ducados*
Lic. Rabanal, attorney general	4,000 *ducados*
Treasurer (vacant)	510,000 *maravedís*
Diego de Ibarra, accountant	510,000 *maravedís*
Juan de Anguciana, clerk	510,000 *maravedís*

Source: Hampe (1986).

judges, who were often elderly royal employees, tried to avoid the harsh conditions of Potosí where everything was much more expensive than at La Plata.

The early salaries paid these men (table 2.2) were considered opulent for the times and as a result officeholders were strictly forbidden to engage in any form of commerce. But as we shall see, even these generous salaries did not always insulate judges from bribes and corruption.

Since table 2.2 uses terminology specific to accounting, we must convert *ducados* and *maravedís* to assayed pesos in order to get a clear understanding of just how much these viceregal judges and royal officials were being paid. With a *ducado* equivalent to two assayed pesos, each worth 450 *maravedís,* we immediately see there was a great discrepancy between the salaries of judges earning 8,000 to 10,000 pesos (4.5 million mvds.) and that of officials on the *maravedís* payroll at only 1,133 *pesos de a ocho* (308,176 mvds.) per annum. No wonder judges of the High Court could better resist temptation than mere clerks who were locked in a daily struggle to make ends meet. See Appendix A (List of Equivalencies) for other Spanish terms of value, measurement, distance, and the like.

Purser (1971: 310–11) offers a more detailed insight into these salary problems. He points out royal officials often had contracts that required them to be paid in *pesos ensayados.* If they were paid in coins, they demanded the full 13.25 reales each such peso was actually worth. Viceroys then insisted they receive only 12.5 reales in coins because the one real difference (approximately 6 percent) was the cost of minting. Since everyone knew the actual cost of minting was not this high, there were continual quarrels over this issue. Evidently some officials had stipends actually paid in silver bars and a *peso de a nueve reales* (a peso of 9 reales) was used in calculating what they were owed. The extra real was compensation for the inconvenience of accepting ingots instead of coins.

After 150 years of scandalous operation at Potosí under a series of venal officeholders, incompetent and dishonest employees, counterfeiters, and worse, the Council of the Indies strongly recommended to King Felipe V that the old system of selling rights to mint positions be abandoned, thieves thrown out, and complete control taken over by a new team of Spaniards sent over for that purpose from Spain as Crown employees with fixed salaries.

In the Royal Ordinance of July 16, 1730, were new regulations for "the making of coins of gold, silver, and copper that are made in the royal mints of Spain; ministers, officials and operators that are to occupy them; salaries they are to enjoy; responsibilities and obligations of each of them; rights to help bear the costs of making them; assays that are to be made of them, and the ingots, and also the sponge metals, and everything that is to be observed." All were spelled out in great detail, closely following traditional methods developed over the years from successful operation of the Mexico mint but without consideration of special circumstances that prevailed in other parts of South American viceroyalties.

Both the cost of living and cost of mint operation at Potosí were ignored by the 1730 Ordinances. Officials in Spain never once recognized there could be such differences and sternly insisted all colonial mints should emulate the example set by Mexico. This document has great historical value and a wealth of information on early mint practices can be gleaned from descriptions of its content, the principal points of which are as follows:

> Motives for this new Ordinance; the earlier ones shall be observed if they are not contrary to it. All labor with gold, silver and copper shall be charged to the account of the Royal Treasury. What must be observed when buying metals, and the fineness, weight and design of gold and silver. Skills required of mint employees, the form in which their titles shall be sent to them, how they and their dependents shall swear allegiance. Formalities of receiving and buying metals for the treasury; the assays that must precede this and the assayer's fees for this. Gold coins must be made of 22 karats and silver coins of 11 *dineros.* Until further notice provincial [cob] coins may continue in use with their own fineness. Milled coins will be made circular with a laurel leaf design on the edge. The proportional value between gold and silver and the prices the mints are to pay for them. Weights of gold and silver coins, consideration of *señorage* and *braceage* and justification of the weights. Allowable tolerances for over/underweight coins and separation and melting of those exceeding the limits. Formalities to be observed when coining gold and silver from acceptance until they are passed on to the foundryman (*fundador*) and custodian. What must be done by the foundryman and custodian (*guardamateriales*) in smelt-

ing metals and concurrence of the assayers; metal for planchets to be locked up in a strongbox of three keys. Duplicate and separate assays to be made and the formalities of turning them over to the inspector (*fiel*), relieving the foundryman and custodian of any more responsibility. What the inspector must do after taking charge of the metal until it is ready to be coined. What must be done with underweight coins; a quarter of them to be made into small denominations. How coins are to be struck; examinations that are to be made to separate the perfect from the imperfect, the latter to be placed in the strongbox with a record of what is kept there together with their disposition. At the conclusion of a job the inspector is to be paid two-thirds of his fees, the last third being kept for a final accounting until it is done. Formalities to be observed when converting silver scrap to coins.

This long document continues by detailing all duties, responsibilities, and privileges associated with mint positions of superintendent, accountant, treasurer, assayers, weighmaster, inspector, foundryman, materials custodian, die guard, door opener, door closer, porter, servant, royal scribe, sergeant-at-arms, and guards. These attempts at micromanaging such a complex operation seem astonishing to us today. Many of the rules and regulations were not taken seriously or simply ignored by mint workers faced with daily problems of their jobs that could only be solved by expedient, commonsense means.[10]

Mexico began to produce beautiful milled coins in 1732,[11] but officials at Potosí could not manage to have heavy equipment installed and working properly until 1767, and in fact continued to strike crude handmade cobs concurrently until 1773. We do not know exactly why both grossly different forms of coinage were struck in the mint at the same time during this interval but we can assume it was related to the economics of mint operations.[12]

Nevertheless, mint workers were now direct employees of the Crown, and as we see from the standard salaries listed in table 2.3, no effort was made to compensate for the high cost of living at Potosí, which was said to be as much as thirty times that of employees in Spanish mints.

Table 2.3 shows that in spite of the well-known high cost of living at Potosí there were notable decreases in the salaries of royal officials of this mint between 1750 and 1776. Although archival records at my disposal do not directly speak to this point, my opinion is that by 1776 these royal salaries had been parsimoniously reduced because some officials now had living quarters for their families inside the new mint building.

Some featherbedding may have been present at the Lima mint where, about 1755, no great quantity of coins was being processed. Various

Table 2.3. Annual Salaries in Pesos of Mint Employees, 1730–1776

Position	All Mints 1730	Potosí 1750	Lima 1755	Potosí 1776
Superintendente (director)	1,875	6,000	5,000	
Contador (chief accountant)	1,900	3,440	4,000 + 200 (for paper, pens, and ink)	3,500 + 200 (for paper, pens, and ink)
Oficiales de contaduria (3) (bookkeeper)			2,000	300
Thesorero(treasurer)	2,625	3,240	6,446	3,500
Cajero num. 1 de thesoreria (3) (asst. treasurer)			600	600
Cajero num. 2 (cashier)				400
Ensayador mayor (chief assayer)	1,250	1,900	3,000	1,800
Ensayador segundo (asst. assayer)	1,000		1,500	1,400
Balanzario (weigher)	687		1,400	1,400
Ayudante (helper)	275		800	800
Fielatura (inspector)	625		800	1,500
Fundidor mayor (chief smelter)		3,000	3,000	2,600
Asistentes (3) (asst. smelters)		1,000		no fuel expense
Fundidor de cisallas (scrap smelter)	750	800		700
Asistente de cisallas (asst. scrap smelter)				400
Guarda vistas de la fundizión mayor (foreman of the main smelter)			800	1,000
Guarda materiales (supply guard)	412	1,400	1,400	1,200
Guarda cuños (die guard)	375		1,400	
Tallador (engraver)	1,000		1,800	
Oficial de la talla (asst. engraver)			400	
Tallador aprendiz (apprentice engraver)			91	
Contador de monedas (2) (coin counter)			1,500	
Asesor (legal adviser)		100	200	400
Portero marcador de barras (porter in charge of stamping ingots)	275	350	350	360
Portero de la calle (street porter)			400	
Guarda de noche (2) (night watchman)			204	
Escribiano (scribe)	250		1,000	
Peon libre de aseo (janitor)			144	

Sources: For 1730, Ordenanza de S.M. de 16 de Julio. Reimpresa por orden Supremo Consejo de Indias, 1745; AGI Charcas 679 for 1750 and AGI Charcas 678 for 1776; the Lima data are from AGI Lima 1258, document of November 11, 1755.

salaried positions being paid in Lima were not listed for Potosí. Since Lima was the seat of the viceroy's court, presumably more pomp and circumstance was required of mint employees' comings and goings. A "cleaning man" at 144 pesos is the last thing one would expect to find in the Potosí mint. Other discrepancies are very hard to interpret without new research, but probably they reflect local differences in how each mint actually operated.

CHAPTER 3

Mint Scandals

Don Juan Carvajal y Sandé: A Most Unusual Investigator

Charges of crimes against the Crown were often made anonymously by writing directly to the viceroy, the Council of the Indies in Sevilla, or even to the king himself. If the situation warranted, it resulted in the appointment of a *visitador* (special investigator) who might be one of the judges of the nearest High Court. However, in a few of the most serious cases, particularly where counterfeiting or diversion of monies owed the king was involved, inspectors might be sent over directly from Spain under secret orders, and even in mufti so not even the viceroy would know what they were about. These secret investigators were empowered to undertake investigations of anyone, even High Court judges and possibly the viceroy himself, if it was believed they were involved in a case. But commonly an inspector was widely announced and his arrival well publicized so that his laborious task of collecting depositions, hearsay, and cross-examination could begin promptly. But in practice the process was often ponderous and dilatory.

While such an investigation was under way, all expenses of the inspector were charged to the High Court, in this case at La Plata. Such a carte blanche expense account was easily abused as was the power to make arrests out of hand, using the *alguacil* (sheriff) to effect the seizures. It was these extraordinary powers that made a *visitador* greatly feared by the guilty.

After some preliminary background research into the alleged offense, the inspector compiled a lengthy list of direct questions and began to interrogate anyone suspected (or suggested by informants) of involvement. Buried within these questions were what seem today to be obvious attempts to elicit the same response but couched in different language. These answers constituted the only "evidence" forwarded to higher authorities in support of the verdict rendered on the spot by the inspector. Of course, all accused were presumed guilty until proven innocent by means of findings revealed by *autos* that were heard in private and recorded in private.

By the 1620s, perhaps even earlier, some mint employees and silver merchants were in collusion. Rumors filtered back to Spain and resulted in the appointment of Don Juan de Caravajal y Sandé, Caballero de Calatrava, Visitador Plenipotentiare, to investigate the counterfeiting that was issuing from the very mint itself on a truly massive scale.

Everyone in Potosí was aware of the circumstances. Assayers at the mint were believed to be working after hours to add large quantities of copper to the silver alloy so that coins struck with legal dies had the necessary overall weight, but not the required amount of silver. Silver saved was used to repay their debts to silver merchants who had loaned them money. Debasing coins reached such proportions that legitimate merchants of Potosí would refuse to accept products of their own mint. Eventually, attempts to dump large quantities of debased coins on ingenuous Mexicans resulted in *peruleros* (as these coins were known) being forbidden entry into this viceroyalty.

Caravajal y Sandé was obviously a lawyer of importance and a man held in profound trust by the king. Archival documents indicate he was comparatively young (about thirty-five when appointed). He arrived openly in Lima sometime in 1630 and was viewed from the beginning as a most unusual royal official.

From the earliest days appointees sent over from Spain were required to be married and bring with them their families at the first opportunity. Bachelor officials were considered (with good reason) to be a threat to the fragile stability of the newly formed colonial society where Spanish women were in exceedingly short supply. Many officials arrived in the New World with a highly developed sense of the importance of their offices and themselves. Their public actions were watched closely and most behaved accordingly; many were models of probity and moral rectitude. As we shall see, none of these qualities applied to our audacious *visitador,* who was something of a physical athlete in contrast to the usual effete dandy produced from the Spanish court.

Don Juan moved briskly from Lima to Potosí where his every move was watched by nervous eyes. We know from later archival accounts he immediately began to act in a manner so shocking, it is without parallel in the records. If there were more accomplished roués in the viceroyalty, their exploits have not come to my attention!

Potosí, like every boisterous mining town before or since, had fostered development of numerous "dancing schools." In fact there were twenty-three of these brothels available to Don Juan. The proprietress of the most famous was Doña Juana Manrrique with whom Caravajal soon forged a close, personal relationship.

It seems our hero went with "indecent habit to the houses of Suspect Women." Skulking through darkened streets of Potosí during this era of sudden swordfights was in itself a highly eccentric and dangerous behavior for a royal official. But there is some internal evidence he was an accomplished swordsman as well.

Late one night while Caravajal was ensconced with Doña Juana, his presence there was detected by another "dancing instructress" with whom he had also "generated great friendship." She took umbrage at his infidelity and began to create an awful scene outside the house of Doña Juana, screaming for the *visitador* to extract himself from the clutches of that woman and to come and abide with her instead. When her arguments failed to raise any response, she attacked the house of Doña Juana, smashing out windows with rocks.

At this serious insult, the owner flew out the door and fell upon her competitor. While the two women grappled and fought in the street, Caravajal was seen to hurry away from this scandalous scene under cover of darkness.

Evidently Doña Manrrique emerged the victor in that contest because we know he became her increasingly frequent guest. In an indignant letter written to the viceroy in Lima, the clergy describe how it became the duty of three of them to break into the house of Doña Juana early one morning and forcibly drag Don Juan out of her bed in order to "preserve public morality." Reading this document carefully, I suspect Caravajal was unable to reach his sword in this assault of three against one.

The Plot Thickens

Caravajal y Sandé's behavior became more erratic as time went by and several years of strange incidents were recorded while his own investigation languished. On one occasion he went with a mixed group of townspeople on an excursion to visit the nearby thermal spring of Tarapaya. While viewing this pleasant scene, the inspector suddenly stripped off all his clothes and "threw himself naked into the water." He then began to swim about and declaim to the scandalized men and women. (At this time it was uniformly believed swimming and bathing were nothing short of a death sentence from the health standpoint and a kind of lunacy practiced only by Englishmen.)

On another occasion it is documented he went hunting birds for sport with a group of common Indians who had become his cronies in this form of dissipation. His "concept of propriety was so eroded" he allowed these Indians to use his fowling piece, "knowing full well it was strictly forbidden for any Indian to use any kind of firearm under any condition."

Under circumstances that are not clear, in the midst of all this profligacy, Caravajal was awarded presidency of the Audiencia of La Plata (chief judge of the High Court) and given full control over the division of Indian conscript mine workers. Now he could issue death warrants for his enemies and dole out valuable Indian laborers to any mine owner who curried his favor.

Shortly thereafter, he seduced Doña Gabriela, wife of Don Diego de Zárate—whom he had just sentenced to death for the murder of Juan Martel (because Martel had also taken her as his mistress). As president, Caravajal was aided somewhat in this convoluted mélange by the fact it all happened in the town of Chuquisaca (Sucre), where he had moved because it was the seat of the Audiencia.

During his next two years as president, he was accused of engaging in business deals, something strictly prohibited for high officials. From this source he was accused of making great profits which he bestowed on his new mistress, Catharina Ximénez.

Meanwhile, Diego de Zárate escaped from jail in Lima and word reached Caravajal the much-abused husband was on his way back to Potosí to seek vengeance after languishing more than a year in prison. On arrival he discovered his wife had given birth to a child by the president. The charge against Zárate was expunged and Caravajal tried to bribe him with ten extra Indian workers to use in his mine or rent out to others, but Zárate refused to be mollified.

So he was arrested again on new charges and thrown back into prison where he could not interfere with Caravajal's access to Doña Gabriela, who by now was pregnant once more by him. The husband was eventually released from false charges and stubbornly returned to Potosí a second time to discover his wife had just given birth to a second bastard.

Don Diego de Zárate again made a nuisance of himself by confronting the president of the High Court. His patience for the cuckold at an end, Juan de Caravajal y Sandé had the hapless husband summarily murdered.

No doubt it was this last outrageous act in 1633 that turned the entire community against him. When they realized he had both power and inclination to put to death the innocent as well as the guilty, it became obvious something had to be done.

To bring this sad story to a close, we find Juan de Caravajal y Sandé was accused of high crimes (about sixty) by a new *visitador,* Juan de Lisarazu, who had him swiftly condemned, divested of all his personal possessions and properties, and sentenced to life imprisonment on board the galleys of Spain. At some point on his transfer between Lima and Panama he escaped from his shackles—and from the pages of history as well.

Francisco Gómez de la Rocha: Counterfeiter Extraordinaire

No Spanish colonial mint was so beset with scandals as was Potosí. Criminal malfeasance of officials and workers there has been a favorite topic of chroniclers of its history (Cañete y Dominguez 1952a) and writers of romantic fiction (Quesada 1950).

Some of the most amazing accounts of counterfeiting to be found anywhere are recorded on the faded pages of folios in Charcas 113 in the Archivo General de Indias. These documents, written between July 30, 1644, and January 3, 1645, detail a colossal struggle between good and evil in the strong personalities of Don Francisco Nestares Marín, president of the High Court in La Plata, and the utterly amoral Francisco Gómez de la Rocha. As a silver broker who had somehow managed to gain free access to the mint equipment, Rocha was authorized sub-rosa to strike his own coins inside the mint at Potosí.

By any measure, we must consider Rocha to be the most audacious and desperate counterfeiter of coins the world has ever known. Like so many events surrounding Potosí during the seventeenth century, the scope and scale of Rocha's activities seem unbelievable, but the archival evidence is incontrovertible.

Details of his early life have not yet been found. We know by the late 1620s Rocha was living at Potosí where he began to buy and sell silver on a small scale. There were perhaps a dozen or so of these *mercaderes de plata* operating in town on a more or less regular basis. Some of them may have functioned as pawnbrokers, loaning cash in the form of coins to mill or mine owners who needed to pay their Indian workers on a weekly basis. The most common collateral that could be offered was in the inconvenient form of unrefined, unassayed, and therefore unregistered (in other words, illegal) small silver ingots and simple masses of amalgamated sponge silver.

Gradually silver brokers began to look for bigger and better opportunities. They found them in the practice of loaning very large sums of money to appointees of important royal offices. Treasury employees, for example, were required to make payment in advance for a *fianza,* a kind of performance bond or cash surety, not to mention the *media annata* which was a direct tax equivalent to half the first year's salary—also paid in advance. Soon there were petty officials all over town, including those in the mint, who were deeply in debt to the silver brokers. Seldom mentioned in archives is the fact they occasionally charged usurious interest (above 20 percent) on these loans to new officeholders. Even long-established court judges are known to have solicited personal loans from these silver merchants.

Beginning on March 20, 1641, mint records show Francisco Gómez de la Rocha was submitting large quantities of silver ingots to the mint for conversion into coins. In 1644 he was referred to as a *capitán* as well as an *Alcalde Ordinario de la Villa.*[1] Soon we read he was allowed to use mint equipment after regular hours to produce coins made from his own silver. I conclude this could have happened only by Rocha's skills at suborning more than a few mint employees and treasury officials (as it later turned out, a total of 168 such people were involved in his conspiracy). An early sign of trouble was written in 1644 by Alonso Cotel Carvajal, defender of the Royal Hacienda in Potosí, and Gerardo de Leon, lieutenant of the treasury, who formally registered complaints about false coins and bars.[2]

Potosí was a compact and densely built town where everyone's business was studiously noted. Soon legitimate merchants began to receive 8-reales coins that, although they weighed enough, had a distinctly pinkish color. Rumors began to echo in the narrow streets these were the work of Rocha and his after-hours crew in the mint building. In a matter of months, debased coins also were being made slightly underweight. The Indian population of the town began to view them with a jaundiced eye and soon nicknamed them *macuquiñas* (from *Quechua:* something weak or lacking weight) while merchants all over the viceroyalty contemptuously called them *rochunas* and tried to get rid of them by paying off debts owed to their counterparts in Mexico, Guatemala, or Panama. These men also indignantly refused to accept the coins at full face value and damned them as *peruleros.* When thousands more poured out of the mint, some no doubt appearing in church offerings and donations, two priests, Padre Franco de Cervantes, S.J., and Padre Hernando de Oçerín, S.J., raised cries for an investigation of Francisco Gómez de la Rocha and secretly wrote to the viceroy Marqués de Mancera denouncing the whole scandal. Finally, a most curious investigation was begun in 1646.

Somewhat reluctantly the defender of the Royal Hacienda reported to the viceroy he was appointing the *corregidor* Blas Robles de Salcedo (see frontispiece) to investigate the matter. Although the *corregidor* represented official Crown interest for the region, he was also one of the secretly accused; this was setting the fox to guard the henhouse. Of course, nothing much happened. On June 30, 1646, Robles wrote to the viceroy with great circumlocution and cleverly warned him this investigation was very dangerous because it would disrupt mint operations of assaying and striking of coins, thus seriously reducing the king's *quinto* and *señorage* taxes. He begged off from his appointment as investigator. He was ignored. He then claimed he was in great personal danger. The viceroy was insistent . . . but later appointed others.

Eventually, from the High Court there appeared a special investigator, Sebastian de Alarcón, together with his assistant investigator, Gaspar Martín de Vargas, and constable Juan Navarro (who no doubt was an excellent swordsman). These two extra members of the secret *visita* point to the extreme importance of this case, but the sudden appearance of three strangers in town could not go unnoticed. Soon a wave of unrest swept through officials and silver merchants alike.

Now the chief investigator had instructions to inquire into activities of *corregidor* Blas Robles de Salzedo, of Alonso Cotel Carvajal, defender of the Royal Hacienda, of Gerardo de Leon, lieutenant of the treasury, of Bartolomé Astete de Ulloa, mint accountant, of Juan Ximénez de Tapia (an assayer whose initial "T" appears on coins of this period), and, most important of all, of Capitán Francisco Gómez de la Rocha. There had never been before, or since, an investigation of so many high-ranking people in the viceroyalty of Peru.

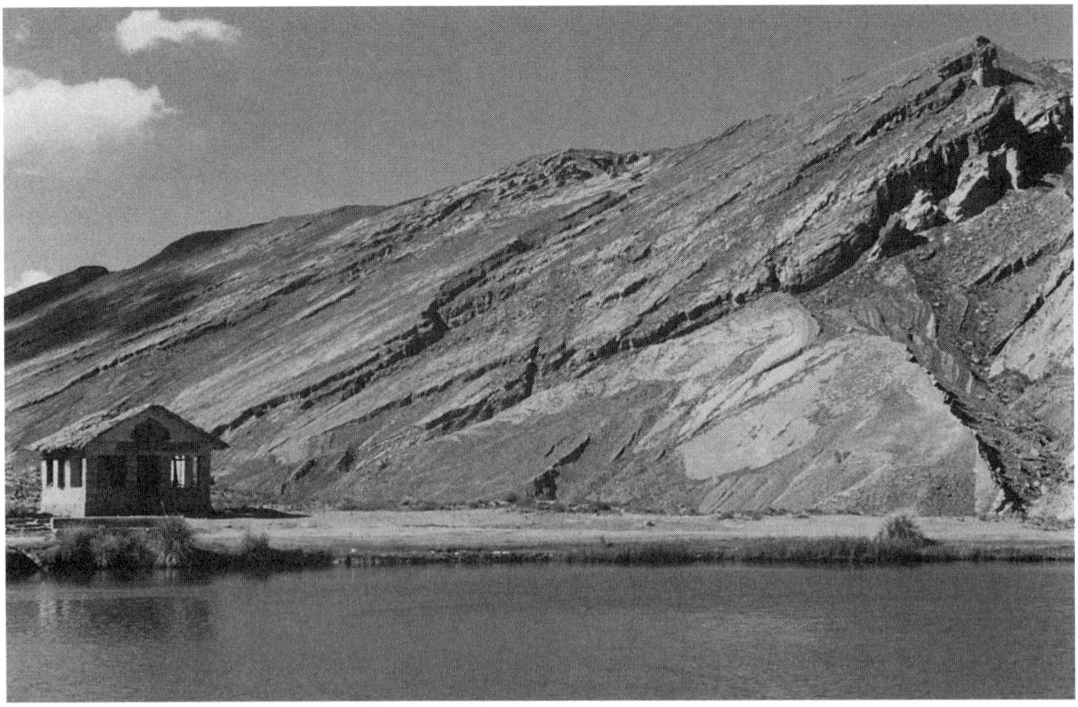

Illus. 3.1. The famous Tarapaya Hot Springs near Potosí was visited by prehistoric Inca rulers for its curative powers. The counterfeiter Rocha is said to have hidden a fortune in coins here in its opaque waters. The steeply dipping beds of quartzite were a source of millstones for the colonial mills of Potosí.

In addition to the above, the papers named Juan de Figueroa, who had purchased the title of assayer of Potosí. In fact he lived in Lima where he was a powerful and wealthy friend of Viceroy Mancera.[3]

The investigation, begun in 1646, was nearly finished by 1649 when 119 people were found guilty of the charges.[4] During this time there was near panic among venal merchants who had loaned out large sums of money at high interest rates to crooked mint officials and treasury administrators. These too were members of the Rocha gang who were involved in turning out large quantities of debased coins with the connivance of officials who wanted to skim from shipments of silver enough to repay their loans. Even judges of the High Court at La Plata were believed to be implicated as we see in the investigation of Dr. Merlo and his vigorous defense as revealed by the documents presented later in this chapter.

But they all knew counterfeiting was considered *lesa magestad* for which the only and ultimate sentence was to be garroted at the scene of their crimes within the mint and then dragged out and hung from a wooden tripod in the public square.[5] This indeed was the wording of death warrants for Juan Velarde Treviño,[6] *corregidor* of Potosí, and the ringleader Francisco Gómez de la Rocha who was condemned on September 12, 1651, and put to death shortly thereafter in the manner described.[7]

Dr. Nestares Marín's Findings on Potosí Coins

The following document (Craig translation) is AGI Charcas 114, 28–2–1650:

To His Majesty

> Judicial findings of the President and Special Investigator Dr. Don Francisco de Nestares Marín on the coinage of the Potosí mint in response to the acts and notices of the viceroy and general council of Lima.
>
> In the Imperial Villa of Potosí on the twenty-eighth day of the month of February of one thousand six hundred and fifty years Dr. Don Francisco de Nestares Marín of the Council of Your Majesty, your President and Inspector of the Royal High Court of the city of La Plata, Royal Treasury and mint of the said town: Having seen the decrees of Your Excellency, the Count of Salvatierra, viceroy of these realms, I have sent you facts about the assay and weight of the new coins made for Your Excellency, the Junta of General Agreement, and

Treasury, and most recently the decree given by His Excellency on the twentieth of January of the present year. I say that regarding the points contained in the said decrees I gave and give the following answers:

First, so much concern and extreme pain has been caused to Your Excellency and to the Council because it has been found that the new coins have the same imperfections as before the special investigation. I said to the President that the case has developed thusly because of the assays of coins and planchets seized during the said investigation and from more than thirty witnesses in it and for *the acts of Francisco Gómez de la Rocha* [emphasis added] merchant, and of Felipe Ramírez assayer. It is known, and seems that before the investigation, coins circulated with one hundred thirty grains or fourth of alloy and copper per *marco* and now, as the said findings confirm and as can be seen, it does not reach six grains of alloy per *marco* with which it is alloyed. The great difference of the imperfections, and this ratio must be watched and moderated as soon as possible when they are found. The new coinage with the said assay must give the ratios and results noted ahead in these findings since the said President has always been given to understand that it came from the highly justifiable labor of Your Excellency.

In the above passage, Marín's description of the problems he found with Potosí coinage is written in elliptical and opaque syntax typical of a lawyer's prose in messages sent to high officials who were then free to interpret it as best suited their purposes. I believe he is advising the viceroy Potosí coins were being debased with so much copper they were only .725 fine instead of having the required .931 silver content.

Readers confused over differences in details of interpretation of Potosí's numismatic history should be aware some of these differences can be traced to longstanding polemics (for example, Cunietti-Ferrando versus Sellschopp), while others involve use of secondary sources, which in turn are not based on archival documents.

The Defense of Dr. Merlo

While corruption in the colonial administration of Peru was pervasive and of long standing, no official, not even a viceroy, was allowed to retire, leave his post, or return to Spain without being subjected to a *Visita de Residencia*. At this time anyone with a complaint against such an official came forward, recorded the charges, and the accused was required to respond before royal permission to leave his post was granted. The following is a classic example of this unique Spanish institution.

The accusations are against Doctor Don Luís Joseph Merlo de la Fuente, oldest and most senior judge of the Audiencia de La Plata. His is a massive defense of the ninety-three *autos* (charges) against him consisting of 586 handwritten pages bound together as a book in which he comments on each of the 609 paragraphs of the *visita*. It is an extensive direct appeal to the king recounting, among many other things, his fifty years of service to the Crown in numerous places in the Spanish Empire. Merlo was besmirched by the Roca counterfeiting scandal . . . old grudges are now in the open and he reacts violently. But his accuser is the implacable scourge of counterfeiters, Dr. Don Francisco Nestares Marín.

Merlo begins (AGI Charcas 116: 3–10–1651):

> Your Majesty . . . the charges that he made against me were taken, not from depositions, but from testimony of judicial fines which Marín should have sent to the Treasury with the same zealousness with which he viewed his actions as worthy of a prize he hoped to receive and not with the approbation, consultation and order in which an investigation of this case should proceed.

Next Merlo opens his counterattack with a pious invocation:

> *Dirigat Dominus Verba mea*
> *In viam veritatis, et justitiae*
>
> (Lord, aim my speech into truth and justice)

But we are not interested in his alibis; the most revealing are Marin's charges against him, summarized here in order of their listing rather than degree of seriousness:

Charge 1. While investigating the death of Pedro Rodríguez de Mendoza, Merlo jailed Francisco de la Oseja, but let him go for a 2,000 peso bribe.

Charge 2. In the above case, he kept a mistress in his house, gambled with persons involved in the case, and extracted from them so much silver it took two mules to carry it back to La Plata.

Charge 3. In the above case he stayed in the house of one of the parties involved in the murder, and while there they fed him "with ostentation."

Charge 4. A priest claimed he lent Francisco de la Oseja 3,000 pesos to bribe Merlo, who insisted on 11,000 pesos.

Charge 5. During Holy Week of 1648, he went to the house of Luís de Vila (a silver broker at the mint), where he stayed for nine days while he and all his family were feted with revelry that amounted to 3,000 pesos. He caused great scandal by gambling publicly in the house of a notorious counterfeiter (Rocha?), and the gambling was so great that Juan Hidalgo Benitez lost more than 14,000 pesos; the other players were also counterfeiters (no doubt they were gambling with their own debased coins!).

Charge 6. He loaned the notorious counterfeiter Francisco de la Rocha six bars of silver at 4 percent interest instead of 12 percent, thereby giving him a great deal of confidence to proceed in his counterfeiting. Merlo was necessarily mixed up in this business (although the complaint does not specify exactly how) and he must have known about Rocha *because the Fiscal of the Audiencia had denounced him as early as August 29, 1647* [emphasis added].

Charge 7. Again Merlo was accused of loaning money at interest—a practice forbidden to royal officials.

Charge 8. On November 20, 1646, he received a silver pot from Miguel de Casanova, silver broker of the mint—and public delinquent. (Casanova testified it was a simple gift—more like a chocolate cup—and he didn't remember any more about it.)

Charge 9. On New Year's Day of 1646 Merlo went to the house of Lucas López de Zervantes, a mere defender of estates of the dead, and took liberties with his children.

Charge 10. In 1650 Merlo received two loaves of sugar and four little boxes of something unspecified as bribes from someone in a pending case.

Charges 11–14. Involved the taking of miscellaneous bribes in 1650 and 1651 in the amount of 600 pesos, 48 silver censers, and a 20-lb. lump of sponge silver.

Charge 15. On January 18, 1652, he received 300 pesos from his wife, who got it from Padre Francisco Joseph Ortíz, who got it from Marcos Cotrina, owner of mines and a mill in Uncia, who had a case pending against Juan del Moral from whom Merlo had received at the same time sponge silver worth more than 600 pesos.

Charges 16–25. Involve bribes of 16½ lbs. of sponge silver, 200 pesos, 2,000 pesos, 29 lbs. of sponge silver, two riding mules, a bolt of fancy cloth 486 ft. long, a stallion, another riding mule, yet another riding mule and a pack mule, 150 pesos, and another sum of 500 pesos from the governor at Santa Cruz, about which Merlo complained bitterly. The coins were brought to him by a priest, but they were all *debased and counterstamped cobs worth only 7½ reales* [emphasis added].

Here we begin to understand from Merlo's arguments in his defense these long lists of bribes are in reality fines he has imposed on guilty parties in cases he has ajudicated. Evidently Audiencia judges received fines directly and were then expected to deposit these funds in the

Royal Treasury, a procedure that may not have been strictly followed in every case. For example, it was not practical to deposit a riding mule (a very valuable animal at that time) and Merlo may have kept the animal until a buyer could be found. In many cases he claimed to have receipts for monies turned over to the Fiscal.

Another of Merlo's arguments in his defense claimed these accusations were not made directly against him and therefore witnesses were not required to declare themselves "friendly" or "enemy" to him—and being a judge, he had many enemies whose claims were thus invalid. Certainly a fine legal point, but understandable in view of the clouds of litigation that were continually stirred up throughout the viceroyalty.

Other interesting charges that reveal a great deal about the man and his times are summarized as follows:

Charge 30. That on July 8, 1653, he received from Miguel de Mecina (a prisoner in jail) 800 pesos of silver and by way of Padre Juan de Vedia, 200 pesos in reales, and by way of the negress Victoria 600 pesos and that furthermore he received six stools (some were from Paraguay) worth 60 pesos and a fly whisk that was "*mui curioso*" [very curious].

Charge 31. That he received two riding mules from Pedro de Chevelas. (This accusation generated a furious reply of nearly twelve folios.)

Charge 54. On November 19, 1650, Merlo visited the house of Doña Isabel Rosel Maldonado and told her that her case was bad; she gave him 21 lbs. of silver, and he came back and told her her case was good.

Charge 71. In the year 1647, being involved in the investigation of the murder of Juan de Soria, Merlo stayed overnight in the house of Rocha, the notorious counterfeiter, whenever he was in Potosí. But Rocha and his wife accused him of stealing Venetian glass, cream pitchers, and "other curiosities."

Charge 82. That high-stakes gambling was continually going on in his house. Litigants who wanted their cases expedited had to come to his house and gamble, and they lost a lot of money this way.

Charge 84. Although all ministers were prohibited from entering into business, he placed 7,000 pesos' worth of Spanish cloth in the shop of Pablo Rodríguez to be sold for his account.

Charge 85. That as a judge, he practiced law by advising litigants how to proceed.

Charge 91. That he consistently mishandled funds of various kinds. (This accusation generated fourteen pages of protest by Merlo.)

We can conclude from the enormity of charges against him that Judge Luís Joseph Merlo de la Fuente was a corrupt man in many ways who made little effort to hide his misdeeds. While almost any excess was a commonplace in the riotous surroundings at Potosí, Merlo lived in the comparatively quiet and peaceful administrative capital of La Plata (now Sucre) where his activities were more conspicuous. Generally speaking, his colleagues in the Audiencia were men of probity and respected for their diligence.

There is a possible clue to Merlo's contempt for government regulations to be found in one of his many *apologías* to these charges. In recalling his more than fifty years of service to the Crown, he bitterly notes both his sons were swept overboard in a storm and lost at sea while he was being shunted from one colonial post to another.

Mint Scandals of 1668

In spite of the profound coinage changes brought about in 1652 as a result of the Rocha crimes, control over activities of mint workers and officials at Potosí soon dissolved, lapsing back into malfeasance and crooked practices of every kind.[8] The royal inspector, Juan López del Aguila, was furious with what he found. Table 3.1 provides a partial list of the guilty and their punishments meted out that are typical of the legal system of this era.

It is clear that counterfeiting by mint employees had been commonplace in spite of the comparatively recent trial and sentences of execution meted out to conspirators of the Rocha gang. From surnames of those involved in this new scandal, it is evident nearly all mint officials were of Spanish rather than mestizo or Indian origin. However, this does not allow us to determine whether they were Creoles (born in Peru) or immigrants from Spain who often obtained these salaried jobs. Also we see there were three assayers involved in mint operations and none was Alonso de Ergueta, the mysterious individual "E" whose initial appeared on Potosí coinage as assayer from 1651 until 1679.

Ergueta, details of whom seem difficult to encounter in the archives, may have been a wealthy Spaniard who had purchased the office. This was a common speculative practice based on the possibility of profit from charges associated with the position that were credited to the holder's account. In such cases there was little incentive for his assay employees to undertake extra work unless they could devise schemes to augment their salaries—in this case, counterfeiting at the mint as we have seen in the Rocha case.

One such scheme seems to have involved laundering their illegal profits through buying and selling Negro slaves. Never very numerous in Potosí, they were believed to be specially suited for heavy, hot foundry work inside the mint building. Here they were kept as virtual prisoners, living in the attic and only allowed out on Sundays to attend Mass. The Florida Collection contains numerous examples of Potosí 8-

Table 3.1. Results of Investigation of the Mint Scandals of 1668

The Accused	The Punishment
Miguel de Casanoba	Condemned to death with total confiscation of his estate.
Bartolomé Hernandez (treasurer of the mint)	Total confiscation of his estate. He embezzled 266,128 pesos; his estate = 212,910 pesos; the balance owed: 53,218 pesos.
Alonso Sánchez Salvador	Fined 219,800 pesos.
Melchor de Escobedo	Total confiscation of his estate with remaining balance owed of 38,130 pesos.
Don Luís de Vila	Condemned to death with total confiscation of his estate.
Pedro Phelipe de Guadalupe	Condemned to death with total confiscation of his estate.
Diego Fernán Rodríguez	Condemned to death with total confiscation of his estate.
Miguel Ruíz	Condemned to death with total confiscation of his estate.
Franco Ximénez Cerbantes	Imprisoned in Panama & fined 57,993 pesos.
Juan Hidalgo Benítez (silver broker)	While in prison, he escaped owing 20,793 pesos.
Juan de Figueroa (chief assayer)	Fined 30,858 pesos for double-charging the treasury for charcoal.
Gerardo de Leon (asst. treasurer)	Condemned to death with total confiscation of his estate.
Luís de Peralta (assayer)	Fined 15,000 pesos & died in jail.
Francisco Cortéz (coiner)	Fined 3,000 pesos.
Juan López Llorente (coiner)	Fined 4,000 pesos.
Lt. Salbador de Herrera (silver scrap collector)	Fined 400 pesos.
Phelipe Ramírez (assayer)	Condemned to death.
Pedro Sambrano (assayer)	Condemned to death & confiscation of his estate.
Francisco Maldonado (mint foreman)	Condemned to death & total confiscation of his estate.
Favian Sánchez Romero (mint foreman)	Condemned to death & total confiscation of his estate.
Francisco de Balsera and Mathias de las Casas and accomplices in the making of false money are guilty of charging the treasury 800 pesos for the purchase of a Negress.	

Source: AGI Charcas 114.

reales coins from the Jupiter Wreck that may have been made by these same men during the late 1650s.

Although adjudication of this new wave of counterfeiting did not take place until 1668, a major investigation of the sort conducted by Juan López del Aguila often required several years of intense questioning of participants and informants after formal complaints had been filed. When such an investigator was at work, Potosí must have been a tense town, with rumors flying in all directions while the guilty trembled.[9]

Counterstamped Coins

The Florida Collection contains several counterstamped coins, one of which directly reflects the turmoil at the Potosí mint in the 1650s—indeed, no coin in the Florida Collection has a more complicated historical background than that shown in figure 3.1a–b. This is a Potosí 8 reales of 1650 struck under the supervision of Juan Rodríquez de Rodas, and then struck again by someone to reduce its value to 7½ reales. Details leading up to this unusual practice are marvelously complex. The good news is they have been exquisitely documented by Cunietti-Ferrando (1995: 147–182; 237–256). In this exhaustive study he identifies twenty-seven different countermarks used to devalue suspect coins of Rodas, Ergueta, and their predecessors. The mark illustrated here can be seen in the upper-left-hand corner of the shield where it appears as part of a circle with two conspicuous dots over the upper part of a crown. This punch was held at an angle to the surface of the coin so that other possible design features are missing (see fig. 3.1b). All coins in figure 3.1 and throughout the book are enlarged 150 percent for greater visibility.

Massive counterfeiting during the 1640s by the Rocha gang destroyed European confidence in the intrinsic value of Potosí coinage. King Felipe IV issued draconian directives to melt down all coins produced by those criminals using the mint. His orders were ignored outright or modified to lessen the impact on a poverty-stricken Indian population. The new mint personnel were unable to improve quality in the coins of 1650 sufficiently to meet the legal standard, so these, while legitimate mint products, had to be devalued by a ½ real to satisfy commerce in both the Old World and the New.

The countermark on this Florida Collection specimen was made from high-quality dies unlike any others known to me from publications illustrating the many varieties salvaged from the wreck of *Nuestra Señora de las Maravillas,* which sank in Bahamian waters. Nevertheless, the striking was careless and the stamped devaluation rendered poorly. We must not discount the possibility that the devaluation mark itself is counterfeit (as many were) on a legitimate but grossly underweight coin.

Several counterstamped Potosí 2-reales coins are present in the Florida Collection and illustrated in figure 3.1c–h. Although these are very interesting coins, they are not related to the mint scandals. The coin shown in figure 3.1c–d illustrates a simple crown device stamped into a previously well-circulated fractional coin produced by assayer "R" during the 1640s.

There is speculation this countermark was used to authorize its acceptance in the Danish West Indies but no archival confirmation has

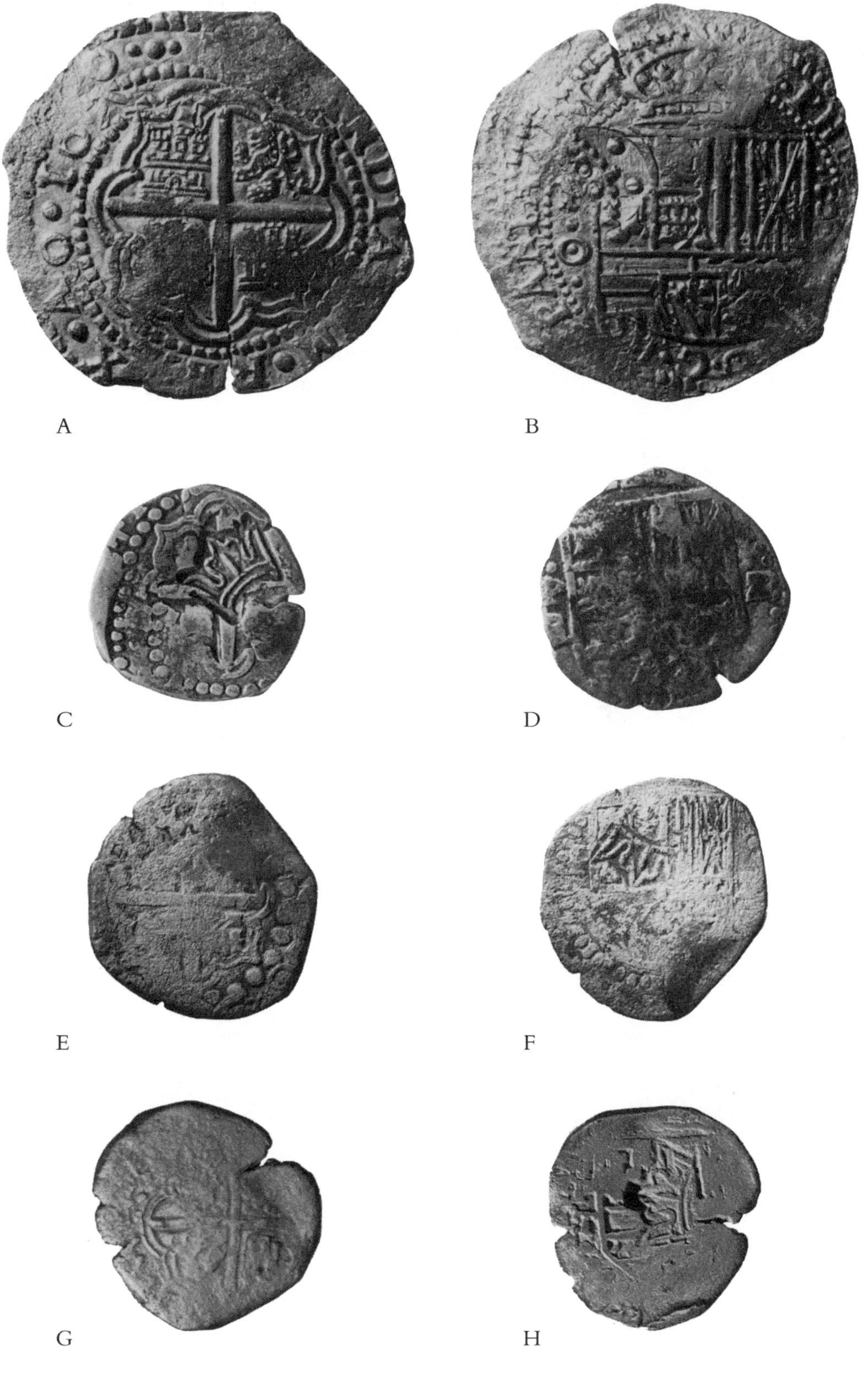

Figure 3.1. Counterstamped Cobs

come to my attention. Other specimens of this type have appeared from time to time in auction sales, always of the same denomination (2 reales) and mint.

Future research may well disclose the basis for devaluation (if any) or, as is more likely, a legal conversion rate into another European monetary system. There are several well-known examples in French and Dutch Caribbean possessions of use of minor foreign coins and carefully cut Spanish colonial silver coins when small change was scarce.

From evidence in hand we can say this is not a Spanish crown. Therefore we have the interesting case of a Spanish colonial coin falling into possession of a foreign government that appropriated it for its own use, only to have it return to Spanish control on board a Spanish vessel wrecked in Florida waters. More intriguing is the question, Were these exchanges by peaceful commerce or were they caused by force in warfare or piracy?

When we hold such a coin in our hands and consider all these possibilities, it becomes easier to understand the pleasure treasure coin collectors receive from their study of these historic artifacts. In a hobby grown much too expensive for most of us, we can still participate in the romance through our own Florida Collection, carefully preserved for all of us to enjoy.

CHAPTER 4

From Mountain to Monarch

All Spanish silver coins in the Florida Collection share a remarkable evolution; it is a pathway more complicated than you may have imagined. To illustrate how coins were made we will follow Potosí silver from the mountain (illus. 4.1) to Spain. Although mines, refineries, mint, and treasury were all very close together at Potosí, the basic processes, with minor variations, were the same for all New World mining districts and mint operations. The practices developed there took place over a considerable period of time and represent what was being done at Potosí about 1652, shortly after the coinage reforms were in force.

Mining Methods

Illustration 4.2 diagrams these processes as a flowchart beginning with the deep shaft shown in Cerro Rico silver deposits. Station 1 is the mine where very hard work begins. All Spanish colonial silver mines were located underground beneath rectangular mining claims measuring 60 x 40 *varas* (165 by 110 ft., 1 *vara* = 33 in.) and extending indefinitely vertically downward from the surface. This meant an ore deposit was exploited by a series of shafts with only a limited opportunity legally to follow veins horizontally before reaching the claim boundaries. At Cerro Rico the mines deepened rapidly such that within three years of its discovery in 1545, some shafts were already 80 *varas* (220 ft.) deep. At the very bottom skilled *barreteros* used their long iron pry bars to break out ore by the light of a tallow candle, gunpowder not yet being in common use until early in the eighteenth century. During the course of a 10-hour work shift, these miners never left the hot, damp, poorly ventilated

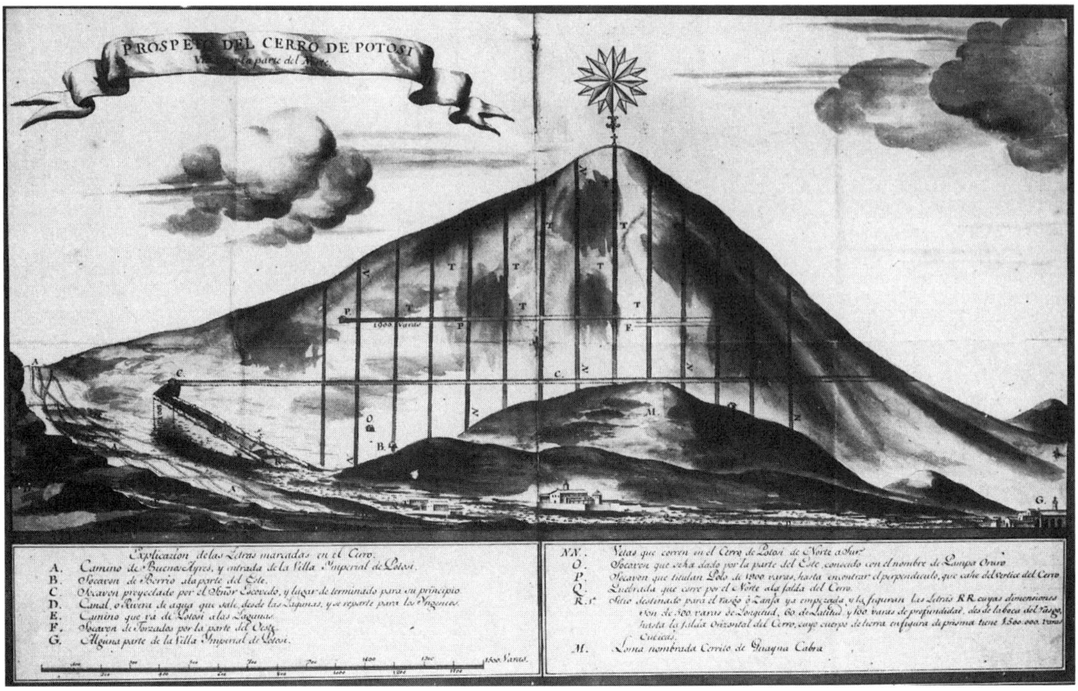

Illus. 4.1. Hypothetical cross section through Cerro Rico showing proposed draining tunnels and indicating the benefits they would provide.

darkness. Chewing dried coca leaves was their only means of alleviating these grim conditions.

It was the task of *apiris* (or *tenateros* as they were known in Mexico) to climb down to the working face and slowly back up again with a leather bag full of ore. These agile young Indians made a fixed number of trips each day along a leather rung ladder, something like the rope ladder ratlines in use on tall sailing ships. Eventually regulations required that a resting platform be constructed every 10 *varas* so that men on the way up could rest and allow others to pass them on the way down. This was always dangerous work because of rocks and bodies falling down open shafts.[1]

On the surface, ore was dumped out of bags and hand-sorted by keen-eyed *palladores,* often women, who also offered food and drink to miners at the end of their day and night work shifts. Meanwhile, teams of pack animals (llamas) were driven up to the sorting area where selected ore was placed in coarse woolen bags and loaded onto the backs of large, castrated llamas, each capable of bringing down about 20 kilos.

Hundreds of llamas were led down to the base of the mountain, where many water-powered stamp mills known as *ingenios* (station 2 in illus. 4.2) were located along a single aqueduct. Here the ore was crushed and mixed with various reagents before mercury was added to begin a version of the amalgamation process, developed a century earlier in Mexico (Craig 1993). After several weeks of stirring this mixture, the

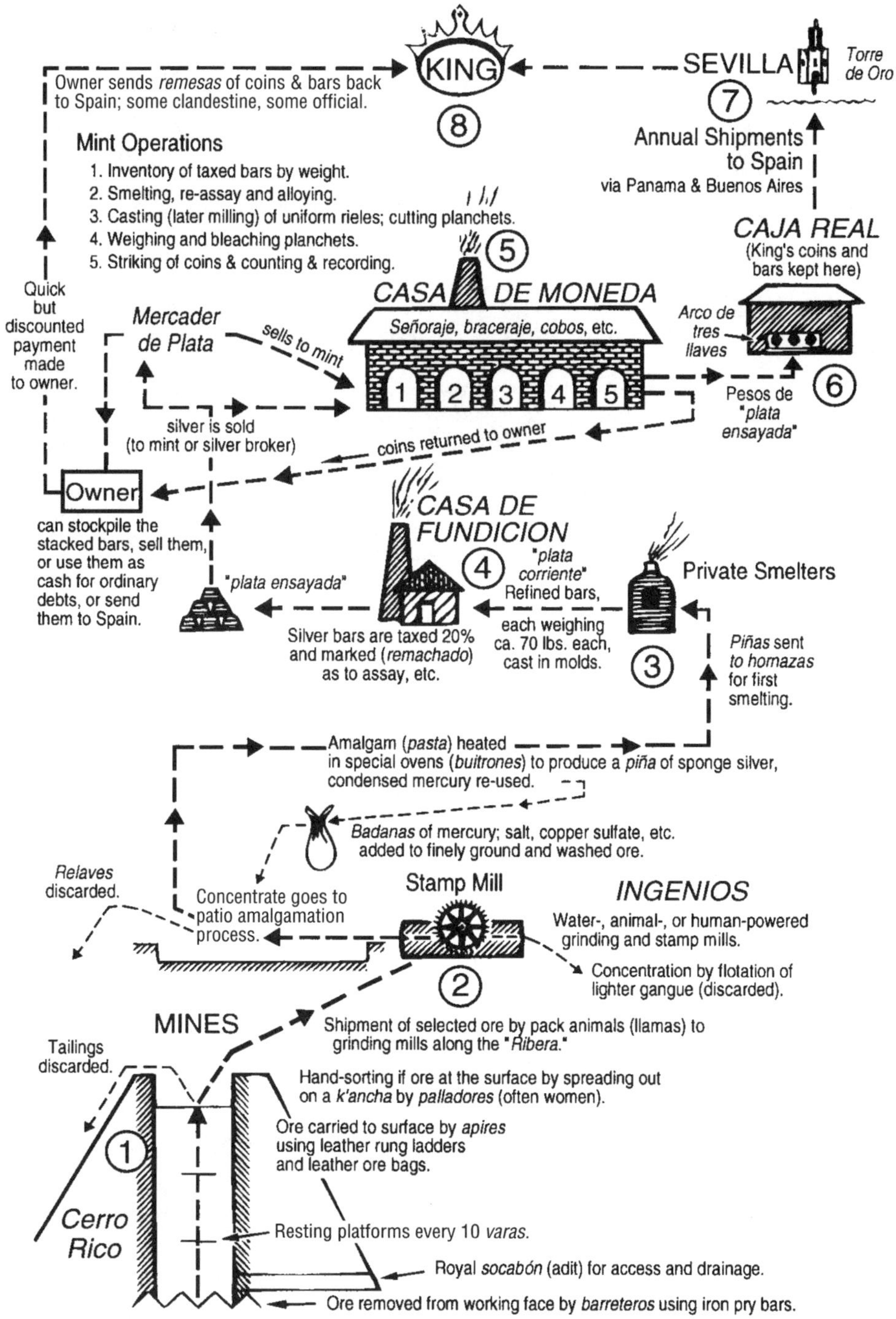

Illus. 4.2. From mountain to monarch: how silver coins were made. A schematic chart traces the process of mining silver ore at Potosí, refining it, converting it to coin and transporting the wealth to Spain. This is a composite of steps that were followed by the late seventeenth century.

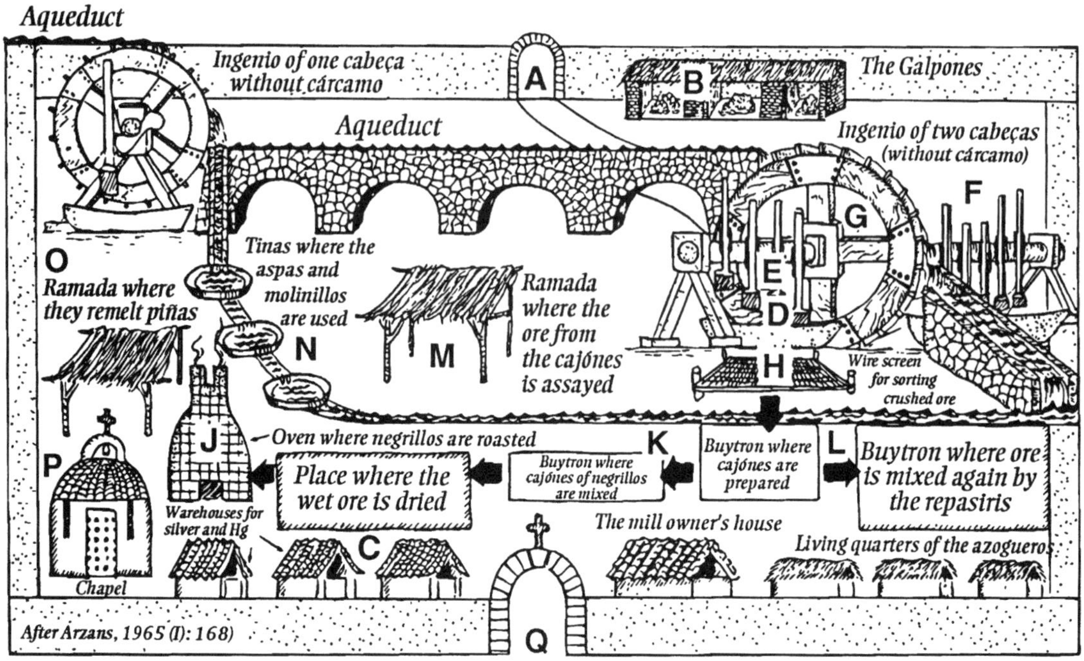

Illus. 4.3. Patio amalgamation at Potosí, ca. 1620. Sketched plan of a silver-refining stamp mill powered by waterwheels.

result was a spongy mass of silver amalgam or *pasta* from which excess mercury had to be expelled in several stages, the first being to enclose the *pasta* in a coarse cloth and twist it with stout poles.

Now it was referred to as a *piña* and was often used informally (and illegally) as a medium of exchange for large purchases and debt payments. More often it was sold as soon as possible to a *mercader de plata* who functioned as a silver broker, buying the still-unrefined amalgam at a substantial discount, smelting it down into a manageable ingot (the so-called *plata corriente*), and taking this to the mint to be assayed, or perhaps converted into coins.

Some mine and mill owners took their *pastas* or *piñas* of nearly pure silver to a private smelter (station 3 in illus. 4.2), then to the official foundry (station 4 in illus. 4.2). Here silver was smelted again and cast into ingots that were assayed, and stamped (*remachado*) with fineness, weight in *marcos,* assayer's identification, year of manufacture, a control number, and numerous royal tax stamps indicating the *quinto* had been paid. If the ingot itself was used to pay taxes it was further stamped with a large "A" for *(h)acienda,* indicating it now belonged to the king. Otherwise, it soon received yet another prominent marking in the form of the owner's private brand, similar in appearance to those used on cattle. After construction of the mint (station 5 in illus. 4.2) in 1576, all these operations involving silver bars were accomplished in the official foundry that had been incorporated into this building.

At this point silver was considered legal tender or *plata ensayada.* Most silver bars were refined until they contained 2,380 parts of silver out of

2,400 possible. These extremely fine bars were then smelted and carefully alloyed with copper in order to produce a coin alloy of 11 *dineros* (.916 fine), which was poured into shallow, narrow molds to produce *rieles*. These were thin silver straps from which individual planchets were cut with large steel shears. When a planchet was formed it was passed to the *balanceador* (weigher) who used a balance beam to check the silver blank against a tray with a standard weight for that denomination. Sometimes overweight planchets had to be passed back and forth several times until they were properly adjusted, then tossed into a basket to be carried back to the annealing furnace. Since seriously underweight coins were costly to recycle, the planchet maker (*cortador*) tried hard to make his first cut produce a blank just slightly overweight. Any trim-

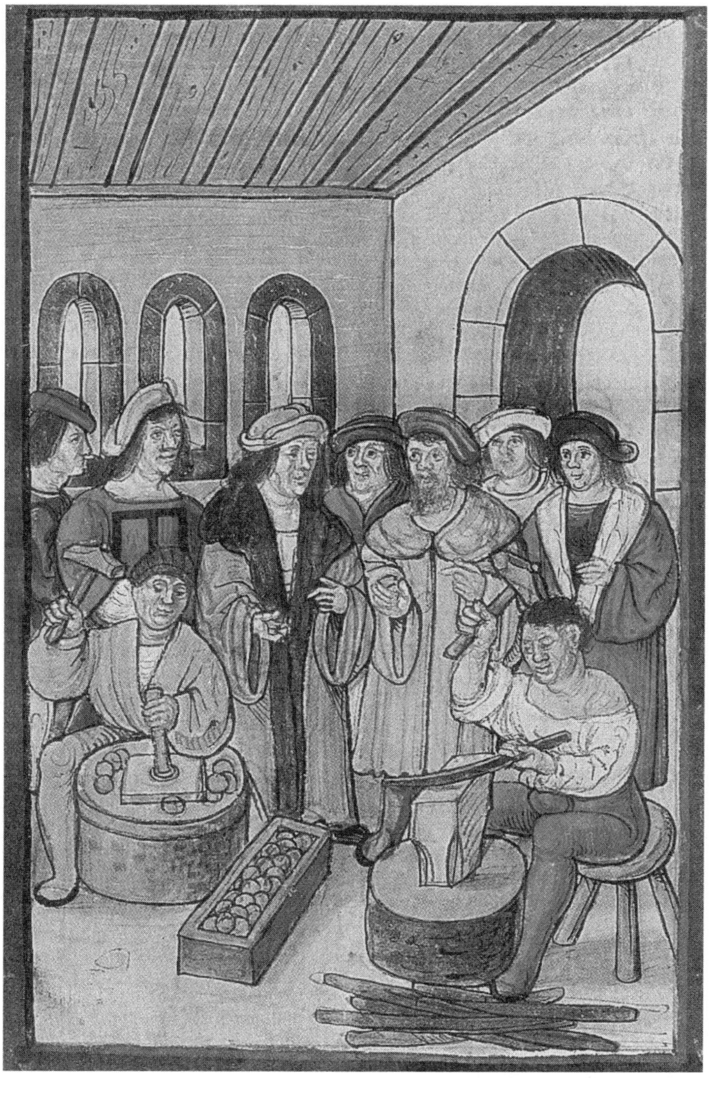

Illus. 4.4. Preparing *rieles* for shearing into planchets. This early sixteenth-century print of a Swiss mint is highly realistic with respect to the long, narrow straps of silver in the foreground being converted into coin planchets.

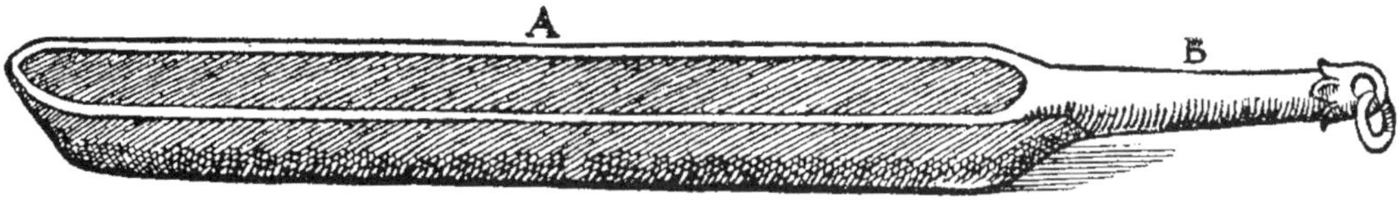

Illus. 4.5. Mold for silver strap (*riel*). Both stone and metal molds of varying sizes were used to create the *rieles* for coins and case ingots.

mings were known as *cizalla* and were of much interest and concern to everyone working in the mint.[2]

After blackish fire scale was removed from the planchets by the *blanqueador,* they were picked up with tongs and placed between dies that were struck a heavy blow with a large lead-filled hammer or hand sledge.[3] Die bounce and occasional extra blows commonly produced multiple partial impressions; at this time tension cracks often developed on work-hardened, poorly annealed planchets. The result was a coin absolutely unique; under these circumstances no two hand-struck cobs can ever be exactly alike. A more detailed description of these subjects is found in chapter 5.

From the mint, the king's bars, unused *rieles,* and any taxes collected in the form of coins and ingots were all sent across the plaza to the Caja Real or treasury building (station 6 in illus. 4.2) where they were formally received, signed for, and placed in a strongbox (*arca de tres llaves*) that could be opened only by three different keys. The viceroy and other royal officials often made withdrawals of these coins to pay for their expenses, but bars that belonged to the king were sent down to Lima once a year, scheduled to arrive in April before winter snows closed the mountain passes.

The trip back to Spain was laborious. Sturdy mules were preferred for bringing the king's bars down to Callao, the port for Lima. Here a silvermaster recorded the loading of all specie on board and eventually turned them over to another official at Panama for yet another transfer by mule train to the Caribbean side of Panama at Portobelo. Here again a silvermaster logged them on board a ship bound for Vera Cruz in Mexico where more coins were added to the cargo. After another stop in Havana, an entire convoy set sail across the Atlantic for Cádiz. The treasure ships then crossed a dangerous bar at the mouth of the Guadalquivir River and slowly worked their way upstream to the dock at Sevilla. At the famous customhouse known as the *Torre de Oro* (station 7 in illus. 4.2) everything was unloaded and the king's share sent as rapidly as possible to wherever he happened to be at the time.

Colonial Refining Methods at Potosí

Step 2 in illustration 4.2 deserves a closer look at this remarkable medieval machinery. Illustration 4.3 represents a facsimile schematic sketch of a typical Potosí *ingenio* (stamp mill) functioning about the year 1600. It has been modified considerably (Craig 1993: 135) from the original to be found in Arzáns de Orsúa y Vela (1965 1: 168) in order to show details of waterwheels and the iron-shod stamps they actuated.

These mills were completely surrounded with high walls of rammed earth having two entrances (A and Q in illus. 4.3). The refining process began at the rear entrance A with the arrival of ore brought down from

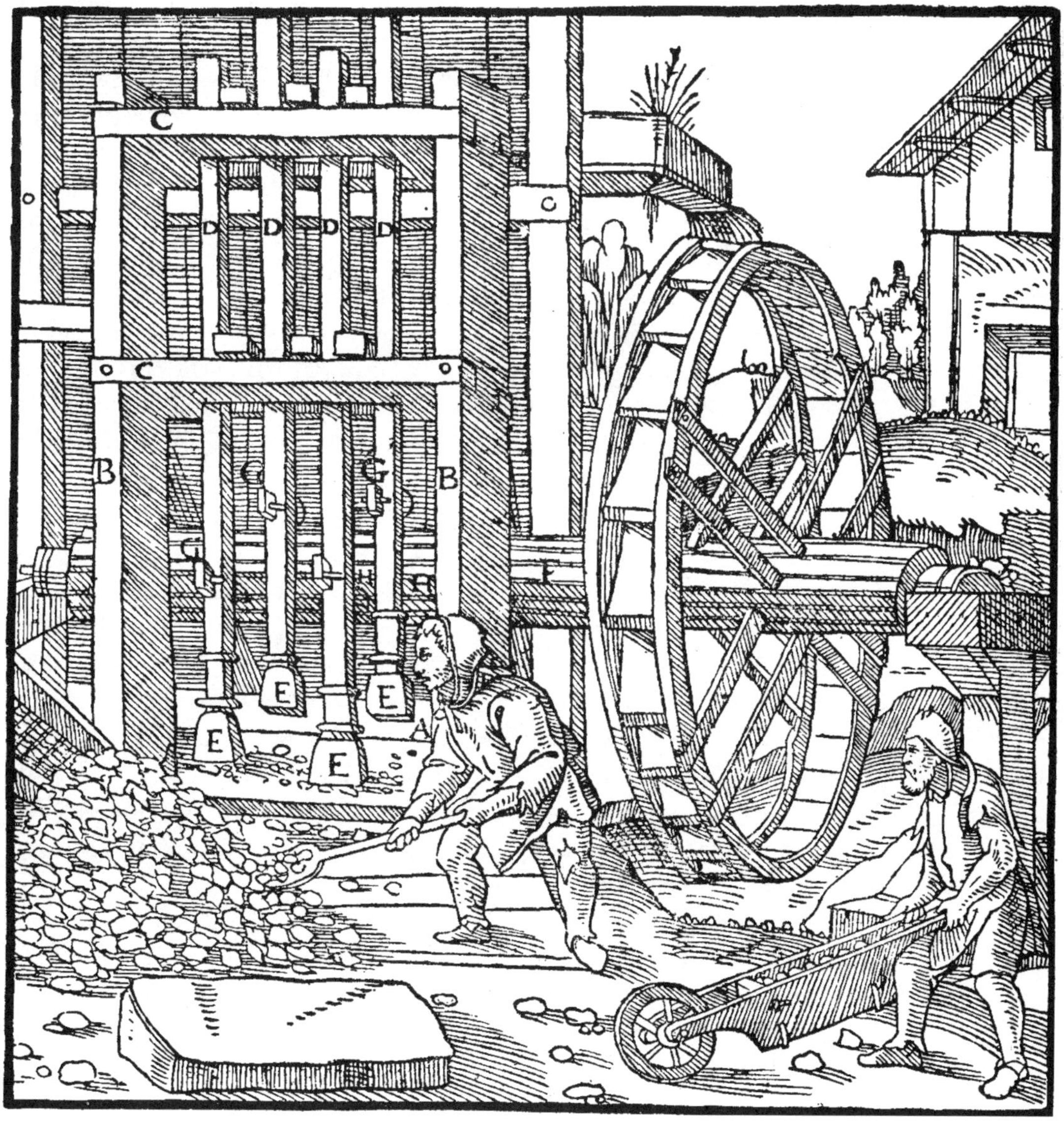

Illus. 4.6. A medieval German hydraulic stamp mill used to crush silver ore.

nearby mines. During winter months (June through September) when the entire hydraulic network was likely to be frozen, silver ore accumulated in covered bins (*galpones*) (B in illus. 4.3) according to the type of mineralization it contained. Especially rich ore, partially refined silver, and extremely expensive flasks of mercury were kept in carefully guarded storage huts at (C). When flowing water was again available and waterwheels could turn, chunks of ore were carried to the large stone *mortero* (D) where they were crushed by falling iron shoes known as *amaldanetas* (E) attached to the bottoms of tall wooden *mazos* (F). In reality waterwheels (G), shown exposed in this sketch, were tightly enclosed in a narrow *carcamo,* or double-sided stone wall, which directed aqueduct water onto wooden blades of the wheel. Two wooden bearings were inset into stonework to help support a heavy wooden axle turning its battery of as many as ten stamps. When a batch of ore was sufficiently crushed, the flow of water was diverted around the waterwheel by closing wooden gates. When the stamps stopped, finely crushed ore could be removed for sifting through large iron screens at H. This was recognized as dangerous work because of silica dust, so it was relegated to Indian women and children who wore cloth masks. If a load of ore (*cajón*) became wet before amalgamation started, it could be dried in a simple adobe oven (J) that could also be used to roast sulfide ores (*negrillos*). Otherwise it was carried to a rectangular, stone-lined pit or *buytrón* (K) where a great deal of stirring and mixing with mercury and other reagents took place. If the ore was rather low grade or difficult to work with for any reason, it was transferred to L where it was trodden, much like wine grapes, by barefooted workers called *repasiris* and even gently heated from below in some of the more elaborate mills.

In about two weeks, mercury was already amalgamated with silver and worked its way down by gravity toward the bottom of the pits. This bottom layer was removed and a small sample (*pella*) of amalgam was brought to an open-air lean-to (*ramada*) for a rough assay by boiling off mercury. From the pure silver left behind it was possible to calculate total value contained in the remainder of the load. If this was too low, more crushing, more mixing, or more reagents could be added, and the whole process begun anew. If the assay proved favorable, all the bottom layer was carried to large basins (*tinas*) (N) where sponge-silver amalgam was carefully panned out. These small bits of pasty amalgam were gathered together and placed in a retort to be heated under another open-air lean-to at O. Here some of the mercury vapor was condensed to be used again; left behind was a large lump (*piña*) of very pure silver. At last, the fruits of this arduous labor appeared.

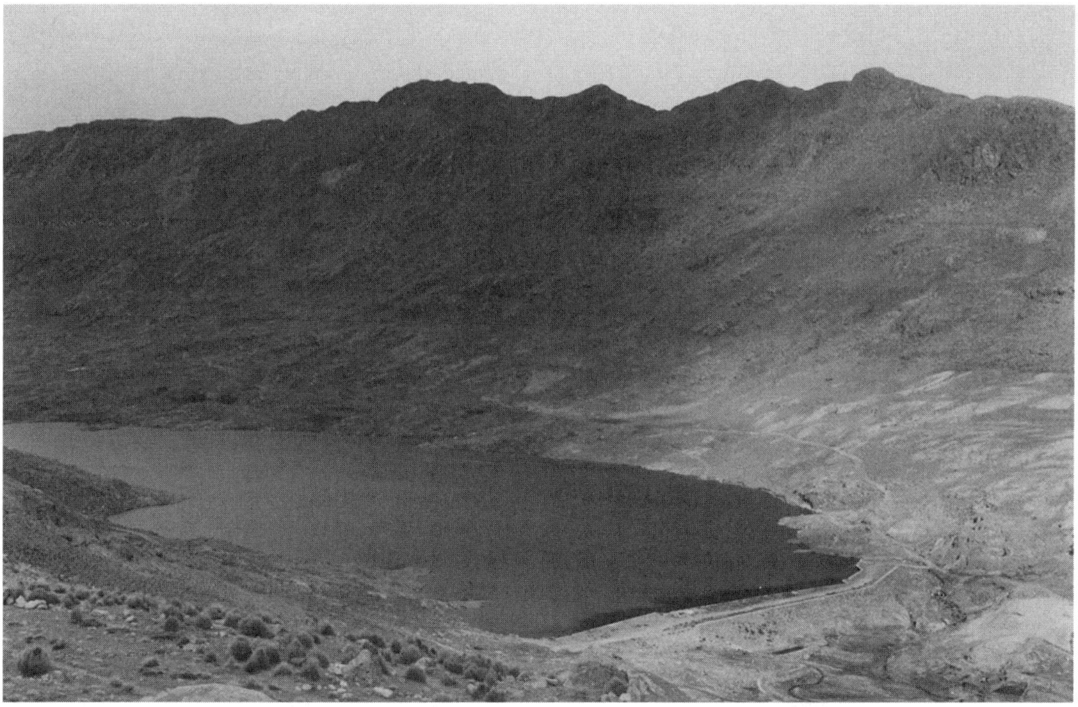

Illus. 4.7. View of the San Idelfonso reservoir today, high above Potosí. In 1626 the dam burst and destroyed many of the stamp mills located below it.

Most miners had this work done on a custom basis in mills they did not own. Since this refining method was understandably slow and costly, only a few wealthy miners operated their own mills. Anyone who owned a mill and had a certain number of Indian laborers assigned to him was eligible to buy a fixed amount of mercury supplied and priced by a government monopoly. Only these men were the famous *azogueros* (handlers of mercury). There were never more than about two hundred of them in the Potosí district. A few of them, such as Antonio López Quiroga, became both politically and economically powerful (Bakewell 1988).

In 1626 a reservoir dam burst, releasing a disastrous *huaico* (mud avalanche) that destroyed many refining mills in the city and the aqueduct that supplied the waterwheels; this left the entire mining economy in shambles, from which it was very slow to recover. This in turn left the Royal Treasury strapped for funds and mint workers disgruntled at being behind in their pay.[4]

After the avalanche of 1626 many *ingenio* owners did not have the means to rebuild and miners did not have enough rich ore left to supply them. But an *ingenio* owner did have other valuable assets: his quota of Indian workers and his ration of mercury were both commodities to be bartered with an ever-present trickle of optimists who wanted to try their luck on the famous mountain.

CHAPTER 5

Finding Your Way around Cobs

Growing up in a modern society we soon learn to recognize coins we use by their distinctive sizes and designs. During our lifetimes these designs change slowly, if at all, and we feel confident these coins are going to be accepted when we spend them. On the other hand, we are suspicious and doubtful of any coin that looks strange or damaged. These human reactions have remained constant since rudimentary coins were first used several thousand years ago in Asia Minor.

Because the vast majority of coins in the Florida Collection are salvaged Spanish colonial cobs, these sunken treasure coins definitely fall into the "strange or damaged" category. Therefore, the purpose of this chapter is to provide readers with an introduction to the sometimes bizarre world of coins known to English speakers as "cobs."

There is no credible explanation of the origin of the word "cob" and it certainly was not used by Spanish colonial people who made these rough and savage-looking coins.[1] Although they invented numerous contemporary slang terms for them, these nicknames did not suggest anyone thought well-made cobs were ugly.

Truly beautiful coins were made by early Greeks from the fifth century B.C. onward. This tradition continued under the Romans until artistic quality of most coinage degenerated during the Middle Ages. By the time cobs from Spanish colonial mints began to pour into Spain, people in Europe were already accustomed to accepting similar, crudely made coins from their own mints. When Europeans discovered some New World coins had slightly higher silver content than their own coinage they gladly received them, sometimes even paying a small premium.

How Cobs Are Made

By definition, a cob coin is made by hand under circumstances such that no two of them can ever be exactly alike. If you think you have two that are precisely alike, look more closely and you will find that one, or both, are cast counterfeits. This must be so because authentic cobs are made from cutting out a slightly overweight blank from a narrow, rather thin strap of carefully alloyed silver, often of uneven thickness. This flan is then further trimmed down with large steel shears or chisels until it falls within legal weight limits for its denomination. When these irregular pieces of silver have been processed to the point they are ready to be struck with coin dies, they are technically called planchets. Often some heavy hammering was done on the larger ones to make them appear more rounded, like some of the better-made coins minted at that time in Europe using screw presses. Before being struck between dies, planchets were inserted into a special annealing furnace to relax the work-hardened silver that may have become brittle.

When poorly annealed cob planchets were finally inserted into iron dies and struck with a heavy sledge hammer, they often developed fine tension cracks around the edges, or deep jagged splits, or both. But if the coin was still within legal weight limits, such a cob was put to use no matter how cracked and battered it appeared because it was too costly to recycle it.

Fairly soft iron dies were used in Spanish colonial mints, which allowed use of steel engraving tools and punches by the die sinker who cut the required designs. A few of these men, especially those who came over after long training in Spain, were skilled at this work and produced excellent dies. Others who were Creole (in other words, anyone of Spanish origin born in the New World) apprentices were sometimes not so clever. But any die, no matter how perfectly rendered, was subject to varying rates of immediate wear and deterioration depending on how well it was case hardened. This hardening or tempering was done by repeated heating and quenching. If a die was not properly case hardened, it could shatter after a few coins were struck. When this occurred the remaining image was ground off the surface of the cylindrical iron rod and prepared for engraving again.

Sometimes in the course of a single year it is possible to identify dozens of distinctive dies made by several engravers used to strike the same denomination coin. Indeed, in the Florida Collection it is difficult to find several cobs with the same date made from the same die; however, it is possible to recognize distinctive die elements or punches from certain coins. When there was no silver to be processed at the mint during certain times of the year, these costly dies and iron rod stock were set aside and often rusted. If not cleaned immediately before use, rusty and worn dies produced another endless variety of poor-quality cobs that appeared worn the very day they were struck.

With the lower cylindrical die set into a massive wooden base, a planchet was placed between it and the upper cylindrical die, held by a coiner using large iron tongs. His partner then struck the upper die a mighty blow with a lead-filled sledge hammer. This commonly caused the hammer to bounce. If the upper die was not firmly held in place when the hammer came down again a split second later at a slight angle, a partial second impression of the coin design could occur. But during that same brief interval the planchet itself might become dislodged so that when the bounce blow occurred yet another partial die impression was transferred. On occasion a struck planchet shot out from between dies, was picked up and placed between them again, without regard to its original orientation, and promptly struck a second time. Of course, this produced bizarre and sometimes amazing results. Examples exist in the Florida Collection that show at least three separate bounces of the die on different planchet orientations.

In early colonial days cob making in the mints was brutal work. It was done under constant pressure from foremen to finish a day's production run and shut down furnaces in order to save on expenses they were obligated to pay. As long as there was molten silver to be poured, the coining team was expected to expedite all its particular tasks.

Die engraving was also done under trying circumstances. Poor light, poor eyesight, and poor education must have caused many of the awkward errors and irregularities that are so conspicuous in the dies used to make cobs. As described earlier, these dies were then case hardened but quickly became worn or shattered, producing another quality problem. So many dies were needed that much of this work was given over to apprentice die sinkers who did a great deal of grinding and retooling of worn dies, again leaving distinctive markings between one cob and another.

As a result of these rather crude minting procedures, it is possible to look at many cobs in the Florida Collection and tell at once in which mint they were made without examining details of the design itself to find the mint mark and assayer's initial. Deeply cracked and split cobs are often characteristic of the Potosí mint (see fig. 5.1b). Smooth-edged cobs are typical of the Mexico and Lima mints, but Mexico coins (fig. 5.1a) show distinctive hammered facets around the edges that often emphasize their rectangular shape. Lima coins (fig. 1c), like those from Potosí, may show annealing cracks and splits around the edges, but these are less pronounced compared with those on Potosí coins. Colombian

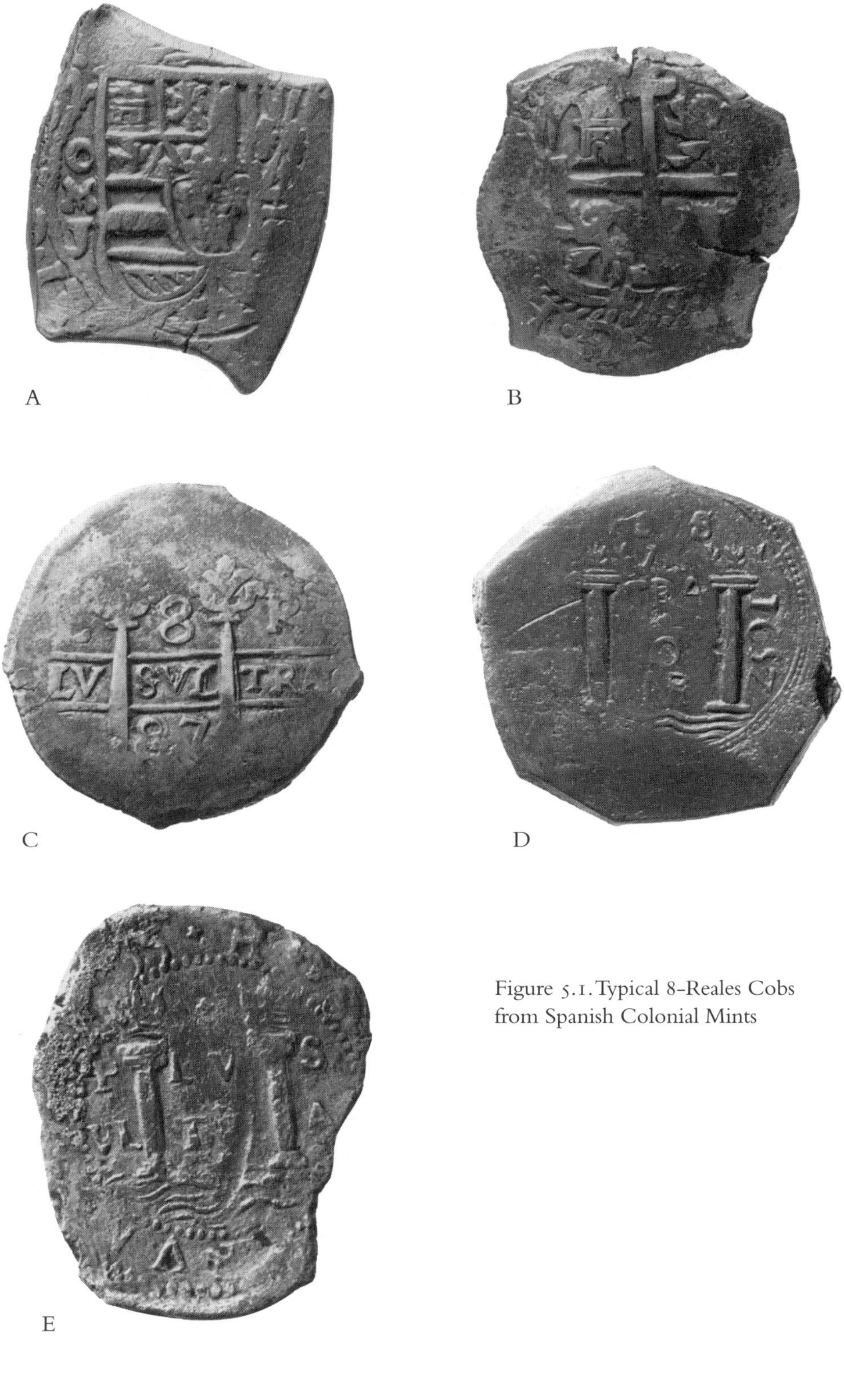

Figure 5.1. Typical 8-Reales Cobs from Spanish Colonial Mints

mints at Santa Fé de Bogotá (fig. 5.1d) and Cartagena (fig. 5.1e) produced a comparative handful of silver cobs typically made on thin planchets that often have a polygonal shape.

You might well ask, Why would Spanish colonial mints essentially using the same hand methods each produce coins that have a distinct appearance, not to mention their radically different die designs? The answer as far as cracks are concerned has to do with fuel. Coins made at the high-altitude (14,750-ft.) Potosí mint were often poorly annealed by assayers who were trying to save money on expensive charcoal for their furnaces. Fuel was cheaper at other mints, and so was the cost of living. At Potosí, grossly underpaid mint employees were anxious to cut corners by any means . . . fair or foul.

This brief overview does not do justice to the incredibly complex steps involved in making cob coins. Readers are invited to experience the complete process by joining a "Virtual Visit to the Potosí Mint in 1700" offered as Appendix B in this book.

How Many Kinds Are There?

Since the 1530s, when the first cobs were made in Mexico, New World mints have produced them in ¼-, ½-, 1-, 2-, 3-, 4-, 8-, and 10-reales denominations. Forget about the 3- and 10-reales coins—not only are they absent from the Florida Collection, you will never find one and may not even see a photograph of one. Figure 5.2 illustrates the comparative sizes of common cobs ranging from the ½ real to the 8 reales. Cob ¼-real coins are so tiny they usually are damaged, or corroded, or both, and are very scarce from any mint by any assayer. Indeed, there are none in the Florida Collection. However, very attractive milled ¼-real coins in beautiful condition are still available in the private market, but prices are steadily rising.[2]

Galanos

Nothing has stirred more excitement among cob collectors than their desire to own outstanding specimens dealers used to refer to as "royals." I objected (Craig 1988) to use of this term with its implication they were made expressly for the king. There is abundant evidence these were actually extraordinary coins prepared for several special purposes and I suggested it would be more accurate to call them "presentation pieces." They all stand out from the ordinary round of battered, hand-struck coins to such an extent Spanish writers (for instance, Lázaro, 1996) now refer to them as *redondos* (round ones) for lack of a better word. However, one exists: Lazo García (1992, 3: 79) has published a 1646 Potosí mintage document proving contemporary scribes listed

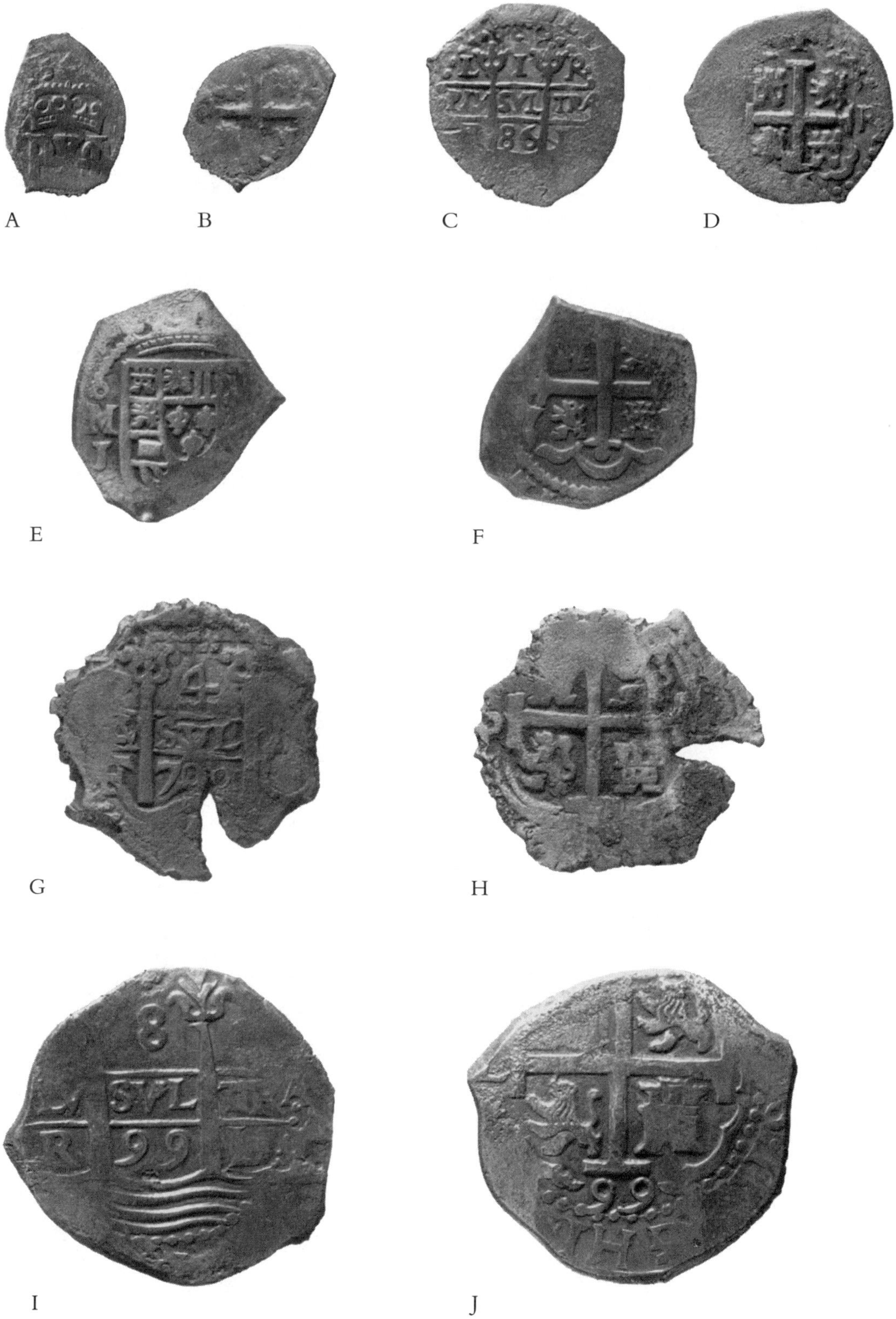

Figure 5.2. Cob Coin Denominations

them as *galanos* (handsome, fine-looking). No finer example from Potosí is known to me than the famous Norweb specimen of 1657 (fig. 5.3a–b). It is indeed a gallant coin that displays all the necessary criteria: (1) broad, very round planchet; (2) full legal weight; (3) carefully executed, correct engraving; (4) complete design impression including the outermost circle of denticles on both sides; and (5) no doubling caused by die bounce.

This exquisite Potosí 8 reales of 1657 is arguably the finest known silver presentation piece, or "royal," ever produced at this mint. It was donated by Mr. and Mrs. Henry Norweb of the American Numismatic Society, which has authorized its reproduction here. In my opinion it represents the very pinnacle of the colonial cob die cutter's art. Nothing made at Potosí before or since in the handmade cob series equals the technical skills inherent in this coin. Even so, it has a glaring problem that leaps out at the viewer of this photograph. Although similar specially prepared large silver coins were occasionally made at Mexico, and more rarely at Lima, after the mint reforms of 1728 everyone became direct employees of the Crown and the practice stopped. Every so-called royal I have seen with a later date is only a sad attempt by auction houses to inflate the value of vastly inferior coins whose only claim to such fame is their approach to partial roundness.

By now you have probably found the egregious error on the Norweb coin. If not, read on. From the illustrations in this book of ordinary coins produced at Potosí after the reforms of 1652, it is obvious the coin design itself was still in a state of flux. In any year during the period 1650–1658 it is possible to encounter significant die varieties. I am left with the impression that the Norweb coin was made to special order on an unusually large flan in an effort to stabilize these design changes and provide apprentice engravers a clear model for their working dies.

Imagine the chagrin of the master engraver when it was first pointed out to him that in the legends of his masterpiece, with its so carefully spaced letters, he identified it as a coin of King PHILIPVS IIIII. I believe the real king, Phillip IV, would not have been amused to see he was already deposed (and presumably dead) by the hand of an ignorant die engraver who did not know proper roman numerals!

Of course coins that demonstrate all of these qualities are very few, so we are left to consider candidates that are not so perfect, and some that clearly don't belong in the company of *galanos.* In figure 5.3c–d is the best example from the Florida Collection, a 1654 8 reales from Potosí, exhibiting round shape with careful engraving and strikings. What cannot be seen in figure 5.3c–d is the strange edge of this coin. The proper weight planchet, which must have had a slightly irregular outline, was struck with the die, then deliberately hammered by someone (at the

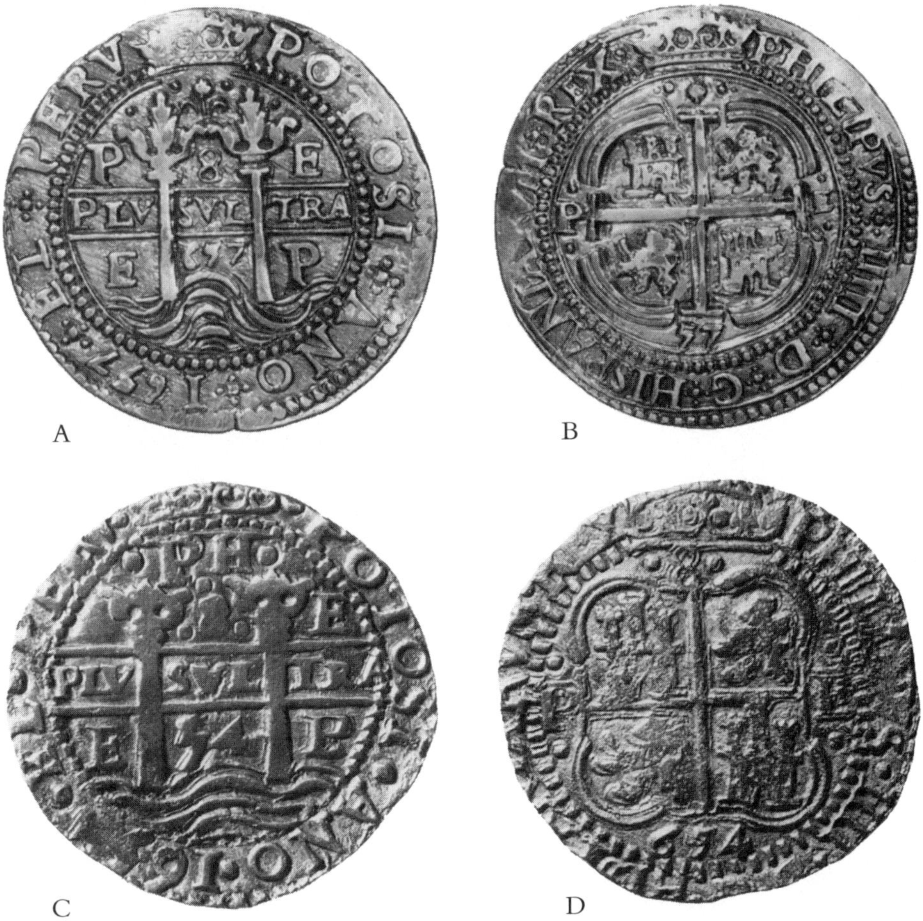

Figure 5.3. The Norweb *Galano* of 1657 *(a, b)* and a Comparable Specimen of 1654 *(c, d)*, both from the Potosi mint. From the Florida Collection

mint?) into roundness by connecting many small flattened areas along the entire edge. This produced the overall roundness seen here, but this is no royal. It failed to be stamped with much of the outer die design and denticulation. More important, it lacks the required mint mark in the upper-left-hand corner above "PLV."

Unfortunately, in my opinion, many of the *redondos* illustrated in Lázaro's 1996 catalog fall into this category. He illustrates many from the Mexico, Lima, and Potosí mints, the earliest dates being 1607, 1684, and 1630, respectively. Most numerous are the Potosí *galanos,* which seem to have been made almost continuously since that date. However, documentation for them only begins in 1646 and remains quite scattered until the record ends in 1757 (see table 5.1). Collectors will recognize that in fact *galanos* are known for many of the years where there are gaps in this record. So far the archives provide no clue as to why there are such fluctuations in the numbers produced from year to year.

In addition to their obvious utility as special presents, ornaments, and the like, I suspect they may have been made on occasion by special order and in relatively large numbers by businessmen who needed them for

Table 5.1. Annual Weight of Silver in *Marcos* Converted at Potosí into *Galanos* (after Lazo García 1992) and Hypothetical Minimum Number of *Galanos* Struck If All Were 8-Reales Denominations

Year	*Marcos*	Number Struck	Year	*Marcos*	Number Struck
1646	86	720	1727	301	2,521
1654	15	126	1728	197	
1661	14	117	1729	92	771
1662	55	461	1730	80	670
1664	30	251	1731	101	845
1672	453	3,793	1732	77	
1673	184	1,541	1733	131	
1674	150	1,256	1734	200	
1679	109	912	1735	242	
1680	222	1,859	1736	182	
1681	46	385	1737	210	
1682	252	2,110	1738	238	
1683	183	1,533	1739	125	
1684	295	2,470	1740	190	
1685	85	712	1741	99	
1686	228	1,909	1742	185	
1687	163	1,365	1743	143	1,197
1688	141	1,180	1744	140	1,172
1689	245	2,051	1745	148	1,239
1690	398	3,333	1746	187	1,566
1691	179	1,499	1747	242	2,027
1692	144	1,206	1748	108	905
1693	136	1,139	1749	131	1,097
1694	98	820	1751	106	
1698	16	134	1752	68	
1699	93	778	1754	49	410
1726	162	1,357			

Note: Since *galanos* were specially set aside for "beauty and extra weight," it does not follow they were all round presentation coins or heart-shaped.
Extracted from Lazo García (1992).

important transactions where their acceptance was critical. This may account for the frequency with which they are found today with counterstamps from later Central American republics. Whatever the motive for their manufacture, these coins simply could not have been made on a cost-effective basis when so much special handling was involved. I conclude that if in 1672 the owner of 453 *marcos* of silver required they be converted into 3,793 *galanos* at the Potosí mint, then he must have paid the coiners extra to have this work done.

Regardless of its lamentable condition, there is one important Mexican 8 reales of 1714 that deserves special mention. This coin, shown as figure 5.4 in obverse and reverse views, was engraved and struck to highest possible standards of that time—fully equivalent to the best

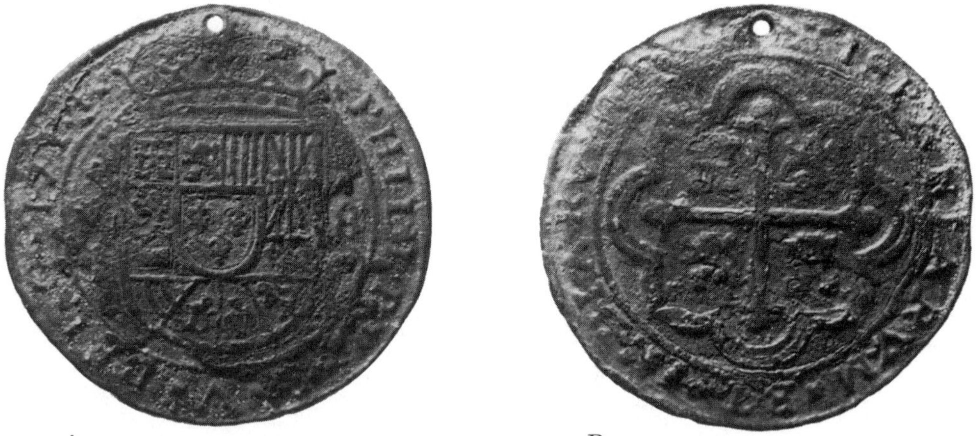

A B

Figure 5.4. Mexican 1714 8-Reales Presentation Piece

workmanship from any European mint. It was carefully prepared to have medallic configuration with both dies having identical orientation, an alignment unnecessary for mass-produced, hand-struck cobs issued from this mint in the hectic days before the sailing of the 1715 Fleet.

Instead this beautiful coin was placed in a screw press allowing the two dies to be brought slowly together by rotating a horizontal arm turning a vertical screw shaft. These coins show no "die chatter" or double-striking of any kind since, indeed, they were not struck in the ordinary sense of the word. Strictly speaking, these coins are not cobs because, being machine made, they are identical. They represent rare precursors of the famous Spanish-milled dollar that appeared in 1732.

This specimen is exceedingly interesting since it has a neat drilled hole positioned near the rim in such a way that when connected by a jump ring to a neck chain, it can be worn with either side correctly oriented toward the viewer, a bold cross for those wishing to proclaim their religious faith, or the shield of Spain to advertise loyalty to the Crown.

Virtually unique among coins in general are South American heart-shaped cobs that have become increasingly popular in recent years. They are related to present-day *milagros* found in some Andean churches. These modern silver miniatures take the shape of some body part or object that is desired and the purchaser leaves it in the church as a token of appreciation for prayers answered or hope for health restored. Although there are no heart-shaped cobs in the Florida Collection, this curious subject is mentioned because there is much numismatic interest in these unusual cobs.[3]

Cob Designs

From 1536 to 1773 details of designs for colonial silver cobs changed many times, but essential elements remained the same. Cut into dies were the current ruler's name and title, denomination, and a way to identify mint and assayer. The assayer's letter is particularly important to locate on early, otherwise undated cobs. Archival records usually make it clear when such a person began and ended his position, thus placing a cob in chronological order with relation to other assayers who worked at the same mint. That single letter taken from his family name could be his death warrant if it was found on debased coins from the mint.

Kings (and I might add, today's collectors) were keen to have an esthetic design in keeping with the dignity of their positions. At first a heraldic shield representing realms under their control occupied the obverse (the most important side) and two conspicuous crowned Pillars of Hercules dominated the reverse. This combination began at the Mexico mint and was later used to begin the series at Lima and in Colombian mints. There is no better place to see details of these designs and their subsequent changes than in the outstanding monograph by Nesmith (1950). The Mexican reverse was changed in 1556 to consist of a large cross with lions and castles (for the kingdoms of Leon and Castile) placed *en echelon* in the empty quarters. This is the design adopted in 1576 for the new mint at Potosí, while the old design had already died in Lima by that time.

These earliest designs are only of academic interest here because the Florida Collection, based entirely on salvaged shipwreck specimens, holds no examples. Fortunately there are ample specimens managed by the state of Texas from artifacts salvaged from the Padre Island shipwrecks.

Dates did not appear on colonial cobs until 1617 when earlier mint scandals at Potosí made this reform a convenient means of detecting the guilty. If you find a cob with a date earlier than 1617 it is either one that was struck in Spain, or one of the rare errors from Potosí with transposed digits such as 1612, but actually made in 1621. At first dates were located in the upper left-hand sector of the reverse legend. Another wave of counterfeiting in the 1640s caused the original pillars design to be reinstituted at Potosí in 1652 with dates placed in three places, two on obverse and one on reverse. Now it was more difficult for corrupt mint workers to escape responsibility for illegal cobs by simply obliterating an assayer's mark with a hammer blow.

A full four-digit date in the 1652 design is found only in the outer rim legend of the pillar (now obverse) side with the word ANO (year)

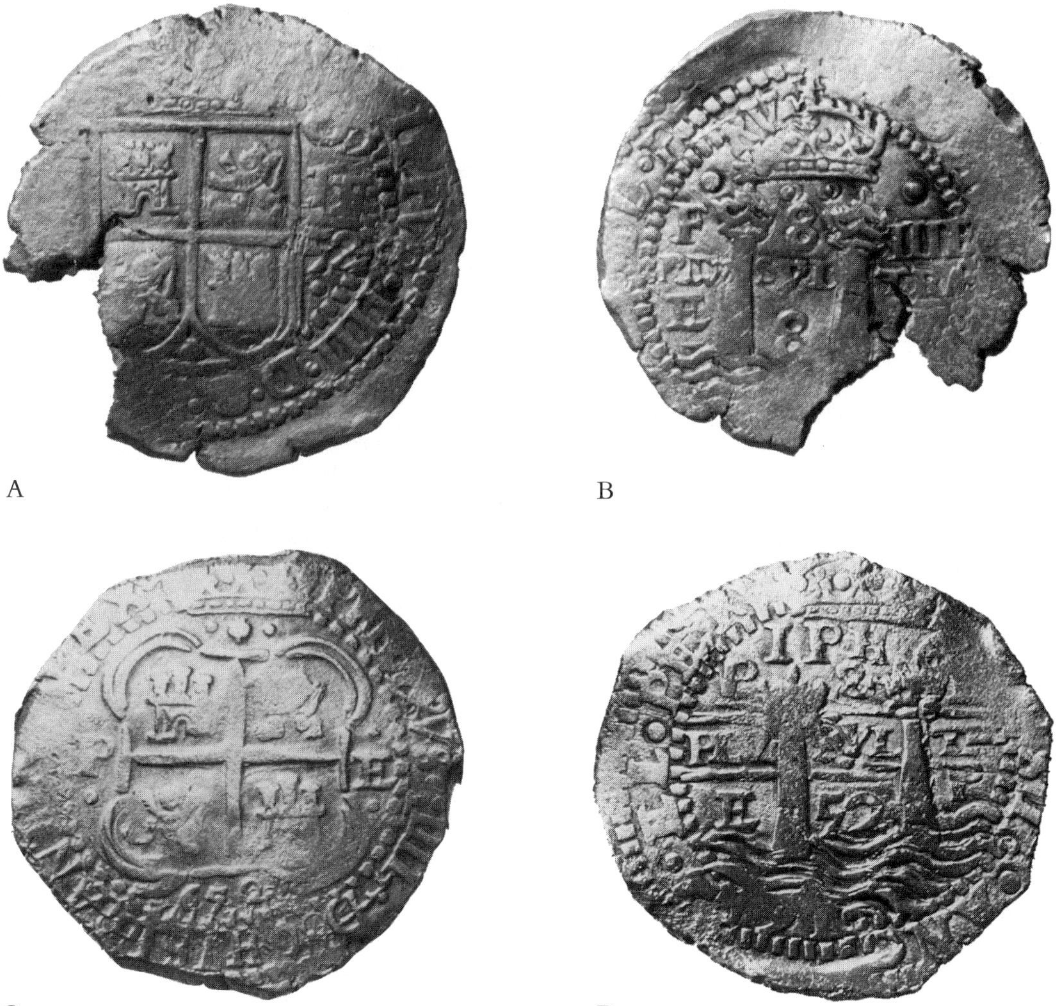

A B C D

Figure 5.5. Potosí 8-Reales Cobs of 1652

preceding it. The last three digits of the same date were placed in the lower-center space between the base of the pillars. And for good measure it was repeated at the base of the cross on the reverse. Often on coins of smaller denomination there was not enough room to include the third digit, but four in the legend were always expected to be cut into dies. But alas, even that has exceptions.

We can see typical examples of this new design with multiple placement of the dates in the nearly round Potosí 8 reales of 1652, two varieties of which are shown in figure 5.5. These were recovered from the Jupiter Wreck site together with numerous others of this transitional date.[4]

We must remember that all colonial mints were subjected to micromanagement by the king's advisors and councilors in Spain. When New World silver production first peaked around 1590,[5] already so many coins were being sent back from the Americas that old quality controls began to plummet. At the same time European merchants and bankers who had loaned the king large sums of money began to lose confidence in the intrinsic value of increasingly sloppy coins from Alto Peru. Finally it became necessary to smelt them down on arrival in Spain and have new assays made by trusted Spanish experts under close supervision.

All basic design features were still required, but royal instructions as to what should be placed exactly where were unclear. The result was a chaotic mixture of design varieties never seen before or since. Die engravers often picked up the wrong size of punch, or forgot on which side to use it, carelessly left out major design elements, and even made a blundered die for a nonexistent king! Assayers' initials might jump from one side of the obverse to the other, be overstruck with another letter, or made retrograde along with the denomination. Generally speaking, die-sinking work was done hurriedly since engravers were usually paid on a piecework basis. However, there is no truth to the canard that ignorant Indians or illiterate, visually challenged Spaniards were employed in this work.

Inexperienced die engravers often had trouble working directly in their mirror-image style so that all letters of the legend were necessarily done retrograde in order to come out normally on struck coins. Errors in spelling form another quaint variation often seen in the Potosí series. Cobs produced during the first half of the seventeenth century at Potosí are notorious for the barbarous eccentricities they display.

Not far behind is the famous "Lima Star," a striking design that suddenly made its appearance in 1659 and again briefly in 1660. Looking at figure 5.6, we can see the Pillars of Hercules have been resurrected in order to firmly support a great crown. Immediately below is a powerful eight-pointed star shining upon the name LIMA. Underneath is the only date in four large digits, all this floating on an ocean of six gently undulating waves. Assayer Villegas' mark (V) is present outside the left pillar and the denomination is opposite on the right. Retrograde N in the legend is a characteristic of this short series. The star, of course, is a reference to the Star of Bethlehem. Lima has been known since its earliest days as the City of the Three Kings.

Evidence points to at least several thousand star cobs having been struck in various denominations, but no royal decree has yet been found officially authorizing them. Nevertheless, it would have been a death warrant for all concerned to strike so many and release them into circulation without regal permission. There is no doubt in my mind these star cobs were made in the old Lima mint facilities, whether authorized or not. Nevertheless, both weights and alloy are suspect.

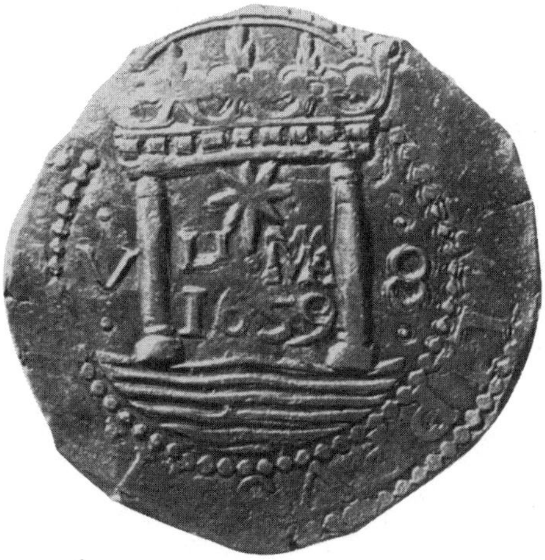

A

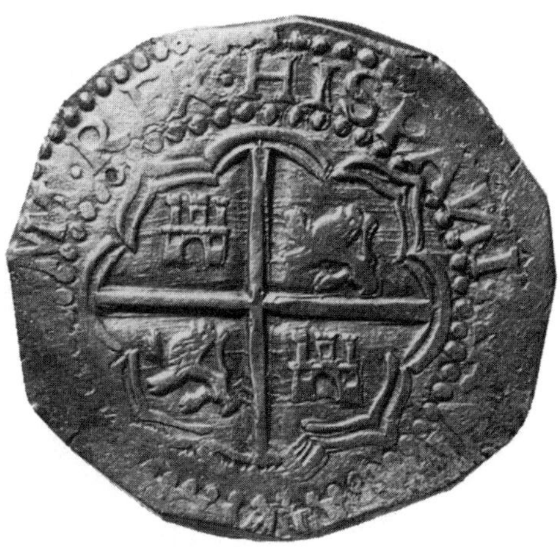

B

Figure 5.6. Lima Star Cob

Parallel archival documentation points to earlier lobbying by the Peruvian viceroy to have a master assayer's office and examining board for provincial assayers established in Lima. This was felt to be urgent in order to facilitate commerce and accelerate revalidation of those Potosí cobs made shortly before design reforms of 1652 were brought about to combat rampant counterfeiting.

The mint at Mexico remained aloof from all this scandal, producing vast numbers of cobs above reproach, if not always esthetically pleasing. Mexicans often hammered their carefully made cobs both before and after they were struck in order to eliminate sharp corners on planchets that could damage heavy canvas storage bags.

So few silver cobs were coined at Bogotá and Cartagena mints that these practices seem never to have been necessary. Instead, workers there appear to have often deliberately obliterated design features that could identify them as responsible for making the coins. These cobs are commonly underweight but since they often began with straight-sheared sides, later clipping as they passed through owners' hands would be difficult to detect.

Not until 1730 do we find high-quality milled coinage prepared from machinery coming from a Spanish colonial mint, although there are no examples in the Florida Collection earlier than 1732. By this date, some silver planchets issued by the Mexico mint were made perfectly round, thus beginning a long series of so-called Spanish-milled dollars widely accepted in commerce around the world (even in the United States until 1857). These coins are distinguished by a new design element, two interlocking globes, flanked by Pillars of Hercules. Milled coins are also characterized by a repeating diagonal pattern of laurel leaves on the coin's edge to prevent shaving or clipping, long a problem with irregular cobs. During this period while milling was being fully implemented, coins with transitional cross designs were still produced on handcut planchets. Milling may have been used to flatten the planchet bar or to impress the design, or both, but the coins are not round and do not have milled edges. Several dozen of the rare 1732 fully milled, pillar dollar coins that begin the historic series are known to have been recovered from state waters. The Florida Collection includes four 1732 fully milled examples, all of which are in poor condition. The best obverse and reverse are shown in figure 5.7.

Modern Counterfeiting

If all the above sounds complicated, it is only because it was. How then, under the circumstances described, can anyone expect two legitimate cobs to be exactly alike? On the other hand, counterfeits were and are being cast from well-made molds using silver of almost any fineness. Serious counterfeiting of cobs designed to mulct collectors exists today from high-tech centrifugal castings that are then "antiqued," or aged, by several means that do not deserve to be described. Some of these fakes are very well made indeed but still can be detected by any competent numismatist with a 30-power stereomicroscope.

If counterfeiters go to extraordinary lengths to make fake dies (by hand, certain mechanisms, or electricity) and spurious cobs are struck from them, even so, there are ways to determine this has happened in a laboratory with trace-element capabilities. If, as has happened recently, legitimate artifacts of the same age (and made from the same silver ores as the coins) are destroyed in order to obtain "authentic" silver, detection is more difficult, but not impossible. It can be done.

To conclude this brief orientation on Spanish colonial cobs in the Florida Collection, let me remind you that anything can happen on a cob. But beware, modern counterfeiters know this too and are busy trying to duplicate these quaint treasure coins.

Figure 5.7. Pillar Dollar

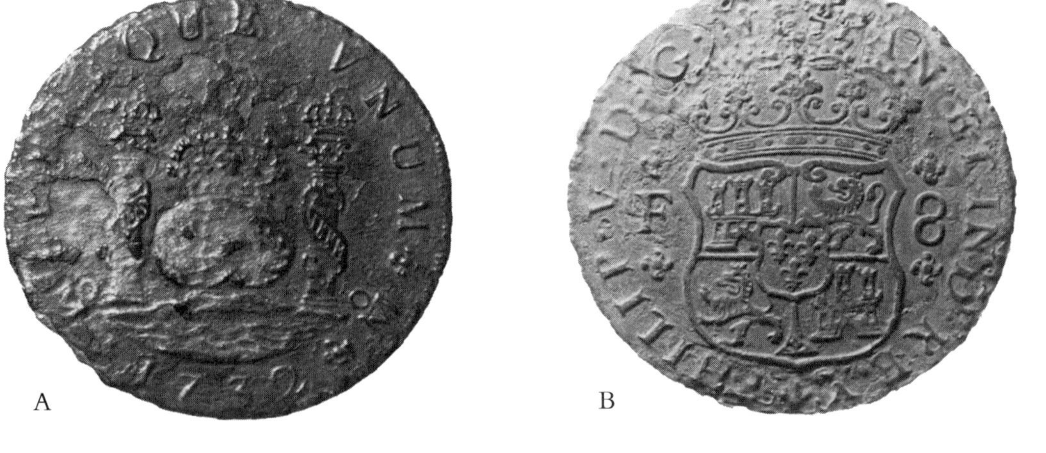

A

B

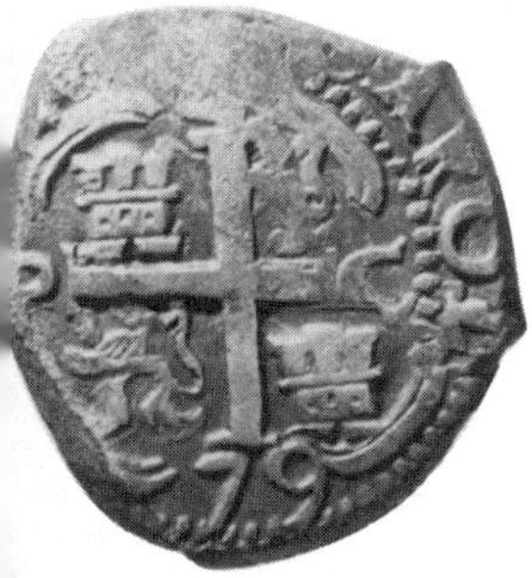

PART II

The Florida Collection

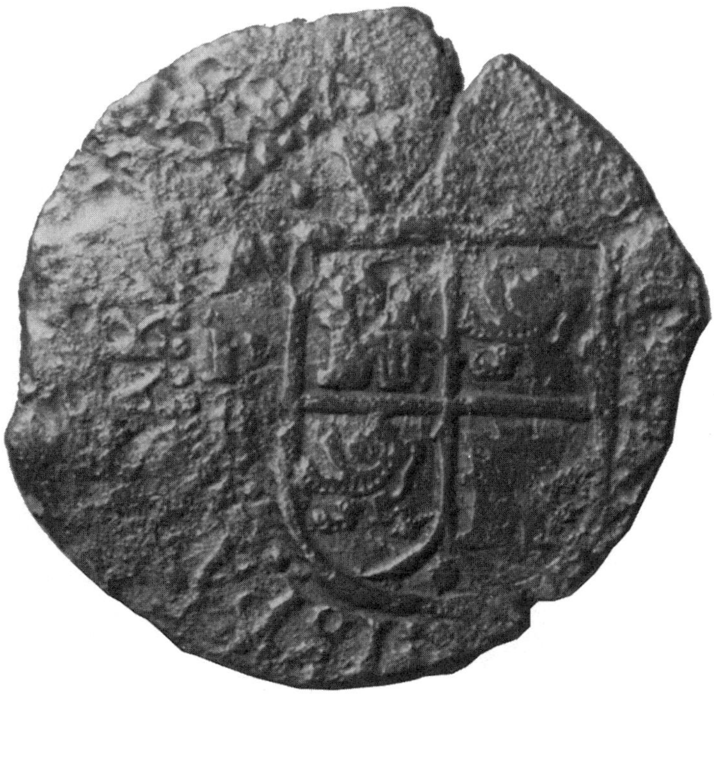

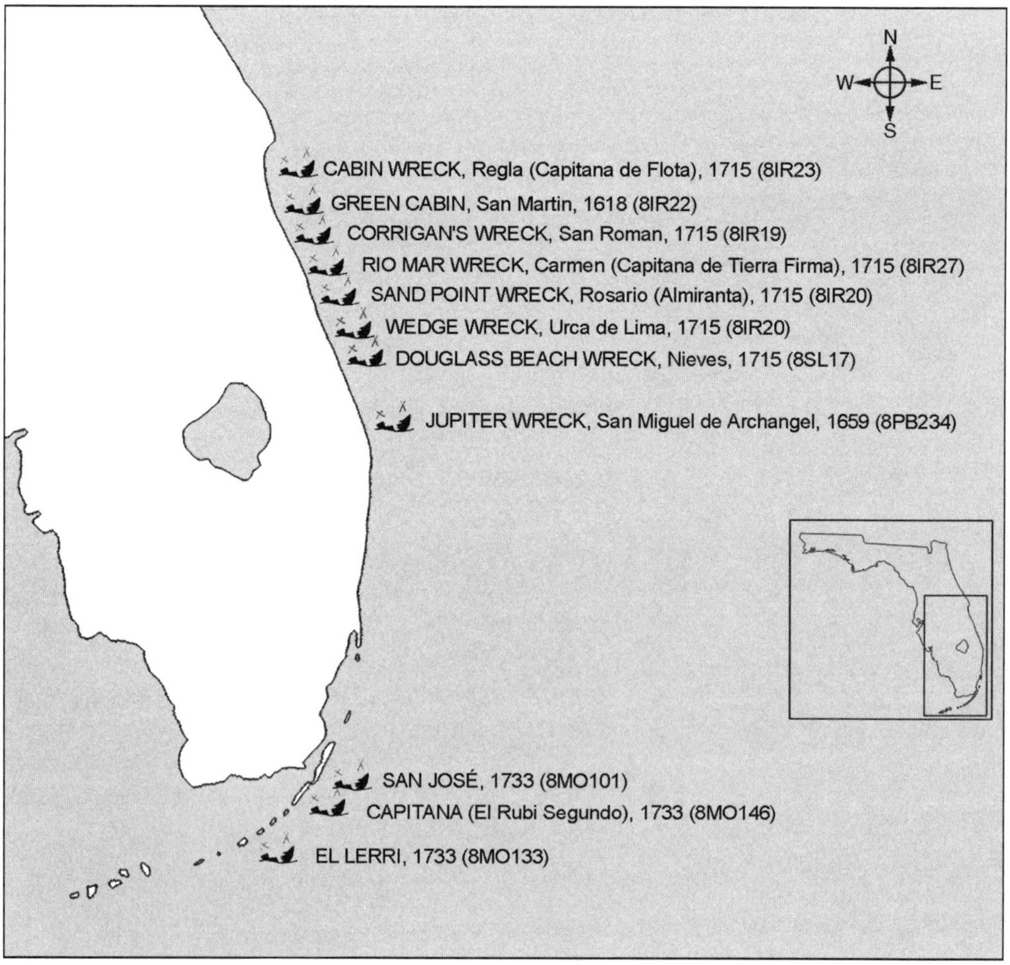

Map 6.1. Florida shipwrecks of the 1715 and 1733 fleets.

CHAPTER 6

Composition of the Florida Collection

In addition to more than 1,400 Spanish colonial gold coins held in the Florida Collection and previously described in my study (Craig 1988), there are currently 23,121 silver coins managed by the state. Of this total, 22,938 are of Spanish origin and form the subject of this book. A few (twenty-three) have been recovered from land-based archaeological sites; seven were donated to the state, as were eighteen modern counterfeits. One coin was recovered by Florida Bureau of Archaeological Research staff. This leaves a total of 22,907 silver coins received by the state as a result of divisions with salvors that have taken place over the years. Exactly 22,478 of these shipwreck coins, equal to 98.03 percent of the total, were added to the Florida Collection before 1983. In that year the present contract salvage system was reinstated following lengthy federal admiralty litigation surrounding wrecks in state waters along the Florida east coast.

A remarkable 21,962 coins, or 95.75 percent, of the shipwreck division total came from a single lease. This lease (1329) extended from 1964 to 1975, a decade in which coin discoveries were so numerous divisions were accomplished by weight rather than by selection for numismatic significance. Under these circumstances coins were divided into four piles of equal weight, one of which was chosen by the state. It was impossible to give these coins an accurate provenience by assigning them to a specific shipwreck or even indicate the year they were found. Records show 8,632 coins fall into this category of "1329 general."

From eleven other contracts in force between 1975 and 1983 have come 525 coins, or 2.29 percent of the shipwreck division total. Since 1983 very few silver coins have been selected for inclusion in the Florida Collection. The state's goal is to strengthen its artifact collection

Table 6.1. Summary of Spanish Silver Coins in the Florida Collection by Site

Date	Wreck Name	Site I.D.	Total by Shipwreck
1618	Green Cabin	8IR-22	127
1622	Quicksands	8MO-141	5
1659	Jupiter	8PB-234	198
1715	Corrigan's	8IR-19	8
1715	Cabin	8IR-23	199
1715	Rio Mar	8IR-27	15
1715	Douglass Beach	8SL-17	13,433
1715	Wedge Wreck	8SL-24	2
1715	Undetermined		8,637
Subtotal			22,264
1733	San Jose	8MO-101	107
1733	Chavez	8MO-102	1
1733	San Pedro	8MO-104	51
1733	El Leri	8MO-133	2
1733	Capitana	8MO-146	1
Subtotal			162
1810	Holden	8SL-20	100
1823	Sunrise	8BD-6911	12
?	Cannon Pile		1
?	Brevard Co.		1
?	St. Johns Co.		13
?	donated, probable shipwreck		2
?	miscellaneous land sites		23
Grand total			22,938

Source: Florida Bureau of Archaeological Research computer database.

with items not already represented. Coins from all shipwrecks received by the state from 1983 to 1997 account for 1.84 percent or 421 coins. Of these, 100 are from an 1810 wreck and 198 are from the 1659 Jupiter Wreck, periods poorly represented previously in the collection.

Fifteen shipwrecks are represented in the Florida Collection of silver coins with sites ranging in time from 1618 to the 1820s. Three additional locations have yielded a few coins, but they are not confirmed shipwreck sites. The comparative scarcity of coins from land discoveries is not surprising. Few land archaeological sites of the historic period investigated by state archaeologists would have any potential to contain the number of coins expected on wreckage of a ship transporting coin and bullion to Europe. Since the 1960s enormous efforts have been made by private contractors to salvage artifacts from sunken wrecks in

Florida waters. Those located within the territorial limits of Florida have supplied the coins listed in table 6.1.

In this table, shipwreck dates shown have been established either by archival records of the disaster or by the less precise means of using dates of the youngest coins found associated with the wreck. In either case relatively few coins will actually bear the same date as the wreck.

From these data we can see immediately that coins recovered from the 1715 Plate Fleet wreck sites form the bulk of the collection. In fact, they constitute 97.19 percent (22,294 coins) of the total. By contrast, only 0.71 percent (162 coins) have come from wrecks associated with the equally large 1733 Fleet, which was clearly not involved in transporting quantities of coins and bullion.

In terms of numismatic significance of individual coins, both fleets have made important contributions although most coins were received at a time when selection was made without help from outside specialists. However, the method of selection did yield a random sample that may be used for certain statistical analyses. Since the mid-1980s silver coins no longer have been acquired indiscriminately in bulk form; instead, they are carefully examined individually to prevent unnecessary duplication before adding them to the collection. This criterion was applied to all 198 coins (0.86 percent) retained from the Jupiter Wreck, which has already added more numismatically interesting material than the entire 1733 Fleet.

Dates given in table 6.1 suggest there are considerable gaps in the chronological sequence of coins in the collection, but they are somewhat misleading. Ships lost in the 1715 hurricane were carrying enough older coins to partially bridge the gap back in time to coins recovered from the Jupiter Wreck. Unfortunately, coins from the 1618 wreck (127 coins representing 0.55 percent) are for the most part poorly preserved and of little interest. As this table suggests, the weakest part of the collection is from the period 1750 to 1850.

Compared with previous decades, only a trickle of sea salvage coins is being submitted to the state for annual division. This of course is a function of the fact that most of the easily recoverable treasure from 1715 wrecks and other known sites has already been found. However, theoretically this situation can change dramatically at any moment with discovery of yet another Florida shipwreck with a cargo of coins.

Composition of the Collection by Denomination and Mints

If all silver coins in the Florida Collection are listed, we arrive at an eclectic mixture shown here as table 6.2. It includes several large clusters of Spanish 4 and 8 reales cemented together whose numbers have been

Table 6.2. All Silver Coins in the Florida Collection by Origin and Denomination

Spanish Colonial		*United States*	
8 Reales	11,779	Half dollar	26
8 Reales (?)	25	Quarter	83
4 Reales	5,366	Dime	22
2 Reales	1,099	Half dime	28
1 Real	2,573	Unidentified	1
½ Real	1,161	Subtotal	160
unidentified	909	*Other Countries*	
Subtotal	22,912	Belgium	1
Spain		Britain	1
8 Reales	2	Denmark	1
4 Reales	0	France	1
2 Reales	11	Netherlands	1
1 Real	1	Subtotal	5
½ Real	9	*Counterfeit*	
unidentified	3	Counterfeit	18
Subtotal	26	Subtotal	18
		Total	23,121

Source: Florida Bureau of Archaeological Research computer database.

estimated by weight. Also included are the remnants of a U.S. Army payroll lost at sea during the Second Seminole War. The remaining odd bits and pieces are mostly of uncertain provenience and may not even be coeval with the wreck where discoverers said they were found.

Of the 23,121 coins shown in table 6.2, more than 99 percent are of Spanish or Spanish colonial origin. Table 6.3 gives a breakdown by mint and makes it clear the collection is dominated by Mexican coins. This

Table 6.3. Spanish and Spanish Colonial Silver Coins in the Florida Collection by Mint

Spanish Colonial		*Spain*	
Cartagena de Indias	3	Madrid	2
Guatemala	11	Sevilla	4
Lima	304	Valladolid	1
Mexico	21,170	Spanish unidentifiable	19
Potosí	515	Subtotal	26
Santa Fé de Bogotá	5	*Spanish Indeterminate*	
Zacatecas	1	Spanish indeterminate	903
Subtotal	22,009	Subtotal	903
		Total	22,938

Source: Florida Bureau of Archaeological Research computer database.

Table 6.4. Totals of Mexico Mint Silver Coins by Denomination and Assayer

½ Real	
Assayers "FF"	1
Assayers "FM"	1
Assayer "G"	2
Assayer "J"	50
Assayer "L"	24
Assayer "P"	5
Assayer not shown	1,073
Subtotal	1,156
1 Real	
Assayers "FF"	1
Assayers "FM"	2
Assayer "A"	2
Assayer "D"	1
Assayer "F"	5
Assayer "J"	84
Assayer "L"	13
Assayer "O"	5
Assayer "P"	11
Assayer not shown	2,274
Subtotal	2,398
2 Reales	
Assayers "FF"	6
Assayers "FM"	9
Assayers "TH"	4
Assayer "F"	5
Assayer "J"	44
Assayer "M"	3
Assayer "P"	5
Assayer not shown	940
Subtotal	1,016
4 Reales	
Assayer "F"	17
Assayers "FF"	1
Assayers "FM"	1
Assayer "J"	427
Assayer "L"	3
Assayer "P"	8
Assayer not shown	4,763
Subtotal	5,220
8 Reales	
Assayers "FF"	3
Assayers "FM"	17
Assayer "D"	1
Assayer "F"	7
Assayer "FT"	4
Assayer "HJ"	3
Assayer "TH"	11
Assayer "J"	1,077
Assayer "L"	68
Assayer "P"	20
Assayer not shown	10,161
Subtotal	11,372
Indeterminate denomination and assayer	8
Total	21,170

Source: Florida Bureau of Archaeological Research computer database.

table does not reflect the historical reality of New World mint production, which we know was mostly from Potosí during the sixteenth to eighteenth centuries. It merely reflects the accidental source of coins from which the collection is derived.

Since the Mexico mint is clearly the principal contributor to the collection, some useful information can be gained from the descriptive statistics of these coins. In table 6.4 we see distribution both by denomination and assayer.

Table 6.4 provides an opportunity to quantify the frequency with which diagnostic assayers' initials are likely to be present on handmade cob coinage from large production runs as opposed to specially prepared coins produced from machinery. These modern milled coins are from the Mexico mint and, except for small denominations, have two

Table 6.5. Dated Mexico Silver Coins with Visible Assayers' Initials in the Florida Collection

"P"	1605	1
"F"	1616	2
"F"	1618	1
"P"	1653	2
"P"	1654	3
"P"	1655	5
"P"	1656	3
"P"	1657	8
"L"	1680	1
"L"	1695	2
"L"	1697	1
"L"	1700	1
"L"	1702	1
"L"	1703	2
"J"	1706	1
"J"	1707	3
"J"	1708	4
"J"	1709	4
"J"	1710	3
"J"	1711	17
"J"	1712	16
"J"	1713	25
"J"	1714	107
"J"	1715	46
"F"	1731	1
"F"	1732	5
"F"	1733	2
"M"	1745	1
"M"	1752	1
"M"	1765	1
"FM"	1772	1
"FM"	1773	3
"FM"	1776	1
"FF"	1778	1
"FF"	1779	3
"FF"	1780	1
"FF"	1781	1
"FF"	1782	3
"FF"	1783	3
"FM"	1784	1
"FM"	1785	1
"FM"	1786	1
"FM"	1787	1
"FM"	1788	2
"FM"	1789	2
"FM"	1791	1
"FM"	1792	2
"FM"	1793	2
"FM"	1795	1
"FM"	1796	1
"FM"	1797	1
"FM"	1798	2
"FM"	1799	2
"FM"	1800	1
"FM"	1801	1
"FT"	1801	1
"FM"	1802	1
"FT"	1802	1
"FT"	1803	2
"TH"	1803	1
"TH"	1804	2
"TH"	1805	2
"TH"	1806	2
"TH"	1807	3
"TH"	1808	3
"TH"	1809	2
"HJ"	1809	1
"HJ"	1810	2

Source: Florida Bureau of Archaeological Research computer database.

assayers' initials present; they have been subtracted from the totals shown for each denomination in order to determine percentages of cob coins with assayers' marks (8 reales, 10.4 percent; 4 reales, 8.7 percent; 2 reales, 5.4 percent; 1 real, 5.1 percent; and ½ real, 7.1 percent).

These calculations show relative scarcity of cob coins with visible assayers' marks in a large, random sample dominated by coins from the Mexico mint. With exception of a slight deviation in the ½-real percentage, they also show a nice progression that increases with increasing size of the coin. In other words, since a 1 real is small, there is a better

Table 6.6. Transitional Mexican Silver Design Types, 173(?)–1733

Date	Transitional (Cross) Design	Fully Milled (Pillar) Design
173(?)	5	
1731	3	
1732	11	4
1733		4
Subtotal	19	8
Total of both designs		27

Source: Florida Bureau of Archeological Research computer database.

chance some details of the round dies will not be transferred to a highly irregular silver planchet. When dates and other diagnostic design features are missing, as is often the case, a coin can still be placed in its proper time interval if an assayer's mark is visible.

Table 6.5 listing dated Mexico coins with assayers' marks displays several interesting relationships not obvious at first glance. The comparatively small number of coins in the 1653–1657 range, all received from the Jupiter Wreck site, is strong evidence this vessel did not load specie from any Mexican port. Instead, these few coins must have come aboard by some indirect means. Most coins from the Jupiter Wreck are from the Potosí mint (see table 8.3).

It is also evident Mexican mint operations began to accelerate in 1711 when it became clear a plate fleet was being assembled. There are fewer coins from 1715 because vessels left Vera Cruz in June, thus curtailing the possibility larger numbers could have been placed on board. Comparatively fewer coins were recovered from 1733 Fleet wrecks. From 1772 to 1810 Mexican coins bear portraits of successive Spanish kings, and, being made entirely by machinery, exhibit no noteworthy varieties.

Shortly after 1728 the Mexico mint installed planchet mills and mechanical coin presses. Most coins recovered from the 1733 Fleet were made by these means. Table 6.6 lists those coins in the Florida Collection from this fleet dating from the 1730s. At present, there are no Mexican coins representing the interval 1716–1730.

Lima coins in the Florida Collection are shown in table 6.7, where they are listed by denomination and assayer. It is obvious this group is much less numerous than Mexican coins. With comparatively small numbers to analyze, very little can be said of Lima coins as a whole. Perhaps they did not arrive at Portobelo in quantities in time to be transferred to the 1715 Plate Fleet. Also, these figures may simply reflect a lack of large quantities of silver available to the mint at that time.

Table 6.7. Lima Silver Coin Totals by Denomination and Assayer

H Real		*4 Reales*	
Assayer not shown	3	Assayer "H"	18
Subtotal	3	Assayer "R"	5
1 Real		Assayer "V"	10
Assayer "H"	28	Assayer not shown	8
Assayer "M"	5	Subtotal	41
Assayer "R"	18	*8 Reales*	
Assayer "V"	5	Assayers "IJ"	4
Assayer not shown	22	Assayers "JP"	5
Subtotal	78	Assayers "MI"	1
2 Reales		Assayers "MJ"	1
Assayers "DT"	1	Assayer "H"	73
Assayers "IJ"	1	Assayer "L"	1
Assayer "H"	5	Assayer "M"	10
Assayer "M"	1	Assayer "R"	35
Assayer "R"	2	Assayer "V"	17
Assayer "V"	2	Assayer not shown	17
Assayer not shown	6	Subtotal	164
Subtotal	18	Total	304

Source: Florida Bureau of Archaeological Research computer database.

Beginning in 1659 unauthorized dated Lima coins were produced for two years, but official activities ceased until the mint was opened again in 1684. Table 6.8 shows holdings of all Lima denominations by date, and table 6.9 presents dated Lima coins with visible assayers' marks in the Florida Collection. Several observations may be made.

Readers are reminded no coins were struck at Lima between 1661 and 1684, which accounts for absence of these dates. Also missing in the collection is a long date run from 1713 to 1775. Coins dated 1713 to 1715 exist, but apparently were not sent forward in time to be placed on board ships of the 1715 Fleet. The remainder of this gap is simply a reflection of coins not yet being present in any group presented to the state by salvors for division.

Clustering of comparatively large numbers in the collection between 1693 and 1699 cannot be explained from this statistically uncontrolled sample. However, experienced Peruvian collectors have long held the view Lima 8 reales become increasingly scarce from the year 1700 onward. Again, abundance of the 1703 specimens obtained from division is by chance and circumstances that cannot be explained.

Collectors who review these tables to compare the assayer-date combinations may find their specimens from the years 1685, 1686, 1687, 1688, 1689, and 1695 differ. These years with multiple assayers are a

Table 6.8. Lima Silver Coins, All Denominations, by Date

1577–1588	1	1703	27
1659	12	1704	7
1684	5	1705	6
1685	4	1706	3
1686	4	1707	1
1687	4	1708	2
1688	4	1709	4
1689	1	1710	7
169(?)	1	1711	6
1690	1	1712	2
1691	6	1776	1
1692	10	1782	1
1693	13	1788	1
1694	6	1794	1
1695	13	1797	1
1696	15	1800	1
1697	19	1801	1
1698	21	1804	1
1699	35	1805	1
17— *	2	1806	1
170-	4	1807	1
1700	11	1808	1
1701	5	No date	22
1702	7	Total	304

Source: Florida Bureau of Archaeological Research computer database.

* Dash indicates numeral indiscernible.

Table 6.9. Dated Lima Silver Coins with Visible Assayers' Initials in the Florida Collection

"V"	1659	8	"H"	1704	6
"V"	1684	3	"H"	1705	5
"R"	1685	4	"R"	1706	3
"R"	1686	3	"H"	1707	1
"R"	1687	4	"H"	1708	2
"R"	1688	2	"M"	1709	3
"V"	1689	1	"H"	1710	6
"R"	1691	5	"M"	1711	5
"V"	1692	9	"M"	1712	2
"V"	1693	10	"MJ"	1776	1
"M"	1694	5	"MI"	1782	1
"R"	1695	10	"IJ"	1788	1
"H"	1696	15	"IJ"	1794	1
"H"	1697	18	"IJ"	1797	1
"H"	1698	18	"IJ"	1800	1
"H"	1699	2	"IJ"	1801	1
"R"	1699	29	"JP"	1804	1
"H"	1700	8	"JP"	1805	1
"H"	1701	5	"JP"	1806	1
"H"	1702	6	"JP"	1807	1
"H"	1703	26	"JP"	1808	1

Source: Florida Bureau of Archaeological Research computer database.

Table 6.10. Lima Silver Coins by Denomination

½ real	3
1 real	79
2 reales	17
4 reales	41
8 reales	164
Total	304

Source: Florida Bureau of Archaeological Research computer database.

function of employee tenure and business decisions of the mint franchise holder.

Distribution of Lima coins by denomination and date is shown in the series of tables 6.10 and 6.11. These data do not reflect actual numbers struck by the mint for any given year; they merely show how many have been divided to the state and less directly indicate how many have been salvaged over the years. Since they were not recovered intact in shipping crates, we cannot infer the coins are indicative of official shipments sent to the king. Some or all might very well be private funds being returned to Spain for a variety of reasons. Generally speaking, these tables again confirm that small-denomination coins needed to facilitate daily marketplace transactions were in short supply and tended to stay in the viceroyalties where they originated.

From data in table 6.11, several observations can be made. Most noticeable is the scarcity of 2-reales coins in the collection. In comparison with other Lima denominations, there are many missing dates. I have no ready explanation for these discrepancies. Since actual mint production records are not available to me, almost any possibility must be entertained regarding their poor representation.

If the Lima mint struck approximately equal numbers of each denomination from year to year (which they most certainly did not), we would expect to see slowly increasing numbers of coins in each denomination as we approach the year 1715. This is the modern analog you would find if you collected a jar full of pennies.

The fact there are seventeen 8 reales present for the year 1703 may have another explanation. From numerous archival sources we know it was the custom of regional Royal Treasury offices to hoard various tax monies in the form of large-denomination coins. When a call came from the king to empty his coffers, many such accumulations may have ended up on board 1715 Plate Fleet ships. Hoard coins usually are in much better condition than coins that have been in circulation for long periods of time. The important datum of condition is missing from this study. This is largely because long immersion in salt water has corroded

Table 6.11. Lima Silver Coins by Denomination and Date

	½ real	1 real	2 reales	4 reales	8 reales
1577–1588	0	0	1	0	0
1659	0	0	3	3	6
1684	0	2	0	2	1
1685	0	3	0	0	1
1686	0	3	0	1	0
1687	0	1	1	0	2
1688	0	1	0	0	3
1689	0	0	0	0	1
169-*	0	0	0	0	1
1690	0	1	0	0	0
1691	0	0	1	1	4
1692	0	3	2	3	2
1693	0	2	0	1	10
1694	0	5	0	0	1
1695	0	3	0	1	9
1696	0	5	1	0	9
1697	0	9	3	1	7
1698	0	4	0	4	13
1699	0	10	1	2	22
17—	1	0	0	0	1
170-	0	2	0	0	2
1700	0	5	0	3	3
1701	0	0	0	1	4
1702	0	3	0	0	4
1703	0	3	0	6	18
1704	0	1	2	2	2
1705	1	0	0	3	2
1706	0	1	0	1	1
1707	0	1	0	0	0
1708	0	0	0	0	2
1709	0	0	1	0	3
1710	1	0	0	1	5
1711	0	0	0	0	6
1712	0	0	0	0	2
1776	0	0	0	0	1
1782	0	0	0	0	1
1788	0	0	1	0	0
1794	0	0	0	0	1
1797	0	0	0	0	1
1800	0	0	0	0	1
1801	0	0	0	0	1
1804	0	0	0	0	1
1805	0	0	0	0	1
1806	0	0	0	0	1
1807	0	0	0	0	1
1808	0	0	0	0	1
Indeterminate	0	10	1	5	6
Subtotal	3	79	17	41	164
Total					304

Source: Florida Bureau of Archaeological Research computer database.

*Dash indicates numeral indiscernible.

every specimen of silver coin to a greater or lesser extent, often obscuring details we use to determine the degree of wear from use.

On the other hand, in spite of the overall large numbers of coins in the Florida Collection, the uncontrolled manner in which they were acquired makes it impossible to arrive at statistically significant conclusions regarding their original abundance and condition at the time they sank.

Additions since 1983 have not come on any predictable basis. The most significant factor is weather, both good and bad. Prolonged calm weather with light winds often results in good shallow water visibility and calm seas where most 1715 wrecks are located. A typical winter season with heavy seas and poor visibility makes diving almost impossible. Consequently, there is a clearly defined diving season from around May through October for wrecks along the southeastern Florida coast (map 6.1). Of course circumstances dictate certain years will be more successful than others. No one doubts the long-term trend for coin recoveries from the 1715 Plate Fleet is sharply declining.

Only one new wreck site of significance, the Jupiter Wreck, has supplied silver coins since 1983. This suggests that, in spite of the enormous diving effort and modern electronics being employed, there is a decreasing likelihood important silver coin treasure remains to be salvaged. If true, this can only emphasize the importance of utilizing what has been conserved and now managed by the Florida Bureau of Archaeological Research.

CHAPTER 7

Mexican Silver Coins

Collectors of Mexican cob coinage have been accustomed to long and often disappointing searches for dated specimens. The single date of the Mexican design, located only on the legend near the rim, was unlikely to be preserved in the normal course of Mexico minting practices. Since planchets were anything but round, chances were not good all four digits would be struck where they could be seen. Mexican coins in the Florida Collection are summarized in table 7.1 by denomination and date. Table 7.2 lists known Mexico City mint assayers.

The small number of fractional coins (traditionally viewed as ½ real to 2 reales) shown in table 7.1 are in keeping with the necessity of retaining as much small change as possible to facilitate daily business transactions while the two large denominations were being sent back to Spain to finance Spanish wars in Europe. This contrast between small and large denominations recovered from salvaged shipwrecks of the 1715 Plate Fleet is easily seen beginning with the year 1710.

Because they were made from much thinner planchets than the 4- and 8-reales coins, fractional denominations were more easily corroded, often beyond proper identification. Consequently, dated specimens of ½, 1, and 2 reales never show more than small totals and their ratios are maintained against larger coins in the subtotals at the end of table 7.1. In view of the large sample, these ratios provide historians with an economic profile that cannot be duplicated from any other source.

By comparing totals of indeterminate coins with subtotals for each denomination, we can calculate the percentage of coins surviving immersion in corrosive salt water to the extent their dates were visible. Visually, we find these percentages were rather small, usually less than 10 percent.

Table 7.1. Mexico Coins by Denomination and Date

	½ real	1 real	2 reales	4 reales	8 reales	Subtotal
—2*	0	0	0	0	2	2
—3	0	0	0	1	5	6
—4	0	0	0	5	41	46
—5	0	0	0	4	12	16
1—	0	0	0	0	1	1
155-	0	1	0	0	0	1
1572?	0	1	0	0	0	1
1605	0	1	0	0	0	1
16-9	0	0	0	0	1	1
1616	0	1	0	1	0	2
1618	0	0	0	0	1	1
162-	2	0	0	0	0	2
165-	0	1	0	0	0	1
1653	0	1	0	0	1	2
1654	0	0	0	0	3	3
1655	0	0	0	2	3	5
1656	0	0	0	0	3	3
1657	0	0	2	1	5	8
1680	0	0	0	0	1	1
169-	0	0	0	0	3	3
1692	1	0	0	0	0	1
1695	0	0	0	0	2	2
1697	0	0	0	0	2	2
1699	0	0	0	0	1	1
17—	1	4	2	16	44	67
17-3	0	0	0	0	1	1
17-5	0	0	0	0	1	1
170-	2	4	1	2	3	12
1700	0	0	0	0	1	1
1702	1	0	0	0	1	2
1703	0	0	0	0	4	4
1704	0	0	0	1	3	4
1705	1	1	0	0	2	4
1706	0	2	0	0	1	3
1707	0	2	1	2	1	6
1708	0	0	1	2	7	10
1709	0	1	2	1	6	10
171-	1	7	1	24	70	03
1710	1	2	0	3	5	11
1711	1	5	1	4	26	37
1712	1	3	3	3	18	28
1713	1	1	1	32	71	106
1714	3	2	2	81	288	376
1715	1	1	2	18	106	128
173-	0	1	0	4	0	5
1731	0	1	0	1	1	3
1732	0	0	3	7	5	15

	½ real	1 real	2 reales	4 reales	8 reales	Subtotal
1733	0	0	0	1	3	4
1745	0	0	1	0	0	1
1752	0	0	1	0	0	1
1765	0	0	1	0	0	1
1772	0	0	1	0	0	1
1773	1	0	2	0	1	4
1775	0	0	1	0	0	1
1776	0	0	1	0	0	1
1778	0	0	1	0	0	1
1779	1	0	1	0	1	3
1780	0	0	0	0	1	1
1781	0	0	2	0	0	2
1782	0	1	2	0	0	3
1783	0	0	1	1	1	3
1784	0	0	0	0	1	1
1785	0	0	0	0	1	1
1786	0	0	0	0	1	1
1787	0	0	0	0	1	1
1788	1	0	1	0	1	3
1789	0	0	1	0	1	2
179-	0	0	0	1	0	1
1791	0	0	0	0	1	1
1792	1	0	0	0	1	2
1793	0	1	0	1	1	3
1794	0	0	1	0	0	1
1795	0	0	0	0	1	1
1796	0	0	0	0	1	1
1797	0	0	1	0	1	2
1798	1	0	1	0	1	3
1799	0	0	1	0	1	2
18—	0	0	0	0	1	1
1800	0	0	0	0	1	1
1801	0	0	0	0	2	2
1802	0	1	0	0	1	2
1803	0	0	0	0	3	3
1804	0	0	1	0	1	2
1805	0	0	1	0	1	2
1806	0	0	1	0	1	2
1807	0	0	1	0	2	3
1808	0	0	0	0	3	3
1809	0	0	0	0	3	3
1810	0	0	0	0	2	2
Indeterminate	1,134	2,352	969	5,001	10,578	20,034
Subtotal	1,156	2,398	1,016	5,220	11,372	21,162
Indeterminate denomination and date						8
Total						21,170

Source: Florida Bureau of Archaeological Research computer database.
*Dash indicates numeral indiscernible.

Table 7.2. Mexico Mint Assayers

Mark	Assayer Name	Term of Office
"R"	Francisco del Rincón	ca. 1536–1560
"G"	Juan Gutiérrez	1538–?
"O"	unknown	1536–1556
"P"	Pedro de Espina	?
"F"	Esteban Franco	1538–1540
"A"	Lic. Aleman	1545
"J"	Juan de San Pedro	1546
"M"	unknown	?
"S"	Gómez de Santillan	?
"L"	Luís Rodríguez	ca. 1560–1570
"F"	unknown	ca.1600–1617
"A"	unknown	1600–1609
"D"	unknown	1618–1634
"P"	unknown	1622–1667
"G"	Gerónimo Becerra	1667–1676
"L"	Martín López	1678–1708
"J"	Juán de Cuevas or Joseph de León	1705–1723
"D"	unknown	1724–1727
"R"	Nicolas de Roxas	1729–1730
"G"	unknown	1730
"F"	Felipe Rivas Angulo	1730–1733
"J"	unknown	1731
"MF"	Manuel de la Peña; Francisco A. de la Peña	1733–1754
"M"	Manuel de la Peña? (single initial "M" seen) on 2 reales in Florida Collection)	1745, 1752
"MM"	Manuel Assorín; Manuel de la Peña	1754–1763
"MF"	Manuel Assorín; Francisco de Rivera	1762–1770
"M"	Manuel Assorín? (single initial "M" seen on 2 reales in Florida Collection)	1765
"FM"	Francisco A. de la Peña; Manuel de Rivera	1772–1777
"FF"	Francisco A. de la Peña; Francisco Arance Cobos	1777–1784
"FM"	Francisco A. de la Peña; Mariano Rodríguez	1783–1802
"FT"	Francisco A. de la Peña; Tomás Butrón Miranda	1801–1803
"TH"	Tomás Butrón Miranda; Henrique B. Azorín	1803–1810
"HJ"	Henrique B. Azorín; Joaquin Dávila Madrid	1809–1814
"JJ"	Joaquin Dávila Madrid; José García Ansaldo	1812–1821

Sources: Calbetó (1970); Pellicer i Bru (1975); Pradeau (1938); Sedwick and Sedwick (1995).

The earliest known dated Mexican cobs appeared in 1609. At least some early examples have been found associated with the *Atocha* Wreck sites of 1622, but as noted in chapter 1, these sites fall outside the legal jurisdiction of the state of Florida and are not represented in the Florida Collection.

In a chronological series of dated Mexican 8-reales cobs shown in table 7.1 and figures 7.1 and 7.2, there are some noticeable gaps as might be expected from a collection structured around inputs from shipwrecks widely separated in time. There is only a short sequence shown in figure 7.1, from 1655 to 1657, of coins recovered from the Jupiter Wreck. From 1715 Plate Fleet wrecks we find a more complete sequence; in figure 7.2, it is unbroken for the interval 1709–1715 (however, the 1710 specimen is a 4-reales example). In all likelihood coin 7.2a dated 1700, assayer "L," is simply an odd example taken from what was in circulation at the time. It happened to be available when a massive effort began to fill the 1715 Plate Fleet with great quantities of long overdue gold and silver, so badly needed by the king.

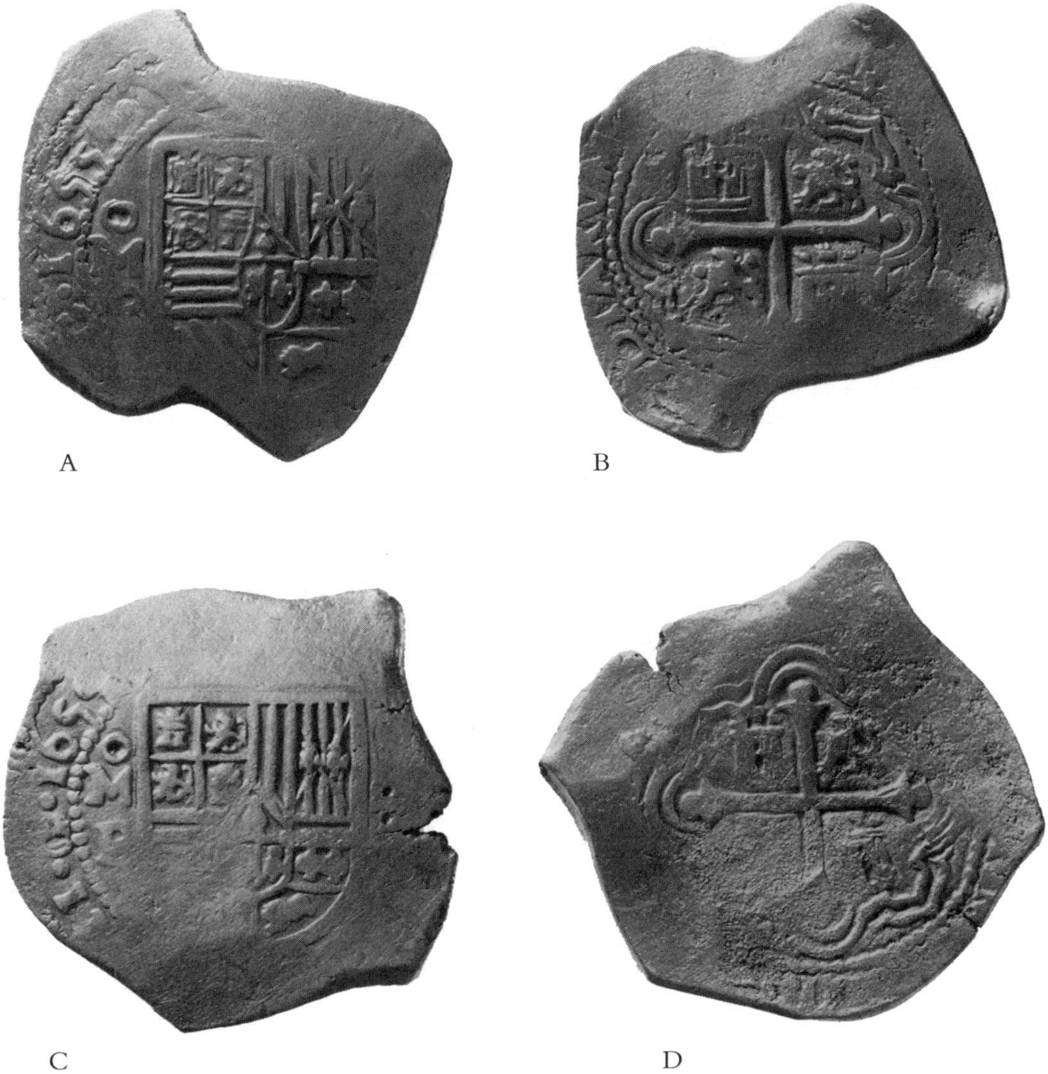

Figure 7.1 A–D. Mexican 8-Reales Cobs, 1655–1657

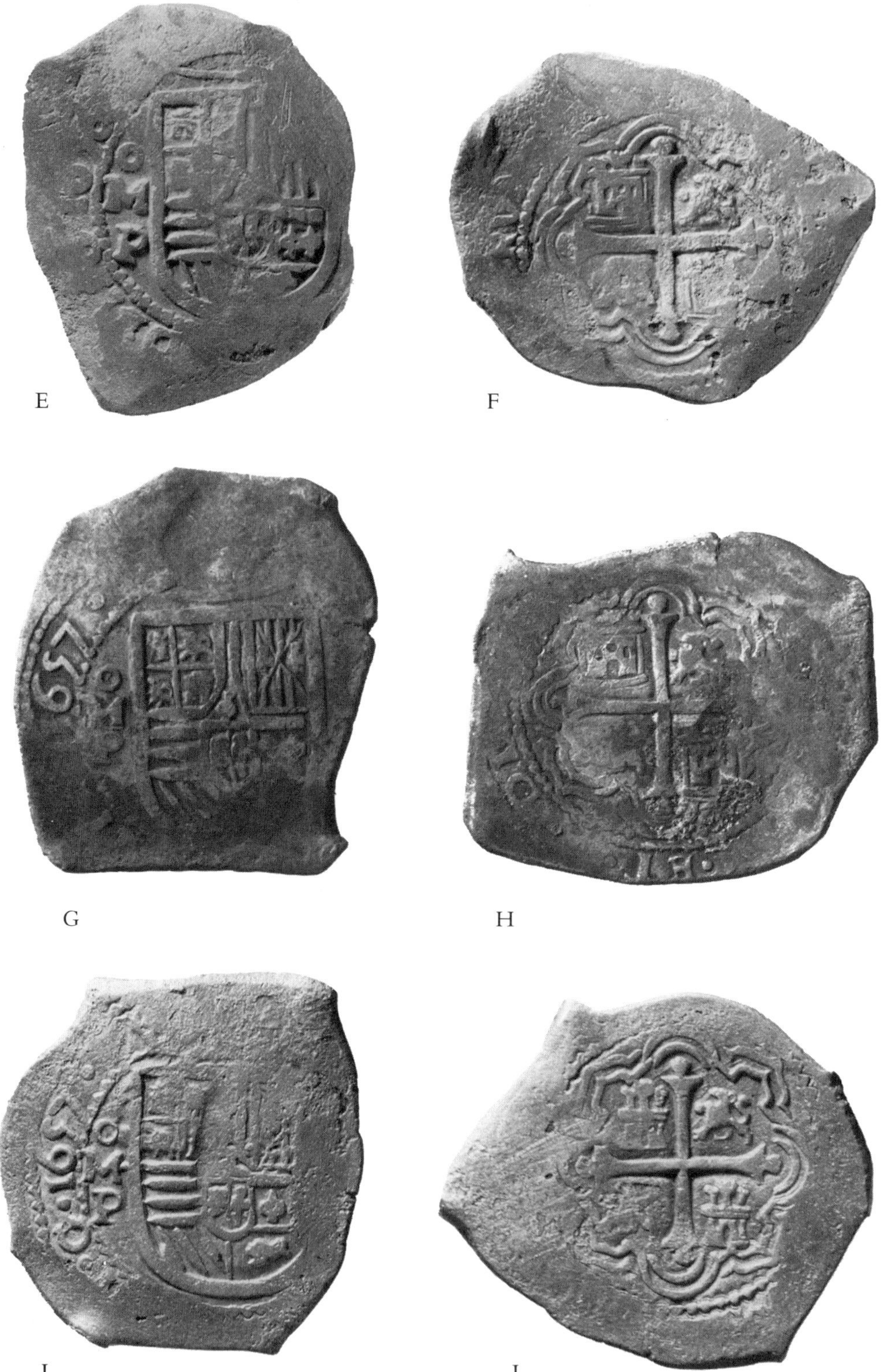

Figure 7.1 E–J. Mexican 8-Reales Cobs, 1655–1657

If we examine the quality of workmanship in dies from this series, we see there is an overall improvement in details between 1655 and 1715. However, having examined more than 1,000 Mexican gold coins in the Florida Collection, I can say by comparison much less attention was given to engraving and striking of silver coins. If dated specimens shown in 7.1 and 7.2 are representative, their occasional double-striking and die bounce suggests minting of the large quantity of silver under assayer "J" was a somewhat hurried matter.

This conclusion is borne out by examples shown in figure 7.3 that, though undated, are most likely from the first two decades of the eigh-

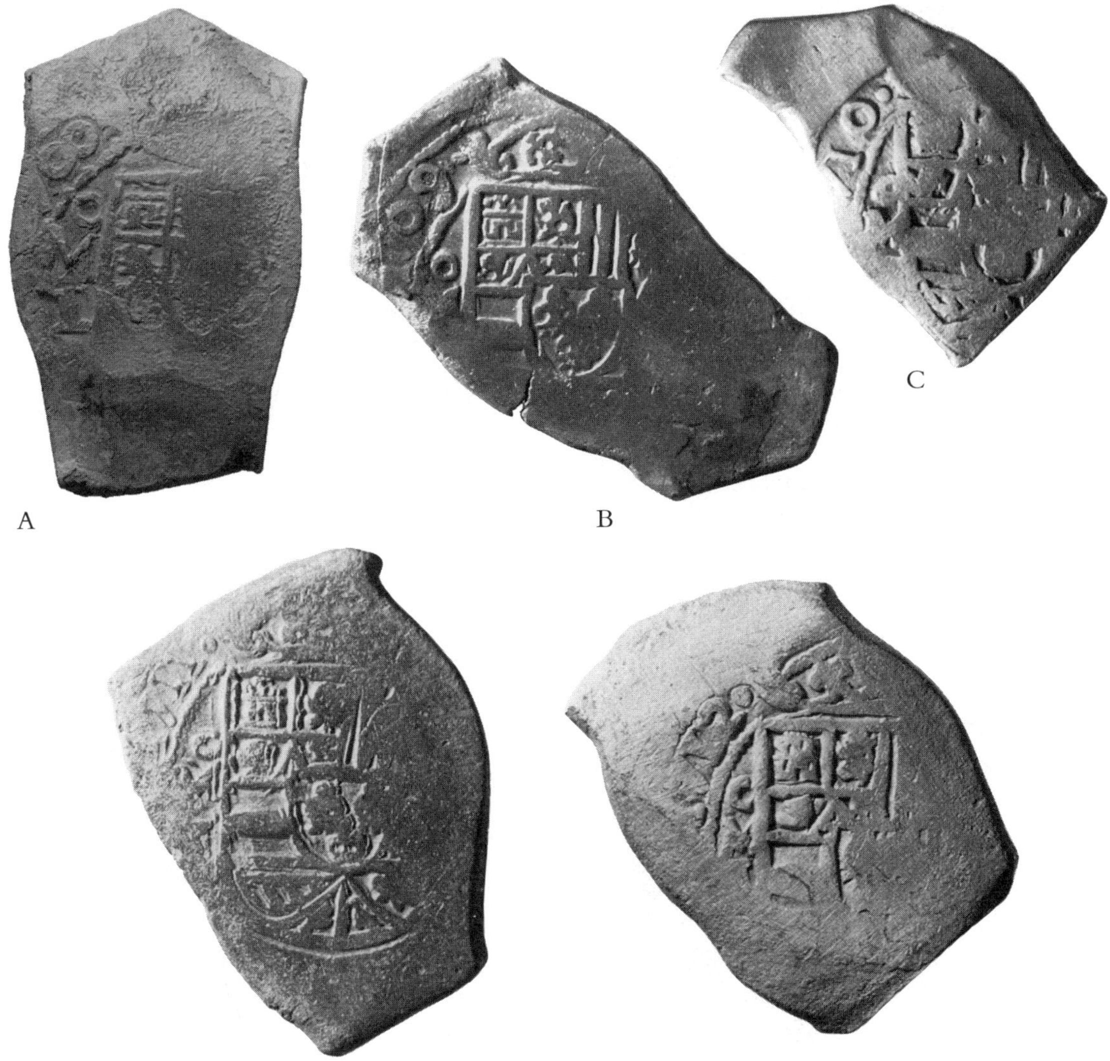

A B C D E

Figure 7.2 A–E. Mexican 4- and 8-Reales Cobs, 1700–1715

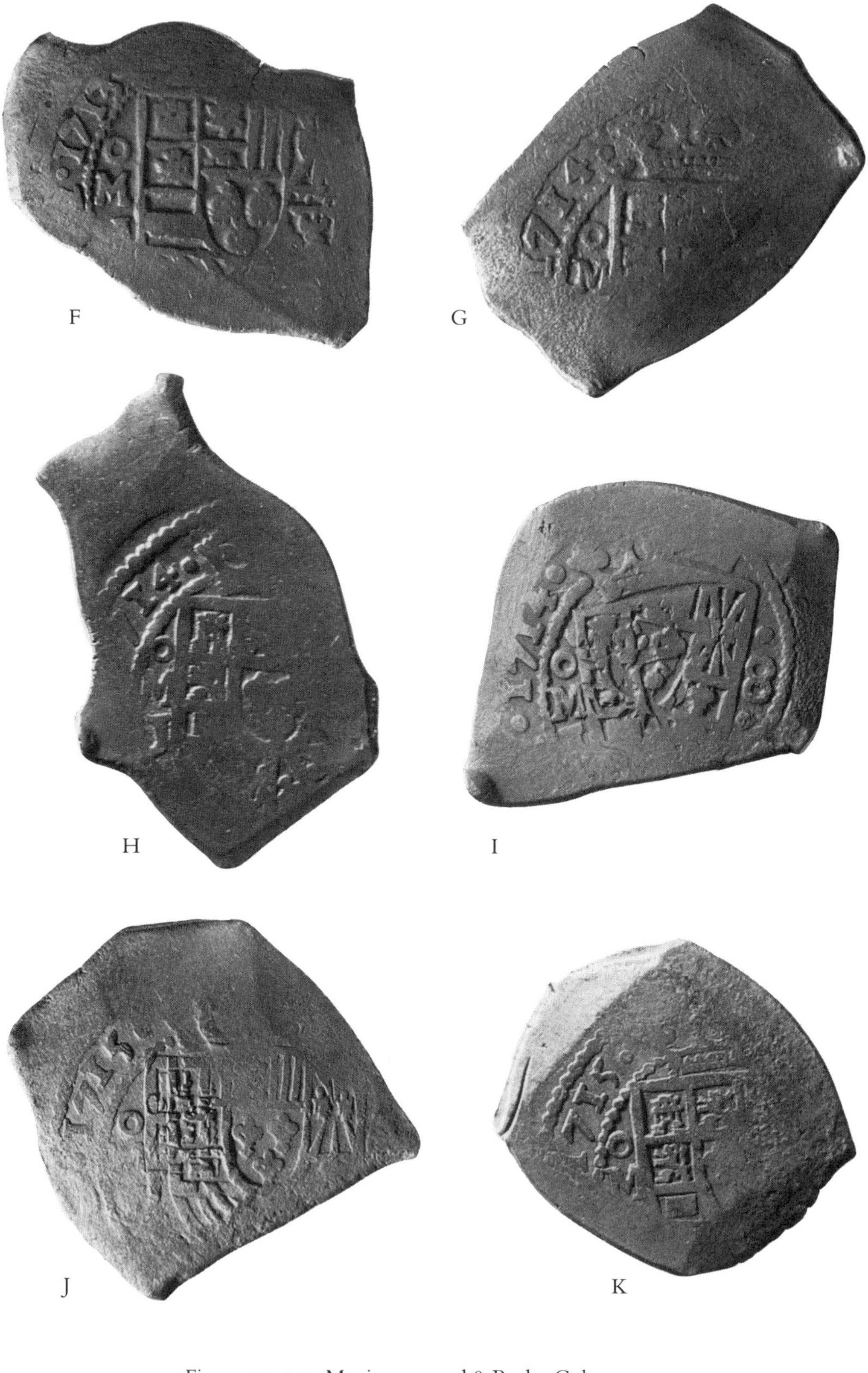

Figure 7.2 F–K. Mexican 4- and 8-Reales Cobs, 1700–1715

teenth century. Coin 7.3g, included for comparison, is a Potosí 8 reales that found its way on board one of the 1715 galleons. Figure 7.3 was organized around aberrant Mexican crosses, and coin 7.3i was included for its curious outlining, something not seen on any other specimen. Since the tressures, lions, and castles are all well flattened, we may assume it was done by reengraving into the field around the original well-worn cross.

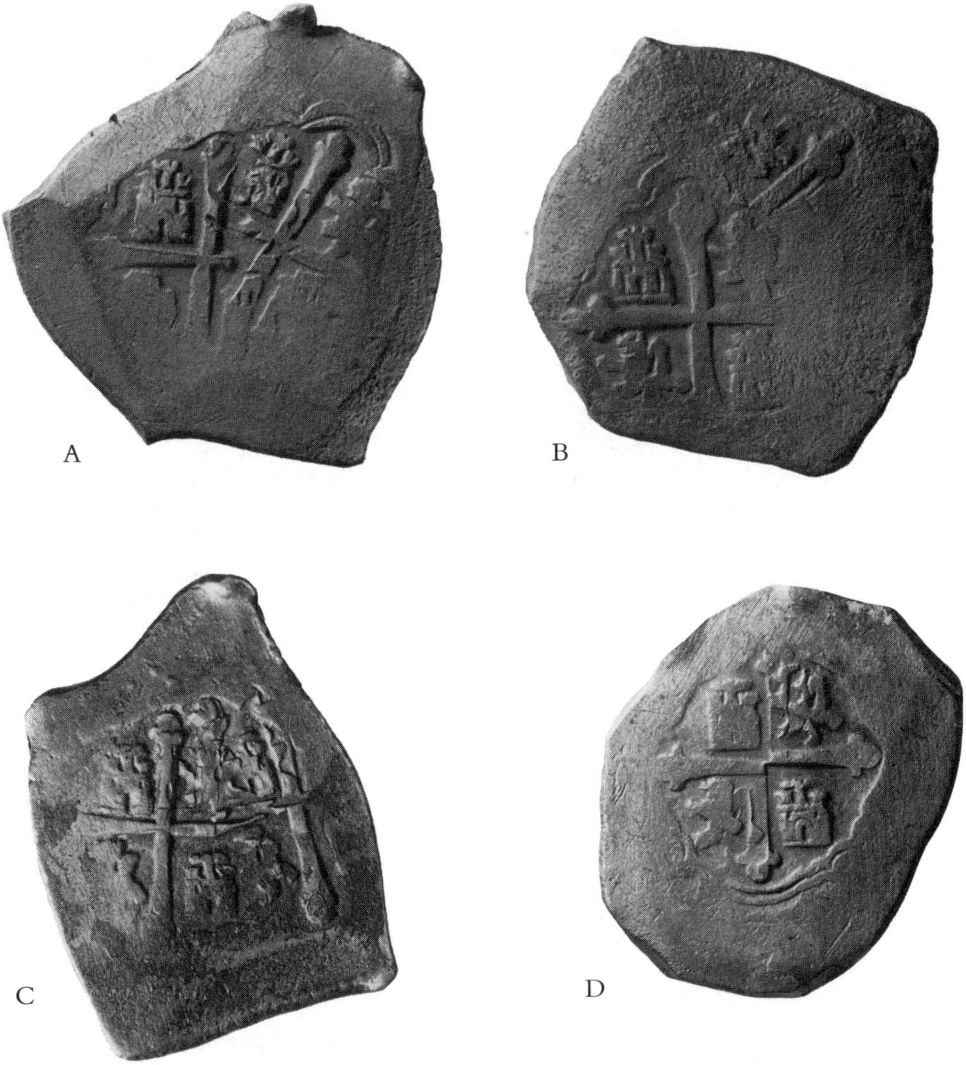

Figure 7.3 A–D. Unusual Cross Displacements on Mexican and Potosí 8-Reales Cobs

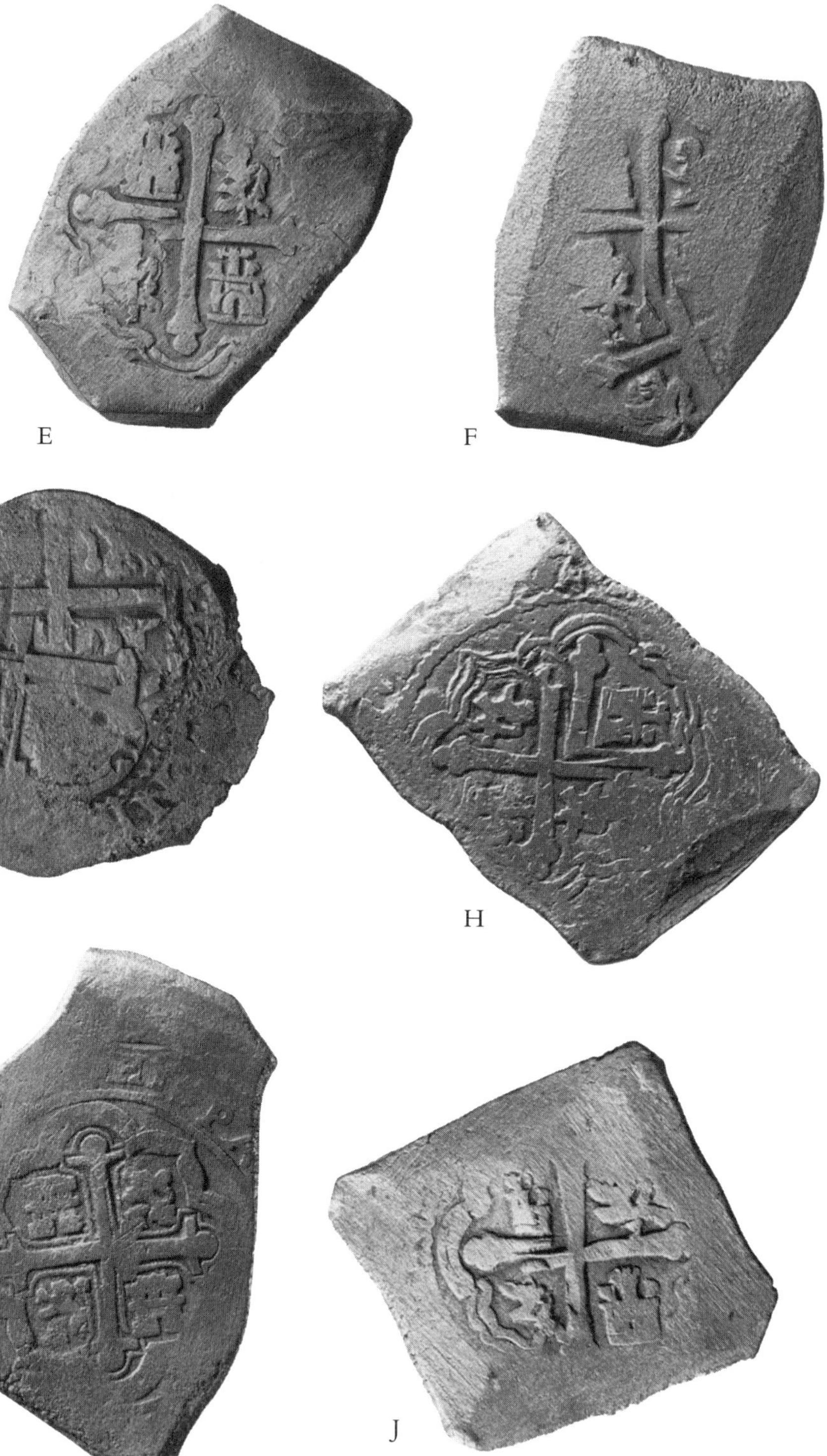

Figure 7.3 E–J. Unusual Cross Displacements on Mexican and Potosí 8-Reales Cobs

Figure 7.4 provides further evidence of Mexican abnormalities during this same period of intense mint activity. Coin 7.4a is a remarkable "sport," in the form of a 4 reales dated 1775 in which the second 7 in the date seems to have been punched in on top of the correctly dated 1715 die. Examples 7.4b, c, e, f, and h provide ample evidence that work was hurried, to say the least. They are all 4-reales coins by weight but struck with 8-reales dies. If this great cargo of coins had stayed in Mexico, such cavalier workmanship would have caused trouble, but it was expected upon safe arrival in Spain that all would soon be converted into other forms of specie and therefore would not become a public problem. While this same large-denomination/smaller-weight error is known in cobs from other Spanish colonial mints (especially Potosí), I do not recall having seen the reverse we find in coin 7.4d. Here we have a remarkable example of an 8-reales cob struck with the proper-sized die but one having an incorrect 4 for denomination. This means someone must have created the entire design with proper dimensions and then carelessly punched in the wrong denomination. Specimen 7.4g is included because it was made in such a way that it

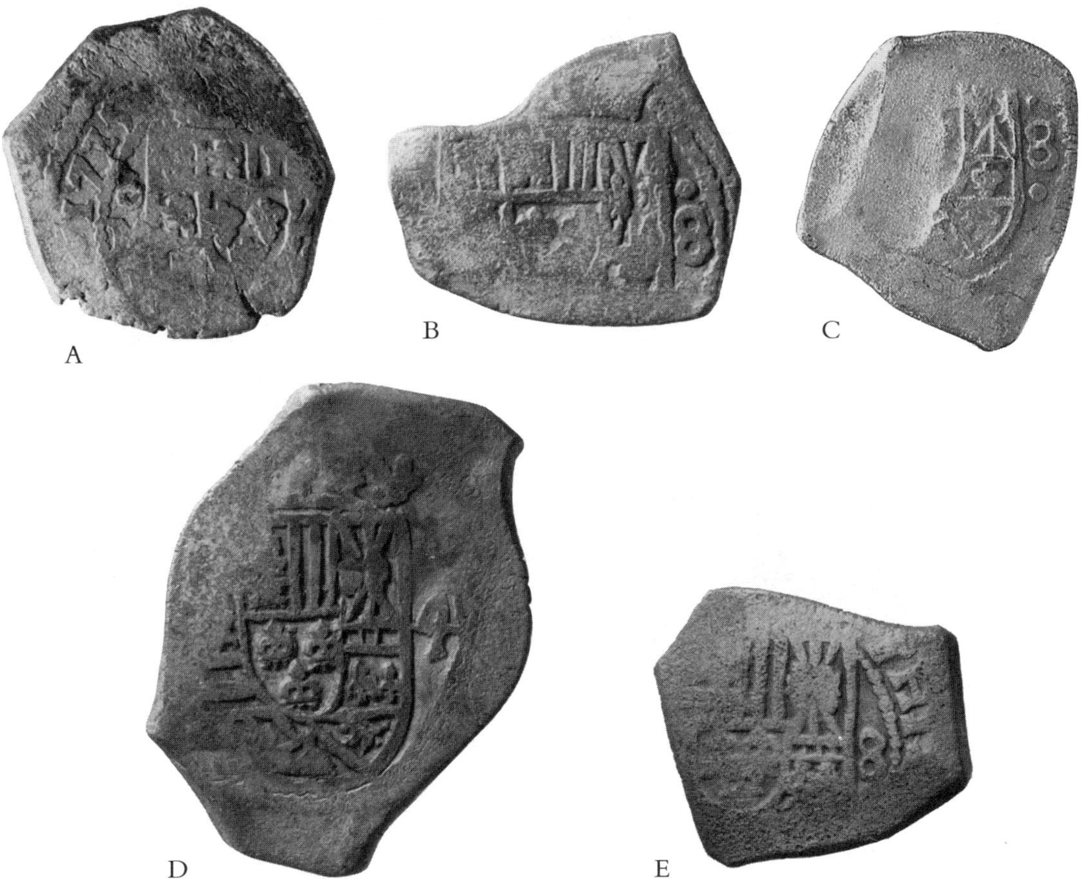

Figure 7.4 A–E. Serious Errors on Mexican 4- and 8-Reales Cobs

Figure 7.4 F–J.
Serious Errors on Mexican 4- and 8-Reales Cobs

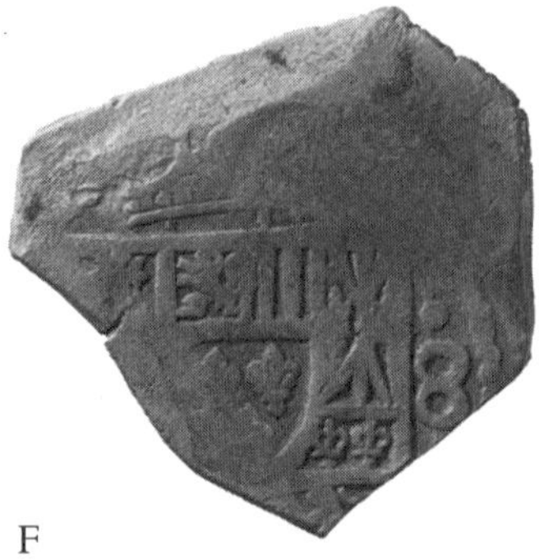

F

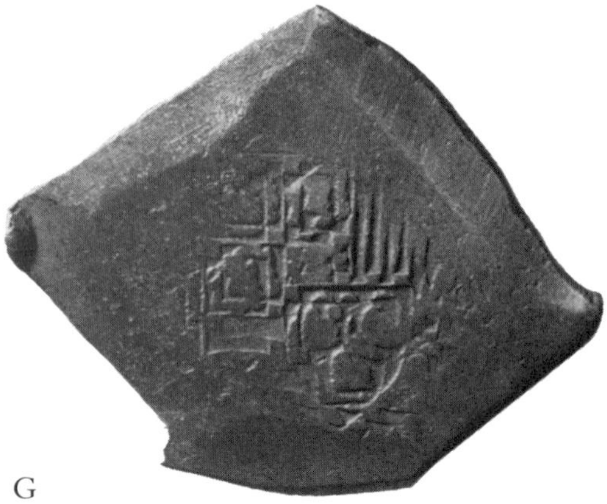

G

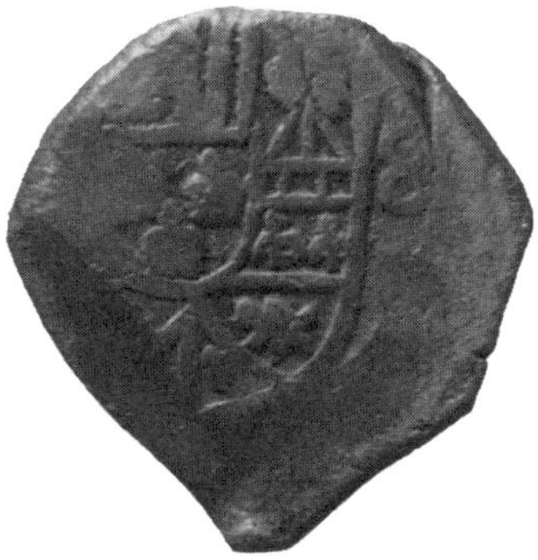

H

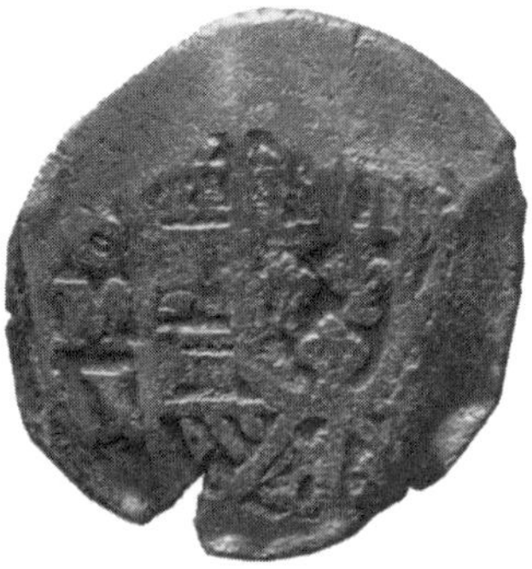

I

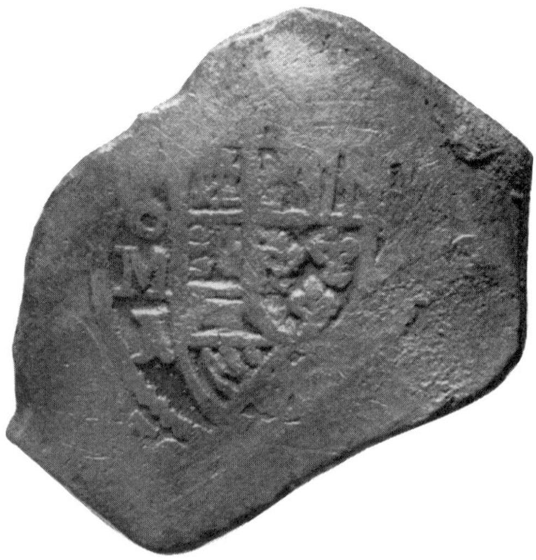

J

completely fails to observe any of the legal requirements except proper weight.[1] A distinctive example of assayer "J"'s hurried work is illustrated in figure 7.4, coins i and j. The assayer's mark "J" is split at the bottom. All such examples in the Florida Collection appear to have been made with the same unique punch.

Figure 7.5 is a grouping of "faceted" specimens illustrating the highly developed Mexican mint practice of hammering planchets after they had been struck with the appropriate dies.[2] A careful examination of these photographs will show numerous examples of hammer blows impinging upon, and partially obliterating preexisting die impressions. This was a very common practice seen in gold coins recovered from the 1715 Plate Fleet. On those coins it is also obvious that similar hammer blows cause sharp rectanglar planchet corners to become blunted, or upturned.

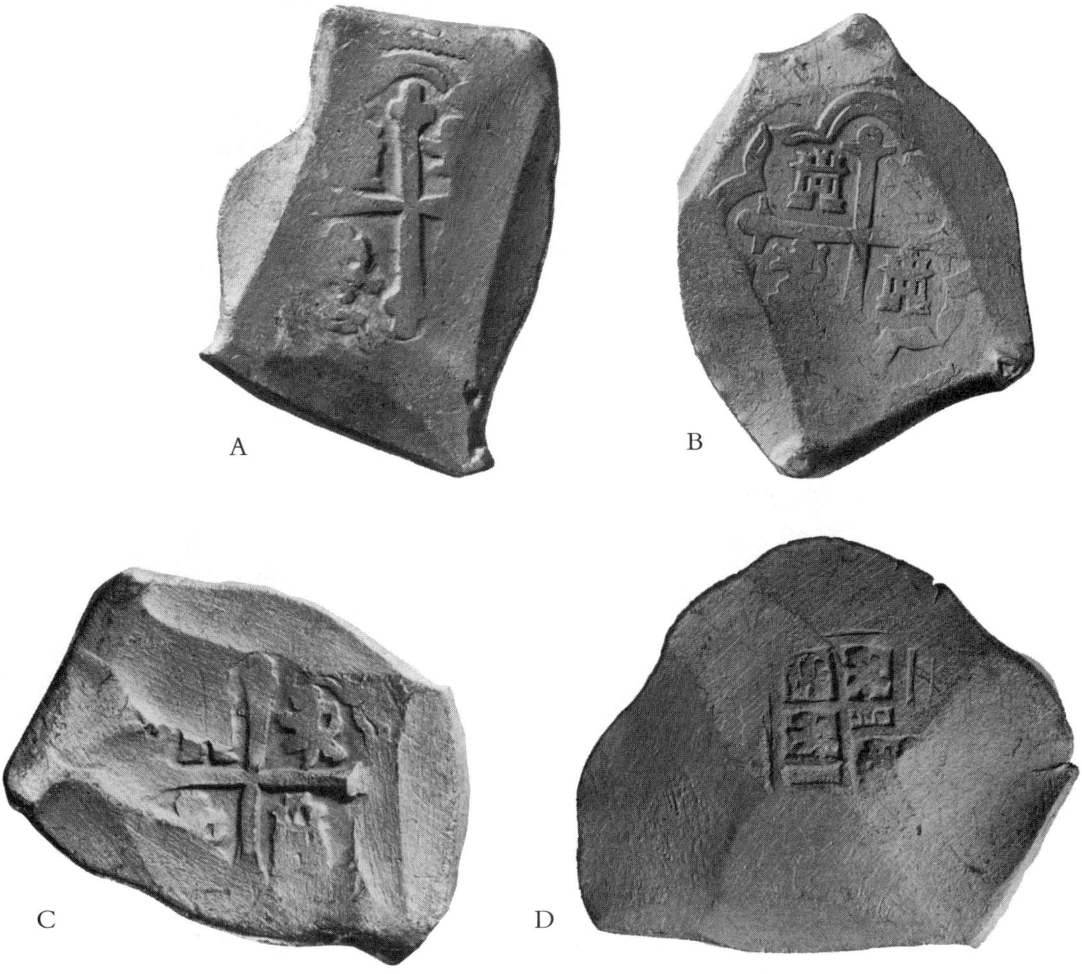

Figure 7.5 A–D. Typical Faceting Blows Struck on Mexican 4- and 8-Reales Cobs

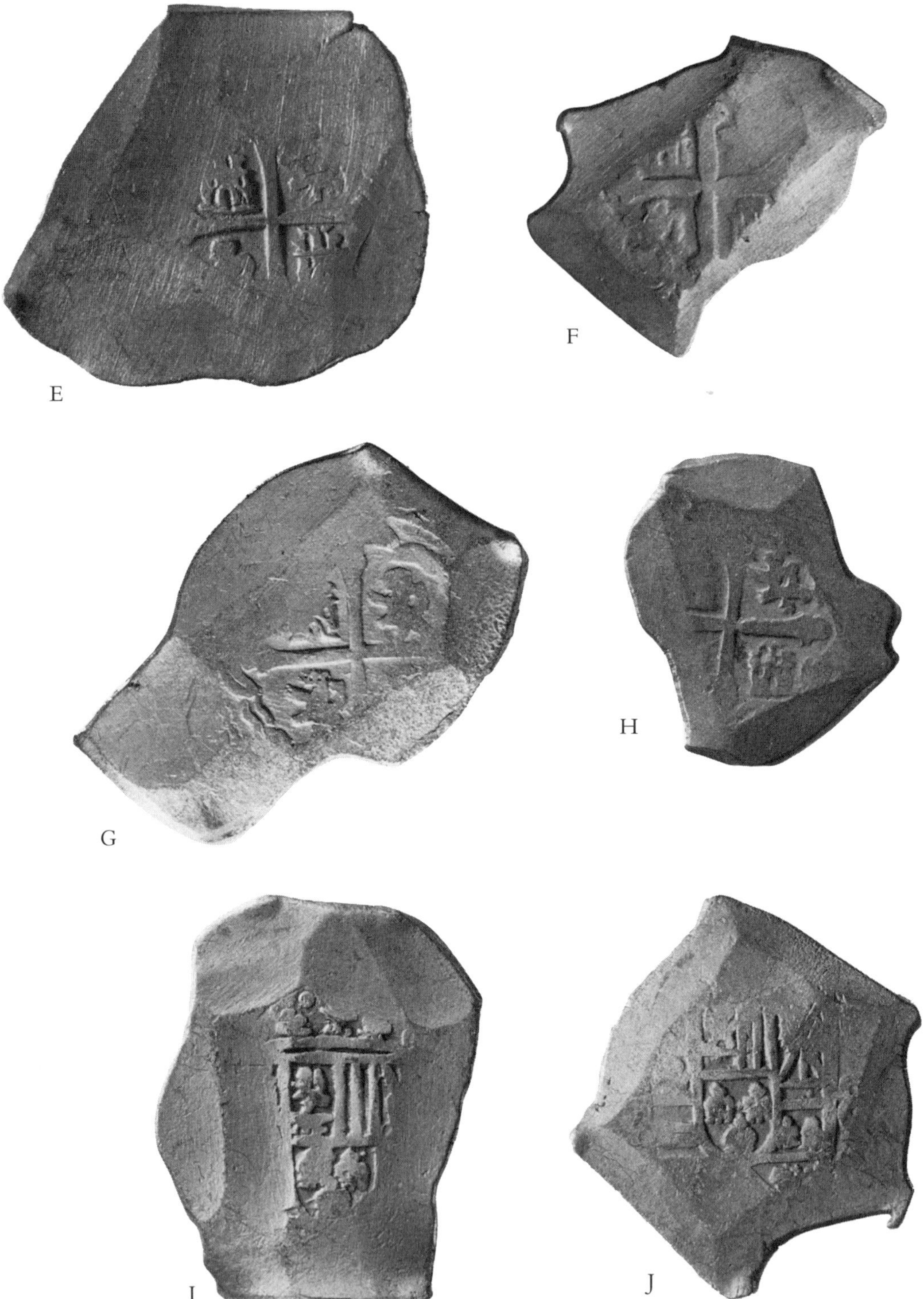

Figure 7.5 E–J. Typical Faceting Blows Struck on Mexican 8-Reales Cobs

The reason for this peculiar work-intensive practice puzzled me for many years until it was made evident during research for this book. While lifting canvas bags of loose cobs from one inspection table to another, I clutched a heavy bag of more than 300 Mexican cobs to my chest and soon felt several sharp corner points were pushing through the cloth. This produced a decidedly unpleasant "porcupine" effect. Later that day results of the same phenomenon were seen on another canvas bank bag, left long undisturbed in the vault; it now had sharp corners of silver cob coins projecting through the corroded cloth.

From this experience, I conclude it was a unique Mexican mint practice developed ca. 1700 to blunt sharply sheared planchet corners of both gold and silver coins to prevent them from damaging their storage bags or owners' purses.

Figures 7.6 and 7.7 illustrate bizarre shapes found among Mexican cobs. In these figures all coins have been positioned with obverse or reverse vertically oriented. These are accidental shapes produced during regular production runs without any overt attempt to create a special figure. Resulting coins were originally within legal tolerances for weight, unlike most of the custom-made animal shapes illustrated with great acclaim in recent auction catalogs where the critical datum of weight is conveniently missing. For weights of all coins illustrated in these figures, see Appendix C.

We conclude from Figures 7.6 and 7.7 that, in spite of their varied appearance, most if not all were produced from relatively narrow straps of silver *rieles*. And these were made by casting into molds of standard dimensions rather than by pouring out molten silver into sheets of irregular shape.

Figure 7.6 A–B. Bizarre Shapes in Mexican 4- and 8-Reales Cobs

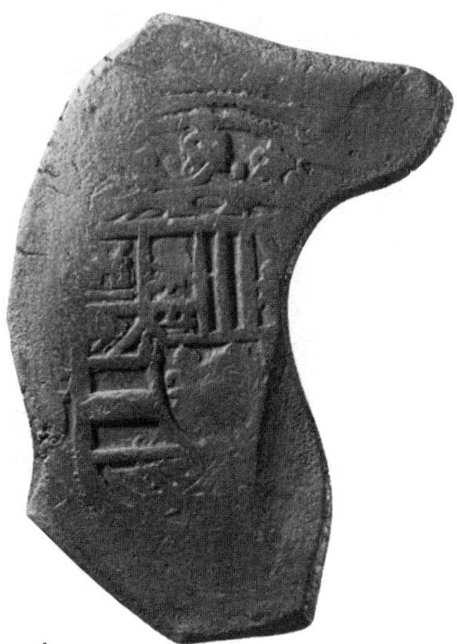

A

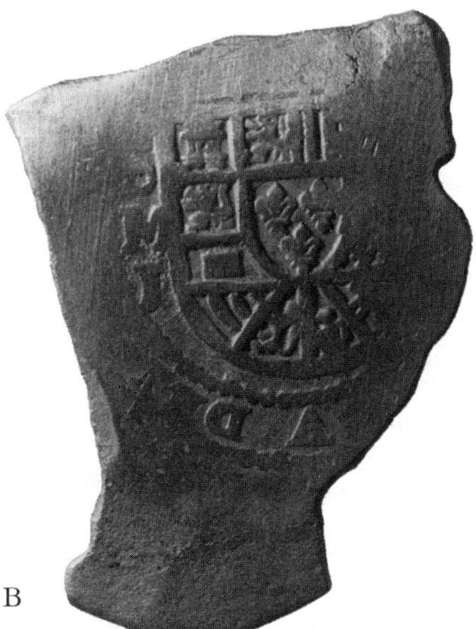

B

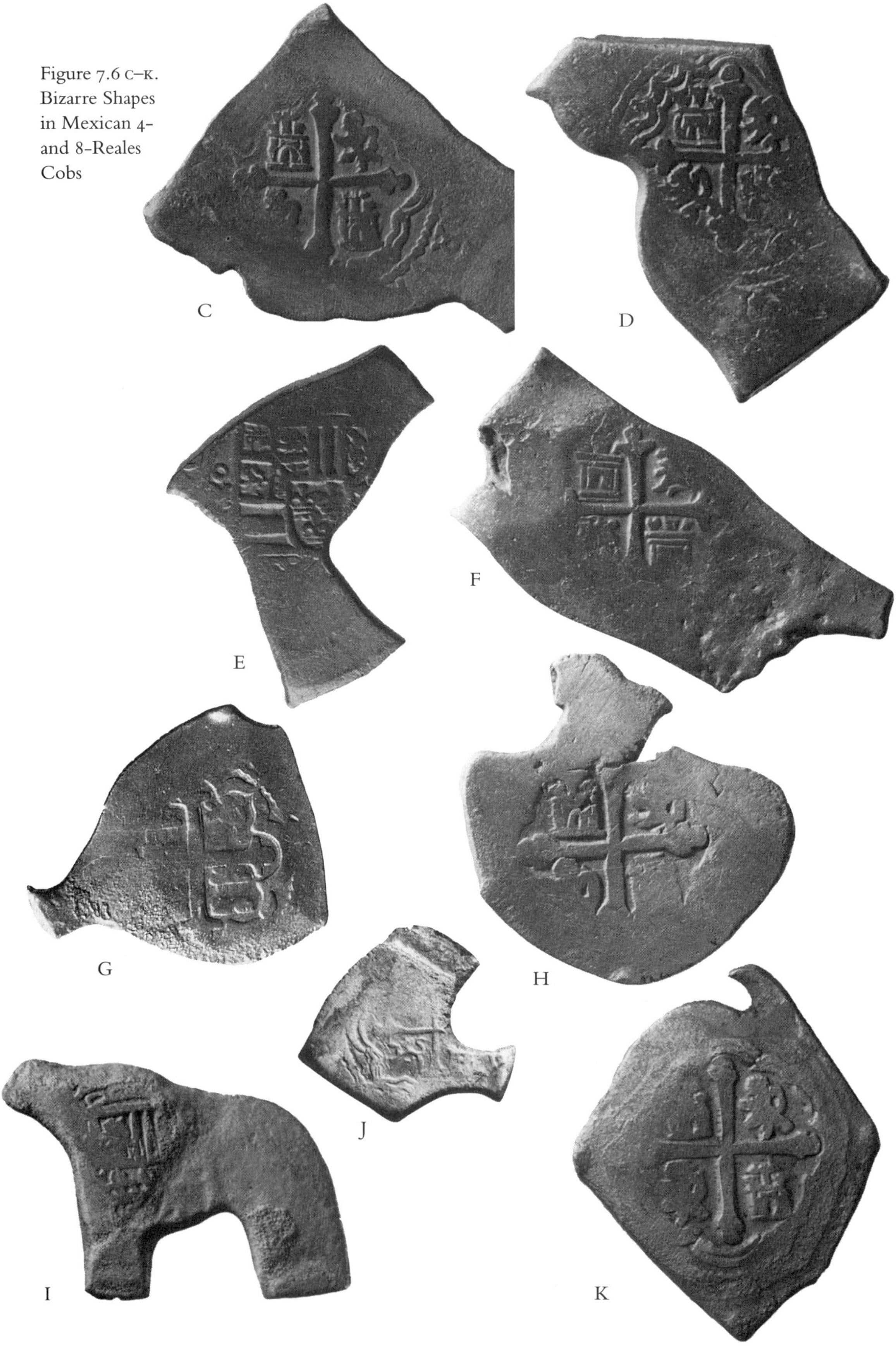

Figure 7.6 C–K. Bizarre Shapes in Mexican 4- and 8-Reales Cobs

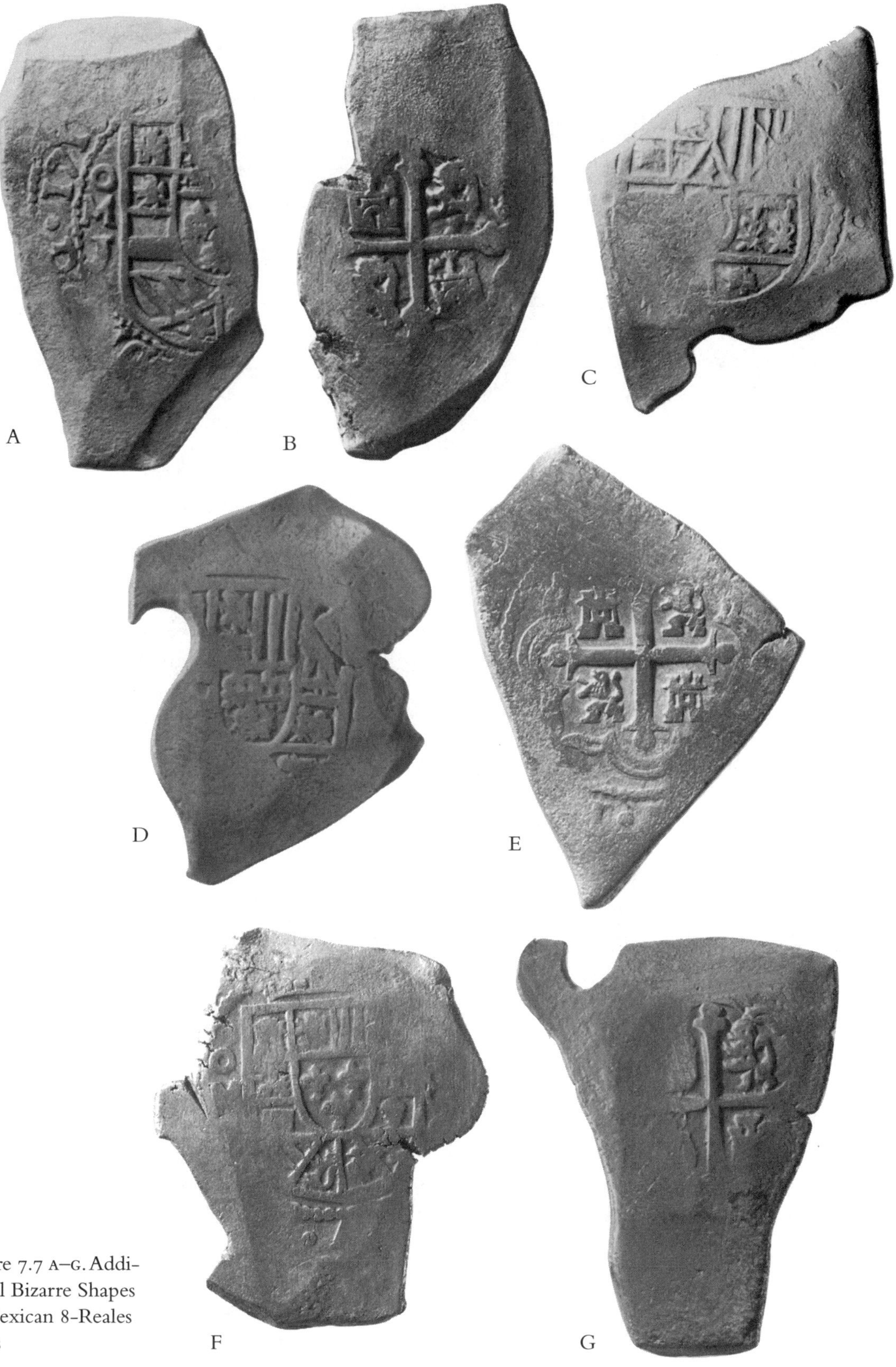

Figure 7.7 A–G. Additional Bizarre Shapes in Mexican 8-Reales Cobs

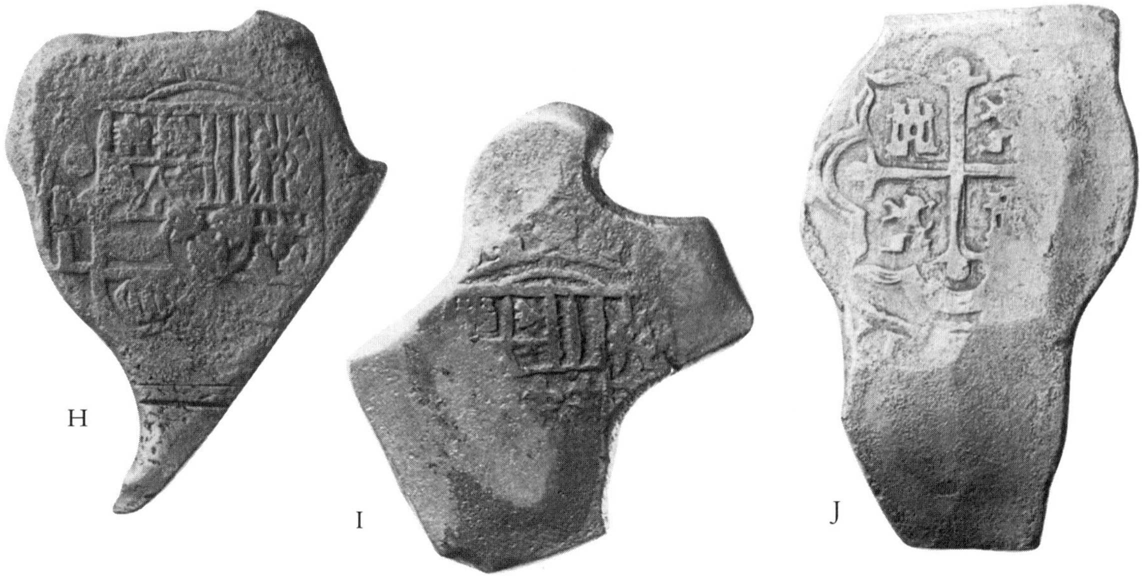

Figure 7.7 H–J. Additional Bizarre Shapes in Mexican 8-Reales Cobs

A special shape I call "spurred" cobs occurred when heavy iron shears used to slice off planchets from the strap were held steady while the silver itself was twisted in order to disengage it. A few of these are quite prickly (7.8a, c, and f) and probably represent exceptions to my hypothesis regarding piercing of storage bags. The extremely fine spur shown on 7.8g subsequently was doubled back on itself by some further application of force; two sharp corners on coin 7.8h were completely blunted, but one still remains.

"Thumbprint" cobs shown in figure 7.9 were a puzzle when they began to appear in our systematic inspection of each coin in the Florida Collection. For several days they were put aside in a box to be photographed along with other more impressive dated specimens. One day, out of curiosity laboratory supervisor David Dickel placed one under the binocular stereo microscope and commented to me that all arcuate grooves began as scoop marks along the sides of the cross but not over the top of it.

By the time we had selected enough photogenic specimens to construct figure 7.9, it was evident how they were made. A rusty and badly worn 8-reales die was picked up by an engraver who carefully recut it. By scraping away rust in long sweeping strokes of his steel *buril* (engraving tool), he created a distinctive thumbprint pattern across all the low-lying areas around the cross. Underlying castles and lions were never repunnched to bring them into sharper relief and the net result was yet another curious variety of Mexican cob.

All but one coin are from the same wreck, the Douglass Beach site, 8SL17, a vessel of the 1715 Plate Fleet. Coin 7.9d is from the same fleet, vessel unknown. A very patient examination by some future researcher

Figure 7.8. "Spurred" Mexican 4- and 8-Reales Cobs

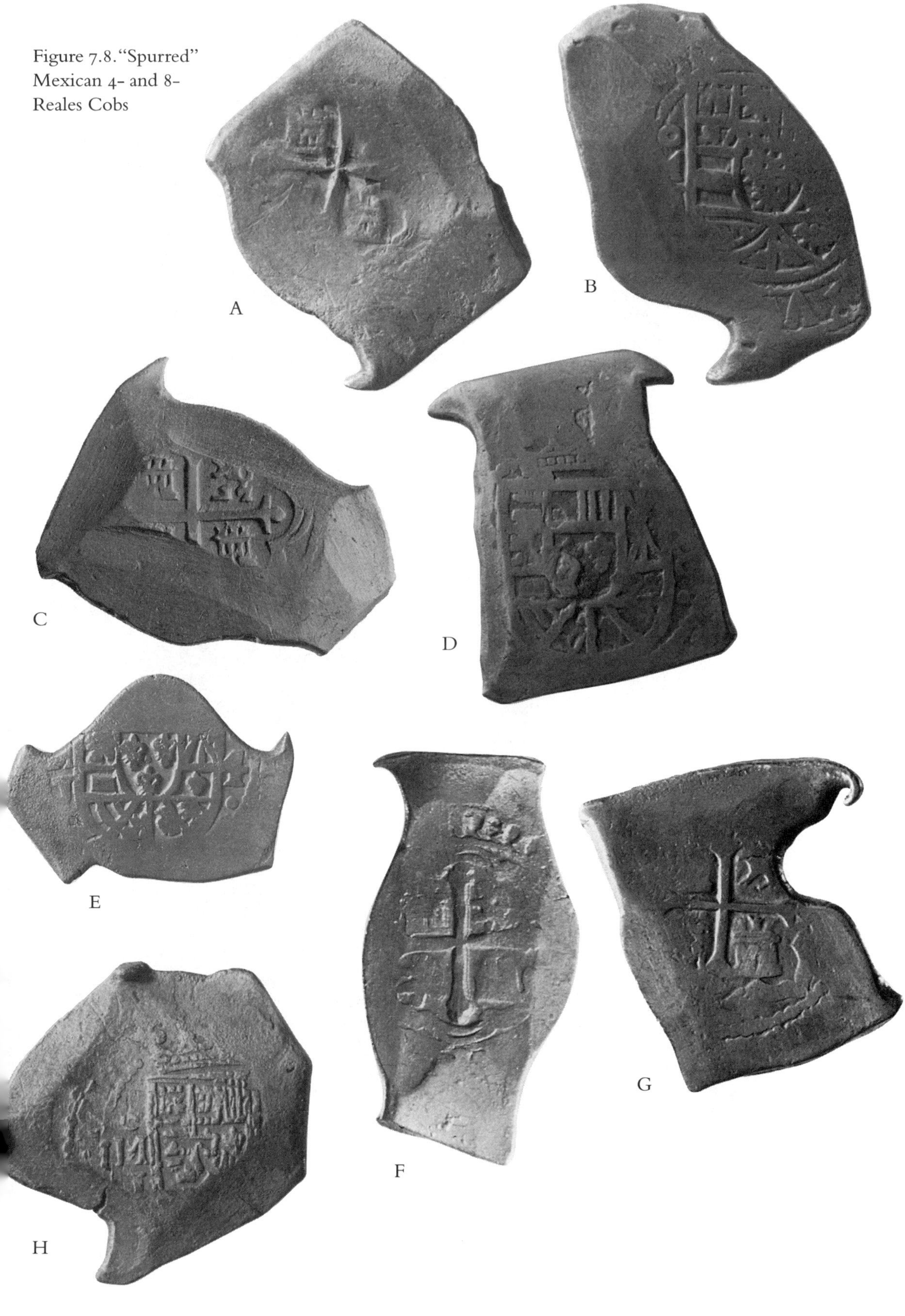

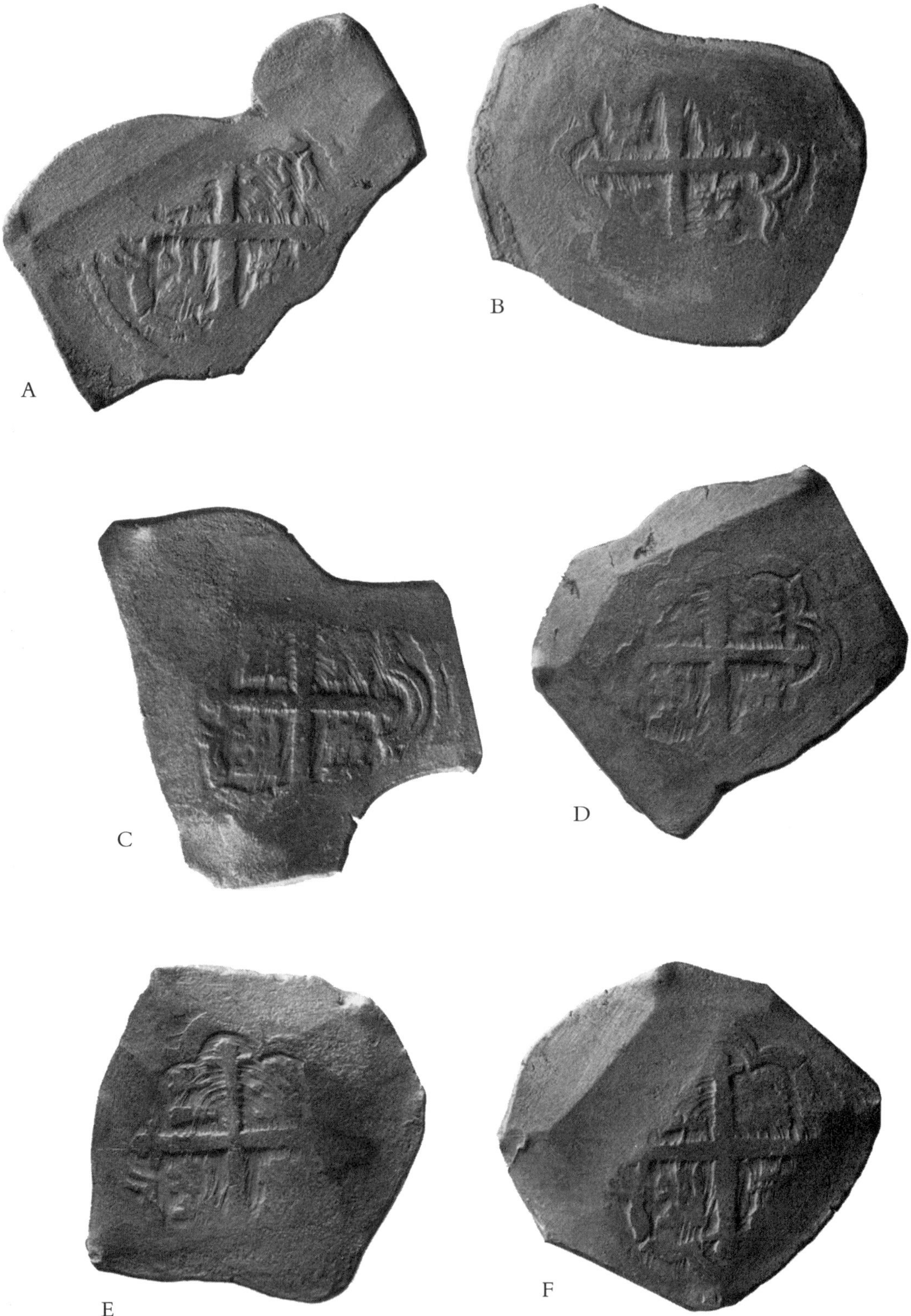

Figure 7.9. A–F. "Thumbprint" Mexican 8-Reales Cobs

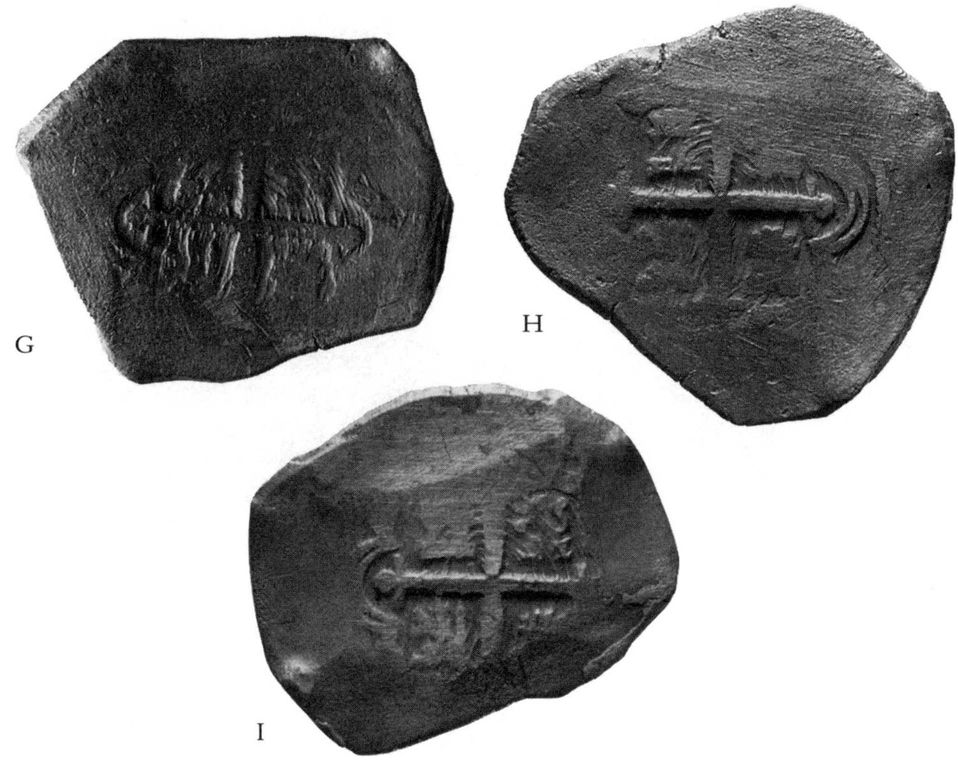

Figure 7.9. G–I. "Thumbprint" Mexican 8-Reales Cobs. The field displays small ridges that were created when the die was scraped with a sharp tool to clean it of corrosion.

may be able to link these specimens in chronological order by measuring slow erosion of these die-polishing lines that form the thumbprint.

Another common Mexican variety we chose to call a "wristwatch" cob is illustrated by specimens in figure 7.10. Again, there was much discussion among us as to why such a distinctive shape should be commonly repeated by the Mexican coining process. These elongated cobs clearly were made by shearing off appropriate lengths of a silver strap, then adjusted by more shearing to proper weight, struck with dies, and finally beaten on both sides by an extra-heavy hammer blow, or blows, that spread out the central area, often leaving behind tiny tension cracks.

In a methodical business where no unnecessary work was encouraged, we must ask why this wristwatch shape was deliberately repeated. A possible answer seems to be for stability in counting stacks of these narrow coins when they are placed one on top of the other. If there is another practical reason for continuing to belabor planchets in this manner after they have already been struck with dies, we have not been able to identify it.

The last shape in our Mexican menagerie of cobs is the rather common square form shown in figure 7.11. It is interesting to note all have evidence of deliberately blunted corners, probably to reduce corner spurs left by shearing. Obviously overall dimensions were dictated by width of the silver strap being used. Coin 7.11g is a 4-reales coin that

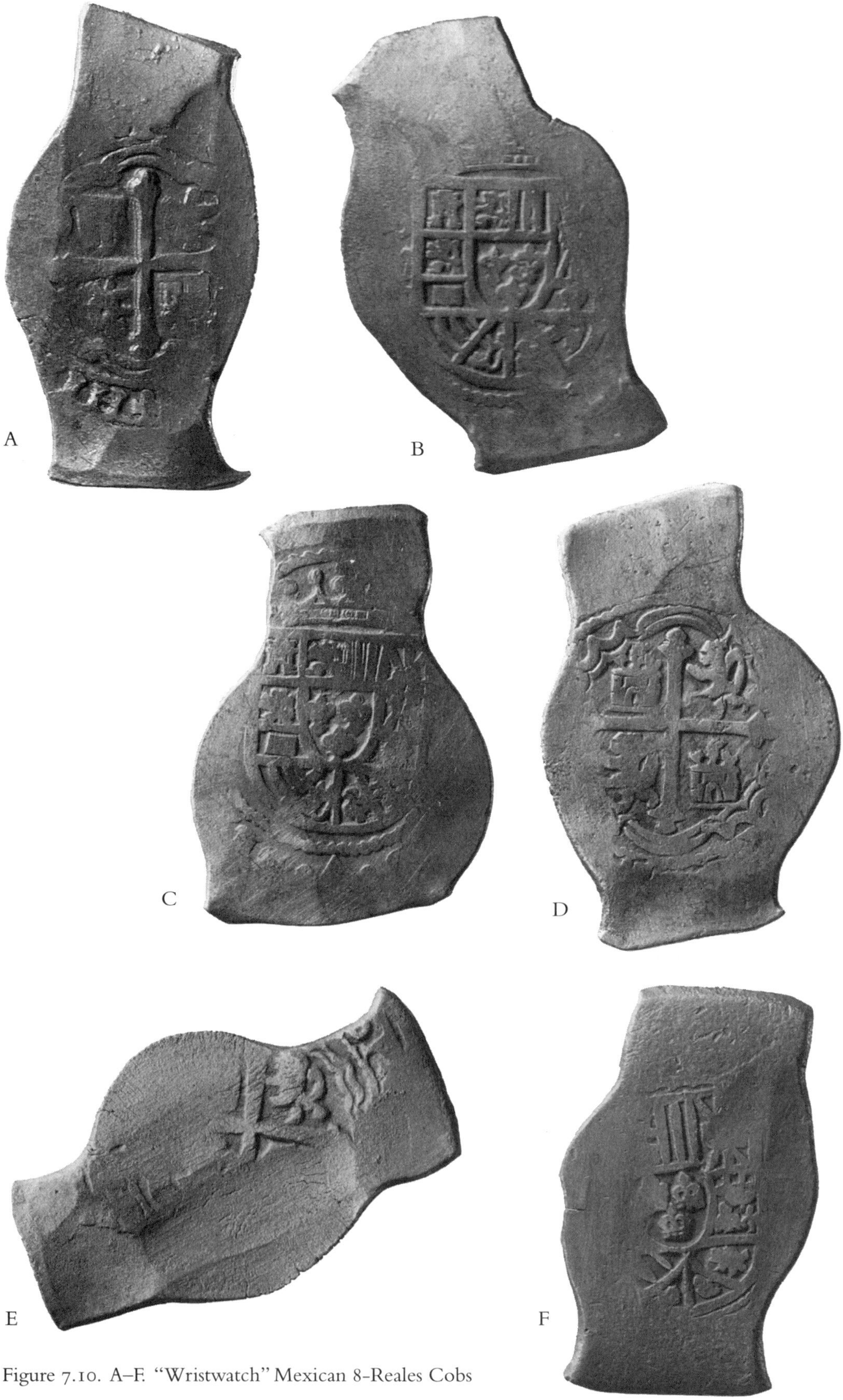

Figure 7.10. A–F. "Wristwatch" Mexican 8-Reales Cobs

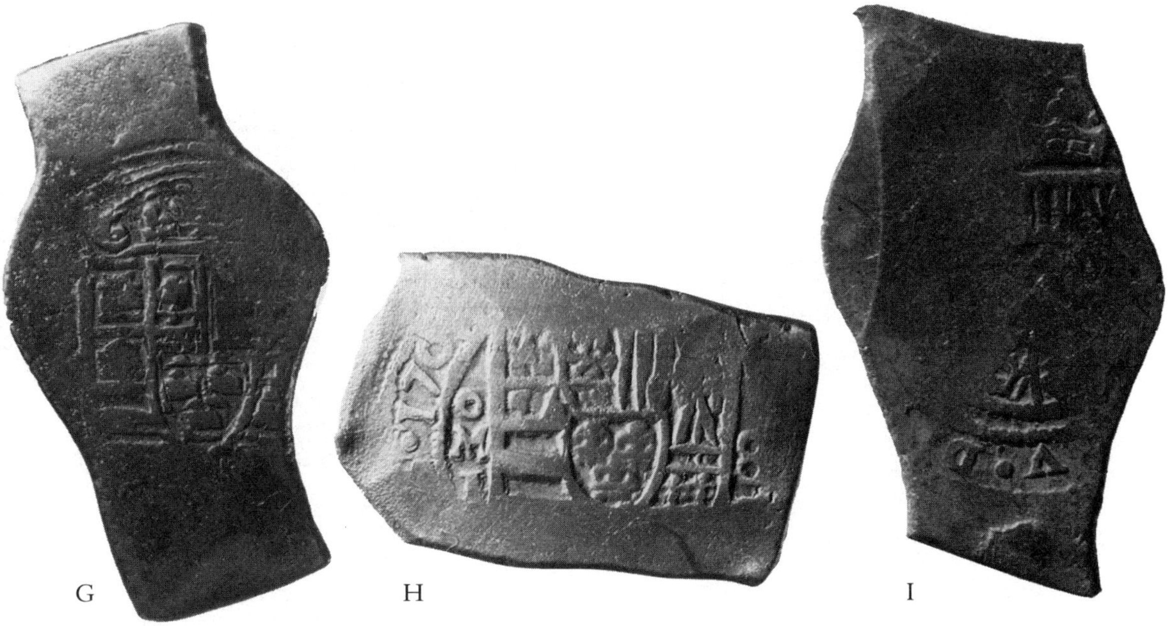

Figure 7.10. G–I. "Wristwatch" Mexican 8-Reales Cobs

may have been made using a narrower strap cast specifically for this denomination rather than cutting one down from a larger-diameter strap.

Saving the most enigmatic variety for last, we find a progressively worsening array in figures 7.12, 7.13, and 7.14. These unsightly planchet defects have been noted before by others who casually dismissed them as "bubbles." Would that everything in numismatics was so simple. From a vantage point of having examined more than fifty such specimens in the Florida Collection, I reject the simplistic "bubble" explanation in a process where no gases are involved.

In the Florida Collection, teardrop defects occur only in Mexican coins. At least one additional example is known. Lot 1005 of the *Association* catalog is an excellent example of a teardrop-shaped hole in a Mexican planchet that is incorrectly described as "pierced." This auction included several other early and scarce coins not expected to be found on a 1707 wreck (an uncirculated 1598 8R of Segovia, a 1676 "royal" 8R of Potosí, and a transitional "double 8" by assayer "E" of 1652).

Remembering these cob coins were all made from thin (ca. 3–4 mm) cast straps or sheets, the photographs shown here suggest several factors may be at work forming these depressions and holes. From their weights we know the coins themselves were made from proper planchets to begin with and are still, with a few exceptions, within reasonable weight limits after long submergence in salt water. In other words,

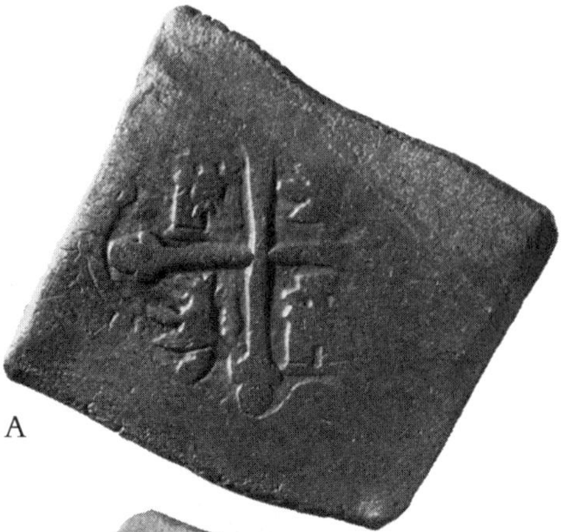

A

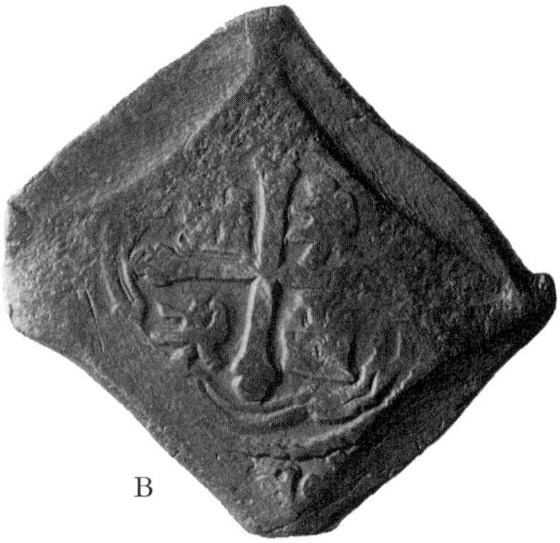

B

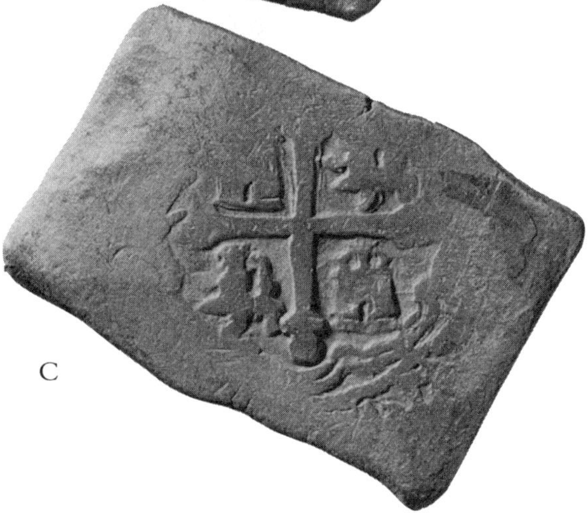

C

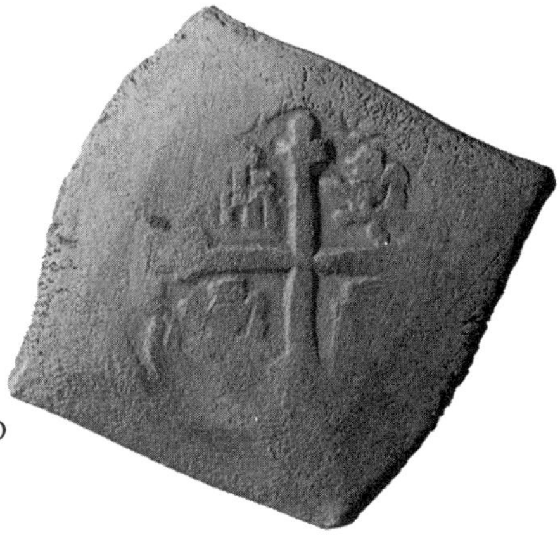

D

E

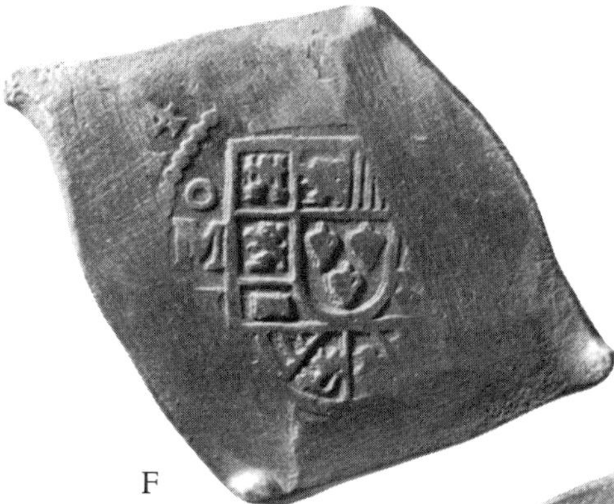

F

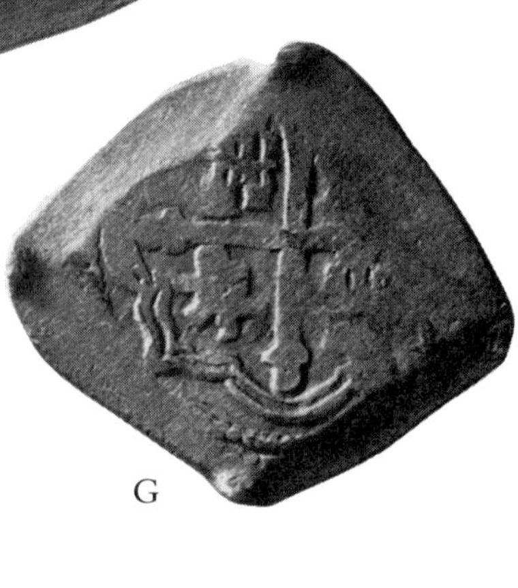

G

Figure 7.11. Rectangular Mexican 4- and 8-Reales Cobs

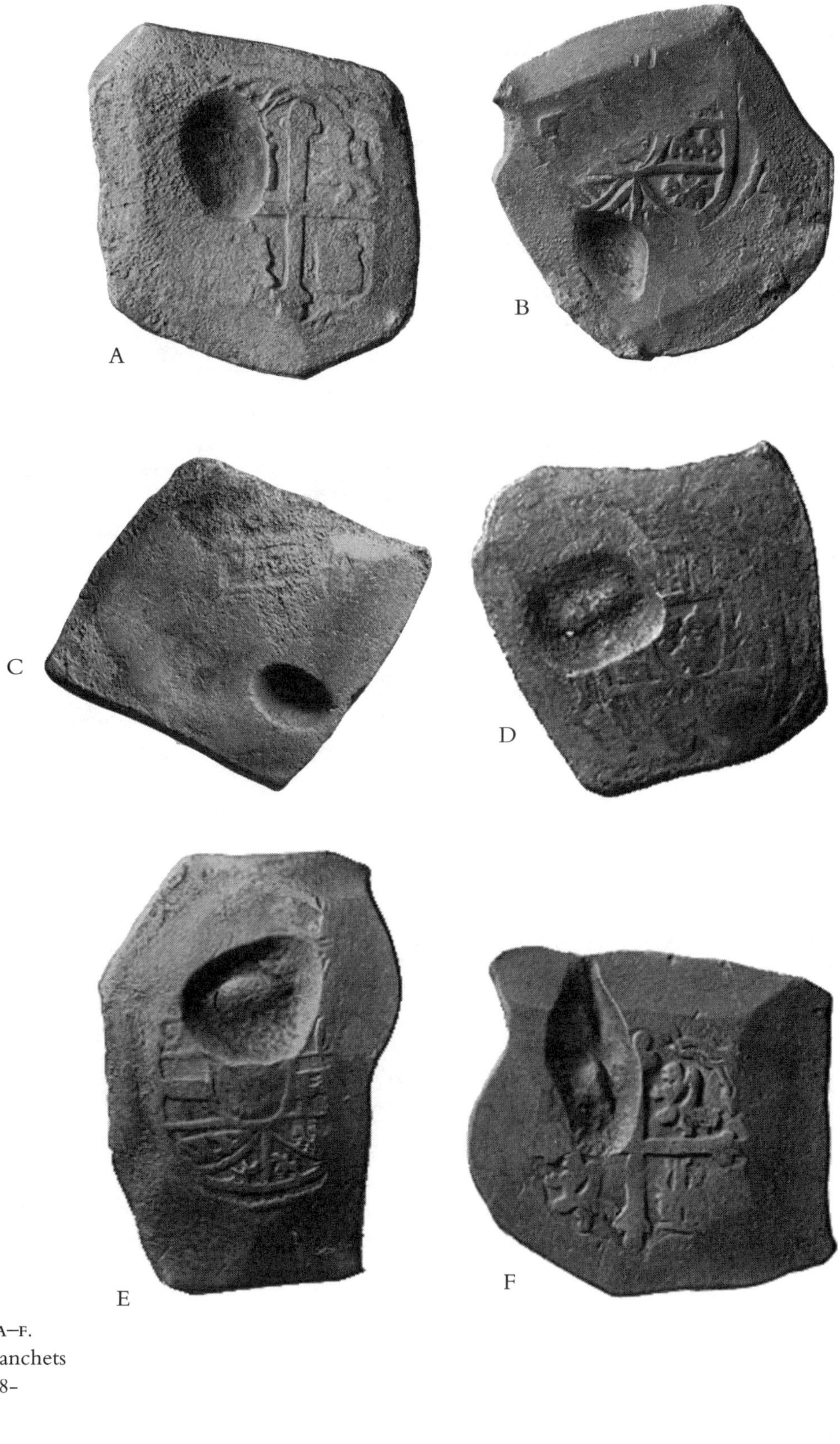

Figure 7.12 A–F.
Defective Planchets
in Mexican 8-
Reales Cobs

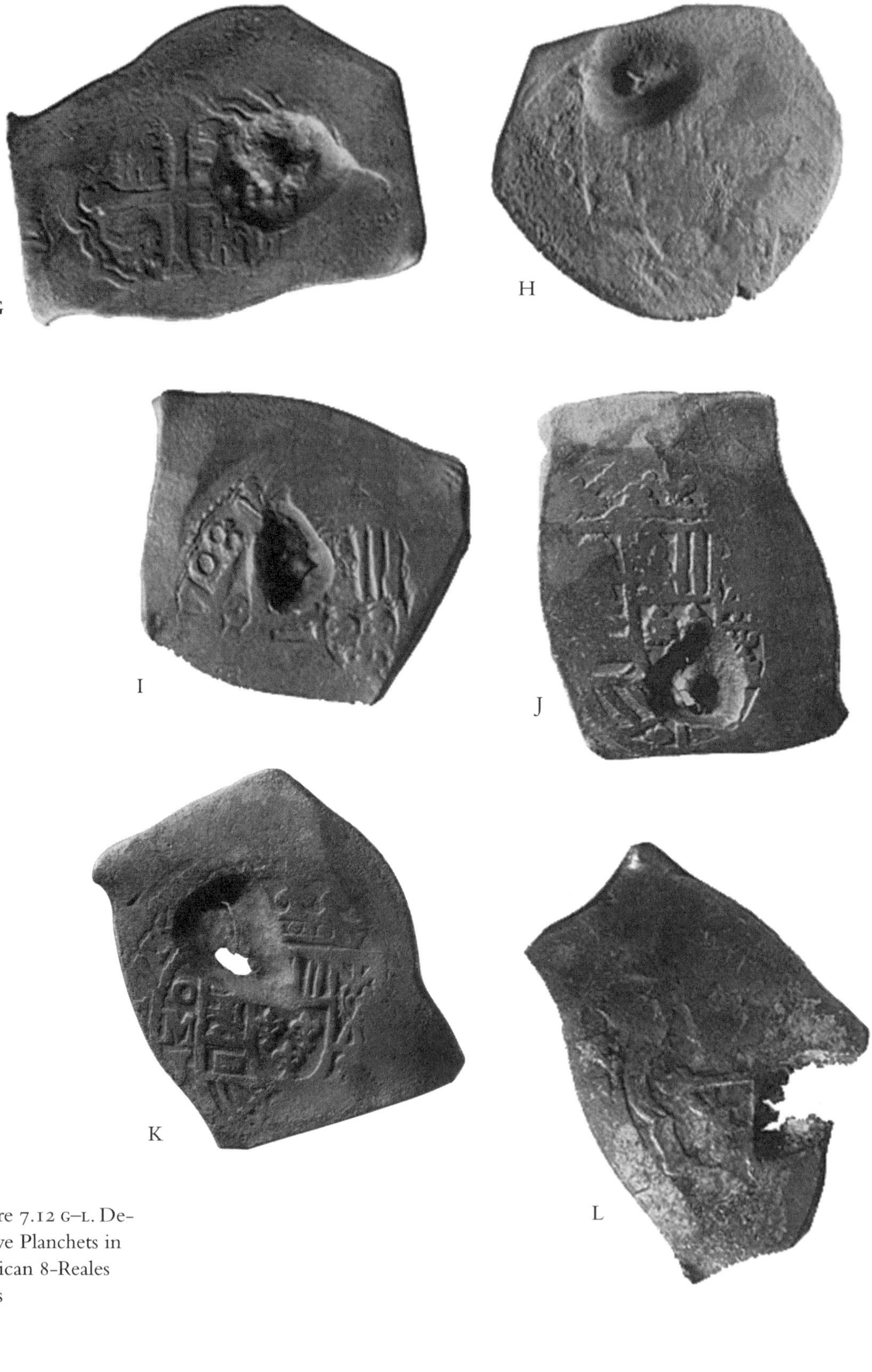

Figure 7.12 G–L. Defective Planchets in Mexican 8-Reales Cobs

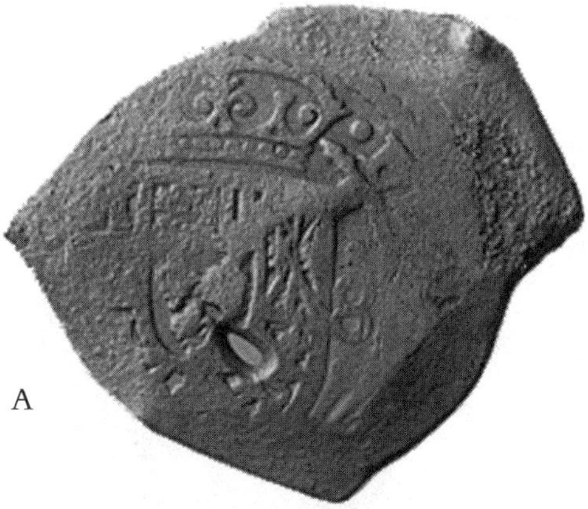
A

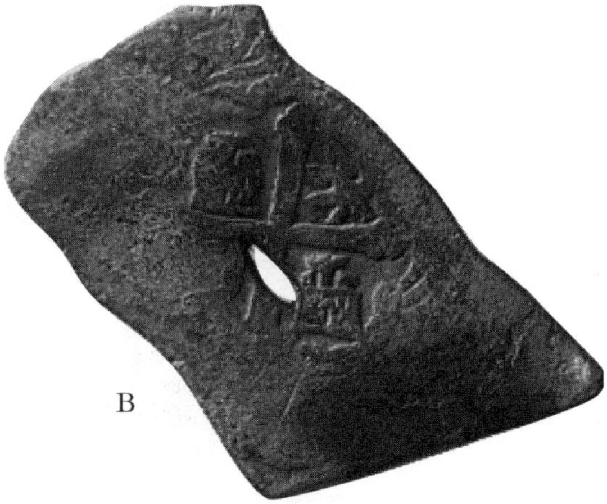
B

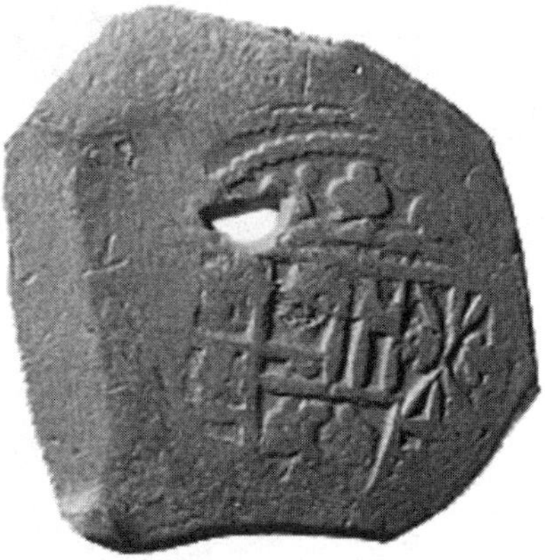
C

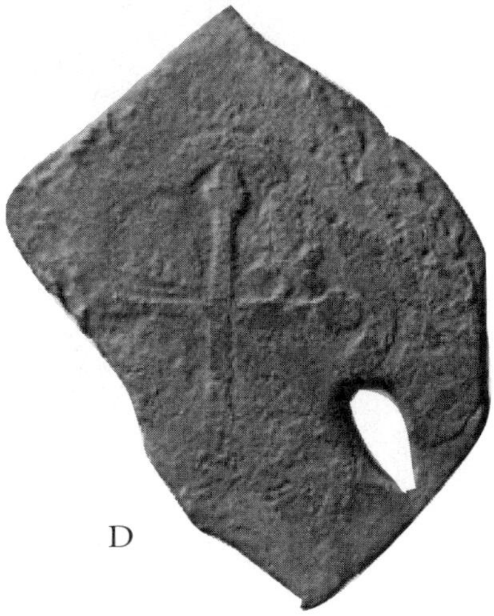
D

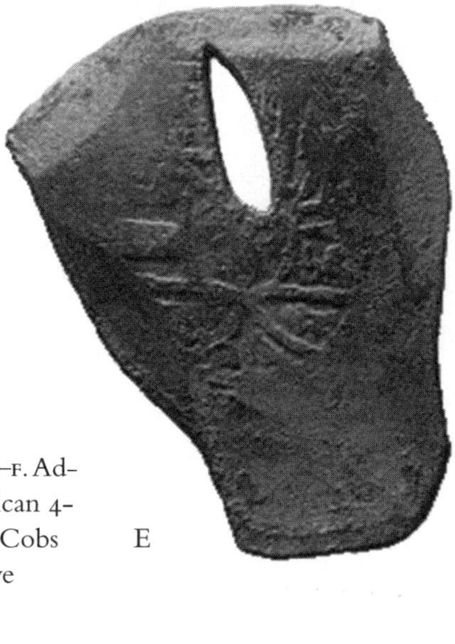
E

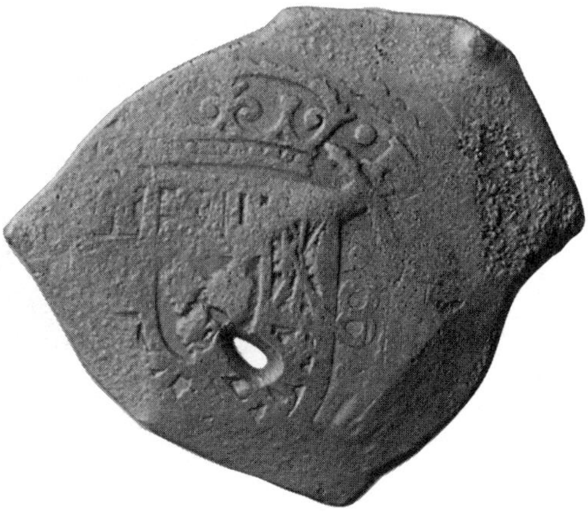
F

Figure 7.13 A–F. Additional Mexican 4- and 8-Reales Cobs with Defective Planchets

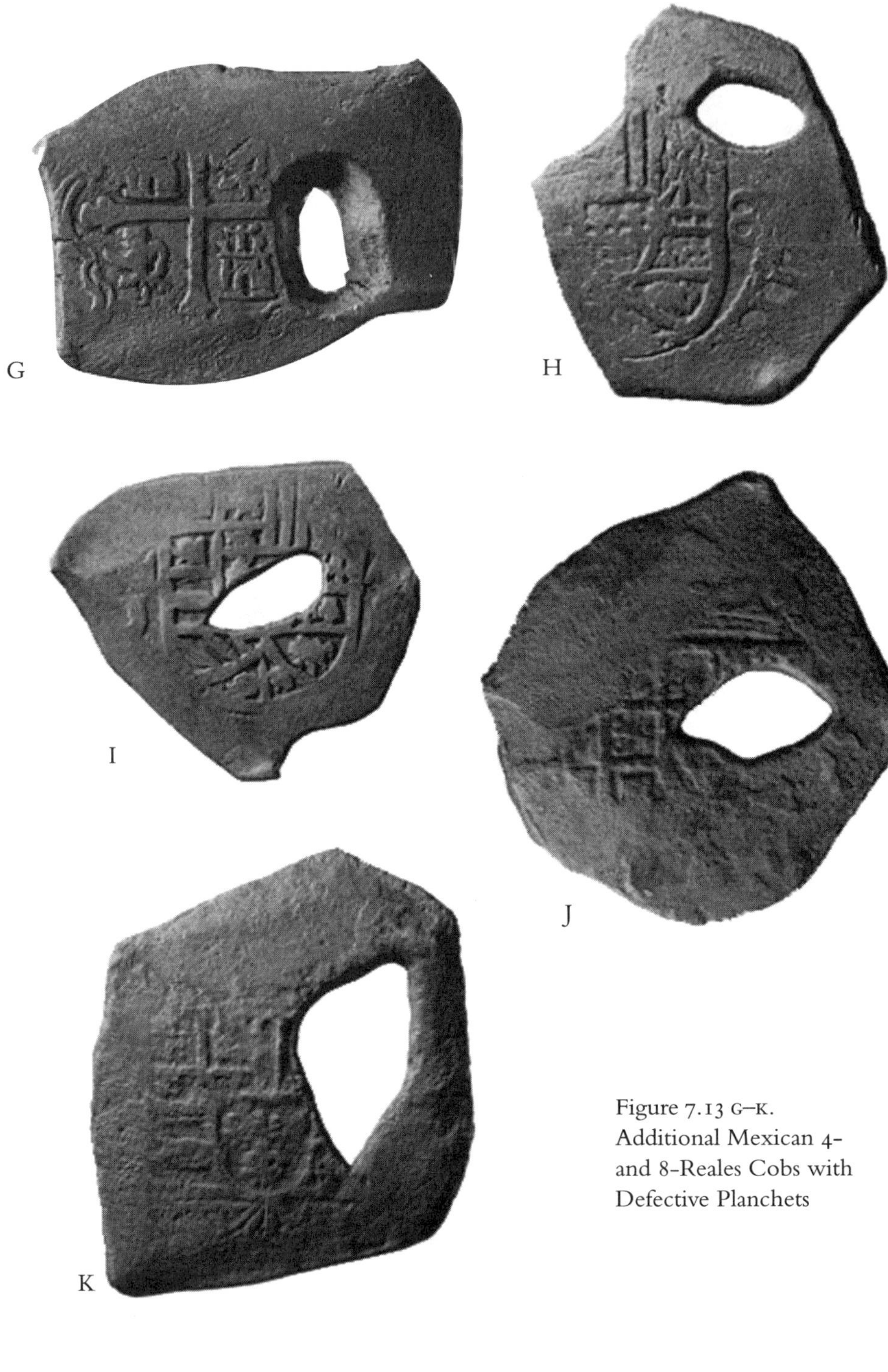

Figure 7.13 G–K. Additional Mexican 4- and 8-Reales Cobs with Defective Planchets

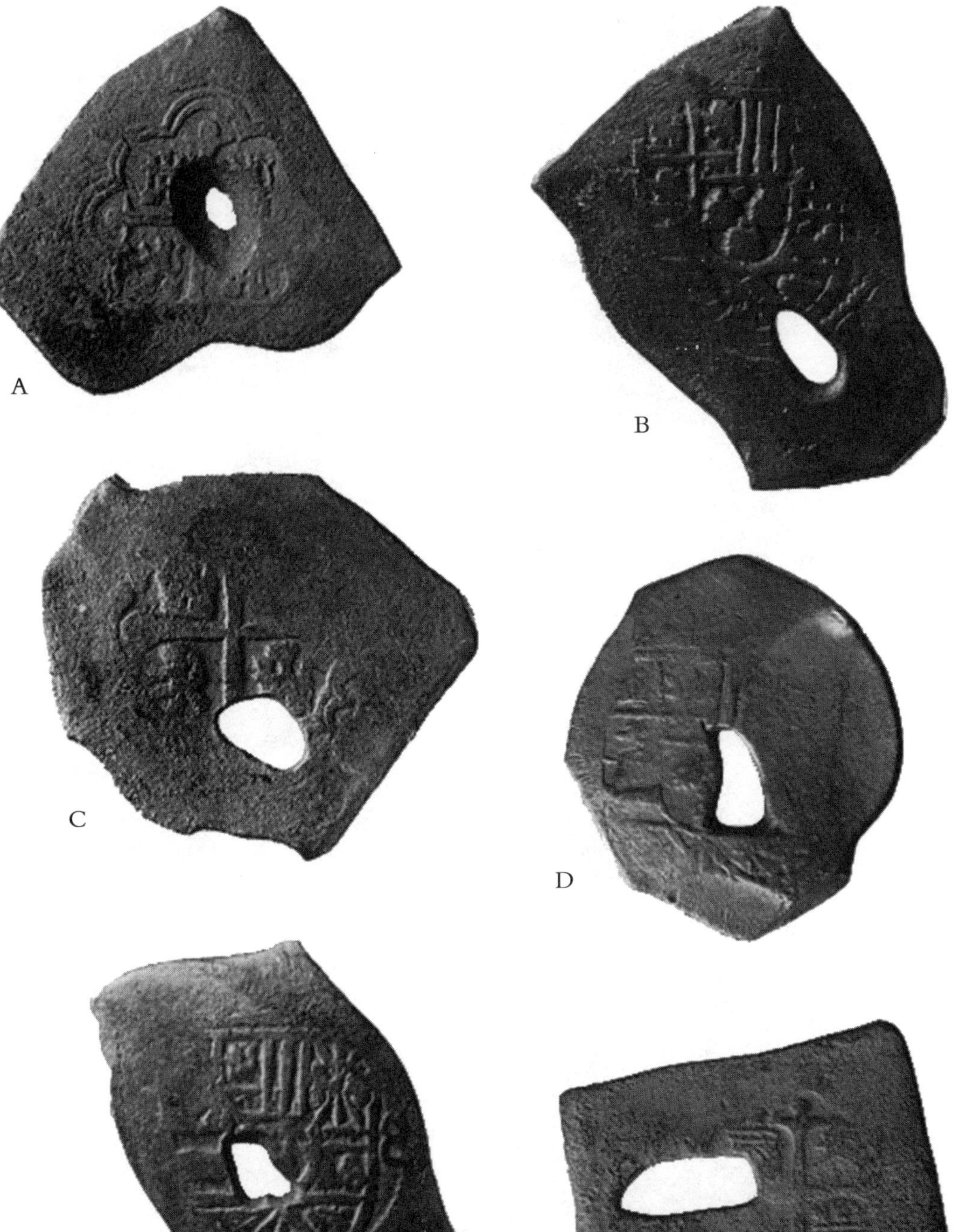

Figure 7.14 A–F. More Mexican 4- and 8-Reales Cobs with Defective Planchets

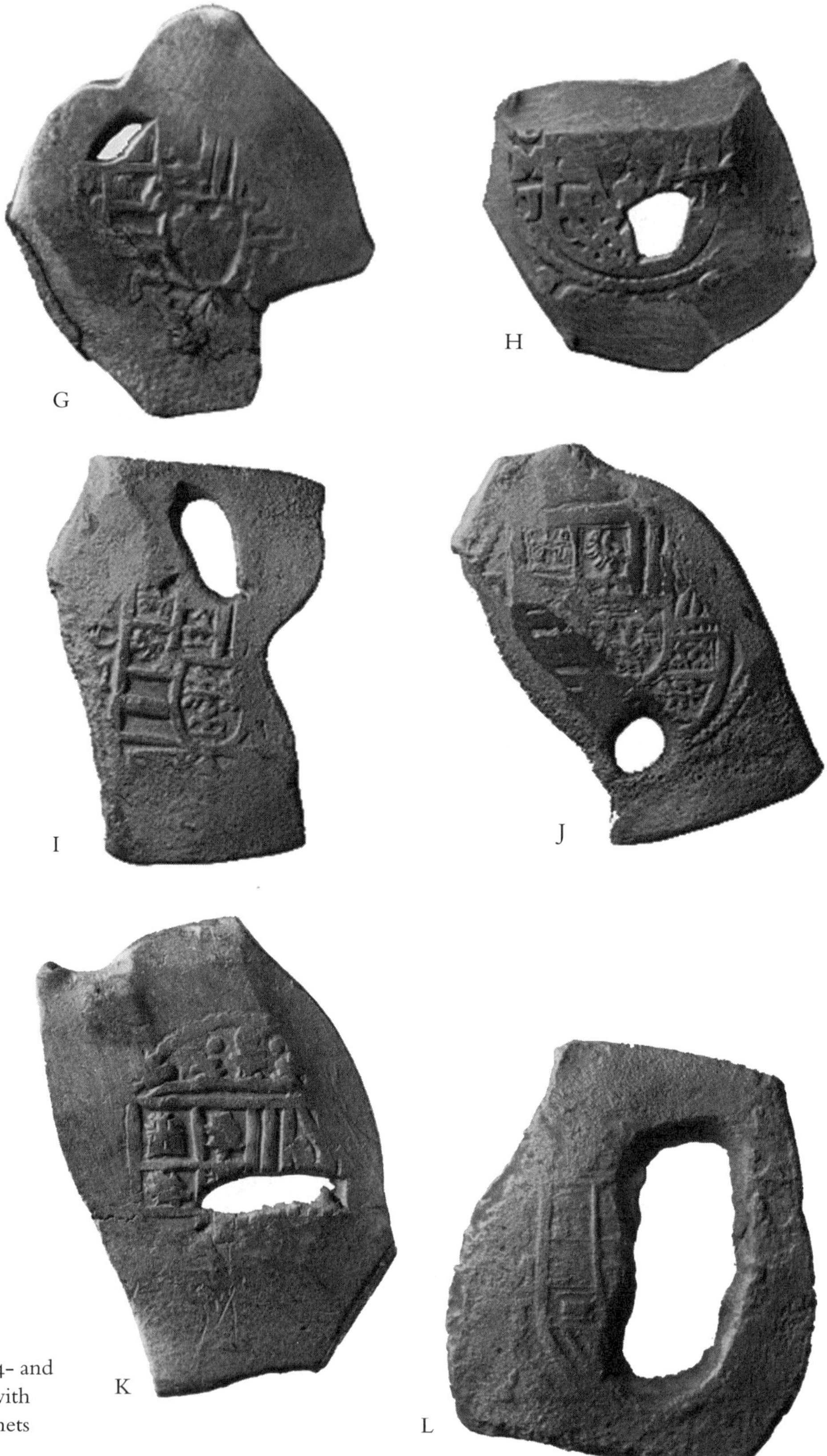

Figure 7.14 G–L.
More Mexican 4- and 8-Reales Cobs with Defective Planchets

these defects were not created by corrosion, although this may have partially enlarged the hole in a few specimens (fig. 7.13k and fig. 7.14l).

We can summarize characteristics of these features as follows:

1. Most are oval or elliptical, or have a teardrop shape.
2. Depressions have sides that slope gently inward; some do not completely pass through the coin and most have rough internal surfaces.
3. There is no relation to die orientation.
4. Size is extremely variable.
5. Some are related to observable laminations.
6. Bottoms of some deep depressions show a reverse bulge.
7. They do not affect the coin's proper weight.
8. The oldest dated is 1708 (7.12i) and youngest dated in this collection is 1715 (7.12k), all under assayer "J."

After reviewing these parameters, we may not feel any closer to solving this mystery, but there are some plausible explanations. For most of the specimens shown in figure 7.12, depressions that do not completely pass through the coin may have been caused by removing dross with a small scoop from the still-molten surface of the silver after it had been poured into the mold. If the clump of dross was deep enough, its removal by the tool may have caused the slightly cooler bottom surface of the silver to be pulled upward when it was removed.[3]

Other defects may have been caused by removal of sprues from the casting if indeed a two-piece mold was being used. Some such molds today have internal bracing between the two halves, possibly accounting for what we see in the cobs where silver could not flow. I find no evidence of anything similar to chunks of charcoal flux that sometimes still can be seen in depressions on the sides of large silver ingots from Mexico and Potosí that might help account for these strange defects.

Elliptical holes with rounded sides passing completely through a coin of approximately legal weight suggest the planchet was cut from a sheet of silver that did not flow evenly onto the mold surface because of contaminants or temperature differences.

Of all the "sport" coins in the Florida Collection, none is more bizarre than coin 7.15a or its companion piece, 7.15b. These two Mexican 8-reales coins were "born" with an appendix, or tabs, projecting away from the main body of the planchet.

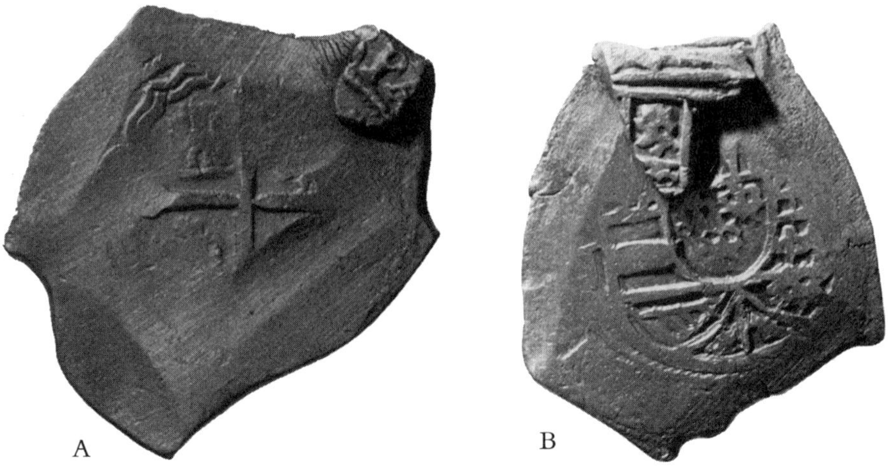

Figure 7.15. Mexican 8-Reales Cobs with Folded Tab Planchet

My interpretation of what happened next is as follows: the appendix was formed accidentally along the edge of a sheet of molten silver when it was poured out and did not completely fill the surface of the mold. Planchets of standard weight were made that included these tabs. The coiners then placed these strange planchets between dies and struck them in the conventional manner. Afterwards, they decided to fold the tabs inward to prevent them from being clipped or broken off. But before doing so they deliberately struck them upside down with the appropriate die and then bent the tabs into the position seen in the photos. This seems to me the most likely explanation for the fact that both tab and underlying coin (which is not double-struck in any way) have the same die strike. By sheer coincidence, the tab of 7.15b is folded over one of the small elliptical planchet depressions. A careful comparison of design features on the tab shows they do not correspond to a missing portion that would have been underneath if there were no depression present. When discussing cobs we should always remember anything is possible. Perhaps such coins were never intended to be allowed into circulation in Mexico. They were products of the haste to complete a production run everyone knew was destined for Spain where this silver would soon be melted into some new form.

CHAPTER 8

Potosí and Its Coins

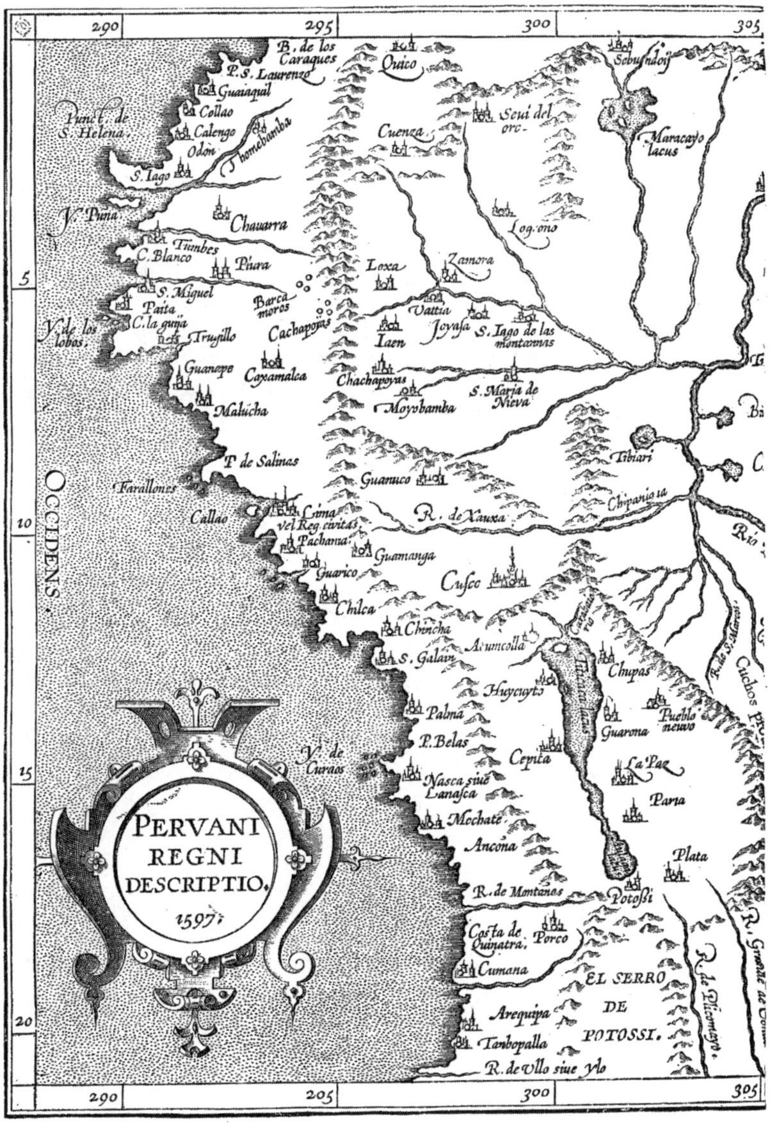

Map 8.1. Peru (1597).

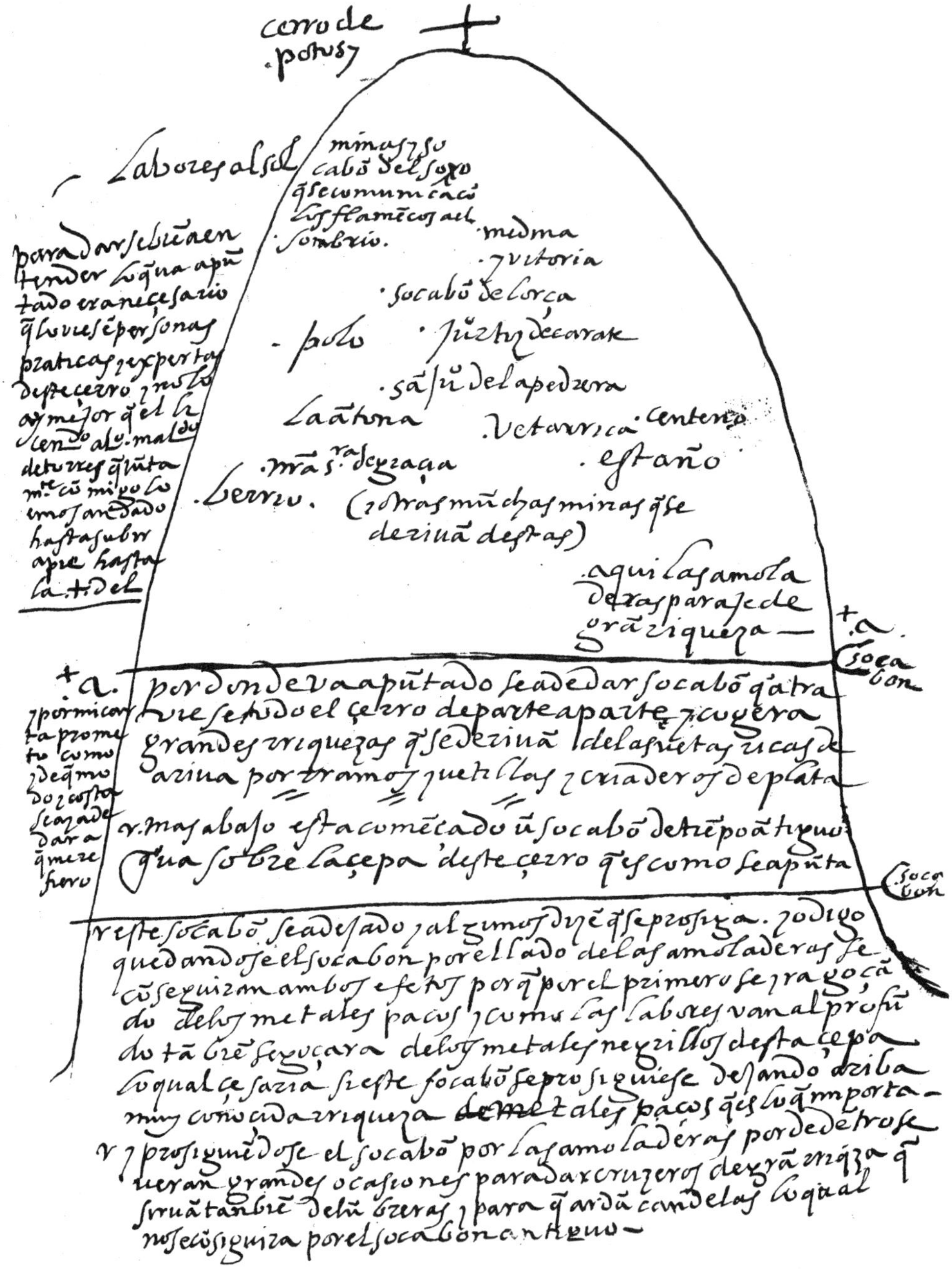

Map 8.2. Earliest known "map" of Potosí Mountain with details of existing and proposed mining activities.

In the year 1600 the sprawling mining community of Potosí, located high in the Andes mountains of what is now Bolivia, may have been the largest city on earth (map 8.3). In that year it was certainly larger than London, Mexico City, or Shanghai. Somewhere between 160,000 and 200,000 inhabitants worked day and night extracting and refining the silver laboriously won from veins in Cerro Rico. This highly mineralized mountain (illus. 8.1 and 8.2) looms up on the western outskirts and

Potosi Mountain
+

Eastern workings — Shallow mines facing east that connect with the Flemish in the shade (west side)

In order to give a better understanding of what is here, it was necessary that expert and practical miners showed me everything, even going up with me to the cross at the top

Medina
and Victoria
.tunnel of Lorca.
Polo — claim of Zarate
tunnel of the tailings
La Atona — .Centeno
Rich Vein
Nuestra Senora de Gracia Tin
Berrio — (and many other mines that are derived from these)
here are the grinding stones—a very rich place.
+a

____(horizontal tunnel)

+.a On my map I promise that Everything I say is true.

where it is indicated [by this line] there should be a drainage tunnel that goes through the whole mountain from side to side and it will encounter great wealth coming from the veins of silver and lower down, a large tunnel has begun as shown

____(horizontal tunnel)

This tunnel has been abandoned and some say it should continue so. I say that bringing it out on the side of the grinding stones will achieve two things; in the first place it will provide silver oxide ores and as the workings go deeper, it will provide silver sulphide ores, of this I know. What is certain if this tunnel is continued it will leave well-known rich silver oxide ores above which is the important thing. And continuing the tunnel by way of the grinding stones there will be many opportunities to find in side tunnels ore of great richness. They also serve to ventilate and help burn the candles, things that cannot be done by means of the old tunnel.

Map 8.2. translation.

from its peak at nearly 16,000 ft. (4,824 m) we can still see the complete and widespread outlines of the colonial city (illus. 8.3). Today fewer than 9,000 people live in the city even though some mining operations continue extracting tin and tungsten ore from deep-seated veins.

This historic mountain is extremely noticeable because of its utterly barren appearance caused by the accumulation of 450 years of mining tailings spread over the slopes in contrasting buff and brick-red rocks.[1]

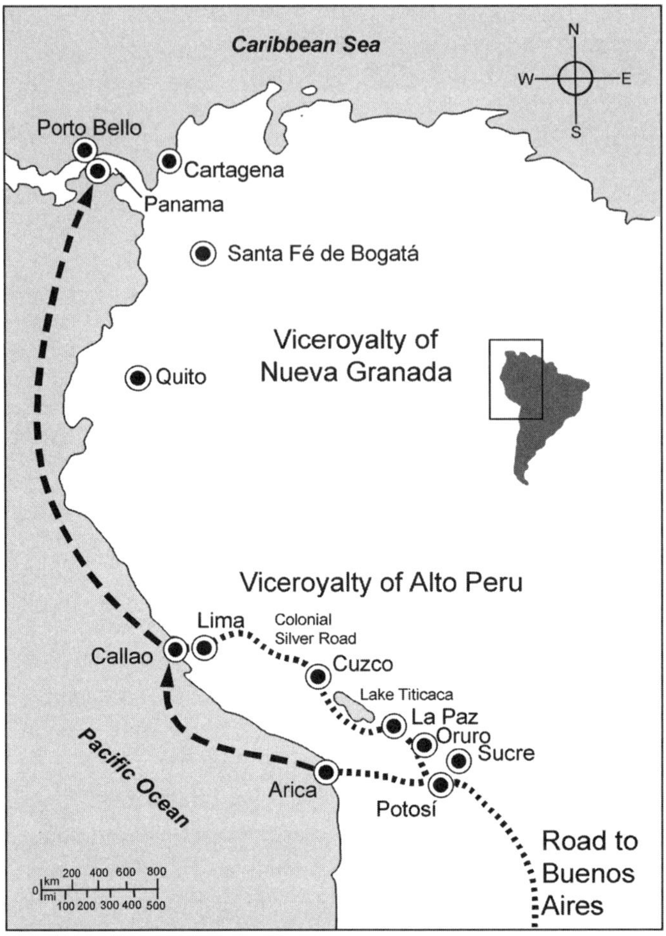

Map 8.3. Map of part of the viceroyalty of Peru.

Illus. 8.1. The western side of Cerro Rico in 1991, as seen along the road to Porco.

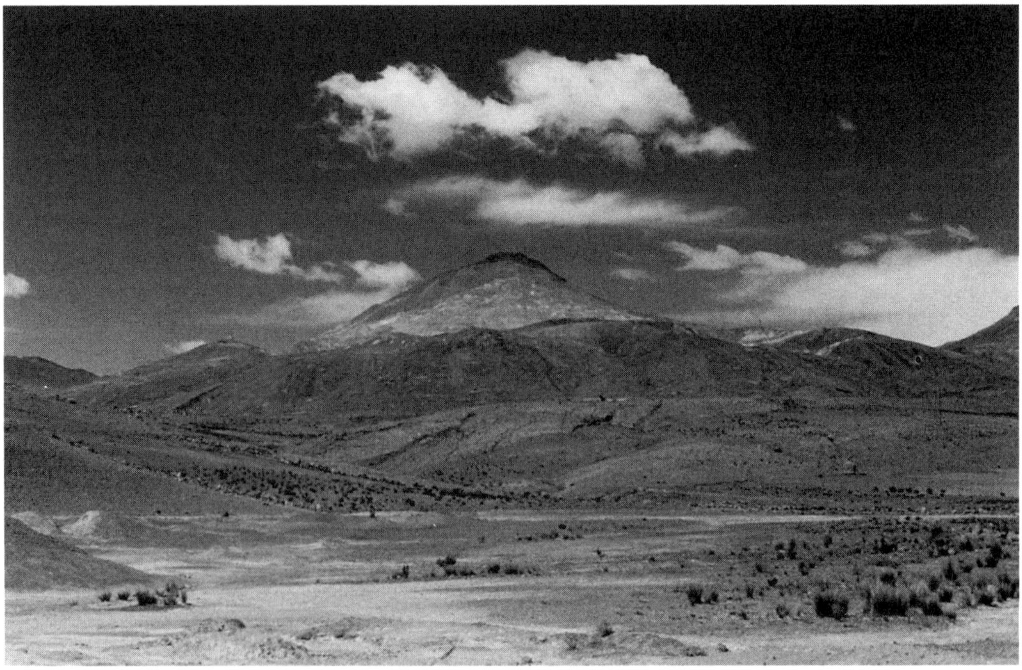

In pre-European times these slopes and the surrounding countryside were covered with a dense carpet of vegetation consisting of coarse grasses, low shrubs, and thickets of low, gnarled *queñua* trees. The pastoral aboriginal inhabitants took no special notice of rocky outcrops on the mountainside where five riblike veins of silver ore emerged and could be traced along the northern side. With dozens of similar, but barren, veins to be seen in the region it is little wonder these particular ones were never exploited.

There are many folk tales lacking substantiation regarding discovery of the silver mountain. My archival research in Sevilla has convinced me these silver deposits were actually discovered by an experienced Indian miner and prospector.[2] Documents make it clear it was an Indian

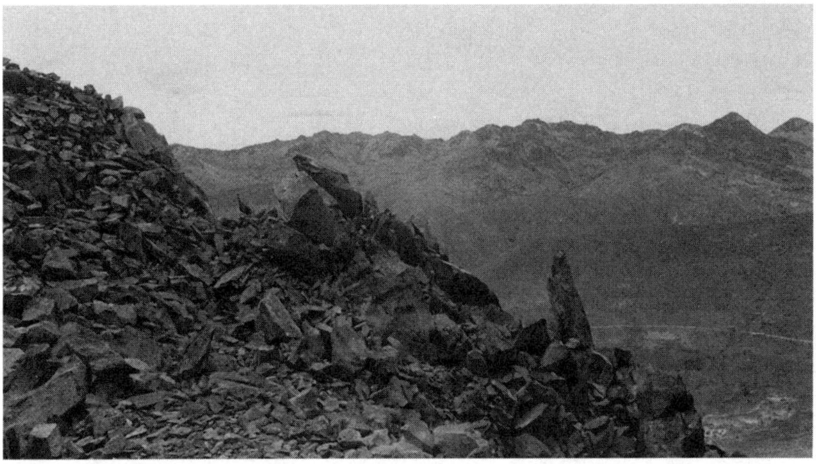

Illus. 8.2. Frost-shattered rocks 10 meters (32.8 feet) below the summit of Cerro Rico and above the discovery of veins of silver.

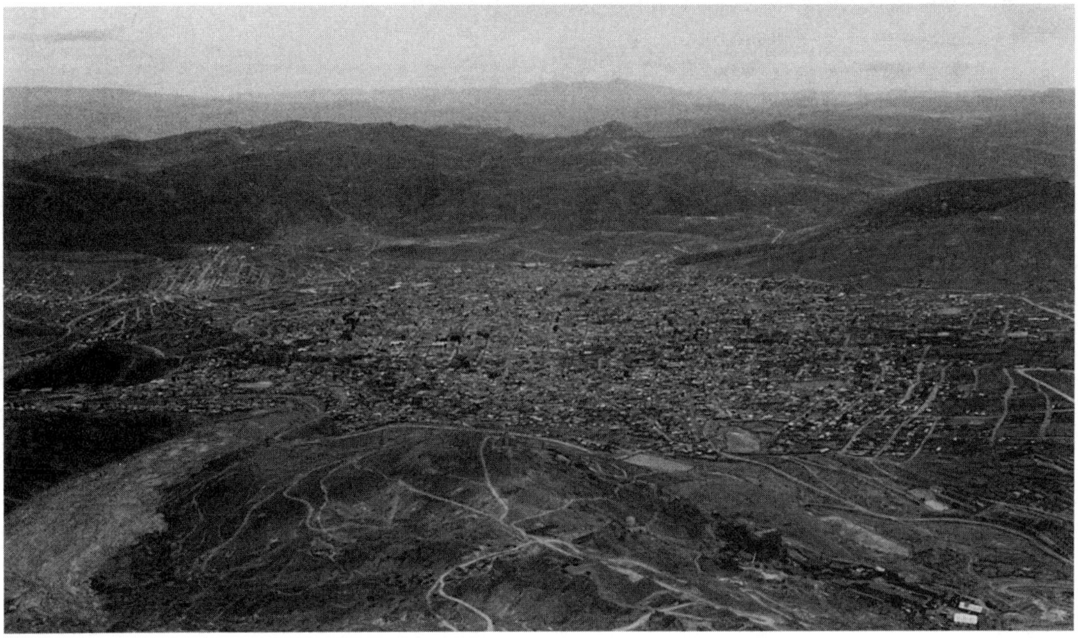

Illus. 8.3. View of the city of Potosí from the summit of Cerro Rico. Mine tailings in the foreground are from the modern Pailaviri tin mine.

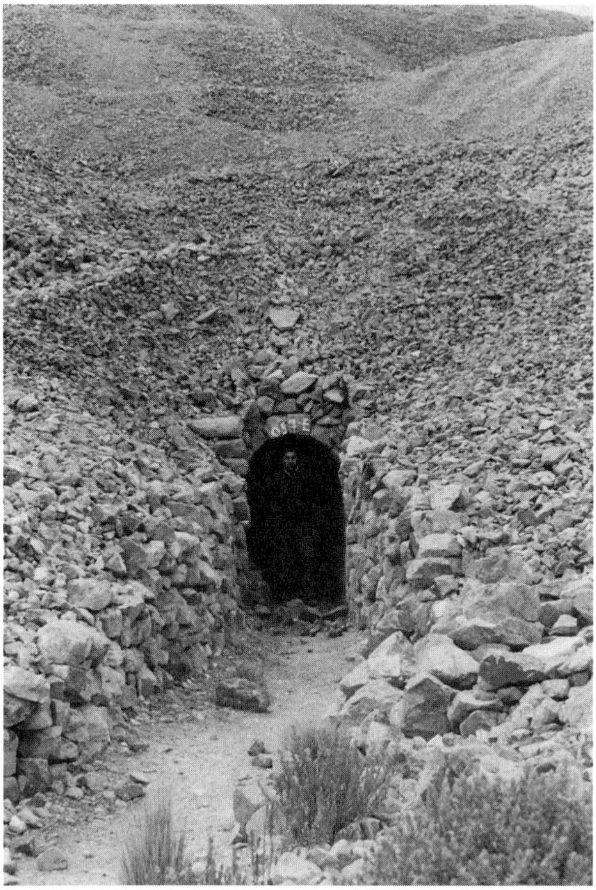

Illus. 8.4. Entrance of an adit on the west side of Cerro Rico. Talus on all sides are old mine "tippings" (debris).

Illus. 8.5. The modern town of Porco with silver mines in the distance. Prehistoric workings are visible in the upper right-hand corner.

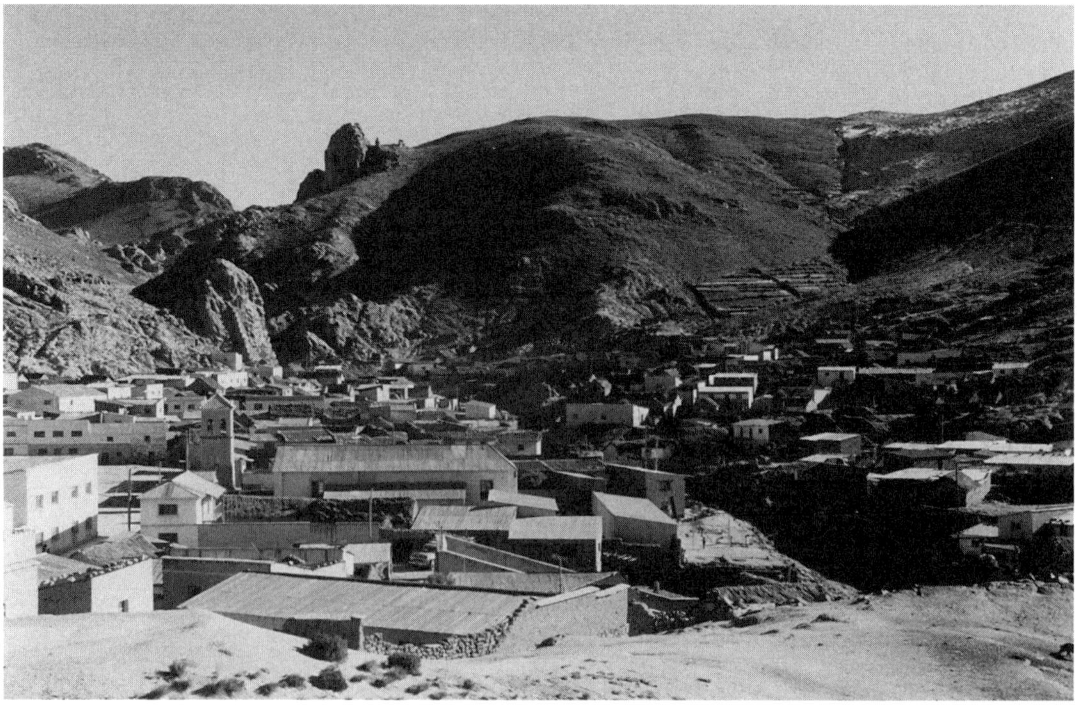

Illus. 8.6. Prehistoric Peruvian metalworkers. An early European illustration of prehistoric Andean ore smelting.

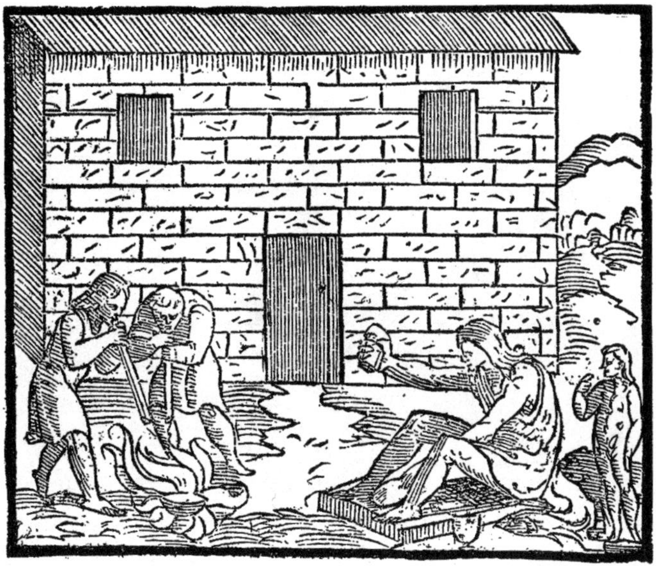

named Guallpa who made the discovery early in 1545. He came from the nearby mining settlement of Porco, where prehistoric silver mines developed by the Inka had been worked about one hundred years before arrival of the first Spaniards. After a few months of trying to keep his discovery a secret from his Spanish patron, Guallpa divulged the location where he had found chunks of pure native silver. This precipitated a stampede of Spaniards out of Porco; others soon arrived from all directions with their Indian workers and the boom town of Potosí was born.

During the next thirty years unbelievable fortunes were made (and lost) stripping away rich surface ores, buying and selling some of the 5,000 claims that were staked, and supplying the burgeoning community with necessities (and unnecessaries) of life. The early years were a yeasty time, and books have been written about excesses of life in Potosí.[3]

Since there were no facilities at this time to strike coins at Potosí, miners and businessmen often used unassayed lumps of more or less pure silver cast into bars of no special shape or size. They were without any marking to indicate the required taxes had been paid. These were the *tejuelos* of Peru of which there are no authentic surviving examples known. This is because they were illegal and eventually most, if not all, were converted into other forms of silver objects that became assayed and taxed.

When Felipe II was crowned king of Spain in 1555, he soon took measures to establish a mint to regularize and tax all precious metal being produced in the viceroyalty of Peru. Most of it was coming from Potosí, but it was decided to locate the mint on the coast at Lima from

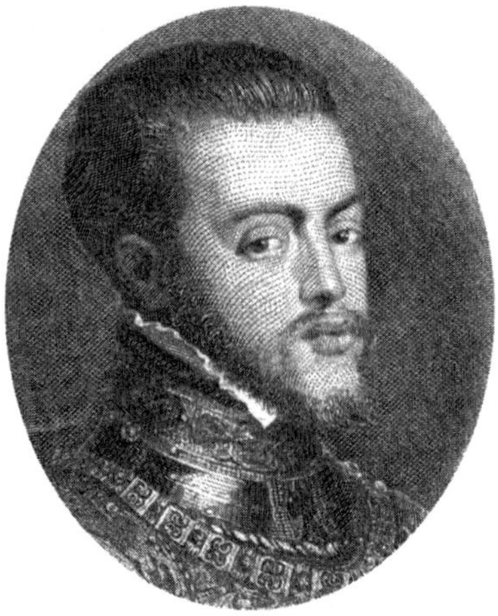

Illus. 8.7. Engraving of a youthful King Felipe II as it would appear on Series of 1920 Spanish currency.

which bullion and specie could be sent north to Panama for transshipment across the Isthmus and then on to Spain on board annual plate fleets.

Bringing silver ingots down to Lima for conversion into coins did not turn out to be a good idea. The costly four-month journey was arduous and dangerous. Although the Lima mint did function briefly in this early period (1568–1570 and 1575–1588) with some employees trained in Mexico, it was decided to move operations to the important administrative center at La Plata where royal officials of the High Court could closely monitor the minting process. Since no heavy machinery was involved, it was a simple matter for dies and hand tools to be transferred there and in 1574, for a few months a new assayer "C" began to strike coins in temporary quarters in this town. But mine owners and operators of newly constructed refining mills at Potosí immediately protested this location for the mint, claiming La Plata was an inconvenient and costly place to transport and process large quantities of silver coming out of Cerro Rico.

The Ephemeral Mint at La Plata

In a letter to the Crown regarding establishment of a mint in La Plata, Dr. Barros, president of the High Court at La Plata, states a site has been purchased from heirs of Thomas Vazquez.[4] Barros originally believed La Plata would be the ideal location for a much-needed mint because more wood for charcoal was available for smelting silver bars preparatory to alloying them with copper to make the required coinage alloy. However, after four months of operations at this location, during which time very few coins were struck (none has been identified in the Florida Collection), it became apparent it was more practical to transport light charcoal up to Potosí than to bring heavy ore down to La Plata, which had no stamp mills for crushing ore.

This struggle between special interests at La Plata and mine owners at Potosí was long and bitter, but Viceroy Toledo sagely decided it was most efficient to bring the mint to the silver rather than the reverse. Consequently, he ordered a mint built at Potosí early in 1572, which became the only center of minting operations when the smelters were finished in 1575. By this time waterwheel-driven stamp mills were already processing accumulated silver ore.[5]

During the three years it took to build the first mint at Potosí it seems very unlikely even a rudimentary mint building was ever actually constructed at La Plata. However, there is archival evidence that "dies and tools" from Lima were transported there. All coins attributed to this location are indistinguishable in design details from Lima cobs except for an obvious clumsy removal on the obverse die of the assayer's letter "B," which was replaced with "C" or even less commonly, "CC." Neither assayer has been identified for this brief time interval during which we have evidence that both 8- and 2-reales coins were produced.

The decision to transfer all refining and minting operations from La Plata to a high-altitude location at Potosí had some surprising and unforeseen consequences not apparent when coins first appeared from the new mint in 1575. With passage of time, however, certain production problems became serious. Something seemed to be wrong with the silver itself; it was not behaving properly.

"Rebellious" Silver

Handmade silver cobs from Potosí often have conspicuous planchet cracks, some so large and extensive the coin seems about to break into pieces. These jagged, irregular tension breaks in the metal actually fol-

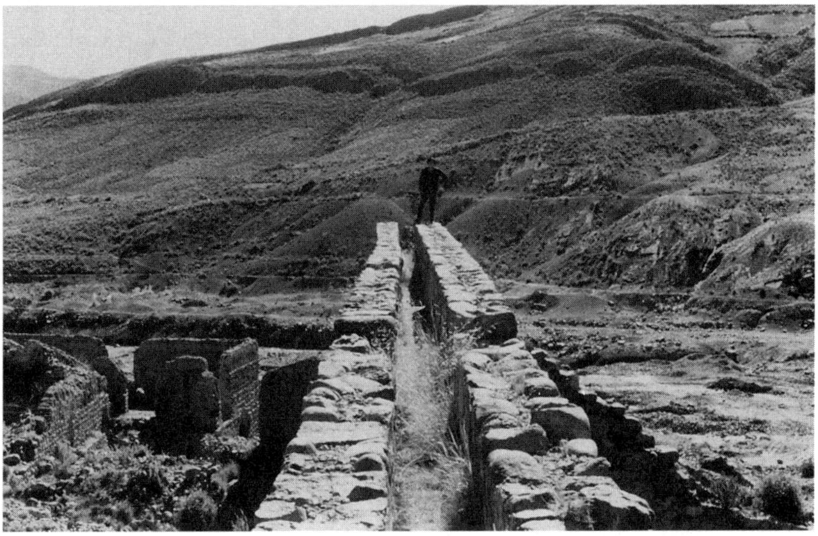

Illus. 8.8. This aqueduct supplied water to the San Bartolomé Stamp Mills, the last in the series built at Potosí.

low the underlying crystalline structure of the alloy along unpredictable lines of weakness. These defects typically radiate outward toward the rim where gaps widen and spread apart. At first glance these cracks make the coin look ragged, brittle, and poorly made. This in turn made them suspect as to weight and fineness. Merchants outside the viceroyalty of Peru were often reluctant to receive them in payment, discounting the coins in some cases even though they were made to legal standards. When widespread counterfeiting of Potosí cobs occurred during the 1630s and 1640s, public confidence in these coins plummeted.

On the other hand, Mexican cobs made from carefully annealed silver usually resulted in comparatively smooth-edged coins. Officials in Spain were accustomed to receiving high-quality specimens annually as evidence of this mint's compliance with royal standards. Eventually they began to demand that other mint superintendents use Mexican coins as examples to which they should aspire. Nevertheless, cracked planchets continued to be so typical of Potosí silver that we can use them today to identify badly corroded wreck specimens that have lost all other diagnostic markings. How can we explain this conspicuous difference between products of two colonial mints that were both following the same rules and regulations?

According to Butts and Coxe (1967: 310) colonial silver alloys used to make coins at Potosí did not successfully deoxidize the metal. In the cobs made there they see "multiple signs of embrittlement in the form of peripheral cracks and large splits in the irregular planchets." In other words, the silver planchets were not very ductile.

Although this is essentially correct, perhaps there is a better explanation. It is clear planchets for Potosí coins were often work-hardened and poorly annealed. Silversmiths of the sixteenth and seventeenth centuries knew perfectly well any silver object becomes brittle if it is hammered without annealing. Slowly heating hammered silver allows the disturbed crystalline structure to relax and return to its normal ductile form. But these same experts in charge of coinage at Potosí deliberately ignored this simple relationship between hardening and annealing of silver for an economic reason that has escaped the attention of previous researchers.

Charcoal was the only practical fuel that could be used to fire smelting and annealing furnaces of the mint. With widespread devegetation since the earliest days of silver's discovery in the surrounding region, charcoal soon became exorbitantly expensive at Potosí. Along with every other staple and commodity, charcoal contributed to the highest cost of living and working in Spanish America.[6]

By 1591 we know Gaspar Ruíz, nephew of the first assayer to operate the new Potosí mint, was complaining bitterly to authorities that the number of Indians assigned to him and his allowance for charcoal were totally inadequate since this strategic fuel now could only be obtained from kilns located 80 leagues away. He pleaded unsuccessfully for an increase of 2 reales per *marco* (0.5 lb.) of raw silver he assayed before adjusting it to the proper alloy for coining.[7]

Evidently Ruíz was unsuccessful in obtaining more charcoal makers and resigned from his post, because in AGI Charcas 43, Doc. 25–4–1594 it appears that Juan de Ballesteros Narváez has been appointed to the position. These two assayers, Ruíz and Ballesteros, functioned at the peak of silver coin production at Potosí, and their initials "R" and "B" are by far the most common to be found on cobs of the late-sixteenth and early-seventeenth centuries. The next time you examine a badly cracked Potosí cob, remember it might have turned out much nicer if only charcoal had not been so expensive and annealing had been performed properly.

If Ruíz felt cheated in terms of his expense allowance, it is not hard to imagine his successors were equally anxious to skimp on fuel. Charcoal continued to increase in cost while assayers' fees remained fixed by suspicious officials who lived at a much lower elevation at La Plata—where life was not so grim, nor charcoal so dear.

Another problem followed from the desire to economize on use of charcoal. When sponge-silver *piñas* were brought to the mint by mine or mill owners, only enough of this expensive fuel was expended to smelt them down into assayed ingots of proper coinage purity (in other words, 2,380 parts silver out of a possible 2,400), the weight and fineness being marked on each ingot and carefully recorded. Nothing happened, sometimes for years, until owners, or the mint, needed to convert these nearly pure ingots into the required fineness by smelting them and adding copper to make a final alloy from which cob coins could be made.

Now the assayer, or in some cases a special foundryman, had to melt down the entire ingot inside a bellows-equipped furnace and pour the barely liquid silver from its iron melting pot into a series of narrow planchet molds to form *rieles.* Since the silver was barely above its melting point, it cooled quickly and unevenly in these standard-sized metal troughs. When planchets were cut from these straps, thickness of metal from various pourings was not always the same. When workers cut planchet blanks from these straps, they deliberately made one that was clearly oversized since it was more cost effective to snip off small pieces (the *cizalla*) until the weighmaster (*balanceador*) was satisfied, than to make an underweight (*feble*) or overweight (*fuerte*) planchet. These would have to be rejected if too light, or subjected to more trimmimg if too heavy. Of course, any trimmings that happened to weigh within the acceptable range for smaller denominations could be put aside to be struck with the appropriate dies, but odd scraps had to be completely recycled—at the cost of yet more fuel. It is interesting to note that during the early days at Potosí, it was the prerogative of the chief assayer to have the floors swept periodically for any silver spatter, fine trimmings, or filings, which then became his property.

But thick or thin, narrow rectangular preform blanks required at least some hammering to help shape them into a more rounded planchet or coin-like form. At this point in the Mexico mint, the planchet was obviously reheated in order to remove most of the internal stresses before actual striking took place. But at Potosí fuel economy was paramont and annealing, if indeed any took place, was brief. There these work-hardened planchets were passed on to teams of actual coin-strikers (*acuñadores*), who held them between tongs on top of the *matriz* while delivering a powerful blow with a large, lead-filled hammer. Both planchet and hammer often rebounded to leave one or more partial impressions from either or both dies on part of the uneven silver surface. At the moment these blows were struck, tension cracks were likely to appear around the thinned rim from whence they might instantly work toward the center if the planchet was unusually hard and brittle. It is easy to understand why no two hand-struck cobs look exactly alike. See Appendix B for a detailed contemporary description of mint activities.

Being silversmiths by long apprentice training, assayers must have known what was happening. Everyone else made excuses for problems encountered in producing coinage and, as often as not, blamed the silver itself for being recalcitrant and "rebellious." Even late in the eighteenth century Superintendent Jorge Escobedo complained to his superiors that "the bad quality of the silver is as irremedial as the ignorance of how to refine it."[8]

K. A. Dym (1969, 1973) made interesting metallurgical analyses of Potosí cobs produced by various assayers. These data reveal considerable fluctuations across time that roughly correspond with known periods of widespread corruption and counterfeiting followed by coinage reform. His data are shown here as table 8.1. However, we should remember all these specimens had some degree of wear since they were placed in circulation long before tests were made.

Even though table 8.1 is based on analysis of single specimens, it shows how carefully planchets could be weighed before striking in order to conform to regulations and, in the case of assayer Rodas, make a handsome profit for the assayer by adding an extra 10 percent of

Table 8.1. Fine Silver Content of Some Potosí 8-Reales Coins

Assayer		% Silver	Weight in Grams
"A"	fourth Alvarez 1586–91	93.3	27.16
"B"	fifth Ballesteros 1591–98	85.5	27.30
"Q"	ninth de la Quadra ca. 1613–16	79.2	27.40
"M"	? ca. 1616–17	93.5	27.21
"M"	? 1617 (dated)	91.1	26.69
"P"	Palencia 1621–27	88.3	26.63
"T"	Tapia 1628 (dated)	90.9	26.77
"T"	Tapia 1645 (dated)	88.9	27.35
"Tr"	Treviño 1645 (dated)	90.9	27.84
"⊙"	Rodas [Rozas] 1650 (dated)	80.0	27.40
"E"	Ergueta 1653 (dated)	90.1	27.20
"E"	Ergueta 1669 (dated)	91.8	26.28

Source: Dym (1969).

copper and pocketing the difference. This of course did not go undetected and is exactly what investigator Nestares Marín complained about in his report to the viceroy.

In another analysis, Dym published the composition results of two cobs from two assayers: Ballesteros, ca. 1582, and Tapia, in 1619. These results are shown in table 8.2.

In spite of the extremely small sample, this table suggests iron and mercury were contaminants introduced during sieving and amalgamation of the ore, as might be expected from steps in beneficiation. However, the amount introduced surely varied from mill to mill as did the amount of lead, tin, and antimony associated with the particular veins being exploited. These constituents of silver ore varied with depth in a given vein and even between adjacent mines following the same vein. Therefore, we cannot necessarily assume the silver that assayer Tapia was working with in 1619 came from any deeper place in the mountain

Table 8.2. Analysis of the Alloy of Two 8-Reales Potosí Coins Showing Percentage Composition by Weight under Different Assayers

Element	Assayer Ballesteros, ca. 1582	Assayer Tapia, 1619
copper	10.20	5.30
iron	0.21	0.75
lead	0.08	0.31
mercury	0.11	0.08
tin	0.02	0.02
antimony	0.14	?
silver	89.24	93.54

Source: Dym (1973).

than ore in 1582, although generally speaking, mines had to become deeper with time. Regardless of these mineralogical factors, assayers had neither means nor inclination to remove such minute quantities; their only concern was to get the copper-silver ratio correct and thereby protect themselves from the death penalty.

Until now there has been much speculation about the actual mintage by denomination each year, given the proportions of denominations found on shipwreck sites. Thanks to research in mint archives by Lazo García and his assistants (1992), nearly complete records of mint production are now available. See table 8.3 for Potosí coin mintage by year.

These figures show ratios between denominations produced over the years at Potosí. When owners of silver and gold came to the mint to have their bullion converted into coinage, as required by law within thirty days of its being refined, they indicated to mint workers just how they wanted it to be struck by denominations.[9] These miners, mill owners, silver brokers, and businessmen were accustomed to keeping their accounts in the largest denomination possible, and there were no regulations requiring them to accept quantities of smaller coins in exchange for their silver. On the other hand, when they brought bullion to the mint to be assayed and transferred to the treasury, government regulations changed through the years but generally specified an "adequate" amount of small change be made to facilitate minor transactions and ensure payment of Indian workers in mines and refining mills.

Since it required substantially more labor to prepare and weigh planchets for striking of small coins as compared with the same weight of silver converted much more rapidly into 8-reales coins, it is easy to understand why mint workers customarily made larger denominations. Although very few cob ¼-real coins were struck by assayer Rincón at the earliest opening of the Lima mint, it was not until 1790 that milled examples were made in Spanish colonial mints, Santiago being the first to do so.

During the late-eighteenth and early-nineteenth centuries disparity in numbers between large-and small-denomination coins from Spanish colonial mints gave rise to severe shortages of small change in many Caribbean islands where Spanish silver was the only readily available medium of exchange. This resulted in the widespread practice of cutting larger coins into smaller pieces counterstamped with the new denomination and place of origin. These "cut and counterstamped" Spanish coins were never very numerous and legitimate specimens are much valued by collectors today, who appreciate them for their often bizarre shapes (see fig. 3.1).

Table 8.3. Potosí Silver Coin Mintage by Date and Denomination, 1626–1773

Year	8 Reales	4 Reales	2 plus 1 Real	½ Real	Taxes in Pesos	Total in Pesos
1626	789,285	166,361	408,097	N.A.*	42,181	942,052
1627	2,031,272	338,266	904,165	N.A.	105,622	2,358,891
1628	1,508,923	317,345	836,026	N.A.	81,660	1,823,758
1629	N.A.	N.A.	N.A.	N.A.	N.A.	N.A.
1630	1,654,900	475,532	1,026,775	157,182	95,402	2,130,657
1631	3,221,485	442,149	2,473,707	?	168,046	3,753,030
1632	1,682,537	493,857	1,227,038	120,332	98,850	2,207,655
1633	1,646,625	545,162	1,262,816	95,944	99,944	2,215,672
1634	1,779,151	503,940	1,314,741	60,970	103,471	2,310,856
1635	1,836,218	516,385	1,298,460	64,454	102,005	2,278,124
1636	2,930,412	586,082	1,469,511	38,458	153,310	3,423,926
1637	1,821,143	311,550	727,553	26,800	93,153	2,080,425

Year	8 Reales	4 Reales	2 Reales	1 Real	½ Real	Taxes in Pesos	Total in Pesos
1638	2,772,845	478,212	136,814	787,853	49,714	141,369	3,157,246
1639	3,255,781	637,337	470,172	598,444	61,506	169,103	3,776,654

Year	8 Reales	4 Reales	2 plus 1 Real	½ Real	Taxes in Pesos	Total in Pesos
1640	3,005,368	563,637	1,825,549	47,704	157,576	3,519,200
1641	3,410,802	574,876	1,961,291	41,540	176,752	3,947,481
1642	4,270,169	582,196	1,739,052	72,762	214,535	4,791,284
1643	4,581,125	720,585	1,738,047	200,866	231,983	5,180,968
1644	3,948,176	756,379	1,935,295	373,994	205,988	4,600,411
1645	4,309,272	527,625	1,961,425	315,704	216,682	4,839,251
1646	4,437,435	546,050	2,168,790	131,052	224,110	5,005,126
1647	3,932,481	501,779	2,407,310	129,712	201,257	4,494,745
1648	4,023,768	539,601	2,096,966	25,874	205,622	4,592,238
1649	4,283,134	662,295	1,925,111	7,370	217,472	4,856,889
1650	3,221,485	442,149	2,473,707	?	168,046	3,753,030
1651	2,925,488	309,690	2,075,727	?	149,558	3,340,134
1652	1,854,543	247,983	1,828,363	200,062	99,427	2,220,539
1653–55	N.A.	N.A.	N.A.	N.A.	N.A.	N.A.
1656	2,717,578	479,401	3,727,746	39,262	137,282	3,429,052
1657	3,155,189	624,172	4,389,036	42,076	160,882	4,018,534

Year	8 Reales	4 Reales	2 Reales	1 Real	½ Real	Taxes in Pesos	Total in Pesos
1658	3,955,772	703,131	345,921	2,969,976	38,324	157,370	3,930,798

Year	8 Reales	4 Reales	2 plus 1 Real	½ Real	Taxes in Pesos	Total in Pesos
1659	3,196,737	813,648	4,027,102	61,238	164,609	4,111,614
1660	2,691,055	624,205	3,358,308	42,478	137,284	3,428,951
1661	2,900,681	502,835	3,222,968	66,062	142,507	3,559,551
1662	2,325,863	489,887	2,711,491	128,104	116,830	2,918,210
1663	2,421,128	462,166	2,746,196	140,834	120,510	3,010,126

continued on next page

Table 8.3—*continued*

Year	8 Reales	4 Reales	2 plus 1 Real	½ Real	Taxes in Pesos	Total in Pesos
1664	2,598,879	489,770	2,831,554	74,638	128,217	3,202,625
1665	2,733,725	564,257	3,104,378	?	136,275	3,403,902
1666	2,672,931	396,740	3,067,930	102,912	130,563	3,261,225
1667	3,090,458	514,677	3,345,891	56,410	150,959	3,770,685
1668	2,898,043	535,665	3,574,175	93,800	144,897	3,619,256
1669	2,415,693	414,780	2,637,254	105,860	118,478	2,959,357
1670	2,257,330	379,605	2,651,793	106,664	111,508	2,785,274
1671	3,196,737	406,824	4,027,102	61,238	164,609	4,111,614
1672	2,547,256	324,112	2,629,549	181,034	121,744	3,049,321
1673	2,363,927	341,113	2,750,484	319,322	116,039	2,898,437
1674	2,062,234	443,875	2,979,624	612,112	108,964	2,721,724
1675	1,948,443	407,343	2,970,646	1,020,410	103,579	2,587,222
1676	1,649,004	371,850	2,805,491	565,346	88,915	2,220,950
1677	1,633,125	426,873	1,297,656	42,478	87,021	2,173,631
1678	1,974,825	486,704	2,730,518	121,136	102,772	2,567,069
1679	2,262,481	516,570	1,628,100	136,412	151,076	2,936,091

Year	8 Reales	4 Reales	2 Reales	1 Real	½ Real	Taxes in Pesos	Total in Pesos
1680	1,784,997	448,079	702,729	1,477,618	495,666	97,247	2,429,060
1681	1,808,413	504,225	778,406	1,462,945	198,856	98,118	2,450,810
1682	2,363,148	619,163	875,857	1,553,797	478,782	124,827	3,117,954
1683	3,558,679	818,756	1,193,002	2,295,889	501,160	183,717	4,588,897
1684	3,095,885	755,575	1,175,146	2,156,127	317,580	162,605	4,061,582
1685	2,702,545	562,230	887,348	1,886,251	306,994	138,568	3,461,178
1686	2,378,474	561,342	829,426	1,740,660	272,958	124,231	3,103,055
1687	2,638,610	790,298	1,091,966	1,876,536	423,172	142,890	3,569,132
1688	2,399,027	728,909	1,035,284	1,809,670	512,014	131,389	3,281,861
1689	2,396,280	692,210	990,494	1,726,456	565,882	129,853	3,243,487
1690	2,848,555	664,489	926,476	1,790,240	334,062	146,545	3,660,411
1691	2,284,055	573,536	804,670	1,580,999	229,542	119,523	2,985,461
1692	1,945,931	472,936	689,932	1,487,266	225,790	103,405	2,582,867
1693	2,179,593	541,326	840,749	1,718,282	183,312	115,617	2,887,893
1694	2,023,860	585,546	803,732	1,632,924	324,682	109,808	2,742,796
1695	2,024,271	565,161	881,552	1,764,646	197,784	117,644	2,938,520
1696	1,876,611	459,754	801,186	1,518,220	517,374	101,255	2,529,158
1697	N.A.	N.A.	N.A.	N.A.	N.A.	40,074	2,700,209
1698	1,771,856	404,579	576,937	1,177,123	175,272	91,146	2,276,668
1699	1,773,582	450.407	634,423	1,173,170	350,812	93,161	2,326,994
1700	1,755,257	523,638	669,866	1,213,638	282,874	94,253	2,354,263
1701	N.A.	N.A.	N.A.	N.A.	N.A.	N.A.	N.A
1702	1,588,654	612,748	735,157	1,188,312	577,004	90,615	2,263,411
1703	N.A	N.A.	N.A.	N.A	N.A.	N.A	N.A.
1704	1,489,493	554,408	750,232	1,184,024	590,672	85,621	2,138,665
1705	1,728,181	682,344	873,780	1,465,424	460,022	100,076	2,499,728
1706	1,834,543	571,175	811,135	1,411,355	229,140	100,634	2,513,656
1707	1,587,481	374,764	574,022	964,934	297,212	82,416	2,058,617
1708	1,829,100	409,554	621,391	1,134,243	250,848	93,949	2,346,683

Year	8 Reales	4 Reales	2 Reales	1 Real	½ Real	Taxes in Pesos	Total in Pesos
1709	1,619,725	333,040	435,600	871,201	231,418	81,316	2,031,139
1710–11	N.A.	N.A.	N.A.	N.A.	N.A.	N.A.	N.A.
1712	(93,733 Reales in unknown denominations were restruck.)					17,098	1,157341
1713	1,101,731	399,906	517,387	962,187	313,158	62,890	1,570,874
1714	N.A.	N.A.	N.A.	N.A.	N.A.	N.A.	N.A.
1715	889,006	315,486	453,221	814,988	546,184	51,888	1,296,065
1716	1,399,588	1,983,066	586,317	980,880	912,607	56,032	1,399,588
1717	1,453,062	508,999	825,440	1,418,725	790,868	88,254	2,204,434
1718	1,391,087	466,286	749,931	1,381,674	451,714	80,576	2,012,655
1719	1,447,618	401,899	715,124	1,288,745	59,053	81,085	2,025,351
1720	999,137	284,984	425,651	800,918	233,026	54,556	1,362,721
1721	945,780	320,997	466,052	812,844	510,004	54,546	1,362,470
1722	838,337	435,851	506,654	837,701	665,310	53,215	1,329,221
1723	N.A.	N.A.	N.A.	N.A.	N.A.	N.A.	N.A.
1724	780,550	563,252	669,732	1,030,862	635,428	55,976	1,398,181
1725	782,978	383,206	536,502	883,596	992,404	51,329	1,282,099
1726	1,036,858	450,256	691,324	1,219,802	835,222	65,191	1,628,351
1727	1,076,329	471,244	623,870	1,157,224	825,172	66,722	1,666,604
1728	1,310,796	444,997	586,149	1,178,463	1,218,060	76,263	1,904,926
1729	723,717	300,109	392,285	724,002	1,207,072	45,615	1,139,397
1730	1,152,140	396,891	512,248	1,024,028	1,266,568	92,690	1,711,658
1731	969,523	398,650	511,947	909,324	1,356,348	82,228	1,518,456
1732	970,201	621,090	715,158	1,144,092	971,768	91,449	1,688,755
1733	987,915	494,996	593,888	1,060,945	1,820,122	89,660	1,655,710
1734	818,790	425,667	497,006	827,182	1,468,640	74,347	1,372,930
1735	1,037,243	435,751	518,915	958,636	1,497,718	87,953	1,624,198
1736	1,074,730	458,983	568,126	1,048,148	1,602,908	92,277	1,704,040
1737	1,219,408	624,356	767,518	1,470,918	2,325,838	113,213	2,090,653
1738	1,060,827	463,640	618,544	1,275,948	2,159,142	95,835	1,769,748
1739	1,220,245	528,613	701,590	1,491,152	2,316,056	109,489	2,021,881
1740	1,371,188	536,402	707,788	1,459,461	2,404,094	118,199	2,182,716
1741	1,385,065	483,003	631,140	1,323,585	1,999,414	114,122	2,107,428
1742	1,432,342	426,672	597,506	1,466,362	2,102,460	116,037	2,142,808
1743	1,357,872	496,838	601,894	1,463,414	2,185,406	114,179	2,108,484
1744	1,300,135	422,820	601,894	1,463,414	2,185,406	114,179	2,108,484
1745	1,404,052	477,023	576,568	1,336,851	2,074,052	114,607	2,116,393
1746	1,606,459	490,389	595,663	1,422,075	2,273,444	127,617	2,356,645
1747	1,659,506	436,454	533,554	1,297,656	2,010,670	126,465	2,335,367
1748	1,687,562	495,314	653,283	1,639,557	2,303,326	134,562	2,484,894
1749	1,790,993	521,327	721,087	1,728,734	2,323,158	142,584	2,633,039
1750	N.A.	N.A.	N.A.	N.A.	N.A.	152,033	2,809,699
1751	2,119,293	719,513	744,269	1,538,655	2,165,440	164,877	3,044,709
1752	1,885,631	816,545	936,224	1,784,277	2,738,156	160,662	2,966,857
1753	N.A.	N.A.	N.A.	N.A.	N.A.	156,522	2,818,010
1754	1,942,162	792,660	883,629	1,788,967	2,903,780	174,406	3,009,170
1755	1,867,206	686,197	838,036	1,844,845	2,329,858	164,472	2,837,768
1756	2,058,993	836,143	1,056,456	2,073,650	2,982,706	187,459	3,234,369
1757	1,991,993	760,818	988,015	1,820,390	2,670,486	177,075	3,058,854
1758	2,173,312	706,682	947,815	1,976,835	2,819,360	187,469	3,234,548

continued on next page

Table 8.3—*continued*

1759	2,151,956	761,220	1,081,447	2,069,027	2,876,310	190,666	3,289,704
1760	1,769,218	539,149	790,231	1,837,341	2,630,286	154,732	2,669,711
1761	2,044,337	749,277	1,023,659	2,031,842	2,197,198	180,370	3,112,063
1762	2,306,893	672,311	942,991	1,327,136	551,142	181,126	3,125,102
1763	2,318,200	601,442	879,274	1,430,651	492,316	179,319	3,093,931
1764	2,164,100	558,428	783,196	1,279,298	539,082	166,634	2,875,060
1765	2,073,231	586,668	797,032	1,245,999	1,118,766	164,206	2,833,174
1766	2,226,912	599,616	784,469	1,300,604	1,291,492	174,478	3,010,408
1767	2,048,525	256,601	770,064	1,234,073	1,030,460	(cob)**	2,959,150
1767	167,441	28,022	32,696	60,568	47,168	(milled)	total
1768	2,368,508	491,679	755,693	1,087,477	516,704	(cob)	3,067,863
1768	36,850	68,675	40,535	70,149	68,608	(milled)	total
1769	2,621,525	448,967	613,686	999,841	2,023,534	(cob)	3,214,411
1769	698,759	69,998	64,923	70,283	70,484	(milled)	total
1770	1,121,487	116,077	307,363	547,926	688,894	(cob)	3,241,839
1770	1,664,355	126,879	91,287	122,476	165,088	(milled)	total

Year	8 Reales	4 Reales	2 Reales	1 Real	½ Real	Taxes in Pesos	Total in Pesos
1771	2,272,045	546,502	711,339	766,815	2,420,576	174,723	3,014,639
1772	2,752,862	624,339	919,307	957,966	2,857,416	211,364	3,646,823

Milled coins with the king's portrait appear, but cobs shown below were also made.

1773	33,918	11,122	14,740	7,638	45,024	2,761	47,639

The last production run of cobs at the Potosí mint took place on July 14, 1773, under the control of foundryman Antonio Figueroa de Quintanilla, resulting in the production of coins worth 47,639 pesos and 2 reales. Thus ended 200 years of continuous production at this site.

Original source Lazo García (1992: vol. 3) presented all values for coins by weight *(marcos)*. This table presents conversion into coins by denomination. The original source presented taxes and totals in pesos.

*N.A. (not available) indicates records are incomplete or missing.

**Milled coins with the *mundos y mares* design, begun in 1767, were abandoned after 1770 and for the next two years only cobs were produced.

Potosí Mint Buildings

According to Alba (1943), as early as 1568 the king was petitioned to open a smelter and mint at Potosí (see illus. 8.9). Construction of the foundation was finally begun on December 8, 1572, at the insistence of Viceroy Toledo. This first building, for which no plans have survived, took a local contractor, Jerónimo de Leto, three years to build at a cost of 8,321 pesos and 1 *tomín,* a modest sum even in those days. This mint is no longer standing, but as recently as 1943, ruins of its furnace and tall chimney were still visible.

Coins were struck in the old mint beginning in 1576 and production continued virtually uninterrupted for decades. By the middle of the seventeenth century it was necessary to expand this old building or erect a new one. Lengthy investigations were made and a new building was finally authorized in a *Cédula Real* of October 3, 1750.

The governor of Potosí, Ventura Santilices y Venero, was made superintendent of this "New Mint of Circular Coins." On September 1, 1751, Santilices was sent instructions indicating a group of expert function-

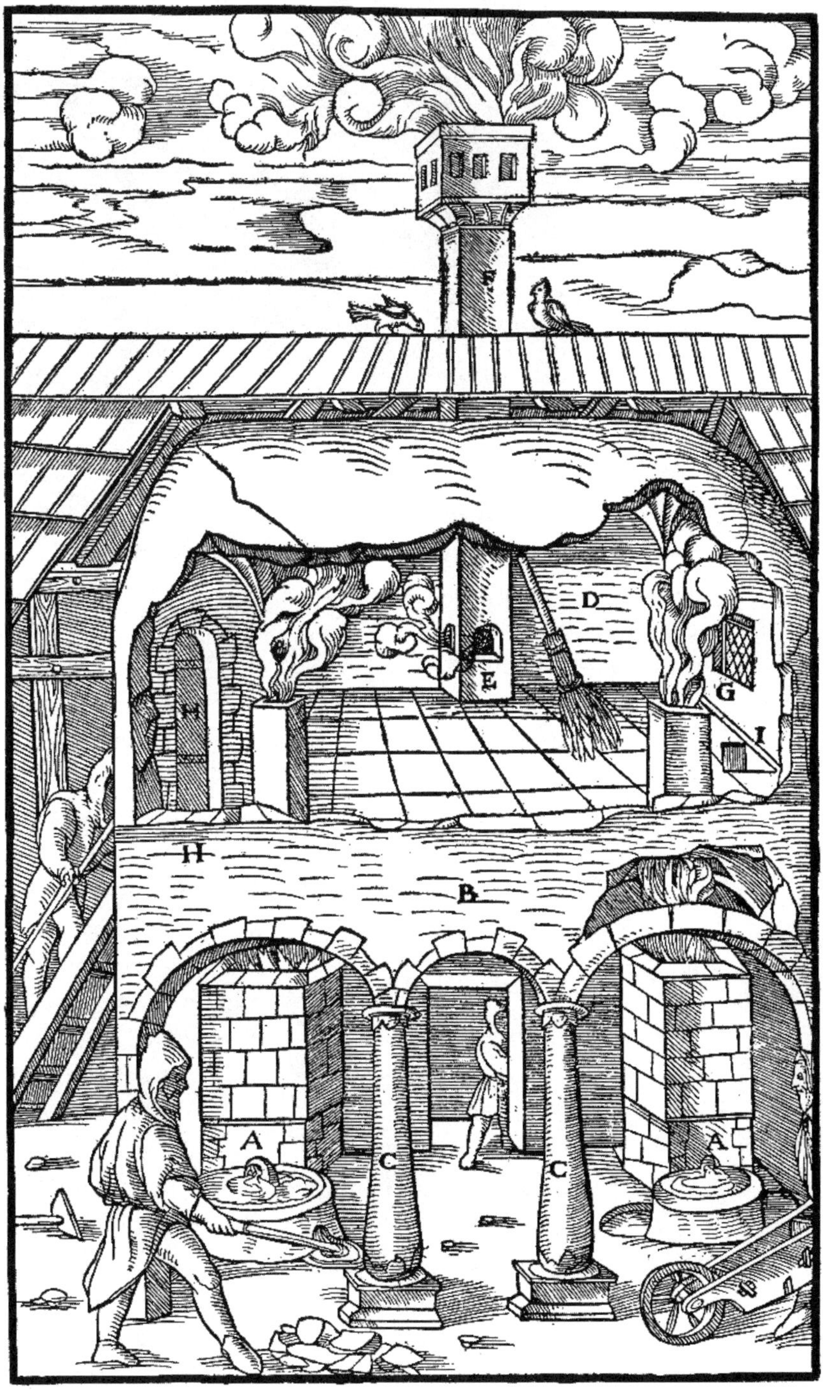

Illus. 8.9. A European sixteenth-century double-smelting furnace. Its construction antedated those built for the mint at Potosí.

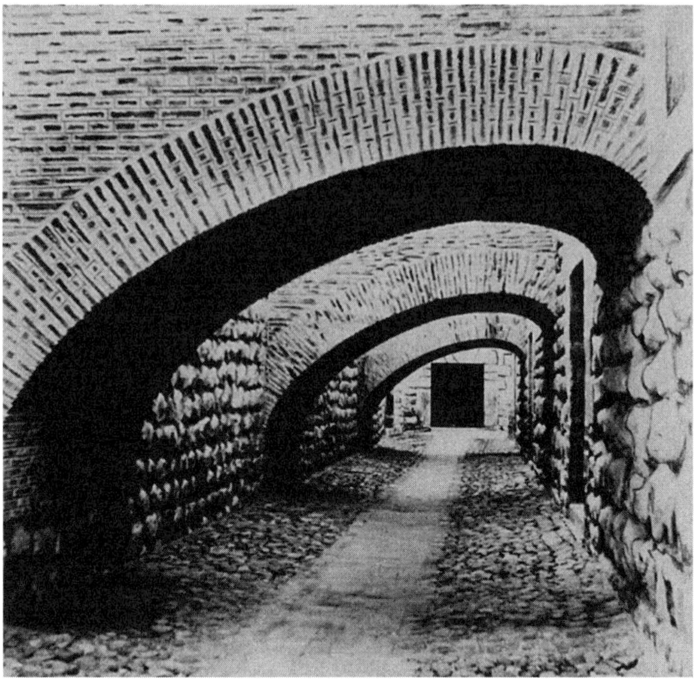

Illus. 8.10. Flying buttresses supporting the massive wall of the Potosí mint.

aries was being sent out from Spain together with special instruments, models, iron, steel, lead, and wooden construction materials to begin the project.

Already in 1752, huge stone walls 24 feet high forming sides of the enormous new building (see illus. 8.10) had been erected at an unexpectedly high cost to the treasury of 200,000 pesos. By 1753 the construction site was being cleared and the count of Carma and the brothers Gambarte were imploring Santilices to stop condemnation proceedings on their luxurious homes that were in the way next to the old mint. Homeowners finally appealed to the viceroy and their bitter struggle only added to the growing accumulation of many other unforeseen delays.

After a series of changes of plans and supervisory personnel, the architect finally decided upon for the new Potosí mint was none other than Salvador de Villa, the same who had been responsible for the designs of mints at Mexico and Lima. Already an old man, and crippled by sciatica, he did not actually arrive at the punishingly high altitude of Potosí until June 1, 1757. After more delays, he asked permission from Santilices to begin actual construction on November 28, 1758; but changes were made to the plans again in 1759. Of course, during all this time silver cob coins were being produced in the old facilities by traditional hand methods. But very little progress occurred toward producing the machine-made planchets and installing the massive geared apparatus for the long-awaited milled coinage (see illus. 8.11).

Eventually the king lost patience and replaced Santilices with Jaime San Just on November 30, 1765. The first Potosí-milled coinage finally appeared in 1767, only to be recalled quickly for an egregious error in design. This was corrected late the same year, but specimens of these 1767 *columnarias* remain scarce.[10] The last cob coinage officially ended at Potosí on November 14, 1771.[11] However, crude specimens dated 1772 and 1773 are known.[12]

Not until July 31, 1773, was the mint declared finished at an astonishing total cost of 1,148,452 pesos, 6 reales—a huge amount for the time. It was and is a massive, awe-inspiring building and the only one by architect de Villa to have survived intact (see illus. 8.12, 8.13, and 8.14). It was acclaimed the *Escorial Americano,* in reference to the famed *Escorial* palace near Madrid. In later years it played an important role in the Wars of Independence, being captured and retaken several times. Today it houses important archives, some of which were used in research for this book. It also is a museum displaying more than 100 colonial paintings, coin dies, machinery, minerals, and archaeological remains. Glenn Murray (1990) has published a splendid pictorial account of the interior of this historical monument.

This long tradition of mint operations at Potosí, second only to that of Mexico, produced an array of silver coins under many different assayers. Their initial letters are listed in table 8.4 as an aid to identification of cobs that may otherwise be poorly struck and lack any dates or other diagnostic features.

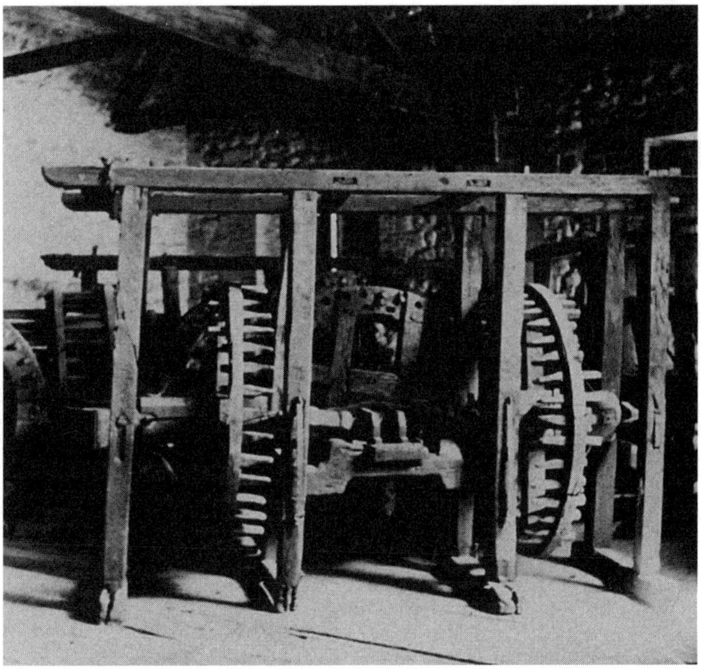

Illus. 8.11. Wooden gear assembly of a milling machine in use after the 1750s to produce milled pillar dollars at Potosí.

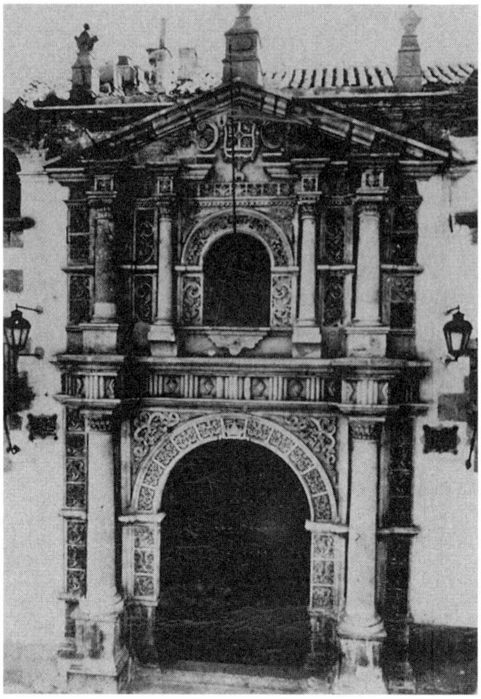

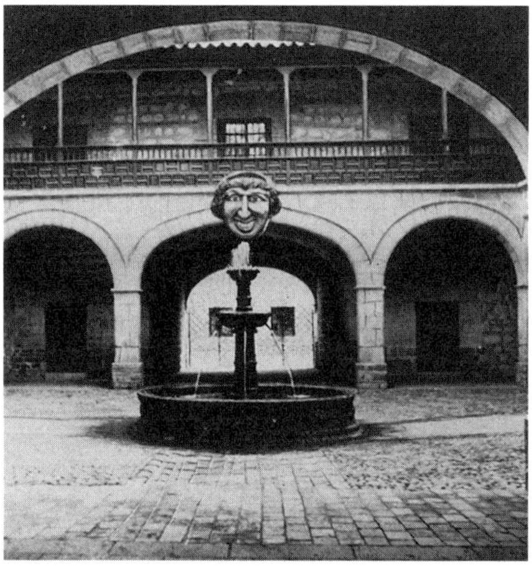

Illus. 8.12. Facade of the front entrance to the Potosí mint.

Illus. 8.13. The patio of the Potosí mint. The bizarre head on the water fountain is a relatively modern gift (early nineteenth century) from a visiting Frenchman.

Illus. 8.14. Passageway leading to the quarters of colonial employees of the Potosí mint.

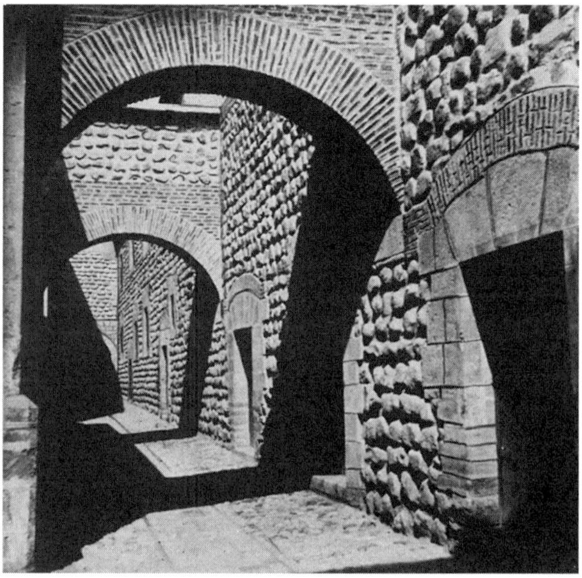

Table 8.4. Potosí Mint Assayers

Mark	Assayer Name	Term of Office
"R"	Alonso Rincón	1573–1576
"B"	Juan de Ballesteros Narváez	1576–1586
"A"	Juan Alvarez Reynaltes	1586–1589
"B"	Juan de Ballesteros et al.	1589–1615
"Q"	Agustín de la Quadra	1610 (?)
"C"	?	1613 (?)
"R"	Baltazar Ramos Leceta	1614
"M"	Juan Muñoz	1615–1617
"RL"	Baltazar Ramos Leceta	1618
"P"	Martín de Palencia	1618
"PA"	García de Paredes y Ulloa ?	1618
"PA + T"	García de Paredes y Ulloa; Juan Ximénez de Tapia	1618
"T/PA" (overstrike)		1618
"T"	Juan Ximénez de Tapia	1618–1624
"M"	Juan Muñoz ?	1621
"P/T" (overstrike)		1621
"P"	Luis de Peralta	1621–1624
"T"	Juan Ximénez de Tapia	1626–1637
"P/T" (overstrike)		1628
"P"	Luis de Peralta	1628
"P"	Pedro Pérez de Carrion	1631
"R"	?	1636–1641
"RT"	?	1638
"TR"	Pedro Treviño	1636–1645
"Z"	Pedro Zambrano	1640
"T"	Juan Ximénez de Tapia ?	1640–1641
"R"	Felipe Ramírez de Arellano	1643–1644
"T"	Juan Ximénez de Tapia ?	1644–1649
"V"	Gerónimo Velázquez	1646
"P"	Luis de Peralta	1646–1647
"Z"	Pedro Zambrano	1647–1649
"FR"	Felipe Ramírez de Arellano	1647
"⊙"	Juan Rodríguez de Rodas	1649–1651
"QZ"	?	1649
"Q"	?	1649–1650
"C"	Manuel de Cejas	1650
"P"	?	1650
"E"	Antonio de Ergueta	1650–1667
"F/E, F, E"	?	1667
"P, F"	?	1668
"E"	Antonio de Ergueta	1669–1678
"C"	Manuel de Cejas	1678
"C/E, C"	?	1679
"V"	Pedro de Villar	1680–1683
"VR" (enlaced)	?	1684–1697
"CH" (enlaced)	Sebastian de Chavarría	1697

continued on next page

Table 8.4—*continued*

Mark	Assayer Name	Term of Office
"CH/VR, F/CH"	Chavez/?; ?/Chavez	1697
"F"	?	1698–1701
"Y"	Diego de Ybarboru	1701–1727
"M"	José de Matienzo	1728–1732
"YA" (enlaced)	?	1732–1733
"E"	Esteban Gutiérrez de Escalante	1733–1737
"M"	Pedro G. Manrique	1738–1740
"C"	José Carnizer	1741–1744
"P"	Diego de Pui	1744
"P" (reversed)	Luis de Quintanilla	1745–1753
"C"	Joseph Maria de Cavallero	1754
"V"	José de Vargas y Flores	1760–1763
"Y"	Raimundo de Yturrlaga	1764–1765
"V"	José de Vargas y Flores	1766–1773
"JR"	José de Vargas y Flores; Raimundo de Yturriaga	1773–1776
"PR/JR"	Pedro Narcisco de Mazondo; Raimundo de Yturriaga	1776
"PR"	Pedro Narcisco de Mazondo; Raimundo de Yturriaga	1776–1795
"JR"	José de Vargas y Flores; Raimundo de Yturriaga	1778
"P"	Pedro Narcisco de Yturriaga	1793
"PP"	Pedro Narcisco de Yturriaga; Pedro Martín Albizu	1795–1802
"J"	Juan Paloma y Sierra	1801
"PJ"	Pedro Prudencio de Esquerrenea; Juan Paloma y Sierra	1803–1809
"PJ"	Pedro Prudencio de Esquerrenea; Juan Paloma y Sierra	1813–1824
"JP"	Juan Paloma y Sierra; Pedro Prudencio de Esquerrenea	1817
"PJ"	Pedro Prudencio de Esquerrenea; Juan Paloma y Sierra	1822–1824
"JL"	Juan Paloma y Sierra, second assayer unknown	1823
"PJ"	Pedro Prudencio de Esquerrenea; Juan Paloma y Sierra	1824
"J"	Juan Paloma y Sierra	1824–1825
"JL"	Juan Paloma y Sierra; second assayer unknown	1825

Sources: Cunietti-Ferrando (1987b, 1995); Sellschopp (1973); Sedwick and Sedwick (1995); Pellicer i Bru (1975); and photographic evidence from various auction catalogs.

If we compare assayers' letters found on coins of Potosí with archival records indicating who held these positions, we must conclude that not only the chief assayer but also assistant assayers were sometimes required to add their initials to the dies. It is also evident there were instances within a given year when different assayers worked on coins of different denominations.

An exact sequence for the period predating 1617 and during the hectic years at the end of the Rocha counterfeiting scandal is poorly understood and subject to revision. In the latter case, it seems possible imaginary assayers' initials were being placed on badly debased coins in a desperate effort to obfuscate the investigation by Nestares Marín.

Lack of background information on the series of Potosí cobs and milled coinage postdating assayer Ergueta reflects the limited collector and research interest in a series of drastically declining cob quality, followed by uniform monotony of the milled coinage. To some extent the mintage figures in table 8.3, published by Lazo García (1992), help alleviate this problem and are welcome additions.

Selected Potosí Cobs from the Florida Collection

Recovery of several thousand coins from the Jupiter Wreck has added more than 150 new dates and varieties of coins to the Florida Collection including a fine study group of Potosí cobs of the transition period beginning in 1652. Distribution of Potosí coins by denominations and date, as shown in table 8.5, reflects the same skewed totals as those from Mexico. Here we see clustering around intervals 1652–1658 and 1690–1703, corresponding to recovery from shipwrecks that took place in 1660 and 1715. The abrupt decline in Potosí coins after 1703 may have multiple explanations although the fundamental reason is a decrease in silver available to the mint. Absence of ½-real coins from such a long time span is more difficult to explain. The anomalously large total of 1-real coins suggests poorly preserved ½-real specimens may have been included.

Totals in table 8.6, Potosí coins by denomination and assayer, basically correspond to the length of time an assayer held his office. This is evident from the example of "E" (Ergueta), who functioned from 1651–1679. Elsewhere we see "VR" (Pedro de Villar) is also strongly represented as a result of his tenure from 1679–1694. On the other hand, assayer "Y" (Ybarboru), who functioned from 1701 to 1727, does not have correspondingly large totals since much of his time in office took place after the 1715 Fleet was destroyed. Another surprise, the result of sheer chance, is the "F/CH" combination with four specimens in the

Table 8.5. Potosí Silver Coins by Denomination and Date

Year	½ real	1 real	2 reales	4 reales	8 reales	Subtotal
—3*	0	1	0	0	0	1
—5	0	1	0	0	0	1
1—	0	0	0	0	1	1
16—	0	0	0	0	1	1
16-6	0	0	0	1	0	1
16-9	0	1	0	0	1	2
162-	0	0	1	0	0	1
1640	0	0	1	0	0	1
1650	0	0	1	0	1	2
1652	0	2	2	3	11	18
1653	0	1	3	4	10	18
1654	0	0	3	9	14	26
1655	0	2	0	3	9	14
1656	0	1	0	4	6	11
1657	0	1	2	3	13	19
1658	0	0	1	5	11	17
166-	0	1	0	0	0	1
1660	0	1	0	0	0	1
1665	0	2	0	0	0	2
1666	0	1	0	0	1	2
1668	0	1	0	0	0	1
1669	0	1	0	0	0	1
167-	0	1	0	0	0	1
1670	0	2	0	0	0	2
1671	0	0	0	1	0	1
1672	0	3	1	0	1	5
1674	0	2	0	0	0	2
1675	0	0	0	0	2	2
1676	0	2	0	1	0	3
1677	0	1	0	0	1	2
1679	0	0	0	1	0	1
168-	0	0	0	0	1	1
1680	0	0	0	0	1	1
1682	0	1	0	0	0	1
1683	0	0	0	0	1	1
1684	0	1	0	1	1	3
1685	0	1	2	1	1	5
1686	0	5	2	0	5	12
1687	0	2	1	2	2	7
1688	0	3	1	3	1	8
1689	0	4	0	1	2	7
169-	0	2	0	0	3	5
1690	0	3	2	7	7	19
1691	0	2	0	3	6	11
1692	0	3	0	2	5	10
1693	0	6	1	3	9	19

Year	½ real	1 real	2 reales	4 reales	8 reales	Subtotal
1694	0	0	0	2	8	10
1695	0	3	3	2	8	16
1696	0	3	0	2	8	13
1697	0	0	1	1	10	12
1698	0	3	1	1	9	14
1699	0	0	1	2	6	9
17—	0	0	0	1	2	3
170-	0	0	0	1	1	2
1700	0	1	1	7	5	14
1701	0	2	0	3	9	14
1702	0	0	1	3	8	12
1703	0	1	2	3	6	12
1704	0	0	1	0	0	1
1705	0	0	0	1	1	2
1706	0	0	1	2	1	4
1707	0	1	0	0	4	5
1708	0	0	0	2	4	6
1709	0	0	1	0	3	4
1710	0	1	0	0	1	2
1711	0	0	0	1	0	1
1712	0	1	0	0	0	1
177-	0	0	0	0	1	1
1775	0	1	0	0	0	1
1776	0	0	2	0	0	2
1786	0	0	0	1	0	1
1788	0	0	0	0	1	1
179-	0	0	0	0	1	1
1794	0	0	0	0	1	1
1798	0	0	0	0	1	1
1805	0	0	0	0	1	1
Indeterminate	1	17	21	7	29	73
Total	1	95	60	101	258	515

Source: Florida Bureau of Archaeological Research computer database.
*Dash indicates numeral indiscernible.

collection, but they could only have been struck during a part of one year.

Relative abundance of certain dates in the Florida Collection cannot be taken as a reliable indicator of original production figures. For example, several design varieties of the year 1652, some quite rare, are included for the total figure of seventeen. The date run 1652–1658 is merely a reflection of the salvaged cargo from a single ship in Florida waters and is not representative of relative mint production. These same comments apply to increased numbers shown between 1686–1696 and 1701–1703 where recoveries were from several galleons involved in the same disaster.

Table 8.6. Potosí Silver Coin Totals by Denomination and Assayer

½ Real		
	Assayer not shown	1
	Subtotal	1
1 Real		
	Assayer "C"	1
	Assayer "E"	11
	Assayer "F"	2
	Assayer "TR"	1
	Assayer "V"	3
	Assayer "VR"	34
	Assayer "Y"	2
	Assayer "Z"	1
	Assayer not shown	40
	Subtotal	95
2 Reales		
	Assayer "CH"	1
	Assayer "E"	17
	Assayer "F"	2
	Assayer "JR"	1
	Assayer "⊙"	1
	Assayer "PR"	1
	Assayer "Q"	2
	Assayer "R"	1
	Assayer "T"	6
	Assayer "TR"	2
	Assayer "V"	1
	Assayer "VR"	10
	Assayer "Y"	7
	Assayer "Z"	1
	Assayer not shown	7
	Subtotal	60
4 Reales		
	Assayer "B"	1
	Assayer "C"	1
	Assayer "E"	32
	Assayer "F"	4
	Assayer "PR"	1
	Assayer "Q"	1
	Assayer "V"	2
	Assayer "VR"	26
	Assayer "Y"	13
	Assayer not shown	20
	Subtotal	101
8 Reales		
	Assayer "B"	1
	Assayer "CH"	2
	Assayer "E"	78
	Assayer "F"	13
	Assayer "F/CH"	4
	Assayer "⊙"	1
	Assayer "PJ"	1
	Assayer "PP"	1
	Assayer "PR"	4
	Assayer "Q"	1
	Assayer "R"	4
	Assayer "V"	9
	Assayer "VR"	71
	Assayer "Y"	32
	Assayer "Z"	1
	Assayer not shown	35
	Subtotal	258
Total		515

Source: Florida Bureau of Archaeological Research computer database.

Table 8.7, showing dated Potosí coins with visible assayers' marks, extends the tenure of an assayer beyond that already published. An 8-reales specimen shown in figure 8.9g extends the range of assayer "VR" to 1698. Since it has escaped attention of previous researchers, it is reasonable to assume this is a scarce coin of very limited production.

In contrast to the Mexican mint's increase in salvaged coin numbers in the years immediately before the sailing of the 1715 Fleet from Vera Cruz, Potosí coins with visible assayers' marks are poorly represented between 1704 and 1711, and missing thereafter. This may be partly explained by known delays in moving specie down from Potosí to Lima

Table 8.7. Dated Potosí Silver Coins with Visible Assayers' Initials in the Florida Collection

Assayer	Date	Total	Assayer	Date	Total
"T"	1645	1	"VR"	1693	18
"⊙"	1650	2	"VR"	1694	9
"E"	1652	17	"VR"	1695	16
"E"	1653	17	"VR"	1696	11
"E"	1654	26	"VR"	1697	4
"E"	1655	12	"CH"	1697	3
"E"	1656	10	"F/CH"	1697	4
"E"	1657	19	"VR"	1698	1
"E"	1658	17	"F"	1698	7
"E"	1660	1	"F"	1699	6
"E"	1665	1	"F"	1700	8
"E"	1666	2	"Y"	1701	10
"E"	1669	1	"Y"	1702	11
"E"	1672	2	"Y"	1703	10
"E"	1675	2	"Y"	1704	1
"E"	1676	2	"Y"	1705	2
"C"	1679	1	"Y"	1706	4
"V"	1680	1	"Y"	1707	2
"V"	1682	1	"Y"	1708	4
"V"	1683	1	"Y"	1709	3
"V"	1684	2	"Y"	1710	1
"VR"	1685	4	"Y"	1711	1
"VR"	1686	12	"JR"	1776	1
"VR"	1687	6	"PR"	1776	1
"VR"	1688	7	"PR"	1786	1
"VR"	1689	5	"PR"	1788	1
"VR"	1690	16	"PR"	1794	1
"VR"	1691	10	"PP"	1798	1
"VR"	1692	10	"PJ"	1805	1

Source: Florida Bureau of Archaeological Research computer database.

in time for embarkation to Panama. However, it is also concurrent with increases in Mexican silver production at a time when Potosí mines were in severe decline.

From 1650 to 1656 there was confusion over details of the design, no doubt because of typical ambiguities in official instructions (see Menzel 1995, 1997, and McLean 1994). Our discussion of these coins begins with figure 8.1 showing obverses and reverses of two "double-8" cobs, produced only in the year 1652. Coin 8.1a–b weighs 24.67 grams, even with a badly cracked planchet. It has a series of distinctive design features, including (1) double rows of rectangular denticulation both inside and outside the rim legend, best seen in coin 8.1b in the lower right-hand corner at either side of Felipe IV's roman numeral IIII; (2) capitals on top of the Pillars of Hercules that are wavelike rather than

Figure 8.1. Potosí 8-Reales Transitional Cobs of 1652

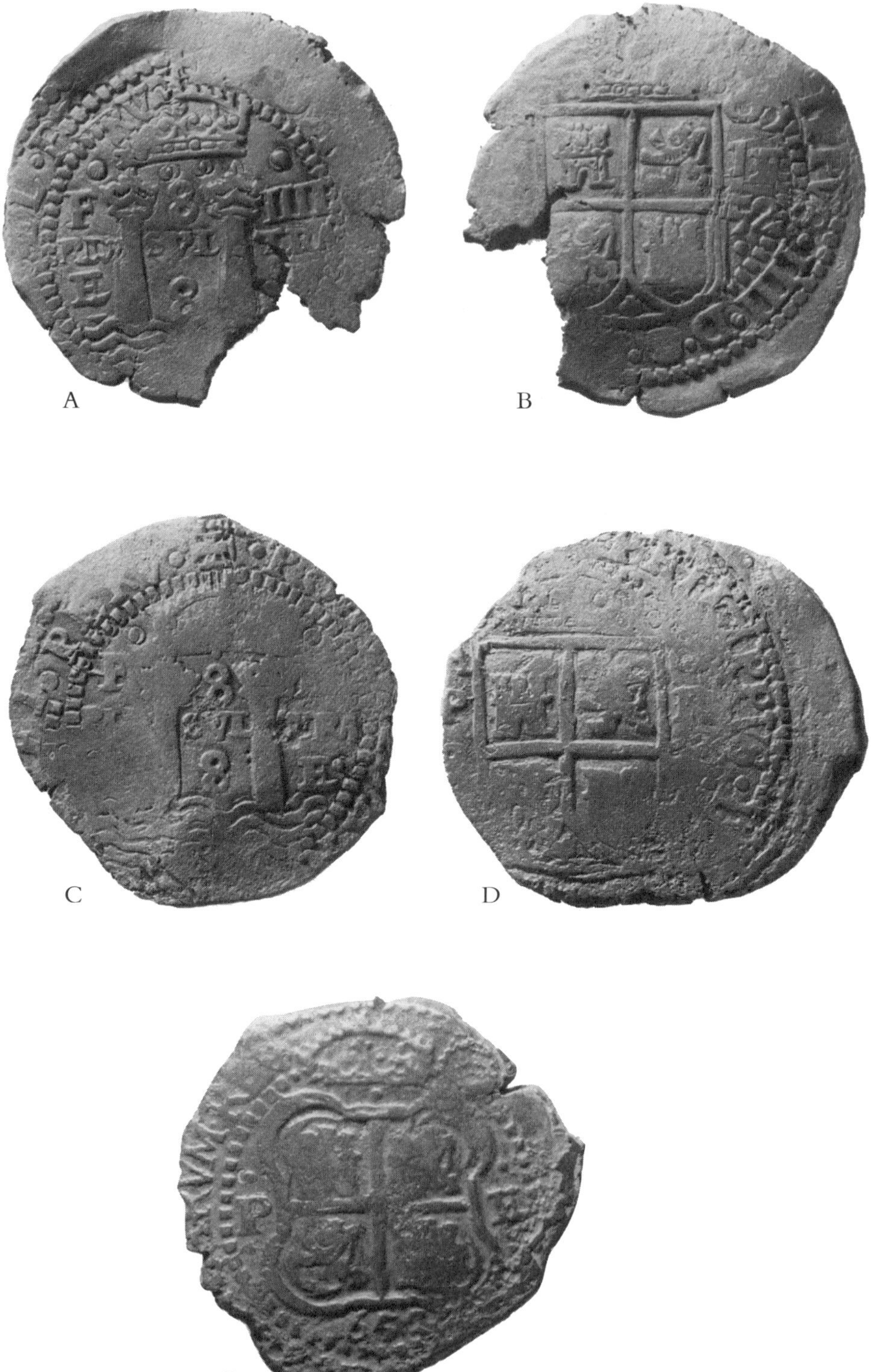

crowns; (3) large dots occupying the space slightly below and on either side of the large crown; (4) space to the left of the left-hand column with "F" over "PLV" over "E"; and (5) space to the right of the right-hand column with III over "TRA," the remainder missing. This resulting combination lacks a mint mark, and the meaning of the letter "F" is clearly linked across the coin with the roman numeral IIII, which can only stand for King Felipe IV. The denomination 8 is repeated a second time at the bottom of the obverse, just above the waves; another "E" may have been in the lower-right-hand quadrant where the planchet is missing if coin 8.1c–d is from the same die. The reverse has a strong, well-made shield similar to Sevilla mint engraving and with "wigged" lions[13] and crisp castles reminiscent of later work at Lima. To the right of the shield we find a letter "E" above a partial date 52, all crowded into two lines; the reverse of this specimen is obliterated. Finally, it is worth noting this rather strange design was made by the third-ranking die engraver, if we can assign the two dots above the uppermost 8 on the obverse to that position (see my explanation in Craig 1988: 33–34 for "secret" die engravers marks).

Coin 8.1c–d is a very similar double-8 design to the first example, except there is only one dot above the upper 8, suggesting it was cut by a different engraver. In figure 8.1e, we have an entirely different reverse with a cross flanked by "P" on the left and "E" on the right and a three-digit date 652 below. This is the familiar arrangement that was to last as a reverse design for many years and it may have been settled upon late in the production year 1652 after some earlier combinations were abandoned.

Quite apart from these curious combinations, we find an amazing variety of obverse dies that mix designation for the king together with part of the date. Coin 8.2 shows "1 PH 6" inserted between the tops of the pillars and base of the crown. The remainder of the date 52 now appears in its customary place riding atop waves between the columns. The reverse design of these coins has become a standard Potosí cross potent with a small, three-digit date 652 tucked in below its base. Coin 8.2c–d is a design selected near the end of the process.

Coin 8.2e–f is a transitional design having only a "PH" over the denomination 8 on the obverse and retaining the transitional shield reverse, but now with a complete date in the legend.[14] Indecision over the basic Potosí die design evidently cleared up by 1653 as we can see from a close examination of the coins in figure 8.3, although coin 8.3c–d has the letters "PH" flanked and separated by large dots.

Figure 8.4 is interesting for "lazy 4's" seen on coins 8.4a and 8.4b that appear to have been struck from the same die, but were not. In this

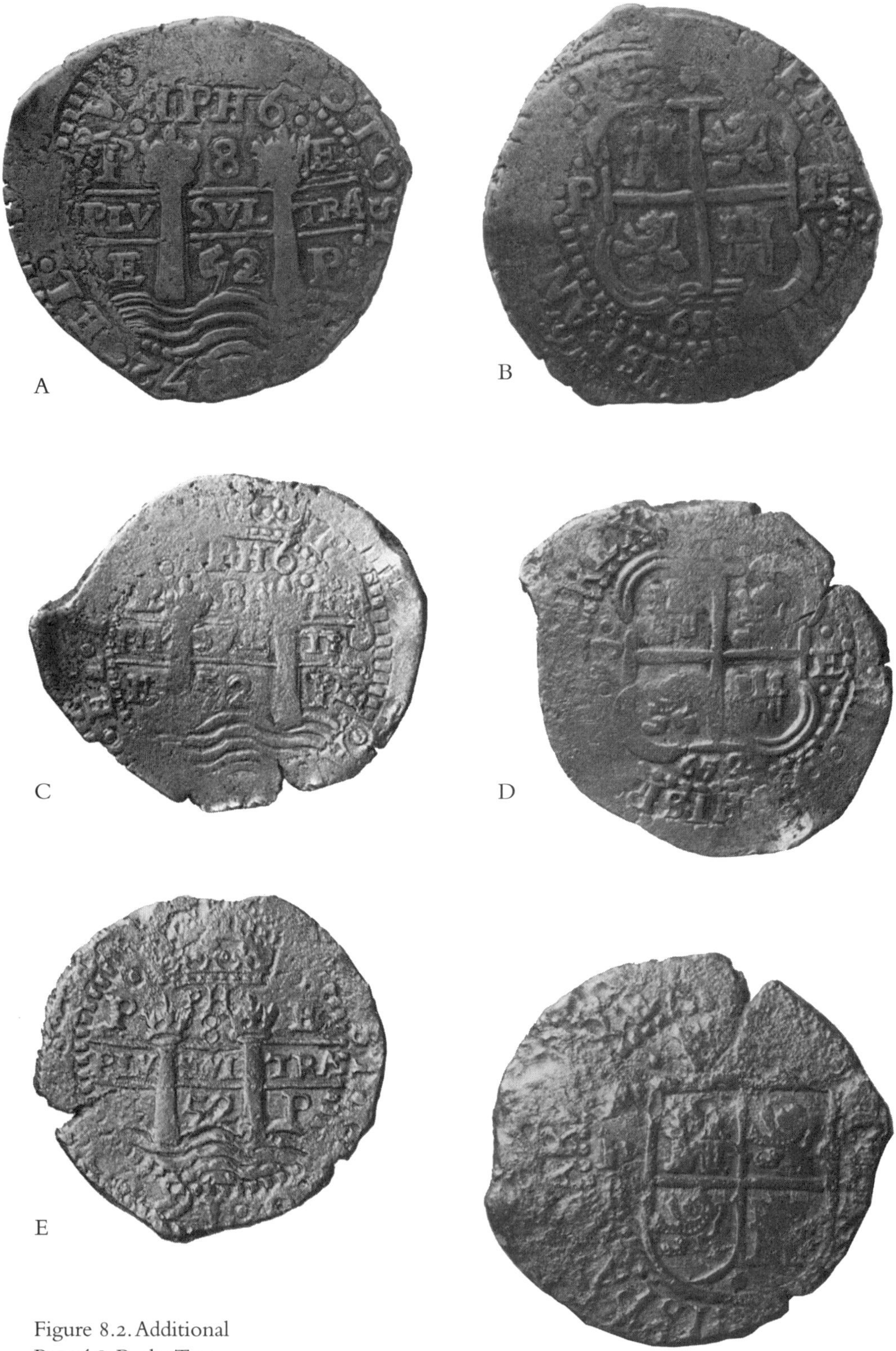

Figure 8.2. Additional Potosí 8-Reales Transitional Cobs of 1652

figure there is a noticeable range of waves in the obverse design from only three to as many as six.[15]

Only two presentable cobs of 1657 could be found for figure 8.6. They are not particularly noteworthy except for shrinking in size and the importance of the king's initials, "PH." Indeed, this is the last year they appear on Potosí cobs.[16] By 1658 all of the "bugs" appear to have been worked out of the Potosí cobs, and the coins shown in figure 8.7 seem well behaved in terms of their design.

Figure 8.8 is a much later grouping of excellent Potosí 4-reales coins salvaged from various wrecks of the 1715 Plate Fleet. These coins are arranged in chronological order from 1687 onward to 1708. One of the best diagnostic features of Potosí coins of this period is the "swollen" 4 of the denomination. It can be used with confidence to identify the mint of origin when all other identifying marks are absent, a situation

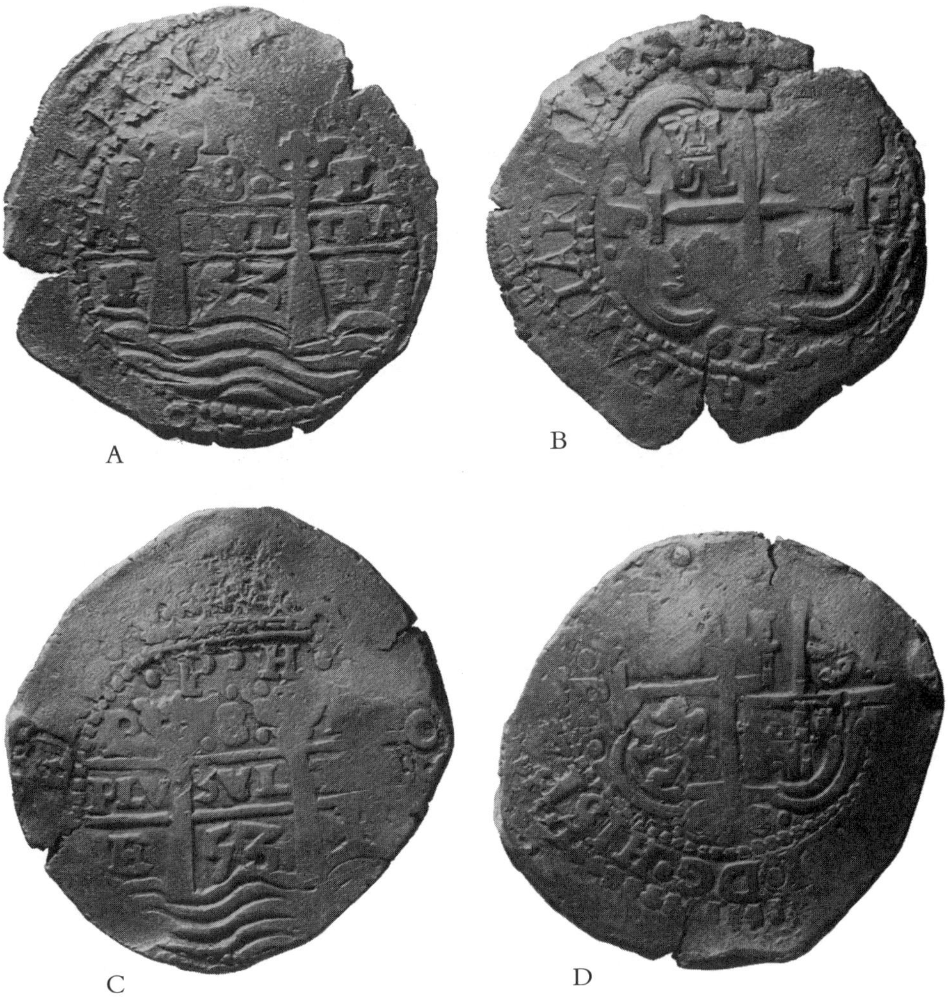

Figure 8.3. Potosí 8-Reales Cobs of 1653

A B C D

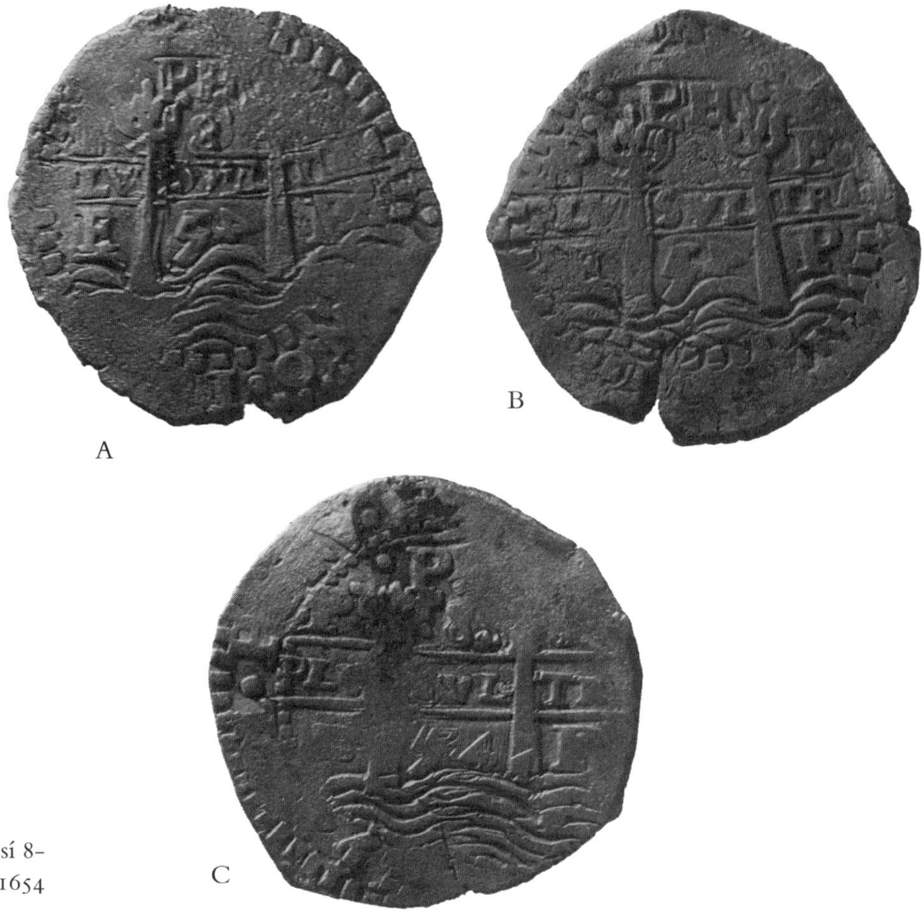

Figure 8.4. Potosí 8-Reales Cobs of 1654

more common than you might imagine. Coin 8.8i is an excellent example; compare the bulging front of the 4 with the sharply executed 4's of the remaining Lima cobs shown in figure 9.3 on page 160.

From these same 1715 wrecks the state has obtained a small but excellent set of dated Potosí 8-reales cobs, selected examples of which are shown in figure 8.9. The date range shown is 1686–1703. Auction records from the last thirty years show the dates 1694, 1695, 1698, 1700, 1702, and 1703 have seldom appeared for sale and must be considered decidedly uncommon, possibly due to losses in the 1715 disaster, although as we have seen Mexican coins are vastly more common. In any event, we find die engraving from this period produced strong, high-quality designs that are usually well struck without the wildly variable results seen during the earlier decades of the 1660s and 1670s.

With enormous quantities of silver being processed at the Spanish colonial mints we can anticipate heavily used coin dies, made from cylinders of soft iron, would quickly become worn by the repeated

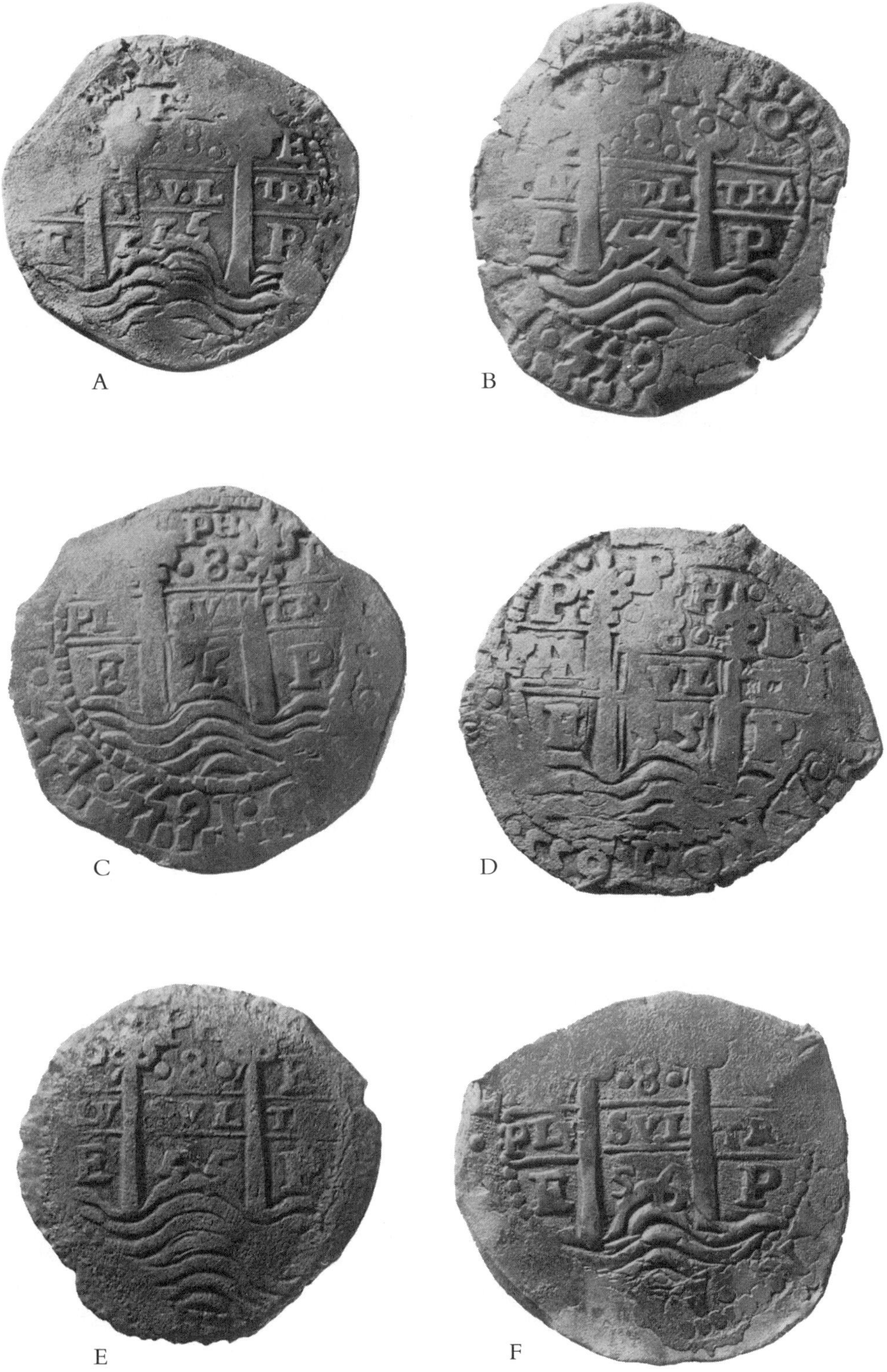

Figure 8.5. Potosí 8-Reales Cobs of 1655 and 1656

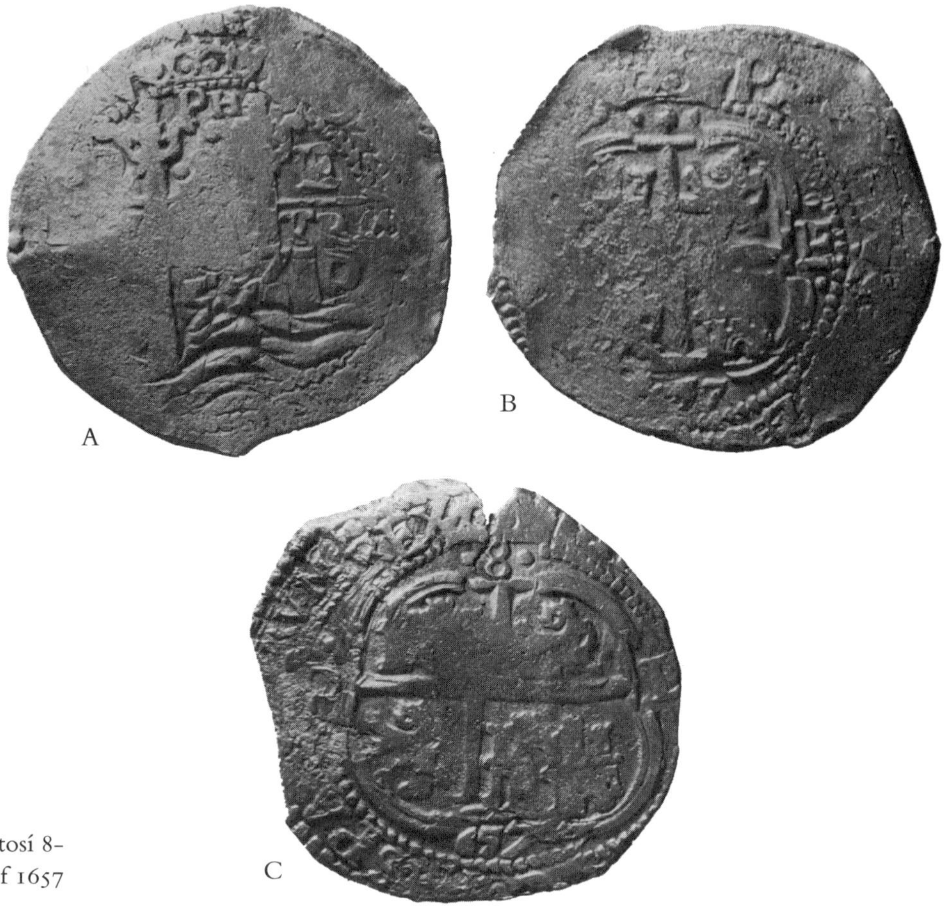

A B C

Figure 8.6. Potosí 8-Reales Cobs of 1657

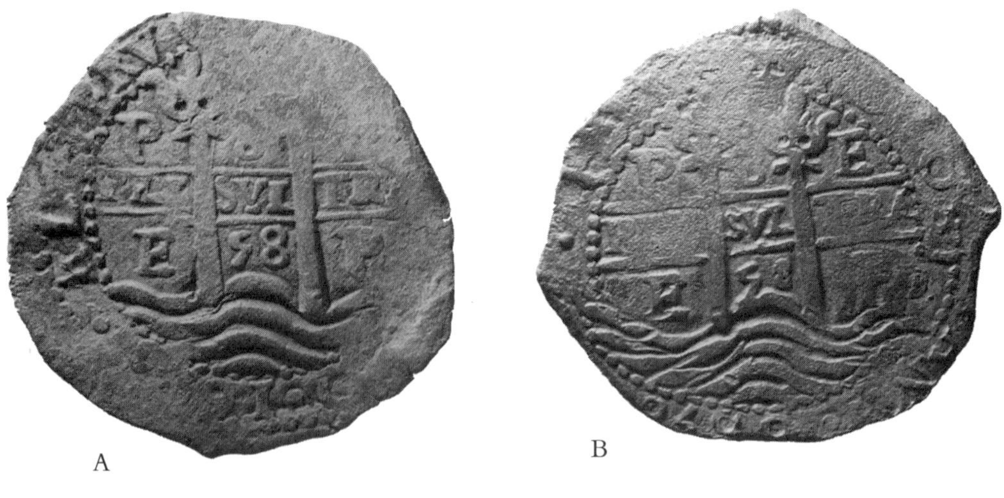

A B

Figure 8.7. Potosí 8-Reales Cobs of 1658

Figure 8.7.—*continued*

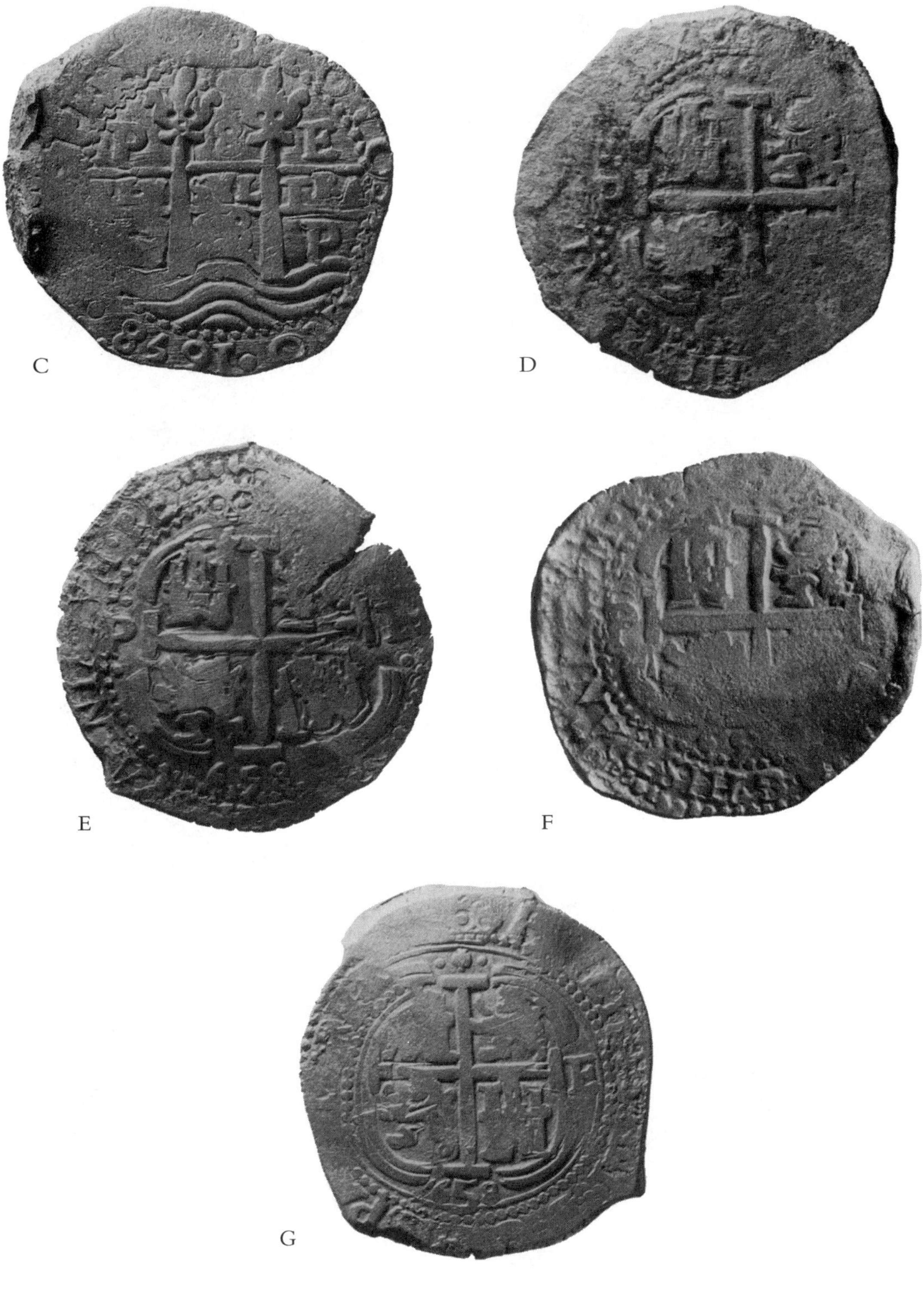

C D E F G

Figure 8.8. Potosí 4-Reales Cobs, 1687–1708

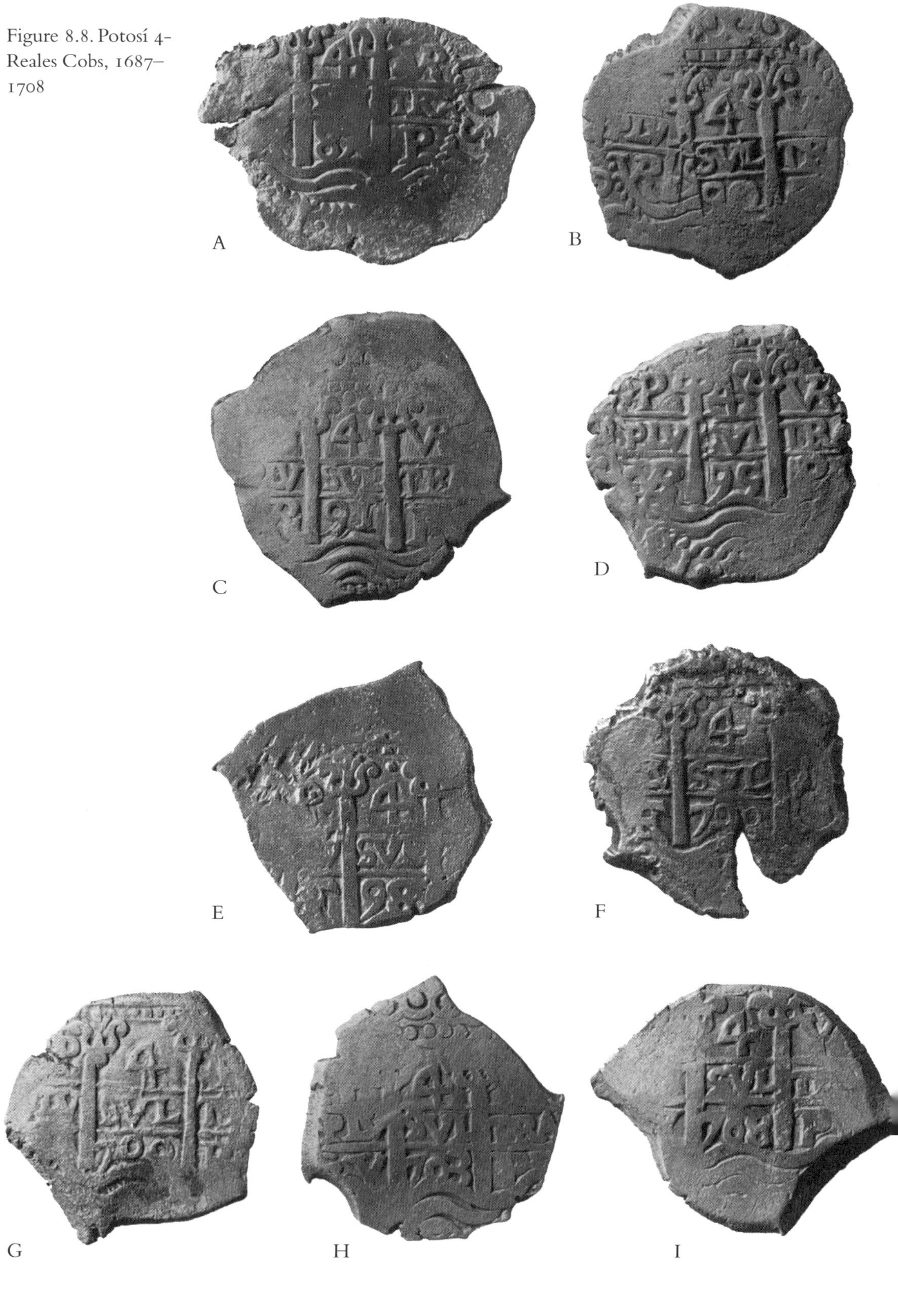

Figure 8.9 A–F. Potosí 8-Reales Cobs, 1686–1703

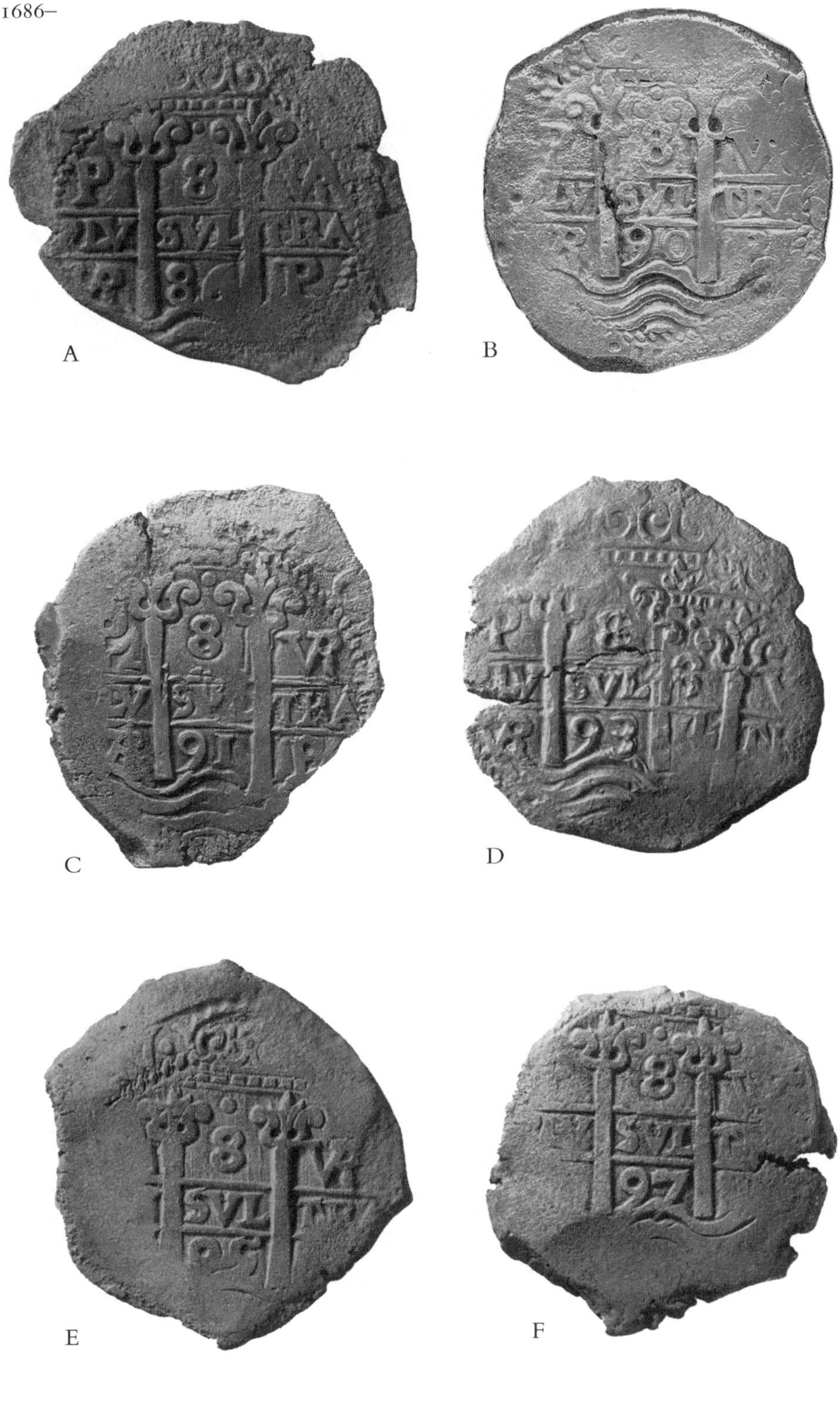

Figure 8.9 G–L. Potosí 8-Reales Cobs, 1686–1703

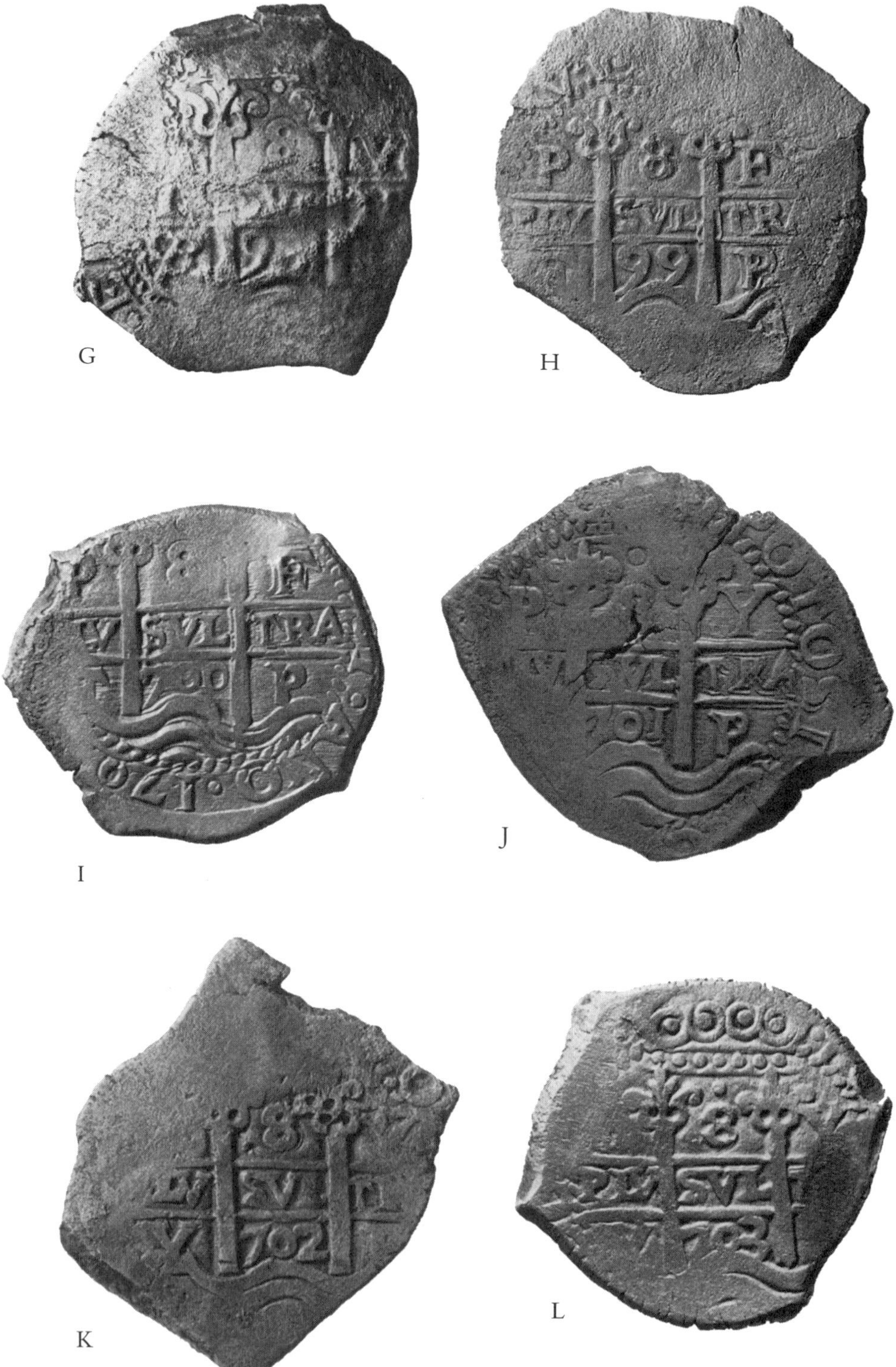

shock of hand-striking silver cobs. This was indeed the case and we can see a gradual softening of design features as a die becomes eroded from impacts. When this became a problem, mint engravers repunched or reengraved dies that were unbroken and still useful.

This is what happened to the die used to strike the coin shown in figure 8.10a, a Potosí 8 reales of 1680. On close examination we find the number 8 of the denomination was repunched four times. Details of the capital on top of the right-hand column have been reengraved one or more times and the two columns themselves have become broadened and flattened through wear of the die's cut edges. Details of the left-hand crest are nearly obliterated—the upper-right assayer's initial "V" is sharpened up, again by repunching. However, the peculiar intersection of two sets of four wave bands below the date is a result of slight die bounce. Although not illustrated, the cross side of this coin has two badly worn lions and a nearly indistinguishable lower-right castle. In spite of these many signs of worn dies, the coin itself still remains an attractive specimen in the Florida Collection.

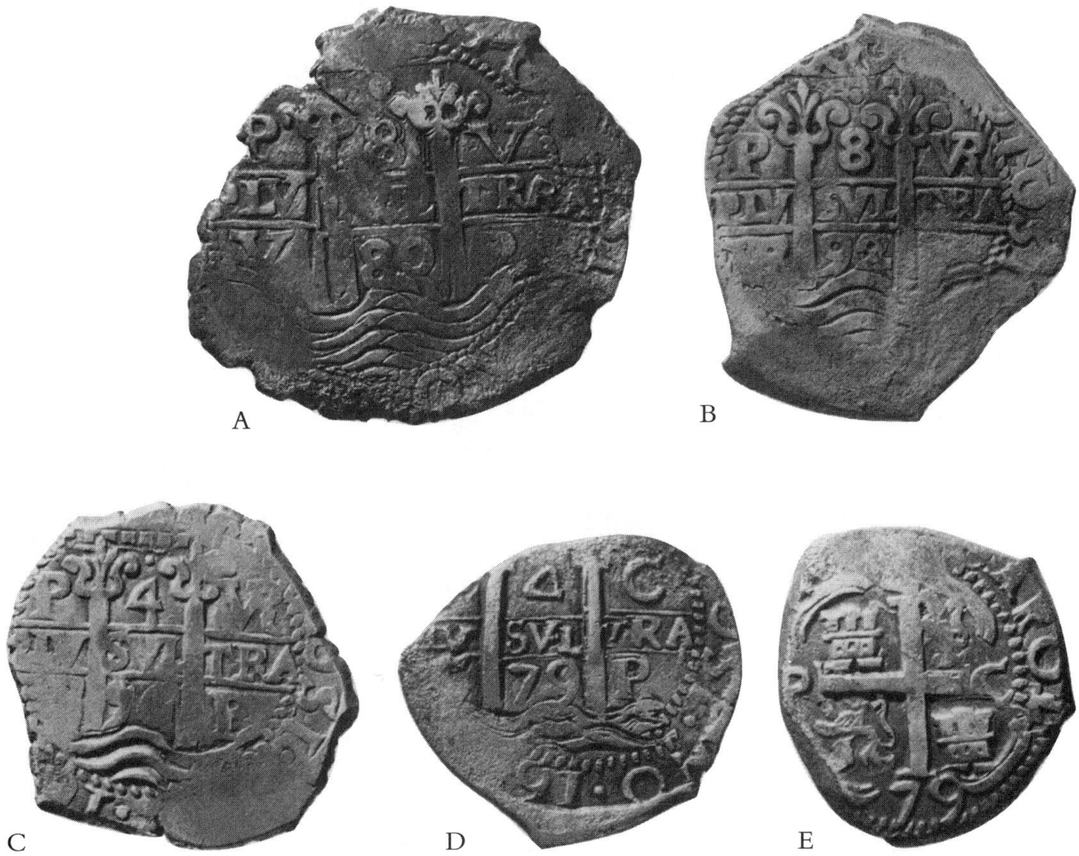

Figure 8.10. Potosí Die Varieties

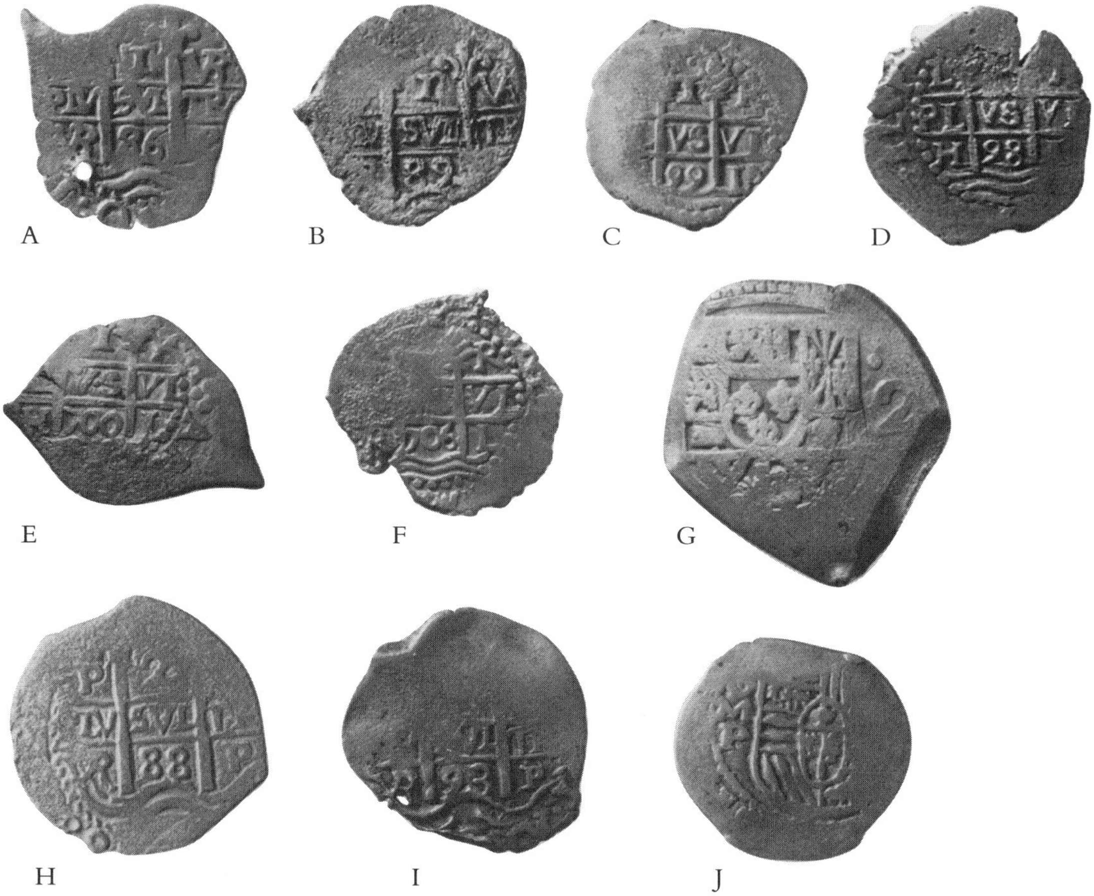

Figure 8.11. 1-Real and 2-Reales Coins from Various Mints, 1686–1706

Late-seventeenth-century Potosí die sinkers often used the same punches to construct design elements of both 8- and 4-reales coins, something not seen in more elegant work done at Lima. Coin 8.10b, a Potosí 8 reales of 1692, and 8.10c, a Potosí 4 reales of 1690, illustrate this practice rather well. When viewed together we might think they were made from the same dies with only the denominations changed and the 4-reales planchet reduced in size. While columns, mint mark, assayer's letters ("VR"), and letters of the motto and legend are all made from the same punches, the 4-reales coin has a field with slightly smaller diameter, accommodating only three waves instead of the four found on the larger coin.[17]

While most die cutters were content to use as many labor-saving punches as possible to finish their dies, we find exactly the opposite to be the case with whoever cut dies for coin 8.10d, a Potosí 4 reales of 1679. For this one year only, assayer "C" was in charge of foundry operations. His engraver was not as skilled as predecessors. His obverse largely comprises numbers and letters noticeable for their clumsy rendition. The reverse die (8.10e) is almost entirely done by hand without punches. Both castles and lions are unequal in size and squeezed into a reduced space. Evidently the lions and castles, mint mark, and assayer's initial were all cut by hand before the cross was added; this was then carved out with grossly unequal horizontal arms due to lack of space caused by poor placement of the castles and lions. The strange, stemless 4 seen on the obverse is faintly visible on the reverse, resting directly on top of the vertical cross arm. There is an oversized 79 date at the bottom. The 9 in this date was clearly added after castle and tressure were in place; then they were both slightly excised to make more room for it. Altogether, this is a most interesting and instructive cob, giving us clear insights into the actual sequence of constructing these dies.

Smaller denominations of Potosí cobs are represented in the Florida Collection but are of relatively poor quality. Figure 8.11 shows a sample of 1-real and 2-reales coins from various mints. As usual, small change tended to stay in the New World, and when on occasion it was sunk at sea on ships returning to Spain, the coins were much quicker to corrode into mere slivers of silver.

CHAPTER 9

Coins from Lima, Cartagena, Santa Fé de Bogotá, and Guatemala

Very early cobs from the first two decades (1568–1588) of mint operations at Lima often are of excellent workmanship. They carry certain design characteristics, such as commas between words in the legend, that help distinguish them from the early Potosí series that are generally similar; coins from both mints may have the same initials, "R," "M," "B," and "L," but they represent different assayers as we notice by comparing table 9.1 with the Potosí assayers in table 8.4.

The Lima Stars

In recent years there has been controversy regarding origin and design of the so-called Lima stars[1] shown in figure 9.1. Before the worldwide search for sunken wrecks that began a few decades ago only a handful of these strange coins were known to collectors. With the discovery of the Jupiter Wreck on the southeast coast of Florida in 1991, choice specimens suddenly began to be offered in European auctions where they attracted great interest and generated much speculation as to their rarity and authenticity. Today so many examples have now been recovered from this wreck that it is evident these were not samples being sent to the king for his inspection. Lima mint records discussed below prove they were produced in large quantities that were clearly meant to facilitate commerce.

Fortunately, Dargent Chamot (1988: 40–45) was able to clarify the situation and show that these coins were produced on orders of the viceroy, Count Alba de Liste, but without direct authorization from the king, making them a very tricky matter indeed. They were struck under supervision of chief assayer of the viceroyalty, Francisco de Villegas,

Table 9.1. Lima Mint Assayers

Mark	Assayer Name	Term of Office
"R"	Alonso de Rincón	1568–1572
"X"	Xinés Martínez	1573?
"M"	Xinés Martínez	1573?
"B"	Juan de Bruselas	1574
"L"	[Baltazar de Leceta?]	1575–1577
"D"	Diego de la Torre	1577–1588
"V"	Francisco de Villegas	1658–1660
"V"	Francisco de Villegas	1684, 1689, 1690, 1692–1693
"R"	unknown	1685–1691, 1695, 1699
"M"	unknown	1694–1695
"H"	José Hurtado	1696–1711
"R"	unknown	1706
"M"	Cristóbal Cano Melgarejo	1722–1727
"N"	Joaquin Negron	1728–1740
"V"	José de Vargas y Flor	1739–1748
"R"	José Rodríguez	1748–1750
"J"	José Rodríguez Carasa	1751–1753
"JD"	José Rodríguez Carasa, Domingo Eyzaguirre?	1754–1755
"JM"	José Rodríguez Carasa, Manuel Iglesia Abarca	1755–1774
"MJ"	Manuel Iglesia Abarca, José Rodríguez Carasa	1773–1780
"MI"	Manuel Iglesia Abarca, Ignacio Zenon Galvez	1780–1787
"IJ"	Ignacio Zenon Galvez, Juan Martinez de Roxas	1787–1803
"JI"	Juan Martinez de Roxas, Ignacio Zenon Galvez	1797
"JP"	Juan Martinez de Roxas, Pablo Cano Melgarejo	1803–1823

Sources: Cunietti-Ferrando (1972); Pellicer i Bru (1975); Lazo García (1992); Sedwick and Sedwick (1995).

whose initial "V" is prominently displayed but in varying locations as design elements seem to change from one die to the next. When we look at the coins shown in this figure we see they are all made from remarkably round planchets, a characteristic that carries through to the smallest denomination.

These coins have radically different obverses from any other Spanish colonial coin because the mint name LIMA is fully spelled out across the field (best seen in figure 9.1a).[2] Without explicit instructions from the Crown this design must be considered a Peruvian invention that can best be described, in my opinion, as having a kind of savage eye appeal.

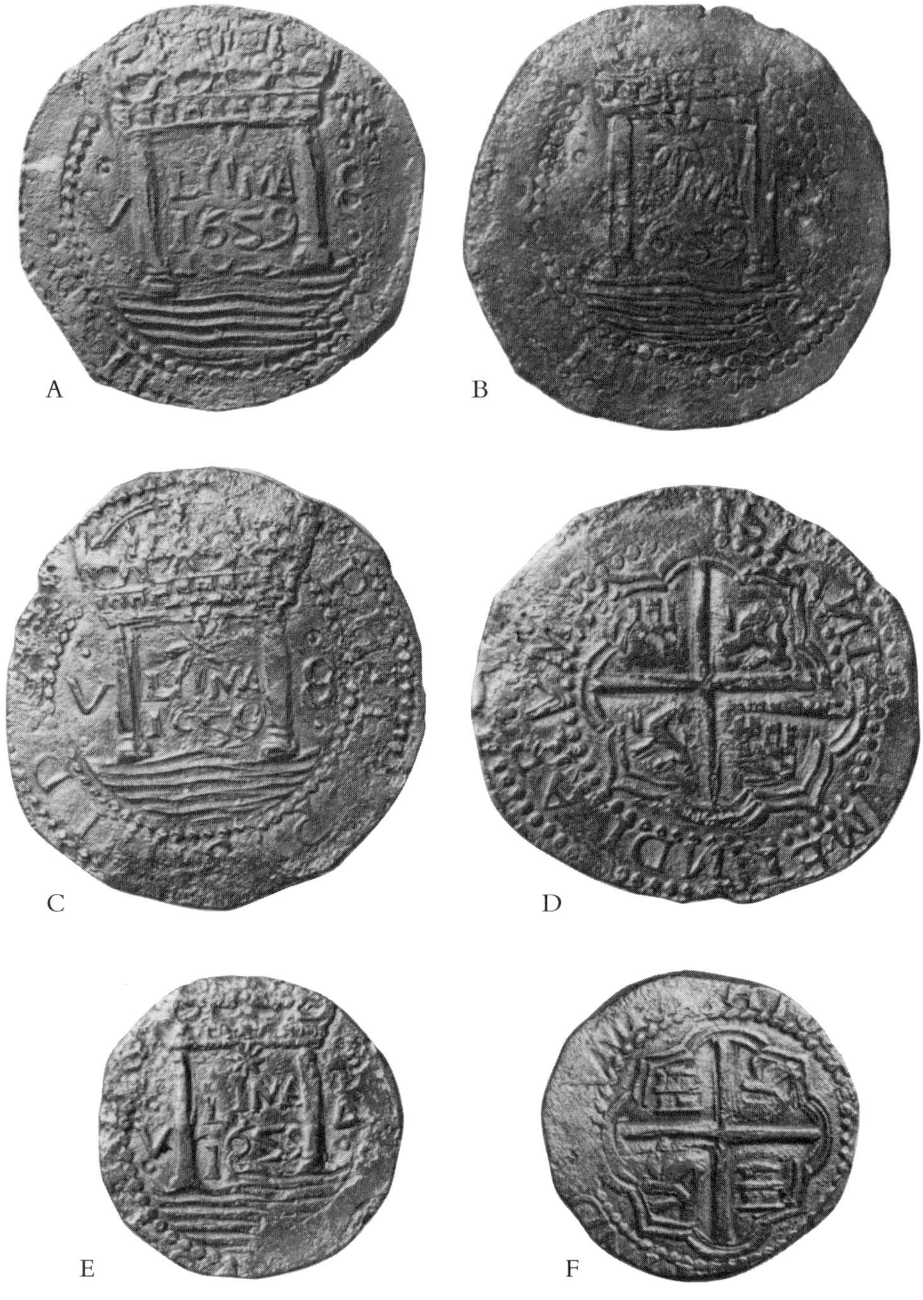

Figure 9.1. Lima Star 8- and 4-Reales Cobs of 1659

In figure 9.1b a conspicuous eight-pointed star appears above the city name.[3]

On the other hand, reverse design is the standard cross with lions and castles surrounded with a legend in the long-established pattern found on silver cobs from Potosí until 1652. In other words, the die maker had instructions from someone to create a new obverse design but was not required to invent a new reverse. Why Lima workers chose to ignore coin design regulations already mandated by an earlier *Cédula Real* and promulgated by a previous viceroy remains an enigma. Whatever the reason, Lima star legends in all denominations are characterized by retrograde "N's," leading me to believe they were all cut by the same engraver.

Data published by Lazo García (1992, 3: 343–345) provide us with exact mintage figures and show preparations to strike silver with this unusual design began on December 11, 1658. It is this date that was first engraved on poorly made dies of the 8-reales denomination. However, there were delays in production, and the 8 of the date was partially removed and overstamped with a 9, traces of the earlier date still being faintly visible on some specimens in the Florida Collection. According to Lazo García's data, the first production run took place on January 21, 1659, when coins worth 22,686 pesos in value were struck. There is no breakdown by denomination for any of the seventy-six days of the year when the mint was producing these new coins. But we do know the total value was a very substantial 2,122,867 pesos from which I conclude it is likely that substantially more than 1 million 8-reales coins were struck.

By comparison, coins of this new design dated 1660 were only made on twenty-six days that year and the total value reached 562,338 pesos, suggesting perhaps some 300,000 were 8 reales. All Lima star coins in the Florida Collection (except for one from Lease 1329) came from divisions of the numismatically important Jupiter Wreck material, which presumably was lost in 1659.

Many fanciful ideas about the nature and mission of the vessel that sank near present-day Jupiter Inlet have been created by the salvage community to explain and enhance the peculiar assortment of artifacts recovered and the presence of so many Lima stars. Some apparently relevant documents from Sevilla have been announced but there is as yet no cargo manifest found to make an unequivocal identification of this vessel. Meanwhile, gold and silver treasure continues to be recovered each season in a pattern suggesting to me more than one wreck is involved in the immediate area.

Although somewhat outside the scope of this book on silver coins, there is relevant and fascinating information in Lazo García (1992, 2: 155–159) regarding the excessively rare gold coins also struck in Lima at the same time as the stars. From a total of 1,234 doubloons of 8 escudos during 1659, a shipment of 1,000 is recorded as having been prepared on September 25 for dispatch to the king. Lazo García (1992, 2: 158) reproduces a photo of such a specimen published by Dargent Chamot in which the reverse design of the gold coin is radically different and clearly copied from those being made at that time from Bogotá.

The letter "N" is not retrograde and the caption implies it is a fabrication.

Spanish catalogers have long maintained at least one such specimen has been known to Spanish collectors since before the time of their Civil War when it disappeared. We are left to wonder where the others are. Did they all arrive safely in Spain only to be melted, or are they still submerged somewhere along the coast of Florida?

Reopening of the Mint

We know less about the Lima assayers' identities than those of assayers at any other large mint.[4] For instance, in 1684 work began under "V" (Francisco Villegas), who was replaced by "R" the next year. These two assayers alternated over the next few years until 1694 when "M" appeared briefly; "R" returned to work in 1695, 1699, and 1706 (but perhaps this was not the same person). In 1696 "H" first began and ended in 1710 when "M" (Cristóbal Melgarejo) also functioned and continued until 1729.[5]

Lima cobs with the standard design required by coinage reforms of 1652 did not appear until the mint officially reopened in 1684. Table 9.2 shows the annual mintage of all cob coins until 1747 when provision for milled coinage was underway. Collectors have long recognized Lima cobs of all denominations are less common than those of the same period produced in Potosí.[6] Lima coins produced before the year 1700, while not common, have been more available than later dates. The scarcity today of Lima silver cobs after 1707, and their rarity in 1713, is reflected in table 9.2; to some minor extent this may be due to losses occasioned by the 1715 shipwrecks. However, we must look to more fundamental explanations for a long-term decline in mint production that does not seem to have been overcome until the last decade of the eighteenth century. These facts are reflected in the distribution tables discussed in chapter 6.

Fortunately, the Florida Collection has a fine run of Lima 8 reales, selected specimens of which are shown in figure 9.2, beginning with the year 1696 and extending to 1711. All these coins came to the collection in divisions of coins salvaged from the 1715 Fleet. None came from other wreck sites or land-based excavations.

In figure 9.2 we see immediately that Lima 8-reales coins are characterized by their uniformity of excellent die engraving, relatively round shape, and lack of striking irregularities that plagued the Potosí mint. There is no escaping the conclusion mint workers in Lima were better artisans in every respect.[7] If we disregard effects of saltwater corrosion on these coins, it is evident they show few signs of having been in

Table 9.2. Lima Silver Coins by Date and Denomination, 1684–1747

All values shown are in pesos. To determine the number of 4 reales multiply pesos x 2; 2 reales = x 4; 1 real = x 8; ½ real = x 16.

Year	8 reales	4 reales	2 reales	1 real	½ real	Taxes	Total
1684	3,848,011	435,436	47,903	91,731	90,341	194,894	4,867,567
1685	2,615,586	266,405	91,508	191,398	63,072	129,234	3,228,043
1686	1,552,095	156,071	84,328	181,679	N.A.*	79,035	1,974,176
1687	1,394,161	155,138	83,339	163,600	N.A.	71,963	1,797,521
1688	788,456	99,503	52,900	101,377	N.A.	41,792	1,043,912
1689	858,656	112,886	51,925	118,657	N.A.	45,726	1,142,175
1690	962,129	122,978	56,799	126,161	N.A.	50,766	1,268,068
1691	547,180	79,939	38,962	60,155	N.A.	29,074	726,238
1692	1,636,475	190,439	112,886	170,930	N.A.	84,502	2,110,731
1693	1,362,897	121,653	81,808	150,449	5,939	68,985	1,723,156
1694	1,518,362	156,486	77,013	178,856	13,400	77,382	1,944,181
1695	1,705,493	182,073	90,357	196,042	12,654	87,614	2,188,434
1696	1,858,085	207,239	107,941	242,959	7,654	97,120	2,425,908
1697	1,402,594	149,016	109,009	108,188	7,163	74,874	1,776,086
1698	1,450,931	170,037	107,040	124,888	6,561	74,444	1,859,459
1699	N.A.	N.A.	N.A.	N.A.	N.A.	N.A.	N.A.
1700	1,113,003	131,407	90,772	104,505	16,999	59,132	1,477,023
1701	1,095,617	124,695	86,488	104,719	19,886	57,336	1,432,162
1702	798,095	96,990	75,869	77,787	18,818	42,933	1,072,390
1703	1,072,402	132,743	96,253	95,248	39,974	57,600	1,483,739
1704	879,383	118,361	83,850	75,308	41,851	48,002	1,199,015
1705	1,023,818	143,242	95,389	89,713	41,130	55,420	1,384,294
1706	967,614	118,816	90,299	89,480	41,933	50,972	1,309,817
1707	690,786	83,327	55,275	62,561	28,014	36,830	919,960
1708	237,774	30,702	18,796	19,905	12,038	12,779	319,217
1709	531,575	61,874	45,170	45,359	26,618	28,448	710,598
1710	435,809	57,645	39,228	35,948	23,815	23,719	592,455
1711	451,379	49,915	36,841	42,829	27,221	24,351	608,259
1712	294,783	39,220	29,722	22,927	19,805	16,512	412,459
1713	74,746	8,693	7,512	6,130	4,705	4,075	101,788
1714	270,051	26,456	22,888	24,563	17,948	14,489	361,909
1715	100,902	8,115	13,492	9,505	6,809	5,557	138,825
1716	210,557	29,482	23,106	24,112	15,316	12,129	302,976
1717	562,917	65,015	53,876	52,667	33,695	30,757	768,256
1718	1,210,489	156,076	120,172	112,122	61,205	66,474	1,660,401
1719	1,205,154	144,828	111,697	114,888	62,414	65,643	1,639,653
1720	914,843	103,255	86,614	83,900	54,998	49,788	1,243,612
1721	744,755	92,711	73,557	69,236	47,642	41,155	1,027,981
1722	817,936	83,163	75,994	78,019	54,033	44,438	1,109,993
1723	1,090,718	102,208	94,448	95,573	70,810	58,361	1,457,761
1724	835,908	77,058	73,758	76,195	54,565	44,739	1,117,503
1725	1,402,427	132,006	125,239	115,851	75,363	74,100	1,850,889
1726	822,533	79,453	71,673	65,969	54,392	43,799	1,094,022
1727	1,153,698	112,635	103,582	92,881	73,855	61,522	1,536,704

continued on next page

Table 9.2—*continued*

Year	8 reales	4 reales	2 reales	1 real	½ real	Taxes	Total
1728	1,134,159	106,052	110,918	86,815	69,508	60,351	1,507,454
1729	N.A.	N.A.	N.A.	N.A.	N.A.	N.A.	N.A.
1730	1,564,739	194,930	164,577	128,766	58,441	114,340	2,111,468
1731	966,671	114,376	114,597	83,784	44,424	71,689	1,323,858
1732	1,088,799	125,154	122,408	94,256	55,191	80,462	1,485,852
1733	958,893	114,352	109,429	87,932	52,972	71,706	1,324,156
1734	1,037,739	127,347	120,980	97,996	57,749	78,007	1,441,813
1735	1,157,198	123,241	117,138	98,617	62,900	84,431	1,559,155
1736	1,062,066	122,502	106,853	83,504	63,716	77,905	1,438,642
1737	1,499,918	169,529	153,212	117,631	89,454	109,918	2,029,809
1738	1,535,389	159,077	146,846	111,112	79,385	110,026	2,031,806
1739	1,863,727	186,872	168,495	129,933	93,313	132,257	2,442,331
1740	1,405,084	127,925	128,222	100,257	81,285	99,790	1,842,775
1741	1,541,891	156,697	145,511	108,553	88,111	110,512	2,040,774
1742	1,404,829	139,969	121,414	94,919	73,593	99,355	1,834,751
1743	1,371,152	104,703	118,524	95,106	69,912	95,275	1,759,398
1744	1,230,511	99,560	109,930	81,770	69,394	86,257	1,592,866
1745	1,267,052	95,531	110,160	86,725	71,017	88,294	1,630,487
1746	1,320,109	92,956	96,483	81,549	71,995	90,110	1,664,020
1747	811,384	74,689	73,984	55,709	45,220	57,454	1,060,987

Note: Cob coins continued to be issued until 1752, when they were replaced by milled coinage. Records for these last years can be found in the source used to compile this table (Lazo García 1992).

*N.A. (not available) indicates records are incomplete or missing.

circulation, especially the coins dated 1703, 1706, 1708, 1710, and 1711 shown in figure 9.2f–j. This raises a possibility they were being kept out of circulation in the Royal Treasury at Lima until such time as the king became desperate for funds and the 1715 Fleet could finally be assembled. In any event, these specimens are some of the finest known.

Figure 9.2. A–B. Lima 8-Reales Cobs, 1696–1711

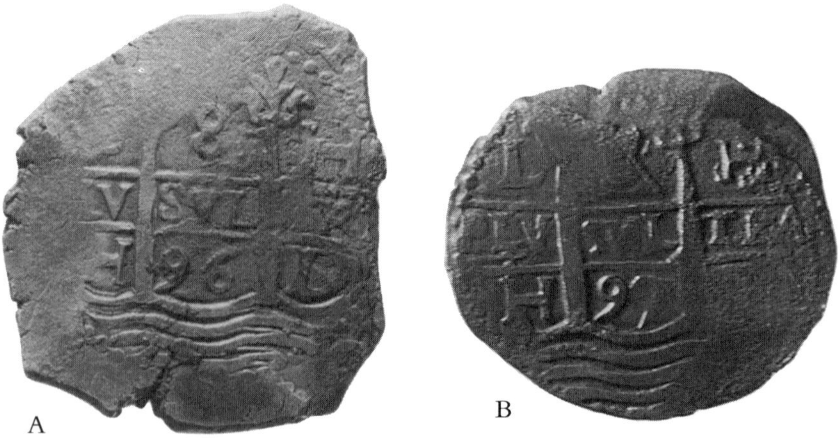

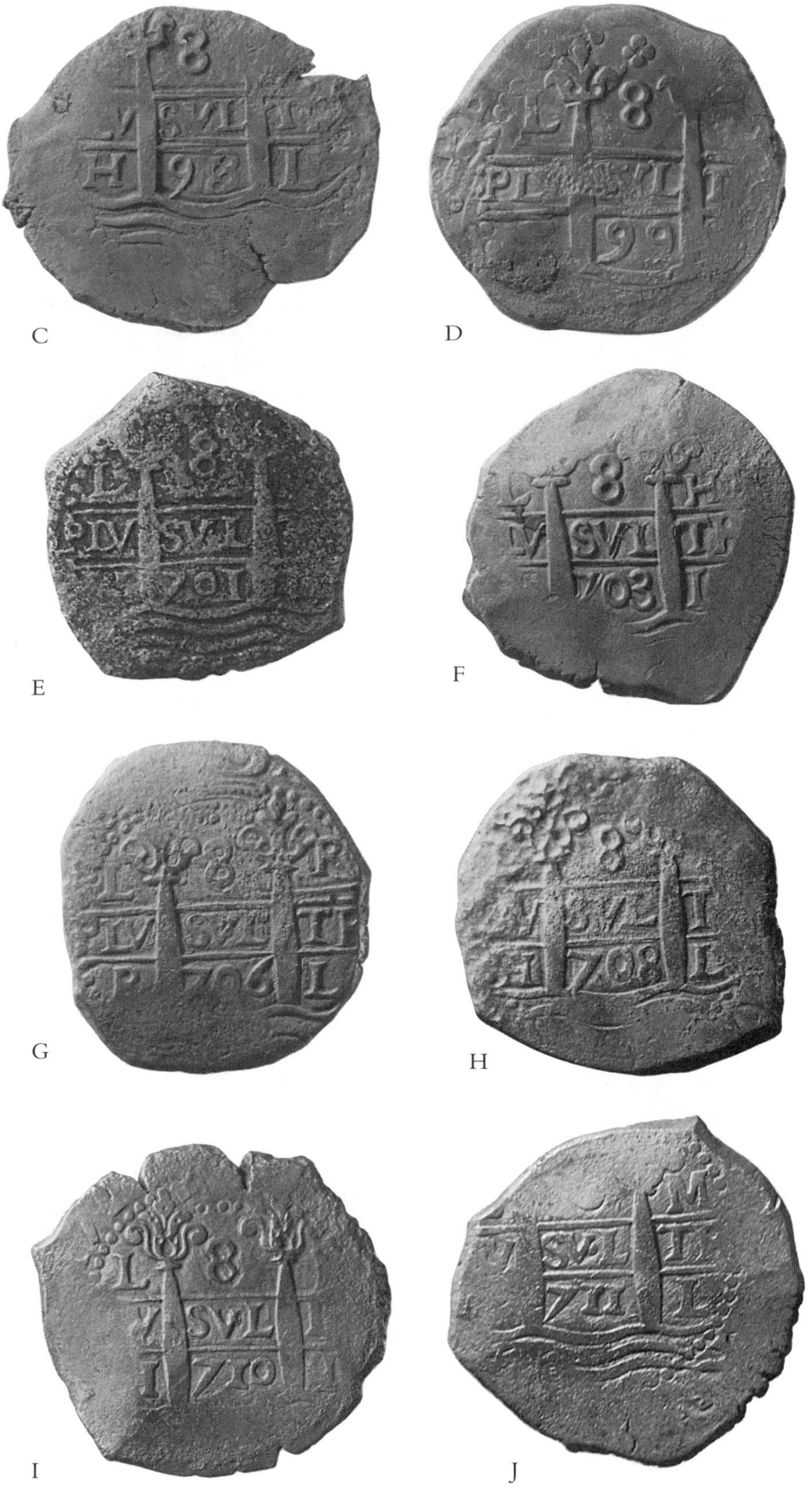

Figure 9.2. C–J.
Lima 8-Reales
Cobs, 1696–1711

Six selected Lima 4-reales cobs are illustrated in figure 9.3. Readers are invited to compare the distinctive "swollen" shape of the Potosí 4's with the typical straight-sided 4's of Lima. The comparatively calm sea waves of Lima coins are another diagnostic design feature helpful in identifying coins where mint mark and assayer have been obliterated.

An inspection of engravers' private marks on coins immediately above the denomination show a wide range, even within this very small sample: 9.3a has a four-pellet cross; 9.3b and 9.3c both have single large dots; details are missing from 9.3d, e but 9.3f is a three-dot variety.[8]

Coin 9.4d, a Lima 8 reales, is an interesting example of a die that once was thoroughly cleaned by tooling to remove rust on two separate occasions. We can determine this because the background field shows two sets of closely spaced, intersecting diagonal striations. They were made with a *buril* blade in order to scrape off a coating of rust or scale from the face of the iron die before elements of the coin design were cut and punched in. As a result, die face cleaning grooves intersect the 3 of the 1693 date, making it appear to be an overdate, which it is not. There is an obvious centering dot to be seen between letters "V" and "L" in the central motto "(P)LVSV.LTRA." This dot was used to scribe a compass circle on the die face that was then used to position and

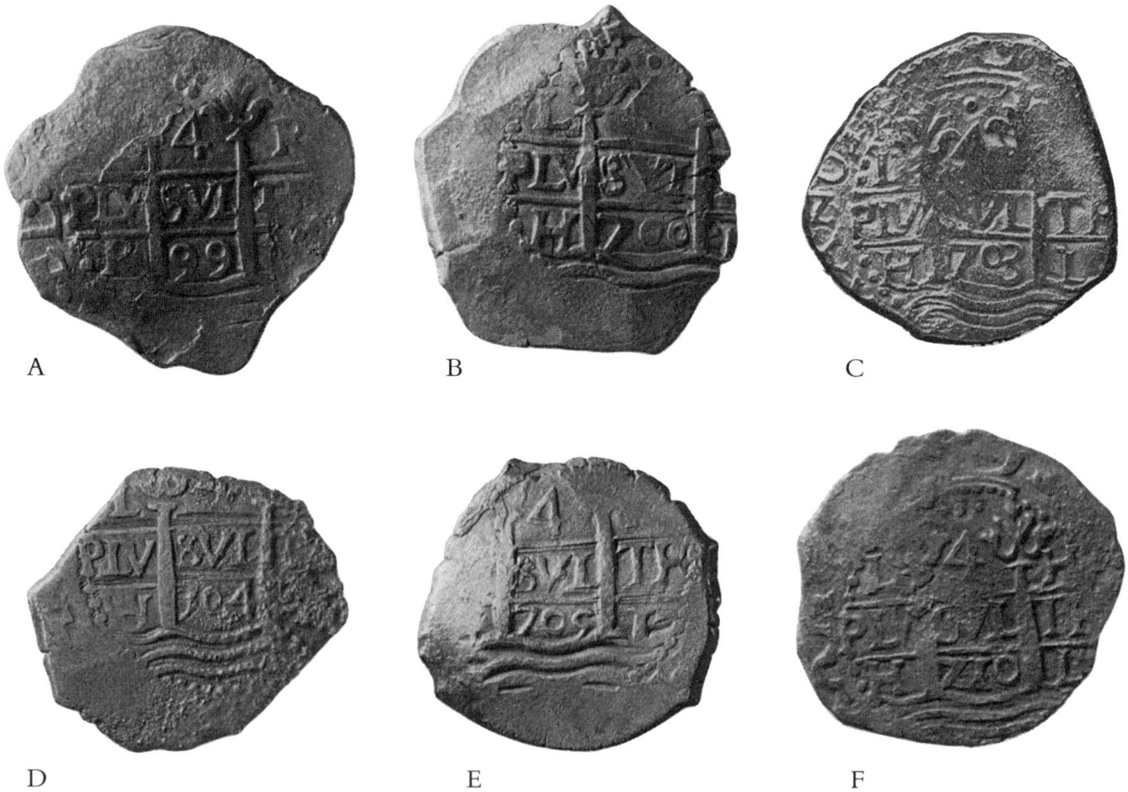

Figure 9.3. Lima 4-Reales Cobs, 1699–1710

facilitate punching in a series of closely spaced larger dots to form the inner border for the legend.

Once this center point was established, denomination 8 and date 93 were positioned equidistant above and below and in vertical alignment. From this moment on design elements were not so tightly controlled and we can see letter punches of different sizes were used to complete the mint mark, assayer's letter, and motto. Lack of any dots above the denomination suggests this die was cut by the chief engraver, who presumably was the most skillful and experienced on the staff of the Lima mint at that time.

Coin 9.4f, a Lima 4 reales of 1695, provides a close look at a clear example of the troublesome Spanish number 5 as it appears in the date. Fives in this old style can easily be mistaken for the number 9, but here we see the downstroke of the 5 is straight rather than curved as is usually the case with 9's from this mint at this time. Additionally, we note the inner border of dots clearly follows a scribed circle which the dots partially obliterate. The distinction between 9's and 5's can be seen to advantage on figure 9.4g, a 1699 Lima 8 reales, with a nicely rendered die where curved tails of 9's are strongly developed in contrast to the straight tail of a similar-looking 5.

The center point pattern is more clearly developed in coin 9.4e, a Lima 8 reales of 1694. The small center point can barely be seen beside the right-hand arm of the central "V." This same feature is less clear in coin 9.4c, a Lima 4 reales of 1692. Another Lima 8 reales of 1684, the first year this design was issued, seems unusually complex at first glance. Perhaps for this very reason someone decided to make a hole in coin 9.4a–b and suspend it as an ornament. Beneath the date we see an upside-down "RV" and to the left of it, the left side of the obverse crown rotated nearly 180 degrees from its usual position immediately above the denomination (figure 9.4a). The reverse (cross) side (9.4b) also has bizarre features. A very large "L" mint mark is conspicuous opposite the left arm of the cross, but assayer's letter "V" has been left out entirely, as has the tail of the upper-right lion. A vague three-digit date appears below the cross and seems to read 688 (hardly possible since the obverse date is clearly 1684), or possibly 683 which is equally unlikely since the mint supposedly did not open until the following year.

How do we explain this coin? Since the reverse is in no way doubled, it seems likely the obverse die was properly placed and fully struck after which the die was entirely rotated, held at a high angle, and tentatively struck again while the planchet itself remained firmly seated. Even stranger things can happen in the world of hand-struck cobs.

Rather poor spacing of an obverse motto is shown by coin 9.4h–i, a Lima 8 reales of 1703, where planning ahead did not result in enough

Figure 9.4. Lima Die Varieties, 1684–1703

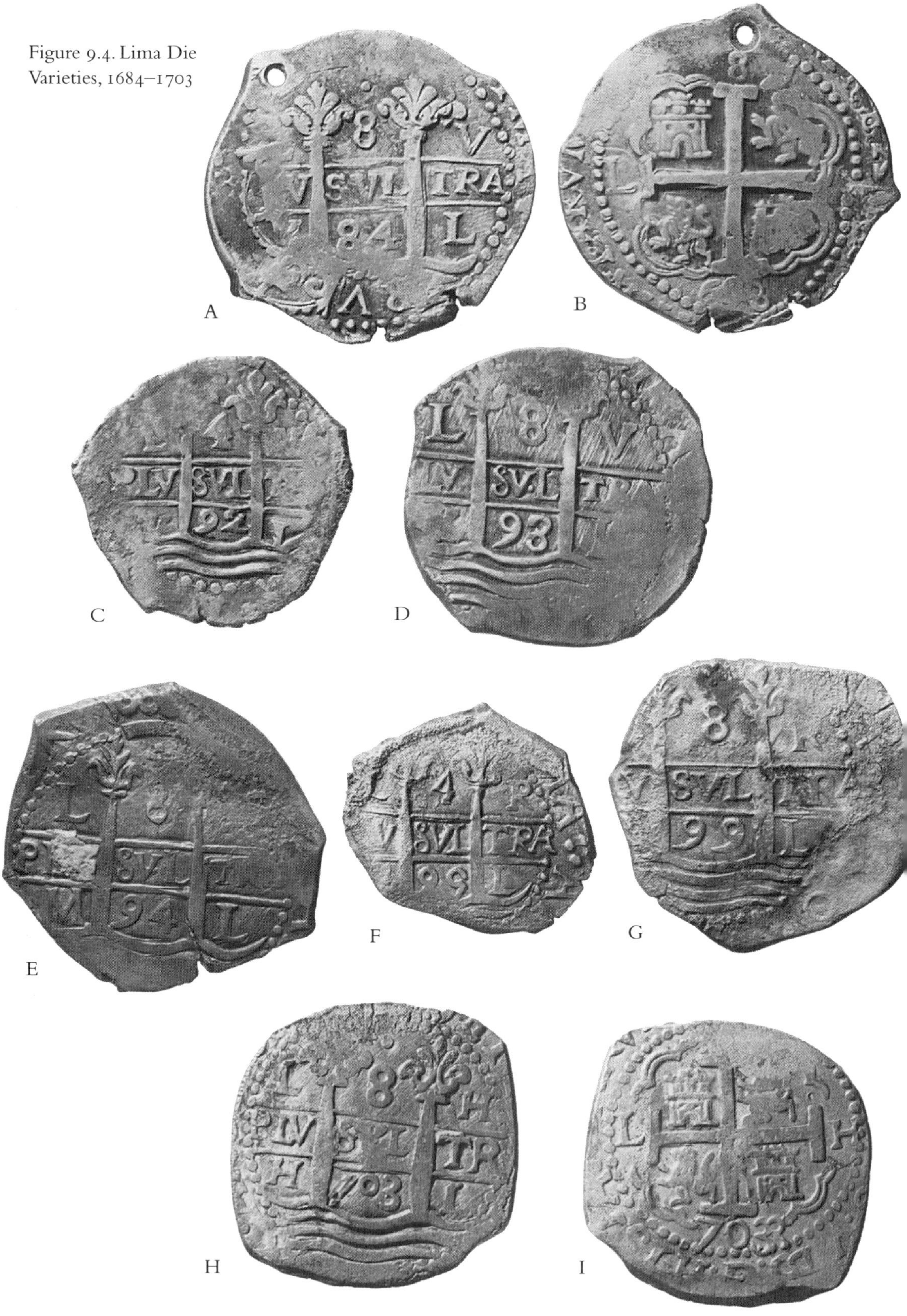

room to fit in the final letter "A" of "PLUS ULTRA." This single-dot assistant engraver was forced to use a very small zero (9.4h) in order to crowd in a full three-digit date of 703. The reverse (9.4i) of this coin shows die chatter in a very narrow diagonal sector of the planchet causing the 3 of the date to be doubled along with the letter "D" of the adjacent legend. Very narrow doublings of this type with the remainder of the design unaffected are not common.

If we compare 1703 dates of coin 9.3c with coin 9.4h, we see differences in workmanship by the same(?) one-dot engraver, especially so in relative size of zeros in the 1703 date. But faint die-cleaning striations on the field of coin 9.4h indicate it was temporarily put aside, became rusty, and had a somewhat clumsy date punched in. The possibility exists this could have been done by yet another apprentice engraver.

Coin 9.5a is a Lima 8 reales of 1704 struck from a worn die in which the number 4 has been punched in repeatedly, enlarging the number but leaving traces of an earlier number still visible. Again, the final "A" of the motto is lost for lack of space.

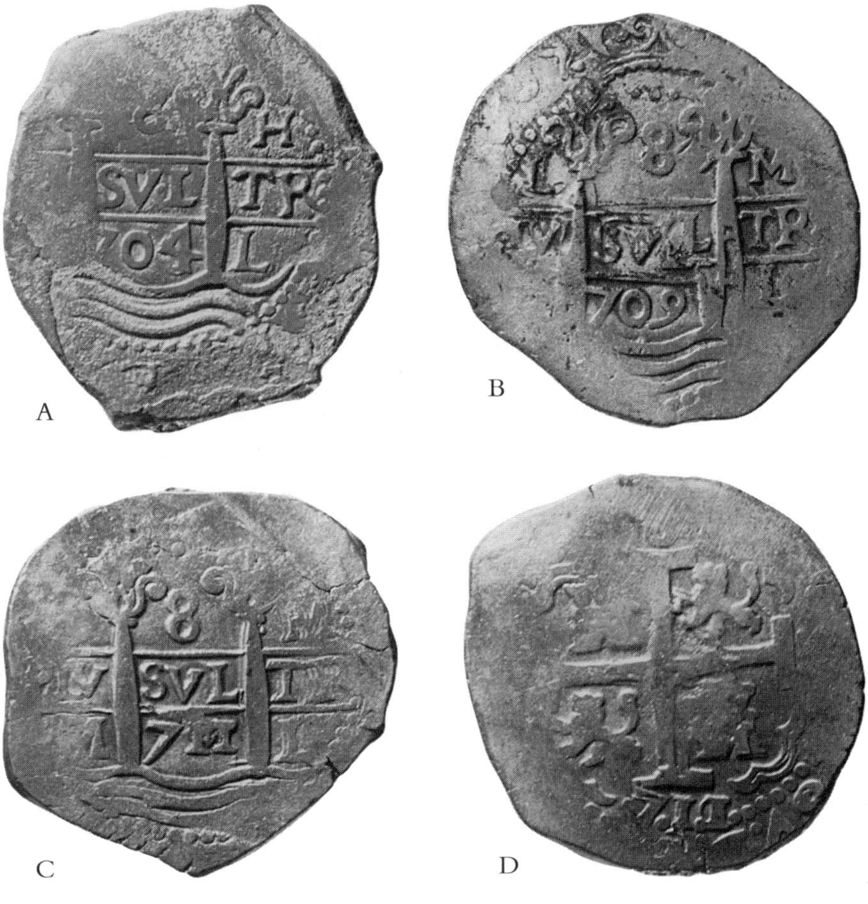

Figure 9.5. Lima Die Varieties, 1704–1711

A B C D

The three-dot assistant engraver who cut dies for coin 9.5b, a Lima 8 reales of 1709, had no such trouble in spacing the date—his numbers are all large and clear—but the Florida Collection specimen shown here is otherwise garbled by partial doubling.

Die bounce has slightly doubled the right side of a Lima 8 reales of 1711 (9.5c) but the most notable feature of the coin is breakdown of the die around the 11, resulting in a flawed date. Another Lima 8 reales (9.5d) has a reverse 1711 date, which is clearly punched in over a die made for the year 1710.

Three Coins from Cartagena de Indias

Of all Spanish colonial mints, none is so well researched and documented as the mint at Santa Fé de Bogotá in outstanding monographs by Barriaga Villalba (1969) and Friede (1963). These scholarly studies are seldom read by North American numismatists, but they contain valuable data on a wide range of topics, including information on other colonial mints as well. They are perhaps most useful for clarifying the matter of a coin workshop opened in 1620 at Cartagena for striking of *vellón rico* (an alloy of one part silver with four parts of copper). The purpose of these low-value coins was to facilitate trade between principal settlements in Nueva Granada (now Columbia) that suffered from a chronic shortage of small change.[9]

Barriaga Villalba (1969: 16–21) describes in detail the design of these coins and the exact number that was struck in Cartagena by the famous Spanish military engineer Captain Alonso Turrillo de Yebra and his assistant, Salazar. But after strong protests from local merchants, these coins were recalled and not a single specimen is known to have survived.

In a lawsuit dated May 22, 1654, there are details showing Turrillo's workers struck up 58,160 *marcos* of silver into 8-, 4-, and 2-reales coins and, without authorization, converted 10,124 *marcos* of gold into 1- and 2-escudo coins. In Turillo's absence, Salazar used the Cartagena workshop to produce 87,459 *marcos* of silver coins and 15,115 *marcos* of gold coins. From the same documents we find that over a period from 1619 to 1654, coins were made from a total of 145,619 *marcos* of silver. At 67 reales to the *marco,* if all were struck as 8 reales, Cartagena and Santa Fé together would have made about 1,219,559 coins if all were pieces of eight. Of course the actual number was more because a few coins of smaller denominations are known to exist.

Losses on board treasure ships of the Atocha Fleet and subsequent sinkings such as the *San José* in 1708 may help to account for the poor survival record of these coins. But we are left wondering why silver cobs of Nueva Granada are the most difficult for collectors to obtain in view of the production totals for Cartagena and Santa Fé de Bogotá.

From Florida waters (but outside its territorial limits) several 1622 gold coins struck in Cartagena by Turrillo have been recovered by salvors including the most remarkable of all, a 1 escudo of assayer "E" dated 1619.[10]

It is fortunate that to date the Florida Collection contains three specimens of the rare and little-known silver cobs produced by successors to Turrillo de Yebra in the year 1655 at Cartagena de Indias in what is now Colombia. These remarkable coins, an 8, a 4, and a 2 reales, are illustrated in figure 9.6a–f. They also came to the Florida Collection from divisions of the Jupiter Wreck artifacts.[11] Silver coins from Cartagena, Guatemala, Santa Fé de Bogotá, and Zacatecas mints are summarized in table 9.3.

The die engraver at Cartagena made a reasonably good interpretation of new design requirements promulgated in 1651 for coins of 1652, and certainly nothing like the bizarre workmanship on the Lima stars. Here there are pillars and waves with the familiar motto "PLUS ULTRA" placed in two lines. The date appears only once in the obverse legend at 11 o'clock as 1655. The reverse contains a simple, but strongly defined shield with rampant lions and castles in the accustomed quarters. However, the lions in both specimens have peculiar recurved tails, the ends of which touch the backs of the lion's heads.

Another interesting feature of the coin shown in figure 9.6a–b is the medallic orientation of the two sides with the dies rotated exactly 90 degrees from each other. This phenomenon has not been seen in any other treasure coin in the Florida Collection. It means a special effort was made to place dies in this position. The large-diameter planchet, now badly corroded, also may have been specially prepared in order to contain the complete design. Slight die bounce of the upper (shield) die is evident.

The 4 and 2 reales (figure 9.6c–f) show a distinct "C" above "S," confirming their Cartagena origin. Neither has a legible date but there is no reason to suppose they were not made in 1655, since no other dates are known for this decade. With so few specimens to study, not much more can be said about this rare issue. The reasons why these coins were struck at Cartagena instead of the better-equipped mint at Bogotá are no doubt to be found someday in archival records.

Table 9.3. Silver Coins from Guatemala, Santa Fé de Bogotá, Cartagena, and Zacatecas Mints by Date, Assayer, and Denomination

Guatemala			
1779	"P"	8 reales	1
1780	"P"	2 reales	1
1790	"M"	1 real	1
1790	N.V.*	2 reales	1
1796	N.V.	1 real	1
1796	"M"	8 reales	1
1804	"M"	2 reales	1
1805	"M"	8 reales	1
1806	"M"	8 reales	1
1807	"M"	8 reales	1
1808	"M"	8 reales	1
Subtotal			11
Santa Fé de Bogotá			
1652	?	8 reales	1
1657	?	4 reales	1
Date unknown	?	8 reales	1
Date unknown	?	4 reales	1
Date unknown	?	2 reales	1
Subtotal			5
Cartagena			
1655	N.V.	8 reales	1
1655	"S"	4 reales	1
1655	"S"	2 reales	1
Subtotal			3
Zacatecas			
1821	N.V.	½ real	1
Subtotal			1
Total			20

Source: Florida Bureau of Archaeological Research computer database.
*N.V. (not visible) indicates the assayer's mark is not visible.

Coins of Santa Fé de Bogotá

The coin shown in both obverse and reverse in figure 9.6g–h is a badly corroded specimen of this rare series. It is one of five from the Nuevo Reino de Granada viceroyalty and one of only two identified as Santa Fé de Bogotá in the collection. A faint pomegranate at the base of the shield and the small cross of five pellets immediately to the right of the shield are the only features that can be used with confidence to distinguish it from yet another of the even rarer Cartagena coins. The char-

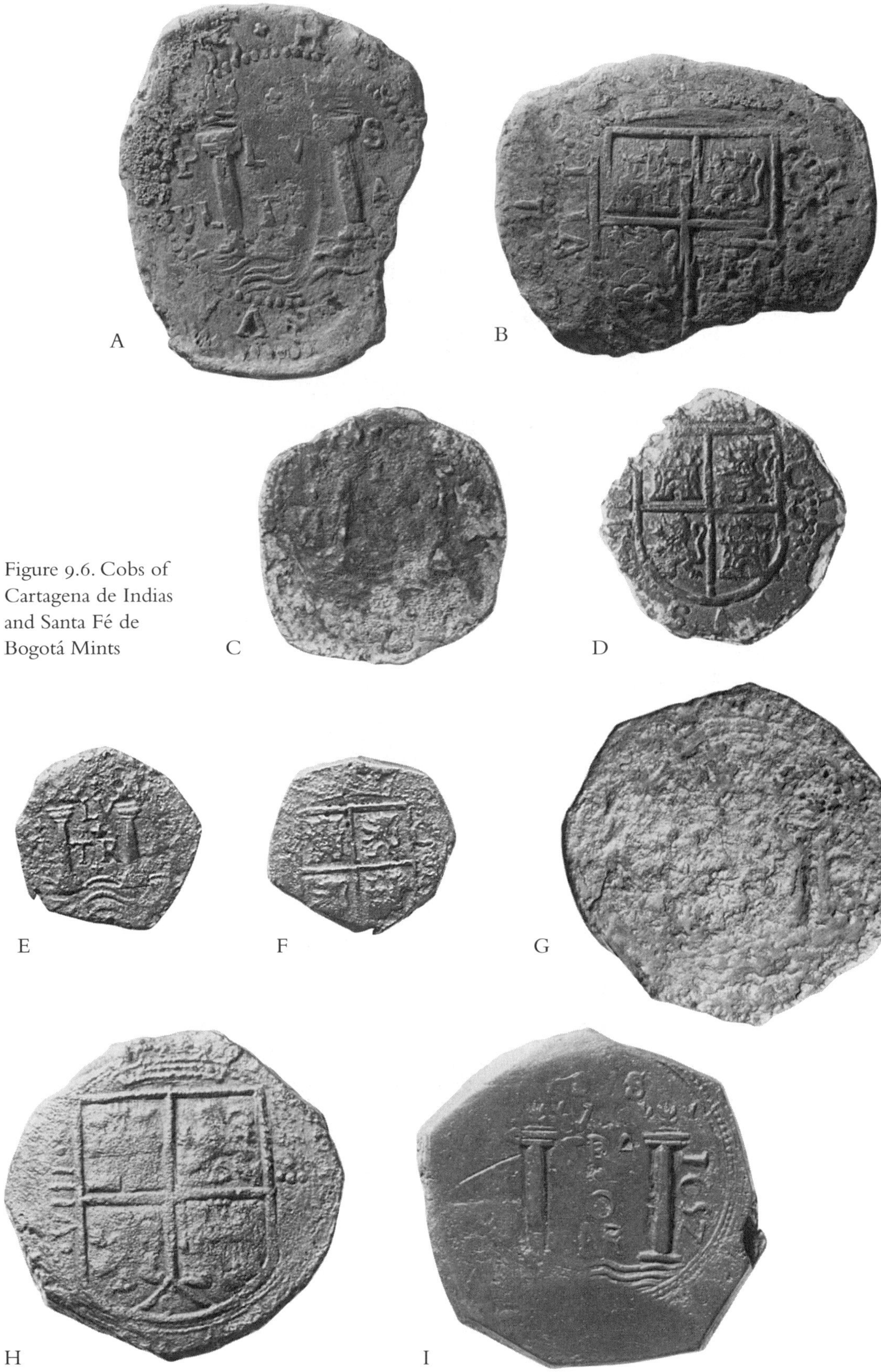

Figure 9.6. Cobs of Cartagena de Indias and Santa Fé de Bogotá Mints

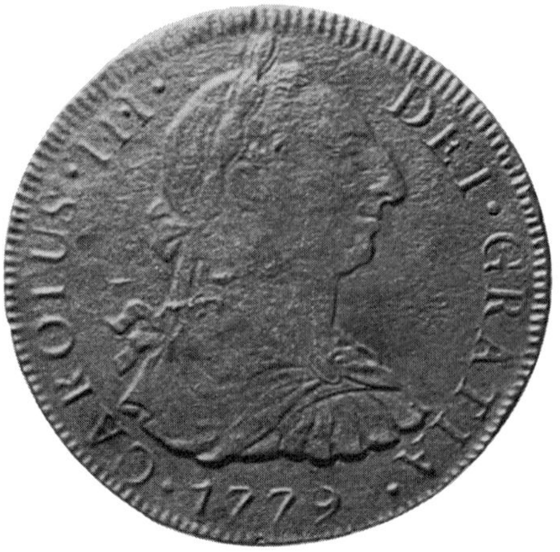

Figure 9.7. Guatemala 8-Reales of 1779

acteristic polygonal sheared sides of the Bogotá planchets are seen here, but with only one year of poorly preserved Cartagena planchets for comparison, this distinction may not prove to be valid.

Unfortunately, it is the more interesting side with Pillars of Hercules that bears the ligature "No Ro" (Nuevo Reino) mint mark and assayer's letters; in this case they were probably some combination of "PoRAS." What is missing here can be seen in the photograph of Tipo 104 on page 265 of Calicó et al. (1994). The overall condition of shield side suggests this was an outstanding, newly minted coin when it found its way on board a ship that was to become the Jupiter Wreck.

From this same wreck site another excellent, fully dated Colombian 8 reales of 1652 from the Santa Fé de Bogotá mint has recently been recovered. Figure 9.6i shows it maintains the same austere design of earlier years that was not required to be changed in 1652 as was the design of corrupt coins issuing from the Potosí mint.

Guatemalan Portrait 8 R's

Only eleven coins from the Guatemala mint have found their way into the Florida Collection. They all came from a single shipwreck that sank off the Florida east coast in 1810. It is not surprising more have not been encountered on other Florida wrecks because this mint did not issue any cobs and only began milled coinage production in 1736, too late for them to have been on board either of the major fleets of 1715 and 1733.

All Guatemala coins held by the state show evidence of considerable saltwater corrosion. An 8 reales of 1779 is the most significant of the group and is illustrated as figure 9.7. This scarce coin does not deviate in any way from the standard design and has no outstanding features, but it is seldom seen in collections.

CHAPTER 10

Numismatic Significance of the Florida Collection

This slowly growing Florida Collection already constitutes the largest group of sea-salvaged Spanish colonial coins in existence. As such, it represents an invaluable historic and scientific resource belonging to citizens of the state of Florida. It is managed and curated by state officials in a prudent and scientific manner so that its educational and historic value will remain intact for generations to come. There is no other state collection in existence with similar scope and purpose. This complex governmental effort resulted from the determination of past and present state administrators to preserve a representative sample of these coins, many of them of considerable historic as well as intrinsic value.

The collection is already known to be largest and most complete in the world with respect to Spanish colonial gold from the first two decades of the eighteenth century (Craig 1989, 2000). Much the same can be said for holdings of 8-reales coins in silver, but only in terms of absolute numbers, because there are many dates and denominations missing both from very early and late colonial periods.

Several private collections exist that contain nearly complete date runs in the smaller denominations (½, 1, and 2 reales) from various Spanish colonial mints, particularly those of Potosí and Lima. Since the Florida Collection is based on samples of bulk specie being shipped back to Spain, it is deficient in these small denominations that were usually retained in the New World to support daily commerce. Those that were placed on board treasure galleons often did not survive well in the corrosive marine environment. The relatively small number of 4-reales coins in the collection reflects the fact they were never struck in such great numbers as 8-reales coins. Eights dominated colonial mint production and consequently make up the strength of the Florida Collection.

Future Research

Individual specimens aside, it is important to mention some of the most significant numismatic research on silver coins from the Florida Collection that may come in the future. Great progress is being made in the field of numismatic archaeometallurgy whereby we are learning some surprising facts regarding identification of source of metals involved and their diagnostic trace elements. A recent example (Craig and Gordus 1993: 133) is the discovery in the Florida Collection of the rare trace element iridium in all early colonial gold coins tested from the Santa Fé de Bogotá mint.

Previous work by Gordus and Gordus (1989) has traced dispersal of Potosí silver into coinage of Europe using the characteristic miniscule traces of gold as a marker. From such research we predict scholarly studies in numismatic metallurgy will provide even more insight into the role of Spanish colonial coins and bullion in the world economy. These testing methods, and other essentially nondestructive techniques (and surely others someday to be developed) will require readily available specimens in numbers for testing.

When a silver coin planchet is struck with dies, force of the blow causes instantaneous compression and expansion of the underlying molecular structure. This causes the die image to be faintly reflected deep into the planchet interior. Sometimes it is still possible to identify the original design on a badly corroded surface of a coin that has lost all of these design elements.

I am confident technology already exists to recover faint die-stamped impressions in ductile metal. It only remains for some dedicated future researcher to apply this methodology and identify hundreds of silver cobs now recorded in the Florida Collection as "unknown." If this process is developed, it may reveal data allowing us to make radical changes in our interpretation of events in Spanish colonial mints and consequences in commerce.

The Florida Collection continues to grow. During preparation of this study, the database was "closed" to create a fixed number of coins. Additions to the collection after the time of this study will be incorporated into future publications.

Appendix A: List of Equivalencies

1 *pie* = 0.27 meters.
1 *palmo* = 0.209 meters.
1 *paso geométrico* = 1.39 meters.
1 *vara* = 0.83 meter = 32.9 inches.
1 *estado* = 1.95 meters (approx.).
1 *toesa* = 1.95 meters = 1 French fathom = 2.13 English yards.
1 *estadio* = 125 *pasos geométricos* = 173.75 meters.
1 *legua* = 20,000 *pies* = 5.5 kilometers.
1 *marco* = 230.04 grams = 2,400 *maravedís* = 50 reales, later 67 reales, and finally 68 reales after the reforms of 1728.
1 *marco* = 8½ *doblones* (after 1755).
1 *arroba* = 25 *libras* = 11.5 kilograms.
1 *quintal* = 4 *arrobas* = 46 kilograms = 101.5 pounds avoirdupois, but also 100 lb. (United States) or 112 lb. (Great Britain).
1 *cajón* = 50 *quintales* = 2.3 metric tons.
1 *carga* = 3 *quintales.*
1 *libra* = 2 *marcos* = 1 pound.
1 *libra* = 460.1 grams = 134 reales.
1 *libra* avoirdupois = 453.6 *granos.*
1 *tomín* = 1 real = 34 *maravedís.*
1 *cuento* = 1,000,000 *maravedís* = 2,666 *ducados* = 2,000 *doblas de oro castellano.*
1 *dobla* = 2 *escudos.*
1 *doblón* = 880 *maravedís* (in 1609); = 35 reales (in 1652).
1 *peso* = 272 *maravedís.*
1 *peso ensayado* = 450 *maravedís* = 13.25 reales.
1 *peso de oro* = 1/50 *marco* = 1/100 pound of gold.

1 *peso corriente* = 8 reales.
1 *ducado* = 5/6 *peso ensayado* = 11 reales (approx.).
1 *dinero* = 24 *granos.*
1 *gramo* = 15.43 *granos.*
1 *onza troy* = 31.1 *granos* = 20 pennyweights.
1 pennyweight = 1/20 *onza* = 31.1 *granos.*
1 kilo = 32.15 *onzas troy.*
1 *frasco azogue* (mercury) = 76.5 *libras* = 34.7 kilos.

Mexican Weight Standards

1 *marco* = 8 *onzas* = 230.20 grams = 7.40 troy ounces.
1 *onza* = 8 *ochavos* = 28.765 grams = 0.92 troy ounces.
1 *ochavo* = 2 *adarmes* = 3.595 grams = 0.116 troy ounces.
1 *adarme* = 3 *tomínes* = 1.798 grams = 0.058 troy ounces.
1 *tomín* = 12 *granos* = 0.599 grams = 0.019 troy ounces.
1 *grano* = 0.049 grams = 0.0016 troy ounces.

Appendix B: A Virtual Visit to the Potosí Mint in the Year 1700

An extremely rare archival document published by Lazo García (1992) and translated here for the first time forms the basis of this unique opportunity to follow in great detail the exact process used at that mint to convert a consignment of silver into silver coins exactly like those in the Florida Collection. Most noticeable is the prodigious amount of hand labor and huge amount of fuel needed to accomplish these tasks.

1. A consignment of ingots ordinarily consists of twenty-four silver bars of 70 lbs. each, these entering the mint by way of the treasure room where they are placed in a row in presence of the treasurer, assayer, weighmaster, and scribe who brings from his archive a file known as the book of stampings (*remaches*). On a page he writes: "In the Potosí mint on xxxx day, there being present (certain people) there to mark the bars." And then the weighmaster in a loud voice immediately describes the inscriptions of each bar showing the year it was cast, the tally number of the foundry, the Royal Treasury where it was taxed, the fineness and the weight, these data being recorded by the scribe in his book. If by chance there is any doubt, the weighmaster repeats them and the total weights are recorded at the bottom of the page. The royal mark ["A"] and the mark of this mint are then punched into the bars and the page is signed. That is to say, the scribe himself takes an iron hammer and with the sharp side defaces the royal tax (*quinto*) marks made by the treasury where it was first taxed, and he pounds in with the other side of the hammer the full-sized coin die with its columns.
2. On the following day after these markings, all the bars are carried to the foundry workshop, which consists of a long and wide hall with

equipment to be mentioned and a great chimney [see illus. B.1] with a big blacksmith's bellows [see illus. B.2] and nozzle which is prevented from being scorched by a wrapping in a sleeve of baked clay and copper smeared with mud which they call an *alcribiz* [a tuyere or protective fireproof tip]. Leaning against the chimney is a large clay crucible seated on a moveable brazier called the *callana,* which has two large iron bars on either side in order to lift it so that a lot of charcoal can be placed underneath to produce a strong fire. A round iron hoop or rim *(cerco)* four fingers wide curves around the crucible like a ribbon to keep the charcoal from spilling into it when the bellows are used to cause it to change into glowing embers. Four bars are placed in this crucible where they melt. Then the assayer who is in charge of alloying with copper pours on top of the molten silver enough to create the proper fineness by lowering it to coin fineness which is 11 *dineros,* 4 *granos* [.910 fine] plus a measured amount to make up for the loss from vaporization, which they call "realloying." This melt of both metals weighs 300 lbs., more or less, and is called the *crazada.* The smelting requires three quarters of an hour and can be recognized when ready by the smelter who watches the color of the flames. When the silver and copper are properly mixed, he orders an Indian to heat

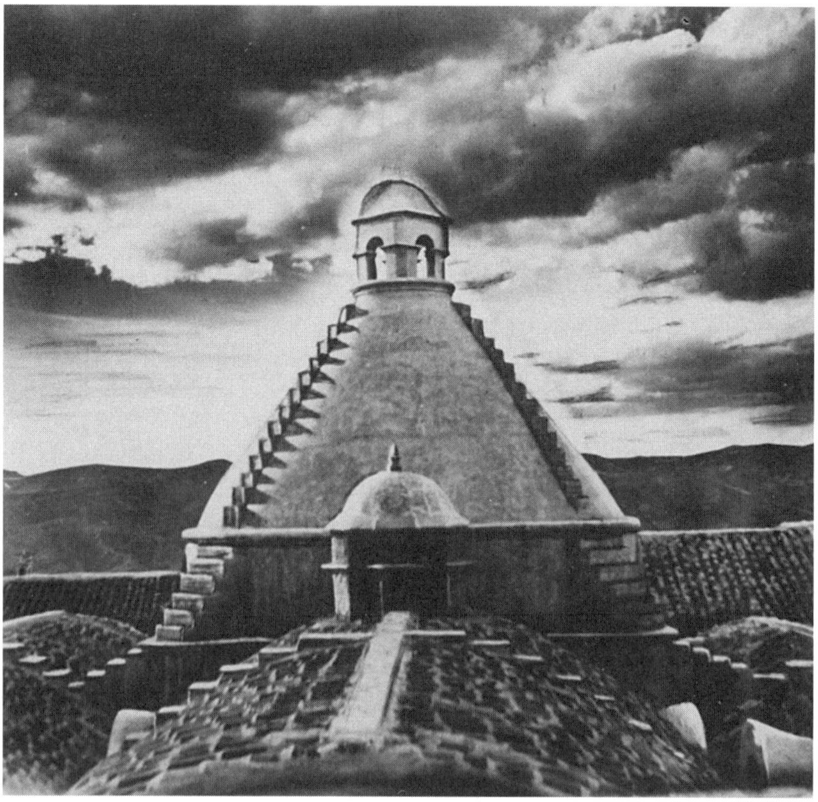

Illus. B.1. Rooflines and central chimney for the mint furnaces at Potosí.

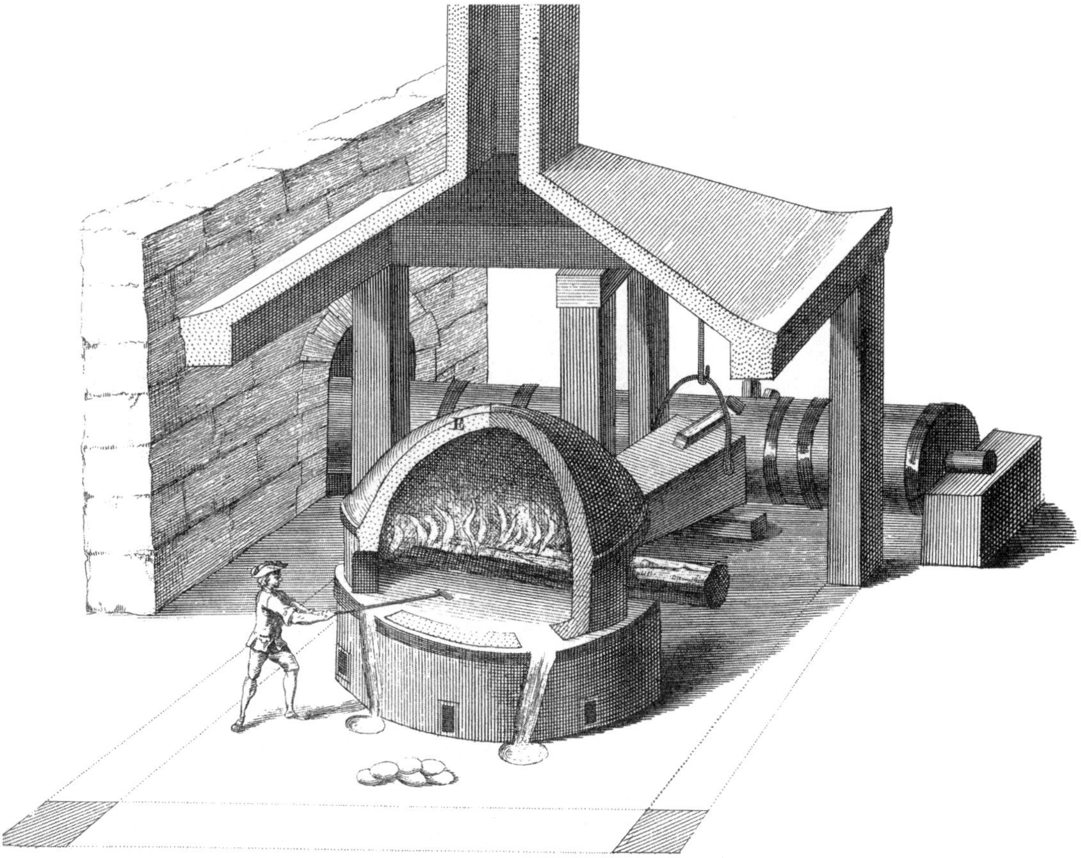

Illus. B.2. A bellows-assisted, wood-fired furnace smelting high-grade silver oxide ores. Puddles, like those shown here, were sometimes found on shipwrecks and are assumed to have been smugglers' contraband.

a large iron instrument called the *espetón* [poker or prong] used to stir the mixture in the crucible. The bellows are stopped, and six or eight Indians lift it and place it over a hole in a thick stone block a yard long with a trough half full of water on the same level. Near the suspended crucible are some iron molds for making the *rieleras* [narrow straps] a yard and a half long with a little trench in the middle an inch wide and high [see illus. 4.5], and with a mop soaked in melted grease these trenches are greased so the silver will flow smoothly and not stick. In each mold the silver is poured, little by little, in a stream coming out of the spout. When a mold is full the Indian empties it out onto the floor and instantly picks up another, this being done with six or seven molds kept nearby. This operation is done by two or three Indians and by this means they continue until the crucible is empty. At the end of this job they gather up the drops of silver spattered around and that fell within the basin, which they wash and recover in a basket. Together with floor spatters, these small drops are known as the sweepings. When the assayer arrives he cuts off a small piece from a new silver strap from the middle of the pile, takes it to his assay office which is next to the foundry and in his own little furnace he assays it.

(In Lima these assays are done each day without adding or changing the circumstances described for Potosí.) If the assayer finds the silver adjusted to the proper coin fineness he tells the smelters it passes, but if he judges it considerably defective, he orders it enriched, which is to say it must be melted again and brought to the correct fineness. In this manner the process continues until all twenty-four bars have been smelted in six melts which require two hours each. The silver straps are gathered up in a medium-sized box with two long poles on each side like a carrying litter, and they take them to the treasure room. The clay crucible is broken up in order to extract any silver it has soaked up. These are called *corpus* and together with the sweepings are remelted with the next production run. The Indians employed in these labors are generally called *servires* and those who specifically carry water to the water trough are called *aguatires* and those who load and empty the crucible are called *cargadores* and *variadores* and those who dump out the silver straps are *tiradores,* and *sopladores* are those who operate the bellows.

3. When the silver straps are taken to the treasure room they are placed on a large table where there is a balance scale made of copper hanging from a small crank with its own set of weights, the larger ones of 25 and 12.5 lbs. being called troughs because of their shape, and they continue down in size to a half ounce. The weighmaster places 53 *marcos* of weight on one pan and on the other a Negro or Indian places silver straps until they are equal in weight, adding ounces until they are balanced. Then they are said to be in the treasury, and the weighmaster sings out in a loud voice . . . so many *marcos* and so many ounces . . . while the scribe writes them down in his book of straps, which narrative says: "straps of assayed silver which in the ___ day of ___ month of ___ year were delivered by _______ to the treasurer proceeding from the lot of bars which were marked on that day, or the said treasurer turned over to _______ foreman in order that they all be made into coins." And at that moment, without repeating the weight himself in his book, the foreman receives the silver straps and carries them to his furnace. The treasurer must be present at all these functions and the assayer, two guards, the weighmaster, and the scribe. The treasurer duplicates in another book what the scribe has put down in his. The reason for putting 53 *marcos* on the scale is for the adjustment of any total shortness in the delivery and summaries.

4. After the silver straps leave the treasury, they are brought to the furnace, being placed on the floor of it and covered on top with a quantity of burning charcoal covering them and are heated on a slow fire until they all have a fiery glow which takes four or five hours, which they call the first baking [annealing]. When this time is finished

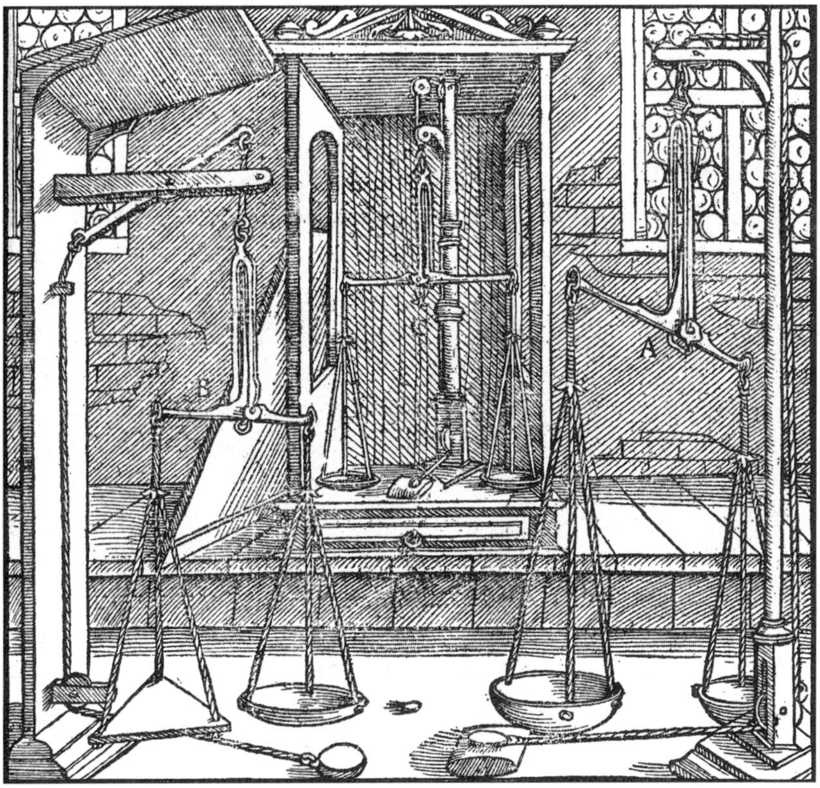

Illus. B.3. A European mint weighing room with various scales and balance beams similar to those in use at Spanish colonial mints.

they rake them apart with a large hoe to cool them, and being cold, they lift them onto a table next to a shears 2 *varas* long and thick as a man's wrist, which are called *tallones.* These shears are sharpened with a thick rod they call the *cureña,* and are held tightly together with a broad, beaten leather belt, and are used to cut the straps one by one into little pieces which are cut to the weight of a *patacón* (8 reales) and weighed against a weight named the *dineral patrón.* They begin by cutting slightly oversize and are adjusted and weighed again by a Negro worker who checks the weight and places any underweight planchets apart to be made into 4-reales coins. The proper planchets are passed to twenty hammer workers who are seated along a wooden bench and facing each of them in front is part of a tree trunk a half *vara* tall placed firmly into the floor with its upper flat part wrapped in iron which swerves as an anvil. Each planchet is placed there and strongly struck with a steel hammer to spread it out until it is the thickness of a coin, and this is called "cleaning." Immediately they place all the planchets that have been flattened into a second furnace like the first, and pulling them out from the embers and cooling them, place them back on the table with the shears where five or six workers called "slicers" cut off any excess metal until they are the proper weight, some being sent to the slicers again, this work being called "rounding." When finished, they are all put aside in the workplace with the 8's separated from the 4's. All the cut-off pieces are gathered up and are called *cizalla,* from which the larger pieces are used to make 2-reales coins and smaller ones for 1-real and ½-real coins. These are all reprocessed, going through all the previous operations. But there is always a surplus of very small pieces from which no coin can be made and these scraps are kept [by the assayer]. After all the coins are divided into classes they are placed in the third furnace like the previous times, and the silver being reheated, they take them out and carefully let them cool. Then each piece is carefully inspected again and each piece that is still defective they place in an iron instrument they call a "buoy" like iron tongs, and there they shape it with a small hammer known as the *muleta.* When all these tasks are finished the workers toss the coins into copper cauldrons the size of a large, well-spread-out plate known as a *rallete.* They pick these up with both hands, tossing the coins in the air and catching them again while shaking, they blow the ashes away. Some ounces are set aside in favor of the owner of the silver by the foreman plus something more for the loss of the multitude of fragments that resulted from cutting up the whole lot. Some tiny grains of dirt and silver called *lises* whose accounting losses may amount to as much as 8 pesos per *marco.* These credits, together with the *cizalla* and the total of coins must be adjusted against the debt of the weight of straps and are written into the book to the satisfaction of the foreman. After all the coins have been weighed they carry them all to be blanched.

5. The blanching workroom is medium-sized in which there is a chimney large enough to hold two or three large copper cauldron-like basins. These are placed over fires from underneath where sufficient firewood is stacked to produce a violent fire that heats the basins. These are filled ⅔ full with water prepared in some open-mouthed jugs into which is poured a sufficient amount of *millo,* this mixture being emptied into the basins where it is vigorously stirred with a paddle. They skim off the fine *millo* while the coarse, too much of which may stain and dull the silver, remains in the basin. This *millo* forms naturally in veins of special mines where it is like pieces of white earth or spongy yellow with greenish and bluish bumps [marcasite?] and has the ability to clean all the ashes [firescale] or soot from the silver. They pour into each container four or six baskets of large coins and wait for them to come to a boil, stirring them with wooden paddles. And if at the end of a half hour the silver has been blanched and brought to its luminous color, they take it out and dump it into a small brick well where they use a lot of clean water to wash the coins because they always come out with some *millo.* When this is

finished the coins are placed on copper sheets the thickness of an 8 reales and a *vara* long by a half *vara* wide that are resting on some bricks well fastened to the wall. Below these sheets they place a quantity of glowing coals to heat the sheets and dry the planchets. When dry, they place them in sacks and when the batch is finished they place another. This process takes eight to ten hours. After blanching, drying, and sacking, the planchets are taken to the treasury where they are guarded by the blancher in a special box made for this purpose.

6. Once they are in the treasury the treasurer comes in and on the top of his desk, opens a book titled *Book of Coinings* and in it he enters the production lot prorated among all names involved and that which each one has earned. A note of this list is sent to the weighmaster who weighs in his balance the *marcos* assigned to each coiner, who receives them in little bags placed in the sacks in each lot which are taken to the coining room. And leaving them there, he hurries back to the treasury to receive from the guards all the tools that are needed for the job which are taken out of a box he must then guard. And counting them piece by piece, he receives them and takes them to his dies to begin his work in the following manner. This journey to the dies is a moderate distance through a doorway where there are numerous workplaces, as have been named, that ordinarily are twelve or fourteen in Potosí and eight or ten in Lima. These workplaces are benches ½ *vara* high and one and a half long, made of wood fastened to the floor with a smooth concave seat in front of which is a thick tree trunk called the *cepel.* It has a hole cut in it into which fits an iron spike from the base of an anvil having a circular mouth with engraved castles and lions and this instrument is called the *pila.* On it the planchet is placed and on top of this is placed on the left of the coiner another tool they call the *troquel* being a *jeme* [the distance between the thumb and the end of the forefinger when both are extended] long and a width that matches the *pila.* On the *troquel* are the columns of this same coin stamped in the iron of the mouth. With the force of some blows that are given with a hammer called the *mallete,* it comes out impressed from one side to the other. When the coin is taken out another is put in its place until all have been coined. Then the tools are taken away and replaced with those that correspond to the 4 reales and so forth for each class of coin alternating with the smaller sizes. There is a proviso: the coiner is not required to strike planchets he sees are badly made, very stained, underweight, or overweight which are all called *remalatos,* and sorts them out to be returned. In the middle of this workroom, set very firmly in the floor, is another iron anvil and bench they call the *descasonadera* (separator). With a hammer

they break them up and take out the pieces that have been broken or stuck in the dies during the blows on the upper part where the mallet strikes. And if the mouth of the die or hub becomes worn away or jumps out, the coiner takes it to the guard to be exchanged for a new one. At sundown the guards gather up the tools, piece by piece just as they were handed over and lock them up in the same box of two keys. The coiners leave, taking up the coins and the hammers, and put them in some boxes they have for their custody in the entry to the treasury. If any planchets are left over, they repeat the same delivery and receipt of tools from the guards and lock up the coins until they are told the delivery is to be made.

7. The day the last batch of the consignment has been finished, the two guards, the assayer, the weighmaster, and the scribe gather together in the treasure room of the treasury. And in order of the first five, they call on the coiner they elect (all having been assembled) to bring before them all the coins he has struck. They are examined and weighed by selecting examples here and there from the various jobs because it would be impossible in that short time to check piece by piece and reiterate that which in the foundries was adjusted with such care. This weight, which they call the *segunda levada* (second weighing), is adjusted to 67 reales to which the scribe testifies. The coiner leaves while the assayer takes one or more coins from the batch that seems to him to have been well struck, cuts it in half [!] with large hand shears. The half having the date and name of the assayer he hands to one of the guards and with the other half he goes to the assay room. Here, with the assistance of the scribe, he smelts the half coin by placing it with two long tongs on top of a little oven, and having purged it with deliberate calm, takes out the remainder with the tongs and places the small pellet on a scale and balances it with the weight for 11 *dineros* and 4 *granos*. And finding it properly adjusted, they return to the treasure room with the assayed pellet. If it fails, they smelt the batch, but if it qualifies well, the scribe recovers the other half of the coin that remained with the guard. On a half page of official taxed paper he writes saying: "In the mint of this city or village of such and such a place on such and such a day of such a month, being present the treasurer, etc., different reweighings of the work of coiner so-and-so of the coins he made of that batch that was assayed on such a day belonging to so-and-so, owner of it, and worked it in such a furnace and the assays were made that the law requires, of which I give testimony that all the said officials signed their names below as witnesses." Whereupon the scribe closes out this document with the two halves of the coin, binds it with a ribbon and wax seal as a summary of the consignment. This written document is called a

libramiento (release). The strongbox of three keys must be opened with three keys, one possessed by the guards, another by the assayer, and the third by the scribe. The document is placed in it and closing it marks the end of this function called the opening and closing of the strongbox.

8. This same day the treasurer makes two little lists on quarter sheets of common paper with the names of the coiners and the weights of coins they must deliver and the amount of the coinage taxes and they take out from the consignment what is owed the officials and the *Real de Señoreaje* (seigniorage). The silver merchant comes who has already arrived to receive the consignment with his baskets and carriers and finding the treasurer and the four chief officials already mentioned, with the scribe the assayer is called and simultaneously the weighmaster with the copy of the list given to him by the treasurer of what is owed. The owner [silver merchant] receiving five weighings of 50 *marcos* making 250 in all and these at 67 reales per *marco* amount to 2,039 pesos, 6 reales unless there are underweight coins they will be more, and less if there are overweights. One coiner enters and delivers his production followed by another until all have done their duty. And if there is any little weight missing with respect to their coining, caused by wear on the silver, they pay for it instantly from the rights they receive for their work, it being taken out by the treasurer from the earnings of everyone involved in processing the consignment. The king's fee is kept in custody by the treasurer until such time as it can be carried over to the Royal Treasury of the king's estate. The sacks of the silver merchant are left on the floor marked with the weights from the scale. If it comes out exactly the scribe opens a book kept annually of special paper and in it he grants a Letter of Payment from the owner of the silver to the treasurer with the individual weights present on the day of the stampings and the quantity of value brought by the owner at 67 reales per *marco* strictly according to law without taking into account any under- or overweight coins. All this concluded, the officials leave and the silver merchant takes out his shipments that regularly are worth 30,000 pesos, with little difference. The defective coins are counted separately and returned to the mint to be smelted and incorporated into the next consignment without having to pay the stamping taxes the second time around. It takes twelve working days to complete the entire process, although this may vary by a day or two.

Appendix C: Illustrated Coins in the Florida Collection

Coins Sorted by Figure Number

Figure	Mint	Year	Assayer	Denom.	Weight	Catalog No.
3.1A	Potosí	1650	⊙	8 Reales	25.13g	97A.005.015795.0001
3.1B	Potosí	1650	⊙	8 Reales	25.13g	97A.005.015795.0001
3.1C	Potosí		R	2 Reales	6.00g	94A.052.000585.0003
3.1D	Potosí		R	2 Reales	6.00g	94A.052.000585.0003
3.1E	Potosí	162-	T	2 Reales	5.50g	94A.052.000585.0005
3.1F	Potosí	162-	T	2 Reales	5.50g	94A.052.000585.0005
3.1G	Potosí		T	2 Reales	4.30g	72A.013.000363.0001
3.1H	Potosí		T	2 Reales	4.30g	72A.013.000363.0001
5.1A	Mexico	1709	J	8 Reales	26.35g	72A.013.000197.0071
5.1B	Potosí	1700	F	8 Reales	25.72g	94A.052.000575.0022
5.1C	Lima	1687	R	8 Reales	26.60g	94A.052.000589.0021
5.1D	Bogotá	1652		8 Reales	25.55g	97A.005.013016.0001
5.1E	Cartagena	1655		8 Reales	20.38g	94A.132.009889.0001
5.2A	Mexico	1715		½ Real	1.20g	94A.036.000778.0298
5.2B	Mexico	1715		½ Real	1.20g	94A.036.000778.0298
5.2C	Lima	1686	R	1 Real	3.03g	94A.052.000557.0024
5.2D	Lima	1686	R	1 Real	3.03g	94A.052.000557.0024
5.2E	Mexico		J	2 Reales	6.57g	94A.052.000582.0014
5.2F	Mexico		J	2 Reales	6.57g	94A.052.000582.0014
5.2G	Potosí	1700	F	4 Reales	12.70g	72A.013.000191.0016
5.2H	Potosí	1700	F	4 Reales	12.70g	72A.013.000191.0016
5.2I	Lima	1699	R	8 Reales	26.40g	72A.013.000126.0005
5.2J	Lima	1699	R	8 Reales	26.40g	72A.013.000126.0005
5.3A	Potosí	1657	E	8 Reales		American Numismatic Society
5.3B	Potosí	1657	E	8 Reales		American Numismatic Society
5.3C	Potosí	1654	E	8 Reales	26.71g	97A.005.014594.0002
5.3D	Potosí	1654	E	8 Reales	26.71g	97A.005.014594.0002
5.4A	Mexico	1714		8 Reales	18.50g	93A.674.000030.0001

Figure	Mint	Year	Assayer	Denom.	Weight	Catalog No.
5.4B	Mexico	1714		8 Reales	18.50g	93A.674.000030.0001
5.5A	Potosí	1652	E	8 Reales	24.67g	94A.132.009893.0001
5.5B	Potosí	1652	E	8 Reales	24.67g	94A.132.009893.0001
5.5C	Potosí	1652	E	8 Reales	25.89g	97A.005.013017.0001
5.5D	Potosí	1652	E	8 Reales	25.89g	97A.005.013017.0001
5.6A	Lima	1659	V	8 Reales	26.94g	97A.005.013325.0001
5.6B	Lima	1659	V	8 Reales	26.94g	97A.005.013325.0001
5.7A	Mexico	1732		8 Reales	18.31g	93A.613.000170.0001
5.7B	Mexico	1732		8 Reales	20.60g	93A.613.000171.0001
7.1A	Mexico	1655	P	8 Reales	27.37g	94A.132.009952.0001
7.1B	Mexico	1655	P	8 Reales	27.37g	94A.132.009952.0001
7.1C	Mexico	1655	P	8 Reales	27.25g	94A.132.009953.0001
7.1D	Mexico	1655	P	8 Reales	27.25g	94A.132.009953.0001
7.1E	Mexico	1656	P	8 Reales	26.05g	94A.132.009892.0001
7.1F	Mexico	1656	P	8 Reales	26.05g	94A.132.009892.0001
7.1G	Mexico	1657	P	8 Reales	26.23g	96A.114.013271.0001
7.1H	Mexico	1657	P	8 Reales	26.23g	96A.114.013271.0001
7.1I	Mexico	1657	P	8 Reales	26.44g	94A.132.009984.0001
7.1J	Mexico	1657	P	8 Reales	26.44g	94A.132.009984.0001
7.2A	Mexico	1700	L	8 Reales	27.10g	72A.013.000207.0035
7.2B	Mexico	1709		8 Reales	26.30g	72A.013.000208.0108
7.2C	Mexico	1710		4 Reales	13.10g	72A.013.000214.0040
7.2D	Mexico	1711	J	8 Reales	24.80g	94A.036.000868.0013
7.2E	Mexico	1712	J	8 Reales	26.00g	72A.013.000209.0136
7.2F	Mexico	1713	J	8 Reales	25.80g	72A.013.000219.0011
7.2G	Mexico	1714		8 Reales	26.80g	72A.013.000746.0211
7.2H	Mexico	1714	J	8 Reales	25.70g	72A.013.000213.0151
7.2I	Mexico	1714	J	8 Reales	26.20g	22A.000.000000.0338
7.2J	Mexico	1715	J	8 Reales	25.70g	72A.013.000219.0039
7.2K	Mexico	1715	J	8 Reales	24.70g	72A.013.000211.0071
7.3A	Mexico			8 Reales	24.40g	72A.013.000209.0105
7.3B	Mexico			8 Reales	22.40g	72A.013.000694.0555
7.3C	Mexico			8 Reales	26.20g	72A.013.000670.0501
7.3D	Mexico			8 Reales	26.30g	72A.013.000205.0012
7.3E	Mexico			8 Reales	26.10g	72A.013.000725.0015
7.3F	Mexico			8 Reales	24.10g	94A.036.000857.0027
7.3G	Potosí	1—		8 Reales	24.50g	94A.036.000880.0010
7.3H	Mexico		J	8 Reales	23.00g	72A.013.000172.0073
7.3I	Mexico			8 Reales	24.90g	72A.013.000209.0106
7.3J	Mexico			8 Reales	25.20g	72A.013.000216.0055
7.4A	Mexico	1715		4 Reales	12.60g	72A.013.000123.0302
7.4B	Mexico			4 Reales	10.80g	72A.013.000218.0115
7.4C	Mexico			4 Reales	11.80g	22A.000.000000.0876
7.4D	Mexico			8 Reales	24.80g	22A.000.000000.0395
7.4E	Mexico			4 Reales	11.80g	94A.036.000857.0039
7.4F	Mexico			4 Reales	12.00g	72A.013.000748.0087
7.4G	Mexico			8 Reales	26.30g	72A.013.000215.0093
7.4H	Mexico			4 Reales	12.20g	94A.036.000894.0046

Figure	Mint	Year	Assayer	Denom.	Weight	Catalog No.
7.4I	Mexico		J	4 Reales	13.20g	94A.052.000583.0003
7.4J	Mexico		J	8 Reales	26.63g	94A.052.000562.0008
7.5A	Mexico		J	8 Reales	26.00g	72A.013.000746.0143
7.5B	Mexico			8 Reales	26.00g	94A.036.000889.0032
7.5C	Mexico	1712	J	8 Reales	26.00g	72A.013.000209.0136
7.5D	Mexico			8 Reales	26.30g	72A.013.000667.0070
7.5E	Mexico			8 Reales	26.30g	72A.013.000667.0070
7.5F	Mexico			4 Reales	12.70g	94A.036.000862.0003
7.5G	Mexico			8 Reales	26.00g	72A.013.000746.0169
7.5H	Mexico			4 Reales	12.70g	94A.036.000781.0078
7.5I	Mexico			8 Reales	26.30g	94A.036.000889.0016
7.5J	Mexico			8 Reales	23.90g	94A.052.000501.0057
7.6A	Mexico			8 Reales	24.90g	72A.013.000213.0053
7.6B	Mexico			8 Reales	24.40g	72A.013.000216.0119
7.6C	Mexico			8 Reales	24.40g	72A.013.000216.0119
7.6D	Mexico			8 Reales	24.80g	72A.013.000209.0098
7.6E	Mexico			4 Reales	14.20g	72A.013.000215.0025
7.6F	Mexico			8 Reales	26.50g	72A.013.000208.0052
7.6G	Mexico			4 Reales	12.30g	72A.013.000191.0005
7.6H	Mexico			8 Reales	23.50g	94A.036.000780.0042
7.6I	Mexico			4 Reales	13.80g	72A.013.000171.0006
7.6J	Mexico			4 Reales	11.20g	94A.052.000580.0007
7.6K	Mexico		J	8 Reales	23.00g	72A.013.000694.0471
7.7A	Mexico	171-	J	8 Reales	24.40g	72A.013.000191.0002
7.7B	Mexico			8 Reales	25.10g	72A.013.000667.0264
7.7C	Mexico			8 Reales	26.60g	72A.013.000191.0018
7.7D	Mexico			8 Reales	26.10g	72A.013.000210.0092
7.7E	Mexico			8 Reales	25.70g	94A.036.000894.0016
7.7F	Mexico			8 Reales	26.20g	72A.013.000126.0016
7.7G	Mexico			8 Reales	24.70g	72A.013.000210.0099
7.7H	Mexico		L	8 Reales	25.60g	72A.013.000126.0063
7.7I	Mexico			8 Reales	24.00g	72A.013.000669.0345
7.7J	Mexico			8 Reales	22.10g	72A.013.000695.0032
7.8A	Mexico			8 Reales	25.30g	72A.013.000696.0025
7.8B	Mexico			8 Reales	25.50g	72A.013.000210.0118
7.8C	Mexico			8 Reales	27.10g	72A.013.000212.0180
7.8D	Mexico			8 Reales	26.70g	22.I
7.8E	Mexico			4 Reales	12.70g	72A.013.000204.0022
7.8F	Mexico			8 Reales	25.90g	72A.013.000746.0177
7.8G	Mexico			8 Reales	23.70g	72A.013.000209.0111
7.8H	Mexico			8 Reales	25.30g	94A.036.000861.0002
7.9A	Mexico			8 Reales	26.30g	72A.013.000217.0022
7.9B	Mexico			8 Reales	25.60g	72A.013.000217.0012
7.9C	Mexico			8 Reales	26.20g	72A.013.000205.0128
7.9D	Mexico		J	8 Reales	25.10g	94A.036.000736.0020
7.9E	Mexico			8 Reales	25.10g	72A.013.000217.0014
7.9F	Mexico			8 Reales	26.10g	72A.013.000217.0003
7.9G	Mexico			8 Reales	25.80g	72A.013.000217.0005

Figure	Mint	Year	Assayer	Denom.	Weight	Catalog No.
7.9H	Mexico			8 Reales	26.10g	72A.013.000217.0001
7.9I	Mexico			8 Reales	25.20g	72A.013.000217.0020
7.10A	Mexico			8 Reales	25.90g	72A.013.000746.0177
7.10B	Mexico			8 Reales	26.10g	72A.013.000191.0008
7.10C	Mexico			8 Reales	26.40g	72A.013.000667.0210
7.10D	Mexico			8 Reales	26.30g	94A.036.000886.0022
7.10E	Mexico			8 Reales	26.00g	72A.013.000208.0003
7.10F	Mexico			8 Reales	25.40g	94A.036.000880.0002
7.10G	Mexico			8 Reales	25.60g	72A.013.000674.0842
7.10H	Mexico	1708	J	8 Reales	26.50g	72A.013.000191.0009
7.10I	Mexico			8 Reales	26.50g	72A.013.000124.0230
7.11A	Mexico		J	8 Reales	25.40g	72A.013.000213.0022
7.11B	Mexico	1713		8 Reales	26.60g	72A.013.000667.0050
7.11C	Mexico			8 Reales	24.40g	94A.036.000868.0005
7.11D	Mexico			8 Reales	24.50g	94A.036.000767.0020
7.11E	Mexico			8 Reales	24.80g	72A.013.000667.0119
7.11F	Mexico			8 Reales	25.50g	94A.036.000780.0006
7.11G	Mexico			4 Reales	12.60g	72A.013.000212.0025
7.12A	Mexico			8 Reales	23.10g	94A.052.000502.0020
7.12B	Mexico			8 Reales	26.50g	72A.013.000207.0087
7.12C	Mexico			8 Reales	21.80g	94A.052.000538.0029
7.12D	Mexico			8 Reales	22.40g	22A.000.000000.0983
7.12E	Mexico			8 Reales	25.70g	72A.013.000191.0004
7.12F	Mexico			8 Reales	26.00g	93A.617.000154.0030
7.12G	Mexico			8 Reales	25.50g	72A.013.000123.0083
7.12H	Mexico			8 Reales	23.70g	72A.013.000214.0152
7.12I	Mexico	1708		8 Reales	25.40g	72A.013.000191.0007
7.12J	Mexico			8 Reales	25.30g	72A.013.000667.0064
7.12K	Mexico			8 Reales	24.40g	72A.013.000209.0097
7.12L	Mexico			8 Reales	26.50g	72A.013.000746.0106
7.13A	Mexico			8 Reales	24.90g	72A.013.000748.0086
7.13B	Mexico			8 Reales	23.98g	22A.000.000000.0687
7.13C	Mexico			8 Reales	27.30g	94A.052.000512.0004
7.13D	Mexico			8 Reales	20.60g	94A.036.000780.0093
7.13E	Mexico			8 Reales	22.70g	72A.013.000691.0015
7.13F	Mexico			8 Reales	24.93g	94A.052.000510.0032
7.13G	Mexico			8 Reales	24.90g	72A.013.000209.0006
7.13H	Mexico			8 Reales	25.10g	94A.036.000861.0001
7.13I	Mexico			4 Reales	13.00g	93A.617.000154.0040
7.13J	Mexico			8 Reales	22.30g	94A.036.000780.0130
7.13K	Mexico			8 Reales	22.30g	72A.013.000214.0151
7.14A	Mexico			8 Reales	21.70g	94A.036.000781.0030
7.14B	Mexico			8 Reales	26.10g	72A.013.000669.0380
7.14C	Mexico			8 Reales	24.20g	94A.052.000506.0016
7.14D	Mexico			8 Reales	25.20g	72A.013.000212.0024
7.14E	Mexico			8 Reales	26.10g	72A.013.000668.0286
7.14F	Mexico			8 Reales	20.20g	72A.013.000694.0538
7.14G	Mexico			8 Reales	25.50g	72A.013.000191.0017

Figure	Mint	Year	Assayer	Denom.	Weight	Catalog No.
7.14H	Mexico			4 Reales	13.10g	72A.013.000746.0112
7.14I	Mexico		J	8 Reales	21.90g	72A.013.000694.0332
7.14J	Mexico			8 Reales	24.30g	22A.000.000000.0085
7.14K	Mexico			8 Reales	26.60g	72A.013.000667.0184
7.14L	Mexico			8 Reales	21.30g	72A.013.000219.0054
7.15A	Mexico			8 Reales	24.50g	72A.013.000194.0089
7.15B	Mexico		J	8 Reales	25.80g	72A.013.000176.0081
8.1A	Potosí	1652	E	8 Reales	24.67g	94A.132.009893.0001
8.1B	Potosí	1652	E	8 Reales	24.67g	94A.132.009893.0001
8.1C	Potosí	1652	E	8 Reales	25.80g	94A.132.009983.0001
8.1D	Potosí	1652	E	8 Reales	25.80g	94A.132.009983.0001
8.1E	Potosí	1652	E	8 Reales	23.10g	97A.086.016691.0001
8.2A	Potosí	1652	E	8 Reales	26.99g	99A.039.021617.0001
8.2B	Potosí	1652	E	8 Reales	26.99g	99A.039.021617.0001
8.2C	Potosí	1652	E	8 Reales	27.93g	94A.132.009939.0001
8.2D	Potosí	1652	E	8 Reales	27.93g	94A.132.009939.0001
8.2E	Potosí	1652	E	8 Reales	21.83g	94A.132.010998.0001
8.2F	Potosí	1652	E	8 Reales	21.83g	94A.132.010998.0001
8.3A	Potosí	1653	E	8 Reales	26.27g	94A.132.009898.0001
8.3B	Potosí	1653	E	8 Reales	26.27g	94A.132.009898.0001
8.3C	Potosí	1653	E	8 Reales	27.15g	94A.132.009891.0001
8.3D	Potosí	1653	E	8 Reales	27.15g	94A.132.009891.0001
8.4A	Potosí	1654	E	8 Reales	26.22g	94A.132.009895.0001
8.4B	Potosí	1654	E	8 Reales	24.12g	94A.132.009946.0001
8.4C	Potosí	1654	E	8 Reales	26.31g	94A.132.009941.0001
8.5A	Potosí	1655	E	8 Reales	26.72g	94A.132.009981.0001
8.5B	Potosí	1655	E	8 Reales	26.72g	94A.132.009982.0001
8.5C	Potosí	1655	E	8 Reales	27.49g	94A.132.009901.0001
8.5D	Potosí	1655	E	8 Reales	26.18g	94A.132.009978.0001
8.5E	Potosí	1655	E	8 Reales	20.04g	94A.132.010732.0001
8.5F	Potosí	1656	E	8 Reales	27.92g	94A.132.009935.0001
8.6A	Potosí	1657	E	8 Reales	25.12g	94A.132.009956.0001
8.6B	Potosí	1657	E	8 Reales	25.12g	94A.132.009956.0001
8.6C	Potosí	1657	E	8 Reales	24.75g	94A.132.009896.0001
8.7A	Potosí	1658	E	8 Reales	26.01g	94A.132.009969.0001
8.7B	Potosí	1658	E	8 Reales	25.14g	94A.132.009900.0001
8.7C	Potosí	1658	E	8 Reales	26.24g	94A.132.009965.0001
8.7D	Potosí	1658	E	8 Reales	26.01g	94A.132.009969.0001
8.7E	Potosí	1658	E	8 Reales	25.80g	94A.132.009968.0001
8.7F	Potosí	1658	E	8 Reales	26.24g	94A.132.009965.0001
8.7G	Potosí	1658	E	8 Reales	27.40g	94A.132.009970.0001
8.8A	Potosí	1687	VR	4 Reales	10.10g	22A.000.000000.0094
8.8B	Potosí	1690	VR	4 Reales	12.20g	72A.013.000171.0047
8.8C	Potosí	1691	VR	4 Reales	12.60g	72A.013.000216.0111
8.8D	Potosí	1695	VR	4 Reales	13.60g	72A.013.000207.0170
8.8E	Potosí	1698	F	4 Reales	13.20g	72A.013.000215.0011
8.8F	Potosí	1700	F	4 Reales	12.70g	72A.013.000191.0016
8.8G	Potosí	1700		4 Reales	13.80g	72A.013.000694.0272

Figure	Mint	Year	Assayer	Denom.	Weight	Catalog No.
8.8H	Potosí	1703	Y	4 Reales	13.30g	72A.013.000191.0014
8.8I	Potosí	1708	Y	4 Reales	13.60g	72A.013.000207.0116
8.9A	Potosí	1686	VR	8 Reales	22.20g	22A.000.000000.0565
8.9B	Potosí	1690	VR	8 Reales	25.80g	22A.000.000000.0063
8.9C	Potosí	1691	VR	8 Reales	20.20g	22A.000.000000.0064
8.9D	Potosí	1693	VR	8 Reales	24.70g	72A.013.000171.0042
8.9E	Potosí	1695	VR	8 Reales	21.10g	72A.013.000171.0032
8.9F	Potosí	1697	VR	8 Reales	24.90g	94A.036.000780.0034
8.9G	Potosí	1698	VR	8 Reales	22.26g	94A.052.000575.0021
8.9H	Potosí	1699	F	8 Reales	23.50g	72A.013.000695.0064
8.9I	Potosí	1700	F	8 Reales	26.10g	72A.013.000191.0011
8.9J	Potosí	1701	Y	8 Reales	25.30g	72A.013.000171.0048
8.9K	Potosí	1702	Y	8 Reales	26.90g	94A.052.000520.0001
8.9L	Potosí	1703	Y	8 Reales	25.40g	22A.000.000000.0567
8.10A	Potosí	1680	V	8 Reales	25.30g	94A.052.000591.0017
8.10B	Potosí	1692	VR	8 Reales	22.70g	94A.052.000591.0003
8.10C	Potosí	1690	VR	4 Reales	13.30g	94A.036.000917.0006
8.10D	Potosí	1679	C	4 Reales	11.00g	94A.052.000590.0005
8.10E	Potosí	1679	C	4 Reales	11.00g	94A.052.000590.0005
8.11A	Potosí	1686	VR	1 Real	2.30g	94A.036.000778.0233
8.11B	Potosí	1689	VR	1 Real	2.60g	94A.036.000872.0032
8.11C	Lima	1699	R	1 Real	3.30g	94A.036.000877.0016
8.11D	Lima	1698	H	1 Real	3.20g	94A.036.000875.0022
8.11E	Mexico	1700		1 Real	3.00g	94A.036.000869.0007
8.11F	Lima	1706	R	1 Real	2.60g	94A.036.000877.0042
8.11G	Mexico		J	2 Reales	6.30g	94A.036.000865.0001
8.11H	Potosí	1688	VR	2 Reales	4.60g	93A.671.000101.0001
8.11I	Potosí	1693	VR	1 Real	3.00g	94A.036.000867.0029
8.11J	Mexico		P	1 Real	3.10g	93A.640.000152.0003
9.1A	Lima	1659	V	8 Reales	23.85g	94A.132.011152.0001
9.1B	Lima	1659	V	8 Reales	25.30g	94A.132.011153.0001
9.1C	Lima	1659	V	8 Reales	24.50g	97A.005.015497.0001
9.1D	Lima	1659	V	8 Reales	24.50g	97A.005.015497.0001
9.1E	Lima	1659	V	4 Reales	11.99g	96A.114.013023.0001
9.1F	Lima	1659	V	4 Reales	11.99g	96A.114.013023.0001
9.2A	Lima	1696	H	8 Reales	25.20g	72A.013.000126.0058
9.2B	Lima	1697	H	8 Reales	22.40g	72A.013.000126.0006
9.2C	Lima	1698	H	8 Reales	20.80g	72A.013.000126.0062
9.2D	Lima	1699	R	8 Reales	26.40g	22A.000.000000.0033
9.2E	Lima	1701	H	8 Reales	22.10g	72A.013.000123.0070
9.2F	Lima	1703	H	8 Reales	26.40g	72A.013.000171.0034
9.2G	Lima	1706	R	8 Reales	22.40g	94A.036.000779.0127
9.2H	Lima	1708	H	8 Reales	21.00g	72A.013.000694.0473
9.2I	Lima	1710	H	8 Reales	21.30g	72A.013.000694.0310
9.2J	Lima	1711	M	8 Reales	25.20g	72A.013.000694.0493
9.3A	Lima	1699	R	4 Reales	12.60g	72A.013.000215.0106
9.3B	Lima	1700	H	4 Reales	12.40g	72A.013.000171.0044
9.3C	Lima	1703	H	4 Reales	11.90g	22A.000.000000.0834

Figure	Mint	Year	Assayer	Denom.	Weight	Catalog No.
9.3D	Lima	1704	H	4 Reales	10.20g	22A.000.000000.0563
9.3E	Lima	1705	H	4 Reales	12.00g	72A.013.000216.0060
9.3F	Lima	1710	H	4 Reales	10.30g	72A.013.000694.0079
9.4A	Lima	1684	V	8 Reales	26.40g	94A.052.000567.0013
9.4B	Lima	1684	V	8 Reales	26.40g	94A.052.000567.0013
9.4C	Lima	1692	V	4 Reales	12.60g	94A.052.000565.0002
9.4D	Lima	1693	V	8 Reales	26.60g	94A.052.000567.0002
9.4E	Lima	1694	M	8 Reales	26.20g	94A.052.000567.0003
9.4F	Lima	1695	R	4 Reales	11.10g	94A.052.000565.0001
9.4G	Lima	1699	R	8 Reales	24.90g	94A.052.000567.0016
9.4H	Lima	1703	H	8 Reales	25.30g	94A.052.000567.0005
9.4I	Lima	1703	H	8 Reales	25.30g	94A.052.000567.0005
9.5A	Lima	1704	H	8 Reales	26.30g	72A.013.000174.0143
9.5B	Lima	1709	M	8 Reales	25.40g	94A.052.000567.0007
9.5C	Lima	1711	M	8 Reales	26.50g	94A.052.000567.0014
9.5D	Lima	1711	M	8 Reales	26.20g	72A.013.000202.0001
9.6A	Cartagena	1655		8 Reales	20.38g	94A.132.009889.0001
9.6B	Cartagena	1655		8 Reales	20.38g	94A.132.009889.0001
9.6C	Cartagena	1655	S	4 Reales	9.63g	94A.132.010195.0001
9.6D	Cartagena	1655	S	4 Reales	9.63g	94A.132.010195.0001
9.6E	Cartagena	1655	S	2 Reales	4.99g	97A.005.013944.0001
9.6F	Cartagena	1655	S	2 Reales	4.99g	97A.005.013944.0001
9.6G	Santa Fé*			8 Reales	20.62g	94A.132.009886.0001
9.6H	Santa Fé			8 Reales	20.62g	94A.132.009886.0001
9.6I	Bogotá	1652		8 Reales	25.55g	97A.005.013016.0001
9.7A	Guatemala	1779	P	8 Reales	20.34g	93A.678.000228.0001

*Santa Fé is Santa Fé de Bogotá

Coins Sorted by Mint, Year, and Denomination

Figure	Mint	Year	Assayer	Denom.	Weight	Catalog No.
9.6I	Bogotá	1652		8 Reales	25.55g	97A.005.013016.0001
5.1D	Bogotá	1652		8 Reales	25.55g	97A.005.013016.0001
9.6E	Cartagena	1655	S	2 Reales	4.99g	97A.005.013944.0001
9.6F	Cartagena	1655	S	2 Reales	4.99g	97A.005.013944.0001
9.6C	Cartagena	1655	S	4 Reales	9.63g	94A.132.010195.0001
9.6D	Cartagena	1655	S	4 Reales	9.63g	94A.132.010195.0001
9.6A	Cartagena	1655		8 Reales	20.38g	94A.132.009889.0001
9.6B	Cartagena	1655		8 Reales	20.38g	94A.132.009889.0001
5.1E	Cartagena	1655		8 Reales	20.38g	94A.132.009889.0001
9.7A	Guatemala	1779	P	8 Reales	20.34g	93A.678.000228.0001
9.1E	Lima	1659	V	4 Reales	11.99g	96A.114.013023.0001
9.1F	Lima	1659	V	4 Reales	11.99g	96A.114.013023.0001
5.6A	Lima	1659	V	8 Reales	26.94g	97A.005.013325.0001
9.1A	Lima	1659	V	8 Reales	23.85g	94A.132.011152.0001
9.1B	Lima	1659	V	8 Reales	25.30g	94A.132.011153.0001
9.1C	Lima	1659	V	8 Reales	24.50g	97A.005.015497.0001

Figure	Mint	Year	Assayer	Denom.	Weight	Catalog No.
9.1D	Lima	1659	V	8 Reales	24.50g	97A.005.015497.0001
5.6B	Lima	1659	V	8 Reales	26.94g	97A.005.013325.0001
9.4A	Lima	1684	V	8 Reales	26.40g	94A.052.000567.0013
9.4B	Lima	1684	V	8 Reales	26.40g	94A.052.000567.0013
5.2C	Lima	1686	R	1 Real	3.03g	94A.052.000557.0024
5.2D	Lima	1686	R	1 Real	3.03g	94A.052.000557.0024
5.1C	Lima	1687	R	8 Reales	26.60g	94A.052.000589.0021
9.4C	Lima	1692	V	4 Reales	12.60g	94A.052.000565.0002
9.4D	Lima	1693	V	8 Reales	26.60g	94A.052.000567.0002
9.4E	Lima	1694	M	8 Reales	26.20g	94A.052.000567.0003
9.4F	Lima	1695	R	4 Reales	11.10g	94A.052.000565.0001
9.2A	Lima	1696	H	8 Reales	25.20g	72A.013.000126.0058
9.2B	Lima	1697	H	8 Reales	22.40g	72A.013.000126.0006
8.11D	Lima	1698	H	1 Real	3.20g	94A.036.000875.0022
9.2C	Lima	1698	H	8 Reales	20.80g	72A.013.000126.0062
8.11C	Lima	1699	R	1 Real	3.30g	94A.036.000877.0016
9.3A	Lima	1699	R	4 Reales	12.60g	72A.013.000215.0106
9.2D	Lima	1699	R	8 Reales	26.40g	22A.000.000000.0033
9.4G	Lima	1699	R	8 Reales	24.90g	94A.052.000567.0016
5.2I	Lima	1699	R	8 Reales	26.40g	72A.013.000126.0005
5.2J	Lima	1699	R	8 Reales	26.40g	72A.013.000126.0005
9.3B	Lima	1700	H	4 Reales	12.40g	72A.013.000171.0044
9.2E	Lima	1701	H	8 Reales	22.10g	72A.013.000123.0070
9.3C	Lima	1703	H	4 Reales	11.90g	22A.000.000000.0834
9.2F	Lima	1703	H	8 Reales	26.40g	72A.013.000171.0034
9.4H	Lima	1703	H	8 Reales	25.30g	94A.052.000567.0005
9.4I	Lima	1703	H	8 Reales	25.30g	94A.052.000567.0005
9.3D	Lima	1704	H	4 Reales	10.20g	22A.000.000000.0563
9.5A	Lima	1704	H	8 Reales	26.30g	72A.013.000174.0143
9.3E	Lima	1705	H	4 Reales	12.00g	72A.013.000216.0060
8.11F	Lima	1706	R	1 Real	2.60g	94A.036.000877.0042
9.2G	Lima	1706	R	8 Reales	22.40g	94A.036.000779.0127
9.2H	Lima	1708	H	8 Reales	21.00g	72A.013.000694.0473
9.5B	Lima	1709	M	8 Reales	25.40g	94A.052.000567.0007
9.3F	Lima	1710	H	4 Reales	10.30g	72A.013.000694.0079
9.2I	Lima	1710	H	8 Reales	21.30g	72A.013.000694.0310
9.2J	Lima	1711	M	8 Reales	25.20g	72A.013.000694.0493
9.5C	Lima	1711	M	8 Reales	26.50g	94A.052.000567.0014
9.5D	Lima	1711	M	8 Reales	26.20g	72A.013.000202.0001
8.11E	Mexico			1 Real	3.00g	94A.036.000869.0007
8.11J	Mexico		P	1 Real	3.10g	93A.640.000152.0003
8.11G	Mexico		J	2 Reales	6.30g	94A.036.000865.0001
5.2E	Mexico		J	2 Reales	6.57g	94A.052.000582.0014
5.2F	Mexico		J	2 Reales	6.57g	94A.052.000582.0014
7.4B	Mexico			4 Reales	10.80g	72A.013.000218.0115
7.4C	Mexico			4 Reales	11.80g	22A.000.000000.0876
7.4E	Mexico			4 Reales	11.80g	94A.036.000857.0039
7.4F	Mexico			4 Reales	12.00g	72A.013.000748.0087

Figure	Mint	Year	Assayer	Denom.	Weight	Catalog No.
7.4H	Mexico			4 Reales	12.20g	94A.036.000894.0046
7.5F	Mexico			4 Reales	12.70g	94A.036.000862.0003
7.5H	Mexico			4 Reales	12.70g	94A.036.000781.0078
7.6E	Mexico			4 Reales	14.20g	72A.013.000215.0025
7.6G	Mexico			4 Reales	12.30g	72A.013.000191.0005
7.6I	Mexico			4 Reales	13.80g	72A.013.000171.0006
7.6J	Mexico			4 Reales	11.20g	94A.052.000580.0007
7.8E	Mexico			4 Reales	12.70g	72A.013.000204.0022
7.11G	Mexico			4 Reales	12.60g	72A.013.000212.0025
7.13I	Mexico			4 Reales	13.00g	93A.617.000154.0040
7.14H	Mexico			4 Reales	13.10g	72A.013.000746.0112
7.4I	Mexico		J	4 Reales	13.20g	94A.052.000583.0003
7.3H	Mexico		J	8 Reales	23.00g	72A.013.000172.0073
7.3A	Mexico			8 Reales	24.40g	72A.013.000209.0105
7.3B	Mexico			8 Reales	22.40g	72A.013.000694.0555
7.3C	Mexico			8 Reales	26.20g	72A.013.000670.0501
7.3D	Mexico			8 Reales	26.30g	72A.013.000205.0012
7.3E	Mexico			8 Reales	26.10g	72A.013.000725.0015
7.3F	Mexico			8 Reales	24.10g	94A.036.000857.0027
7.3I	Mexico			8 Reales	24.90g	72A.013.000209.0106
7.3J	Mexico			8 Reales	25.20g	72A.013.000216.0055
7.4D	Mexico			8 Reales	24.80g	22A.000.000000.0395
7.4G	Mexico			8 Reales	26.30g	72A.013.000215.0093
7.5A	Mexico		J	8 Reales	26.00g	72A.013.000746.0143
7.5B	Mexico			8 Reales	26.00g	94A.036.000889.0032
7.5D	Mexico			8 Reales	26.30g	72A.013.000667.0070
7.5E	Mexico			8 Reales	26.30g	72A.013.000667.0070
7.5G	Mexico			8 Reales	26.00g	72A.013.000746.0169
7.5I	Mexico			8 Reales	26.30g	94A.036.000889.0016
7.5J	Mexico			8 Reales	23.90g	94A.052.000501.0057
7.6A	Mexico			8 Reales	24.90g	72A.013.000213.0053
7.6K	Mexico		J	8 Reales	23.00g	72A.013.000694.0471
7.6B	Mexico			8 Reales	24.40g	72A.013.000216.0119
7.6D	Mexico			8 Reales	24.80g	72A.013.000209.0098
7.6F	Mexico			8 Reales	26.50g	72A.013.000208.0052
7.6H	Mexico			8 Reales	23.50g	94A.036.000780.0042
7.7B	Mexico			8 Reales	25.10g	72A.013.000667.0264
7.7C	Mexico			8 Reales	26.60g	72A.013.000191.0018
7.7D	Mexico			8 Reales	26.10g	72A.013.000210.0092
7.7E	Mexico			8 Reales	25.70g	94A.036.000894.0016
7.7G	Mexico			8 Reales	24.70g	72A.013.000210.0099
7.7H	Mexico		L	8 Reales	25.60g	72A.013.000126.0063
7.7I	Mexico			8 Reales	24.00g	72A.013.000669.0345
7.7J	Mexico			8 Reales	22.10g	72A.013.000695.0032
7.8A	Mexico			8 Reales	25.30g	72A.013.000696.0025
7.8B	Mexico			8 Reales	25.50g	72A.013.000210.0118
7.8C	Mexico			8 Reales	27.10g	72A.013.000212.0180
7.8D	Mexico			8 Reales	26.70g	22.I

Figure	Mint	Year	Assayer	Denom.	Weight	Catalog No.
7.8F	Mexico			8 Reales	25.90g	72A.013.000746.0177
7.8G	Mexico			8 Reales	23.70g	72A.013.000209.0111
7.8H	Mexico			8 Reales	25.30g	94A.036.000861.0002
7.9A	Mexico			8 Reales	26.30g	72A.013.000217.0022
7.9B	Mexico			8 Reales	25.60g	72A.013.000217.0012
7.9C	Mexico			8 Reales	26.20g	72A.013.000205.0128
7.9D	Mexico		J	8 Reales	25.10g	94A.036.000736.0020
7.9E	Mexico			8 Reales	25.10g	72A.013.000217.0014
7.9F	Mexico			8 Reales	26.10g	72A.013.000217.0003
7.9G	Mexico			8 Reales	25.80g	72A.013.000217.0005
7.9H	Mexico			8 Reales	26.10g	72A.013.000217.0001
7.9I	Mexico			8 Reales	25.20g	72A.013.000217.0020
7.10A	Mexico			8 Reales	25.90g	72A.013.000746.0177
7.10B	Mexico			8 Reales	26.10g	72A.013.000191.0008
7.10C	Mexico			8 Reales	26.40g	72A.013.000667.0210
7.10F	Mexico			8 Reales	25.40g	94A.036.000880.0002
7.10D	Mexico			8 Reales	26.30g	94A.036.000886.0022
7.10E	Mexico			8 Reales	26.00g	72A.013.000208.0003
7.10I	Mexico			8 Reales	26.50g	72A.013.000124.0230
7.11A	Mexico		J	8 Reales	25.40g	72A.013.000213.0022
7.11C	Mexico			8 Reales	24.40g	94A.036.000868.0005
7.11D	Mexico			8 Reales	24.50g	94A.036.000767.0020
7.11E	Mexico			8 Reales	24.80g	72A.013.000667.0119
7.11F	Mexico			8 Reales	25.50g	94A.036.000780.0006
7.12A	Mexico			8 Reales	23.10g	94A.052.000502.0020
7.12B	Mexico			8 Reales	26.50g	72A.013.000207.0087
7.12C	Mexico			8 Reales	21.80g	94A.052.000538.0029
7.12D	Mexico			8 Reales	22.40g	22A.000.000000.0983
7.12E	Mexico			8 Reales	25.70g	72A.013.000191.0004
7.12F	Mexico			8 Reales	26.00g	93A.617.000154.0030
7.12G	Mexico			8 Reales	25.50g	72A.013.000123.0083
7.12H	Mexico			8 Reales	23.70g	72A.013.000214.0152
7.12J	Mexico			8 Reales	25.30g	72A.013.000667.0064
7.12K	Mexico			8 Reales	24.40g	72A.013.000209.0097
7.12L	Mexico			8 Reales	26.50g	72A.013.000746.0106
7.13A	Mexico			8 Reales	24.90g	72A.013.000748.0086
7.13B	Mexico			8 Reales	23.98g	22A.000.000000.0687
7.13C	Mexico			8 Reales	27.30g	94A.052.000512.0004
7.13D	Mexico			8 Reales	20.60g	94A.036.000780.0093
7.13E	Mexico			8 Reales	22.70g	72A.013.000691.0015
7.13F	Mexico			8 Reales	24.93g	94A.052.000510.0032
7.13G	Mexico			8 Reales	24.90g	72A.013.000209.0006
7.13H	Mexico			8 Reales	25.10g	94A.036.000861.0001
7.13J	Mexico			8 Reales	22.30g	94A.036.000780.0130
7.13K	Mexico			8 Reales	22.30g	72A.013.000214.0151
7.14A	Mexico			8 Reales	21.70g	94A.036.000781.0030
7.14B	Mexico			8 Reales	26.10g	72A.013.000669.0380
7.14C	Mexico			8 Reales	24.20g	94A.052.000506.0016

Figure	Mint	Year	Assayer	Denom.	Weight	Catalog No.
7.14D	Mexico			8 Reales	25.20g	72A.013.000212.0024
7.14E	Mexico			8 Reales	26.10g	72A.013.000668.0286
7.14F	Mexico			8 Reales	20.20g	72A.013.000694.0538
7.14G	Mexico			8 Reales	25.50g	72A.013.000191.0017
7.14I	Mexico		J	8 Reales	21.90g	72A.013.000694.0332
7.14J	Mexico			8 Reales	24.30g	22A.000.000000.0085
7.14K	Mexico			8 Reales	26.60g	72A.013.000667.0184
7.14L	Mexico			8 Reales	21.30g	72A.013.000219.0054
7.15A	Mexico			8 Reales	24.50g	72A.013.000194.0089
7.15B	Mexico		J	8 Reales	25.80g	72A.013.000176.0081
7.4J	Mexico		J	8 Reales	26.63g	94A.052.000562.0008
7.6C	Mexico			8 Reales	24.40g	72A.013.000216.0119
7.7F	Mexico			8 Reales	26.20g	72A.013.000126.0016
7.10G	Mexico			8 Reales	25.60g	72A.013.000674.0842
7.1A	Mexico	1655	P	8 Reales	27.37g	94A.132.009952.0001
7.1B	Mexico	1655	P	8 Reales	27.37g	94A.132.009952.0001
7.1D	Mexico	1655	P	8 Reales	27.25g	94A.132.009953.0001
7.1C	Mexico	1655	P	8 Reales	27.25g	94A.132.009953.0001
7.1E	Mexico	1656	P	8 Reales	26.05g	94A.132.009892.0001
7.1F	Mexico	1656	P	8 Reales	26.05g	94A.132.009892.0001
7.1G	Mexico	1657	P	8 Reales	26.23g	96A.114.013271.0001
7.1H	Mexico	1657	P	8 Reales	26.23g	96A.114.013271.0001
7.1J	Mexico	1657	P	8 Reales	26.44g	94A.132.009984.0001
7.1I	Mexico	1657	P	8 Reales	26.44g	94A.132.009984.0001
7.2A	Mexico	1700	L	8 Reales	27.10g	72A.013.000207.0035
7.10H	Mexico	1708	J	8 Reales	26.50g	72A.013.000191.0009
7.12I	Mexico	1708		8 Reales	25.40g	72A.013.000191.0007
7.2B	Mexico	1709		8 Reales	26.30g	72A.013.000208.0108
5.1A	Mexico	1709	J	8 Reales	26.35g	72A.013.000197.0071
7.2C	Mexico	1710		4 Reales	13.10g	72A.013.000214.0040
7.7A	Mexico	171-	J	8 Reales	24.40g	72A.013.000191.0002
7.2D	Mexico	1711	J	8 Reales	24.80g	94A.036.000868.0013
7.2E	Mexico	1712	J	8 Reales	26.00g	72A.013.000209.0136
7.5C	Mexico	1712	J	8 Reales	26.00g	72A.013.000209.0136
7.2F	Mexico	1713	J	8 Reales	25.80g	72A.013.000219.0011
7.11B	Mexico	1713		8 Reales	26.60g	72A.013.000667.0050
5.4A	Mexico	1714		8 Reales	18.50g	93A.674.000030.0001
7.2G	Mexico	1714		8 Reales	26.80g	72A.013.000746.0211
7.2H	Mexico	1714	J	8 Reales	25.70g	72A.013.000213.0151
7.2I	Mexico	1714	J	8 Reales	26.20g	22A.000.000000.0338
5.4B	Mexico	1714		8 Reales	18.50g	93A.674.000030.0001
5.2A	Mexico	1715		½ Real	1.20g	94A.036.000778.0298
5.2B	Mexico	1715		½ Real	1.20g	94A.036.000778.0298
7.4A	Mexico	1715		4 Reales	12.60g	72A.013.000123.0302
7.2J	Mexico	1715	J	8 Reales	25.70g	72A.013.000219.0039
7.2K	Mexico	1715	J	8 Reales	24.70g	72A.013.000211.0071
5.7A	Mexico	1732		8 Reales	18.31g	93A.613.000170.0001
5.7B	Mexico	1732		8 Reales	20.60g	93A.613.000171.0001

Figure	Mint	Year	Assayer	Denom.	Weight	Catalog No.
3.1C	Potosí		R	2 Reales	6.00g	94A.052.000585.0003
3.1G	Potosí		T	2 Reales	4.30g	72A.013.000363.0001
3.1D	Potosí		R	2 Reales	6.00g	94A.052.000585.0003
3.1H	Potosí		T	2 Reales	4.30g	72A.013.000363.0001
7.3G	Potosí	1—		8 Reales	24.50g	94A.036.000880.0010
3.1E	Potosí	162-	T	2 Reales	5.50g	94A.052.000585.0005
3.1F	Potosí	162-	T	2 Reales	5.50g	94A.052.000585.0005
3.1A	Potosí	1650	⊙	8 Reales	25.13g	97A.005.015795.0001
3.1B	Potosí	1650	⊙	8 Reales	25.13g	97A.005.015795.0001
5.5A	Potosí	1652	E	8 Reales	24.67g	94A.132.009893.0001
5.5C	Potosí	1652	E	8 Reales	25.89g	97A.005.013017.0001
8.1A	Potosí	1652	E	8 Reales	24.67g	94A.132.009893.0001
8.1C	Potosí	1652	E	8 Reales	25.80g	94A.132.009983.0001
8.2A	Potosí	1652	E	8 Reales	26.99g	99A.039.021617.0001
8.2C	Potosí	1652	E	8 Reales	27.93g	94A.132.009939.0001
8.2E	Potosí	1652	E	8 Reales	21.83g	94A.132.010998.0001
8.1B	Potosí	1652	E	8 Reales	24.67g	94A.132.009893.0001
8.1D	Potosí	1652	E	8 Reales	25.80g	94A.132.009983.0001
8.1E	Potosí	1652	E	8 Reales	23.10g	97A.086.016691.0001
8.2B	Potosí	1652	E	8 Reales	26.99g	99A.039.021617.0001
8.2D	Potosí	1652	E	8 Reales	27.93g	94A.132.009939.0001
8.2F	Potosí	1652	E	8 Reales	21.83g	94A.132.010998.0001
5.5B	Potosí	1652	E	8 Reales	24.67g	94A.132.009893.0001
5.5D	Potosí	1652	E	8 Reales	25.89g	97A.005.013017.0001
8.3A	Potosí	1653	E	8 Reales	26.27g	94A.132.009898.0001
8.3C	Potosí	1653	E	8 Reales	27.15g	94A.132.009891.0001
8.3B	Potosí	1653	E	8 Reales	26.27g	94A.132.009898.0001
8.3D	Potosí	1653	E	8 Reales	27.15g	94A.132.009891.0001
5.3C	Potosí	1654	E	8 Reales	26.71g	97A.005.014594.0002
8.4A	Potosí	1654	E	8 Reales	26.22g	94A.132.009895.0001
8.4B	Potosí	1654	E	8 Reales	24.12g	94A.132.009946.0001
8.4C	Potosí	1654	E	8 Reales	26.31g	94A.132.009941.0001
5.3D	Potosí	1654	E	8 Reales	26.71g	97A.005.014594.0002
8.5A	Potosí	1655	E	8 Reales	26.72g	94A.132.009981.0001
8.5B	Potosí	1655	E	8 Reales	26.72g	94A.132.009982.0001
8.5C	Potosí	1655	E	8 Reales	27.49g	94A.132.009901.0001
8.5D	Potosí	1655	E	8 Reales	26.18g	94A.132.009978.0001
8.5E	Potosí	1655	E	8 Reales	20.04g	94A.132.010732.0001
8.5F	Potosí	1656	E	8 Reales	27.92g	94A.132.009935.0001
5.3A	Potosí	1657	E	8 Reales		American Numismatic Society
5.3B	Potosí	1657	E	8 Reales		American Numismatic Society
8.6A	Potosí	1657	E	8 Reales	25.12g	94A.132.009956.0001
8.6B	Potosí	1657	E	8 Reales	25.12g	94A.132.009956.0001
8.6C	Potosí	1657	E	8 Reales	24.75g	94A.132.009896.0001
8.7A	Potosí	1658	E	8 Reales	26.01g	94A.132.009969.0001
8.7B	Potosí	1658	E	8 Reales	25.14g	94A.132.009900.0001
8.7E	Potosí	1658	E	8 Reales	25.80g	94A.132.009968.0001
8.7C	Potosí	1658	E	8 Reales	26.24g	94A.132.009965.0001

Figure	Mint	Year	Assayer	Denom.	Weight	Catalog No.
8.7G	Potosí	1658	E	8 Reales	27.40g	94A.132.009970.0001
8.7D	Potosí	1658	E	8 Reales	26.01g	94A.132.009969.0001
8.7F	Potosí	1658	E	8 Reales	26.24g	94A.132.009965.0001
8.11D	Potosí	1679	C	4 Reales	11.00g	94A.052.000590.0005
8.10E	Potosí	1679	C	4 Reales	11.00g	94A.052.000590.0005
8.10A	Potosí	1680	V	8 Reales	25.30g	94A.052.000591.0017
8.11A	Potosí	1686	VR	1 Real	2.30g	94A.036.000778.0233
8.9A	Potosí	1686	VR	8 Reales	22.20g	22A.000.000000.0565
8.8A	Potosí	1687	VR	4 Reales	10.10g	22A.000.000000.0094
8.11H	Potosí	1688	VR	2 Reales	4.60g	93A.671.000101.0001
8.11B	Potosí	1689	VR	1 Real	2.60g	94A.036.000872.0032
8.8B	Potosí	1690	VR	4 Reales	12.20g	72A.013.000171.0047
8.10C	Potosí	1690	VR	4 Reales	13.30g	94A.036.000917.0006
8.9B	Potosí	1690	VR	8 Reales	25.80g	22A.000.000000.0063
8.8C	Potosí	1691	VR	4 Reales	12.60g	72A.013.000216.0111
8.9C	Potosí	1691	VR	8 Reales	20.20g	22A.000.000000.0064
8.10B	Potosí	1692	VR	8 Reales	22.70g	94A.052.000591.0003
8.11I	Potosí	1693	VR	1 Real	3.00g	94A.036.000867.0029
8.9D	Potosí	1693	VR	8 Reales	24.70g	72A.013.000171.0042
8.8D	Potosí	1695	VR	4 Reales	13.60g	72A.013.000207.0170
8.9E	Potosí	1695	VR	8 Reales	21.10g	72A.013.000171.0032
8.9F	Potosí	1697	VR	8 Reales	24.90g	94A.036.000780.0034
8.8E	Potosí	1698	F	4 Reales	13.20g	72A.013.000215.0011
8.9G	Potosí	1698	VR	8 Reales	22.26g	94A.052.000575.0021
8.9H	Potosí	1699	F	8 Reales	23.50g	72A.013.000695.0064
8.8F	Potosí	1700	F	4 Reales	12.70g	72A.013.000191.0016
8.8G	Potosí	1700		4 Reales	13.80g	72A.013.000694.0272
5.2G	Potosí	1700	F	4 Reales	12.70g	72A.013.000191.0016
5.2H	Potosí	1700	F	4 Reales	12.70g	72A.013.000191.0016
8.9I	Potosí	1700	F	8 Reales	26.10g	72A.013.000191.0011
5.1B	Potosí	1700	F	8 Reales	25.72g	94A.052.000575.0022
8.9J	Potosí	1701	Y	8 Reales	25.30g	72A.013.000171.0048
8.9K	Potosí	1702	Y	8 Reales	26.90g	94A.052.000520.0001
8.8H	Potosí	1703	Y	4 Reales	13.30g	72A.013.000191.0014
8.9L	Potosí	1703	Y	8 Reales	25.40g	22A.000.000000.0567
8.8I	Potosí	1708	Y	4 Reales	13.60g	72A.013.000207.0116
9.6G	Santa Fé			8 Reales	20.62g	94A.132.009886.0001
9.6H	Santa Fé			8 Reales	20.62g	94A.132.009886.0001

*Santa Fé is Santa Fé de Bogotá.

Notes

Chapter 1. Introduction and Historical Background

1. Numerous coins and artifacts recovered from the *Atocha* were once held in Tallahassee until a federal court determined the wreck was located outside territorial waters, at which time all the material was returned to salvors. Much of it was then distributed to investors, who in turn sold it to treasure brokers, who have sold it to private collectors.

2. Although the 1733 Fleet was not carrying enormous amounts of silver and gold like that that had been lost on board the 1715 Plate Fleet, at least one vessel, the *San José,* had some 250 freshly minted examples of the newly designed Mexican "pillar dollar" of 1732 (Weller 1990: 53, 56). This coin has long been a classic rarity among collectors. However, the few specimens now in Tallahassee are badly corroded and are much inferior to those salvaged from the 1733 wreck.

3. Readers interested in details of Spanish political economy under Felipe II and his successors, as well as strategies developed for transfer of treasure from New World to Old, should consult the recent book by Walton (1994). For rigorously documented nautical details of Spanish galleons and the Spanish navy in general, see Phillips's definitive study (1986).

4. While today we seldom think of Haiti and the Dominican Republic as gold producers, gold dust and fine nuggets are still washed out of the same river gravels that were extensively mined by the earliest Spanish settlers of Hispaniola. It was gold from this island that started an exodus of adventurers out of Spain in hope more was to be found elsewhere in the Caribbean—and it was—during the conquest of Puerto Rico.

5. Fifty-five miles east of Palm Beach marine salvors have recovered more than 200 alloyed silver and gold ingots bearing the tax stamps of Carlos V, as ruler of the Holy Roman Empire. Some of these historic artifacts also bear assayers' marks I have attributed to Bernardino Vásquez de Tapia, whom we know was in Mexico with Cortés (for details see Armstrong 1993).

6. The classic study showing economic effects of this surge of silver on the cost of living in Spain is by Earl J. Hamilton (1934).

7. Francis Drake became the first pirate to sail around Cape Horn into the Pacific Ocean. From 1578 to 1579 he raided the coast of Chile and Peru, capturing more than 25 tons of lightly guarded silver ingots and coins from Potosí. His epic voyage continued across the Pacific and around the world back to England. In his wake, the Spanish began to refer to him in their dispatches as *El Drago* ("The Dragon").

8. Accurate historical details of the trade fair at Portobelo can be seen in a carefully researched painting by Robert McGinnis used to illustrate an equivalent scene of loading Mexican silver ingots on board the Manila galleon (Lyon 1990) while it was anchored at Acapulco.

9. Dargent Chamot (1988:91) claims Lima merchants who brought underweight and counterfeit silver coins from Potosí to pay for merchandise at the Portobelo trade fair were forced to return to Lima empty-handed. Common sense dictates this did not happen very often. The *Atocha* manifest of 1622 shows many large, privately owned silver ingots properly assayed and taxed, and therefore legal tender, were loaded on board at Portobelo. Debased or underweight coins probably were discounted heavily the first time they were detected by sellers from Spain, who were loath to ship their goods back again. The same reasoning applies to Lima merchants: they came to buy with legitimate ingots or good coins to avoid a costly and disastrous trip back home.

10. One of the few such silvermasters for whom we have archival documentation is Jacobo de Vereder, whose sign, a large "V," is found cut into a corner of many silver ingots recovered from the *Atocha*. Silvermasters were responsible for calculating the *avería*, a kind of transportation tax charged to merchants to reimburse the Crown for costs of maintaining guard ships for the convoys.

11. In a few cases the fleet would sail directly to Portobelo and then back track to Cartagena before sailing for Vera Cruz and/or Havana.

12. For more details of Portobelo and particularly photos of its present condition, see Webster (1993).

Chapter 2. Organization of the Spanish Colonial Mints

1. For this responsibility, the treasurer's share of profits (ca. 1650) would have been about $55,000 annually.

2. By an interesting coincidence, the copy of Pradeau obtained by the Florida Bureau of Archaeological Research for its reference library in Tallahassee was in fact previously purchased by Major Frederick Pridmore on May 3, 1956, for a mere £4 while he was in Aden. While it is understandable this famous numismatist might wish to have something to read in that desolate location, the puzzle is, from whom did he buy it in this odd corner of the Arabian Peninsula? However, more important to the theme of this study are his corrections to Pradeau's text, made in pencil at various places where Pridmore disagreed with certain historical statements. For example, on page 61, there is a particularly long notation by Pridmore that deserves publication here as an

example of the extent of his own research; in a small, neat hand Pridmore wrote the following:

> Charles III issued an ordinance from Spain, March 18th, 1771, whereby the Mexico City mint was instructed to strike silver coin of all denominations with dies bearing the portrait of the monarch, to be issued on January 1, 1772. By the same ordinance the striking of coins with the old dies was strictly forbidden. The viceroy of New Spain, Don Antonio Maria Bucareli y Ursúa, published in Mexico City an edict dated January 2nd, 1772, advising the inhabitants of the province of the effected change and that from then on only the new specie, of which the Mexico City mint had a sufficient quantity, was to be the sole legal tender. On April 8th, 1772, the viceroy reiterated the edict of January 1st and fixed a time limit of one year for the exchange of face value of the old coinage. After that time, the previously issued coins were to be purchased by the mint or assay office as bullion.

3. In Letter No. 139 of March 31, 1819, located in Sección Novena of Archivo General de Indias (hereinafter AGI), the viceroy of Mexico reminds the minister of state that apprentice engravers at the mint must comply with the king's ordinance that they attend school daily (but without neglecting their work). This is the only example of instructions regarding mint apprentices found during this study.

4. In Craig (1962) there is an interesting graph reflecting gradual decrease in weights of Potosí cob 1-real coins over the years before sudden increases were brought about coincident with death warrants of notorious counterfeiters.

5. AGI Charcas 16, Doc. 171.

6. AGI Charcas 16, Doc. 67.

7. Originally known as the *Derechos de Cobos,* the fee was a gift from the Emporer Charles V to his secretary Francisco de los Cobos. The rights to these funds reverted to the Crown and were passed on to these mint officials.

8. This practice explains the peculiar triangular silver wedges recovered from the 1715 "Wedge Wreck." I believe these were untaxed *piñas* being smuggled back to Spain, possibly at the bottom of a wooden barrel custom-built to accommodate them. Nine examples are curated by the Florida Bureau of Archaeological Research and available for future study. Three of these thick, pie-shaped wedges along with one of the less common muffin-shaped *piñas* can be seen in the treasure display in the Museum of Florida History located in the R. A. Gray Building in Tallahassee.

9. AGI Charcas 16, Doc. 97.

10. AGI Lima 1258. These sweeping new regulations were published in order to prepare all mints for installation of new milling machinery enabling mints to produce the "Spanish-milled dollar" of uniform weight and appearance.

11. Florida played an important role in the numismatic history of these new so-called pillar dollars made in 1732. For many years the coin was considered

a classic rarity with few known specimens changing hands for many thousands of dollars. Suddenly treasure divers in the Florida Keys began to recover dozens of uncirculated specimens from a sunken galleon that was part of the 1733 Fleet destroyed by a hurricane. Unfortunately, most pillar dollars from the *San José* show considerable seawater corrosion, but a few are known that are still in pristine condition. The state of Florida received no well-preserved pillar dollars even though all from this galleon were found within Florida territorial waters.

12. Technical problems at Potosí seem to revolve around difficulty in milling out silver straps to uniform thickness and then producing a round planchet of proper diameter and weight with an animal-powered wooden gearing system (½ *volante*) in use (see illus. 8.11). Apparently production of milled coinage could not keep up with the quantity of silver presented to the mint by owners who needed it converted into coins. Old-style handmade cobs could be struck up without these problems. However, neither milled nor cob coinage from this period seems to have been produced in quantity.

Chapter 3. Mint Scandals

1. ANB (Archivo Nacional de Bolivia, Sucre), AALP, vol. 13, folio 167, verso.

2. AGI 113, document of June 30, 1644.

3. Juan de Figueroa was also a *regidor* (alderman) of Lima. Judge Nestares Marín investigated him carefully and reported to the king (AGI 114, document of April 12, 1651) that Figueroa had paid 45,000 pesos for the title of *ensayador propietario* of the Potosí mint and during the thirteen-year period of greatest fraud, he had been paid a total of 382,934 pesos. He escaped serious punishment only to become involved in the mint scandals of 1668 from which he emerged with a token fine.

4. AGI 113, document of November 20, 1649. Rocha's reply to the charges against him can be found in a thick set of documents at the end of Charcas 687.

5. AGI 114, document of May 30, 1652.

6. Juan Velarde Treviño, a *caballero* of the Order of Calatrava, was a man of consequence in Potosí before he became embroiled in the Rocha scandals. Judge Marín had him arrested and thrown into jail at Cuzco. He quickly escaped in 1651 and somehow found his way back to Spain where he made many appeals but was fined for leaving Peru without royal permission. He was sent back to Potosí in chains to stand for his *residencia* (formal investigation of his term of office). Finally, a death warrant was issued for his crime of counterfeiting (AGI 114, document of June 5, 1653). He was strangled in the public square of Potosí.

7. Chroniclers such as Arzáns (1945: 169) repeat the contemporary popular belief that at some point in the final stages of the investigation, Rocha spirited away by night an enormous quantity of his accumulated counterfeit coins, hiding them in a cave nearby, or in the case cited, dumping them in the Tarapaya hot springs (see illus. 3.1).

8. AGI 686, *in passim*.

9. Data published by Lazo García (1992) show 218 *marcos* of counterfeit

coins were melted in 1668. Since the last batch of Rocha's counterfeits seems to have been melted in 1656, this relatively small quantity (1,826 coins minimum) must be related to the 1668 scandals.

Chapter 4. From Mountain to Monarch

1. One of the worst disasters on record is described in AGI Charcas 16, document 10–1–1581, where thirty-eight Indian miners were killed inside Cerro Rico by a single large rock falling down a mine shaft. Within hours of the accident Lic. Barros, a judge of the High Court who happened to be in town, rushed to the scene where he met with widows and children of these miners and paid them a 4,000-pesos cash settlement on the spot. I have found nothing in the archives that compares with this act of charity and concern for Indians at Potosí.

2. Generally speaking, very fine trimmings were swept up daily and kept by the assayer to defray his expenses of recycling larger pieces and unacceptably defective coins that had to be melted down. Blatant abuses in cutting and trimming planchets could not be perpetrated on owners of silver submitted to the mint since they knew exactly how many coins should result from the weight of silver they owned.

3. Readers are encouraged to seek out publications of Glenn S. Murray (see references), particularly for their exquisite photographs of seldom-seen mint machinery. Specifically, on page 10 of his "Project: Segovia '92" they will find crisp photos of iron-hammer dies from the Segovia mint, which, through long use, have acquired clearly mushroomed striking surfaces. On the same page are machine-driven roller dies that supplanted them and may have been used much later in some American mints.

4. Although not an eyewitness to the 1626 disaster, the chronicler Arzáns writing some eighty years later presents a vivid description of this destructive natural disaster used as a basis for this chapter. It is interesting to note that the Potosí mintage figures available from Lazo García (1992) substantiate a decline of at least 50 percent for 1626 compared with subsequent years. But the recovery in coin production from 1627 onward suggests both mills and aqueduct were soon repaired. During my own research in 1989 I saw artisanal miners digging through thick deposits of the 1626 alluvium to recover silver ore and any amalgam from the debris. These valuables came from the stockpiles of more than 100 mills that were swept away.

Chapter 5. Finding Your Way around Cobs

1. An often-repeated translation is "from the end of a bar" derived from the Spanish *al cabo de barra.* In stubborn pursuit of this idea, some years ago a Texas collector cast a large silver ingot and attempted to shear off a planchet from the end of it (as you might slice off a piece of salami) in order to replicate the making of a cob. Anyone who has a good Spanish dictionary will soon see that *cabo de barra* means the last payment due on an account. Therefore the word comes from the verb *acabar* (to finish). The only other attempt at translation I have ever read involves crude barnyard humor in the expression "rough as a

cob." There is nothing more to be gained from etymology of the word "cob."

2. Some years ago a well-known Mexican collector obtained a mint-sealed canvas bag containing 1,000 uncirculated 1821 ¼-real milled coins from the Guatemala mint. This hoard has largely been absorbed by the collector market since that time.

3. Heart-shaped cobs have no parallel in numismatic literature. They are known in all reales denominations. The popularity of and the value placed on these smaller hearts are astounding. Their perforations demonstrate they were intended to be worn as personal jewelry or, more likely, sewn to garments of religious figures as are their modern analogs, the *milagros* (small silver medals) purchased from kiosks outside churches in northern Peru. They take the shape of organs that are diseased or wishes for such benefits as travel and wealth, and are left inside churches as votive gifts. From time to time they are recycled back to sellers. They show a clear anatomical resemblance to the human heart caused by accidental shearing of the silver planchets. In most cases this was further enhanced by hand-carving after they were struck with coin dies. These embellishments complicate the matter of authenticating a legitimate specimen from one that has been made recently using any available cob. In other words, neither is likely to be close to its legal weight.

It is not possible to tell exactly when this custom began, but examples made from coins struck before the reign of Felipe IV have never come to my attention, nor are there any made from Mexican or Colombian cobs. I conclude it was a religious culture trait restricted to the Peruvian Andes and probably associated with a *cofradía* (religious fraternity) devoted to the Sacred Heart of Jesus.

4. For many years 1652 coins of Potosí were difficult to obtain and numismatists assumed their scarcity was due to many design changes and general confusion in the mint taking place that year. Actually, mintage was considerable and many such coins are now known to have gone down with several treasure ships that sank over the next few years. Salvage from these wrecks has once again made this date available but it is still much sought after by a new generation of collectors.

5. It may seem strange that silver production from the New World peaked in 1590 when the most prolific source, Cerro Rico at Potosí, was thought to be nearly exhausted. The answer lies in new refining techniques that were then being applied to an enormous amount of earlier mine tailings of relatively high silver content that had been discarded on all sides of this mountain.

Chapter 7. Mexican Silver Coins

1. Cob coins with missing mint marks and assayers' initials because of deliberate hammer blows to the planchet are typical of periods in other mints (particularly Potosí) when we know employee conspiracies were underway. But in the Mexican series where dates also are often missing because of the peculiar planchet shapes, it must have been a relatively easy matter for "contemporary counterfeits," as today's coin dealers prefer to call them, to appear

from the workshops of silversmiths. These debased and/or underweight coins without assayers' marks could not easily be traced back to the guilty parties. Fortunately, there are no such specimens to my knowledge in the Florida Collection.

2. The question may be asked, why did colonial mints all produce cob coins whose design features were often obliterated by hammer blows struck after dies were used? This sequence was dictated by the desire to produce a rounded coin without serious planchet cracks. Hammering causes "work-hardening" of silver, which would make it difficult to get a strong impression from dies without causing the planchet to split.

3. Proof these elliptical depressions in Mexican silver planchets were the result of a long-term phenomenon taking place at the mint can be found in a photograph of lot 672 in the June 4, 1994, auction catalog of Ponterio & Associates Sale No. 69. It is a Mexican 8 reales of the "square-shape" variety with transitional design struck in 1730 and bears no signs of being from sea salvage. The depression is identical to that shown here in figure 7.12c. Still another example can be seen in lot 1,810 of Ponterio & Associates Sale No. 74 in an auction held March 24 and 25, 1995, where an 8-reales "square" of 1731 was offered for sale.

A few months later other professional numismatists of Classical Numismatic Group Inc. offered (lot 1516, Auction 35) a Mexican 2 reales (misidentified as a "real 5.29 gm") with a large area missing from the planchet. They confound the problem with this quaint explanation: "The hole in the center of this coin is not a flan flaw. The flan has been manipulated into a U shape, creating a pair of 'pantaloons' with flared legs. A most unusual piece." Indeed.

These widely separated dates (1708–1731) suggest the phenomenon was not considered serious by mint workers, who continued to use the same production process resulting in these planchet depressions.

Chapter 8. Potosí and Its Coins

1. Hence the name chosen by Bakewell (1984) for his excellent book *Miners of the Red Mountain*.

2. Shortly after conquest, Spanish observers make it clear the Inka regime supported full-time mineral prospectors with local knowledge of metallic deposits in their districts.

3. For details see Hanke (1966) and Cañete y Dominguez (1952a).

4. AGI Charcas 16, file 55; 8/9, 1572.

5. For construction details of hydraulic stamp mills at Potosí see Craig (1993).

6. AGI Charcas 43, Doc. *borrador* [1591].

7. "Gaspar Ruíz, chief assayer and smelter of the Villa of Potosí, says one of the conditions with which these positions were auctioned was that he be given the necessary Indians for smelting and making silver ingots and twelve Indians to make charcoal necessary for proper functioning of the foundry. But not with these twelve, nor with many more, can sufficient charcoal be made because the

region and places where it is made are so far away. I beg Your Highness to send me forty Soras, Casayes or Carangas Indians of Colquemarca each year to make the charcoal." AGI Charcas 43, Doc. 20–10–1593.

8. AGI Charcas 688, Doc. 127.

9. This legal regulation was seldom, if ever, enforced since there was no registry or other means to indicate exactly when a mill owner had processed a given batch of ore, extracted the amalgam, refined out the mercury, smelted the *piña,* and cast it into an unassayed bar. From archival records it is clear even royal officials trafficked in this *plata corriente.*

10. English-speaking numismatists refer to these earliest milled coins as "pillar dollars" because the obverse design contains conspicuous Pillars of Hercules. The Spanish equivalent is *columnarias* or, less commonly, *mundos y mares.* This reference to worlds and seas is derived from the remainder of the design, consisting of globes showing Old World and New World above ocean waves.

11. AGI Charcas 678, Doc. 11.

12. Elsewhere, cobs had ceased to be struck when installation of heavy equipment made it possible to make planchets and strike coins using gear-driven machinery. These improvements began first at Mexico (1730), followed by Guatemala (1733), Santiago (1749), Lima (1751), Bogotá (1755), and finally Potosí (1767). However, true cobs were never made at the Guatemala and Santiago mints before milling machinery was introduced. Potosí cobs of the 1770s have design elements so poorly rendered that often only the central cross is clear. Very little legend can be seen on these peculiar small, thick planchets. They are among the crudest coins to be found anywhere; altogether, a disgraceful end of the line. Lazo García (1992) has found documents indicating these cobs were made by a private contractor working independently inside the mint while regular employees were involved in producing the new design of milled coins.

13. A "wigged lion" is terminology I use to describe the engraver's characteristic style of rendering the lion's mane. It looks very much like formal wigs worn by judges of the Audiencia and wealthy aristocracy, who in turn were known as *pelucónes* (big wigs) by commoners in colonial Peru.

14. Specimens of Potosí cobs from the critical years 1650–1652 were all formerly scarce to rare and few collections had an example. But in recent years several wrecks from around the world (in addition to the Jupiter Wreck) have yielded so many different varieties that a monograph (Menzel 1995) has been written on this series.

15. One of my all-time favorite coins is shown in figure 8.5a, where a slight die bounce caused the left side of the obverse to read 5,5,5, sending the numbers surfing up and over the waves. In figure 8.8b the 5's begin to sink below the waves (perhaps because they are so large and heavy?). Well, fortunately they bob up again in the remainder of this figure, although a tiny 5 in a 1656 coin, figure 8.5f, is almost squeezed out by a large 6.

16. It may be no coincidence that mint employees produced a superb series of the best "royals" or presentation coins in 1657. More than seven have been

auctioned in recent years. Sadly, none seem to have been found in Florida waters.

17. Since Mexican die sinkers used a distinctive obverse design dominated by a large shield, it is not unusual to find them producing 8 and 4 reales interchangeably from the same dies. There are various examples in the Florida Collection of 8-reales dies used to strike 4 reales, and the reverse. In such cases users were left to recognize the difference by weight alone.

Chapter 9. Coins from Lima, Cartagena, Santa Fé de Bogotá, and Guatemala

1. The device of a star was chosen for these coins because Lima was known as the "City of Kings," a reference to the Three Wise Men, and hence it became the Star of Bethlehem. It is an unusual example of numismatic kenning.

2. To view a photograph of a better-preserved Lima Star of 1659 from the identical die, see lot 2,895 of Swiss Bank Auction No. 57, where it reportedly sold for SF 10,000 on January 27, 1995. However, readers unfamiliar with the arcane world of coin auctions should keep in mind the prices reportedly paid for rare coins may not accurately reflect reality and indeed such coins do not always change hands in spite of the "prices realized."

3. Even more controversial and suspect are gold coins purportedly from this same series. They are cataloged in Calicó et al. (1994: 243) as unauthorized trial pieces made with permission of Viceroy Alva de Liste.

4. The colonial archives at Lima have been subjected to fires, earthquakes, and sacking by an invading army, which may account for much of this problem. What we do know is largely due to efforts of modern researchers and collectors such as Sellschopp, Dym, and Dargent Chamot.

5. From a careful study of Lima assayers listed in Calicó et al. (1994) it is apparent Lima assayers during this period had divisions of labor, being assigned to work either silver or gold, and assignments differed within the silver series according to denomination. Probably, experienced assayers were assigned to gold and high-value silver coins. We do not see this happening at Potosí, where gold was not struck until late in the eighteenth century.

6. This relative scarcity is simply a reflection of where the bulk of silver production was located during the sixteenth to nineteenth centuries and the total lack of hydraulic stamp-mill capacity at Lima.

7. Lima was a more urbane and relatively genteel place to work; I am not aware of Indian forced laborers (*mitayos*) or Negro slaves being kept inside the mint at this time.

8. The need to identify which die cutter made a given die may have arisen at Lima if die cutters were hired on a piecework basis. The practice is more evident on dies used for striking gold at this mint.

9. If the earliest coins issued by the Cartagena branch mint were desperately needed to facilitate trade within the viceroyalty, it is difficult to understand why local merchants would try to prevent them from being used. Possibly there was fear the mint might soon issue these coins without any silver at all.

10. Although discussion of this unique treasure coin is far beyond the scope

of this book, readers should be aware of its existence in case others are salvaged inside Florida waters; details of this coin have appeared in Craig and Simmons (1995).

11. In my capacity as numismatic advisor for divisions, I nearly overlooked the badly corroded Cartagena 4 reales of 1655, one of the very few to exist. But when I turned it over, the better-preserved reverse with its distinctive shield caught my eye. At first I believed it to be from Santa Fé de Bogotá like the coin shown in figure 9.6g–h. Eventually it was traced to the small Cartagena mint and this alerted me to look for others in the next division when more specimens appeared. The dated 1655 8-reales companion piece from Cartagena was identified several months later. Even more recently, a 2-reales specimen was added to the collection. With luck, perhaps better-preserved coins may someday be recovered from this increasingly interesting wreck.

References

Alba, Armando. 1943. "La Casa Real de Moneda de la Villa Imperial de Potosí." Unpaginated photographic folder on cardboard with text, on file at Sociedad Geográfica y de Historia, Potosí.

———. 1944. *Archivo de Documentos de la Casa Real de Moneda Potosí.* Sociedad Geográfica y de Historia, Potosí. Buenos Aires: Plantié, Talleres Gráficos.

Alexander, David T. 1978. "Neptune's Bounty," *Numismatic Scrapbook* 41, no. 476: 6–16; 70–72.

Allen, W. Frank. 1967. "History Revealed: Previously Unknown Spanish Gold Coins," *The Numismatist* (February): 1–16.

Almanzar's. 1981. *Mail Bid Auction Catalog: Part 1 of an Outstanding (Lifetime Endeavor) Collection of Hispanic American Coinage.* San Antonio: [privately printed].

Armstrong, Douglas R. 1993. *Tumbaga Silver for Emperor Charles V of the Holy Roman Empire.* [privately printed].

Arzáns de Orsúa y Vela, Bartolomé. 1965. *Historia de la Villa Imperial de Potosí, Riquezas Incomparables de su Famoso Cerro, Grandezas de su Población, sus Guerras Civiles, y Casos Memorables.* Buenos Aires: Fundación "Simon A. Patiño."

Asociacion Venezolana de Numismaticos. 1968. *Ceca de Caracas.* Vol. 1.

Bakewell, Peter. 1971. *Silver Mining and Society in Colonial Mexico: Zacatecas, 1546–1700.* London: Cambridge University Press.

———. 1975. "Registered Silver Production in the Potosí District, 1550–1735," *Jahrbuch für Geschichte von Staat, Wirtschaft und Gesellschaft Lateinamericas* 12: 67–103.

——— 1984. *Miners of the Red Mountain: Indian Labor in Potosí, 1545–1650.* Albuquerque: University of New Mexico Press.

——— 1988. *Silver and Entrepreneurship in Seventeenth Century Potosí: The Life and Times of Antonio López de Quiroga.* Albuquerque: University of New Mexico Press.

Banco de la Republica. N.d. *Casa de Moneda.* Medellín, Columbia: Movifoto.

Barriga Villalba, Antonio María. 1969. *Historia de la Casa de Moneda,* 2 vols. Bogotá: Banco de la Republica.

Beerenson, John L. 1978. "The Treasures of 1715," *Numismatics International* 12, no. 12: 389–395.

Bermúdez Plata, Cristóbal. 1949. *Catalogo de Documentos de la Seccion Novena del Archivo General de Indias.* Vol. 1. Sevilla: Escuela de Estudios Hispano-Americanos.

Bischoff, William L., ed. 1988. *The Coinage of El Peru.* New York: American Numismatic Society.

Bradley, Peter T. 1993. "The Loss of the Flagship of the *Armada del Mar del Sur* (1654) and Related Aspects of Viceregal Administration," *Mariner's Mirror* (November): 383–403.

Brown, Kendall W. 1986. *Bourbons and Brandy: Imperial Reform in Eighteenth-Century Arequipa.* Albuquerque: University of New Mexico Press.

Burgess, Robert F. 1977. *They Found Treasure.* New York: Dodd, Mead.

Burgess, Robert F., and Carl J. Clausen. 1982. *Florida's Golden Galleons: The Search for the 1715 Spanish Treasure Fleet.* Port Salerno, Fla.: Florida Classics Library.

Burzio, Humberto F. 1945. *La Ceca de la Villa Imperial de Potosí y la Moneda Colonial.* Facultad de Filosofia y Letras de la Universidad de Buenos Aires, Instituto de Investigaciónes Históricas. Buenos Aires: Peuser, S.A.

———. 1950. "Ensayo de Catálogo de los Valores Acuñados con Sello Español, en la Ceca de la Villa Imperial de Potosí 1574/75–1825," *Boletín del Instituto Bonaerense de Numismática y Antigüedades* 2: 45–60.

———. 1958. *Diccionario de la Moneda Hispanoamericana.* 3 vols. Santiago de Chile: Fondo Historico y Bibliografico José Toribio Medina.

———. 1959. "La Casa de Moneda de Potosí en el Período Hispánica," *Boletín del Instituto Bonaerense de Numismática y Antigüedades* 6: 29–38.

Butts, Allison, and Charles D. Coxe, eds. 1967. *Silver: Economics, Metallurgy, and Use.* Princeton, N.J.: D. Van Nostrand.

Calbetó de Grau, Gabriel. 1970. *Compendio de las Piezas de Ocho Reales.* 2 vols. San Juan, Puerto Rico: Ediciones Juan Ponce de Leon.

Calicó, F. Xavier 1953. *Aportación a la Historia Monetaria de Santa Fé de Bogotá (Colombia): (Ensaio de Catálogo de las Acuñaciones de Oro con Marcas F.S. o S.F. Erróneamente Atribuídas a Sevilla).* Barceolna: Xavier and Ferrán Calicó.

Calicó, Ferrán, Xavier Calicó, and Joaquín Trigo. 1994. *Las Monedas Españolas desde Fernando e Isabel a Juan Carlos I, Años: 1474 a 1994.* Barcelona: Gráficas Reclam, S.A.

Cancio, Leopoldo. 1978a. "El Tesoro de El Mesuno, Corregido y Aumentado," *Gaceta Numismática* 51: 32–40; 52: 37–49.

———. 1978b. "Una Epoca Anarquia en la Ceca de Potosí," *Gaceta Numismática* 50: 28–33.

Cañete y Dominguez, Pedro Vicente. 1952a [1787]. *Guia de la Provincia de Potosí.* Potosí: Editorial "Potosí."

———. 1952b. *Historia Fisica y Politica de la Provincia de Potosí.* La Paz: Fundación Universitaria "Simon I. Patiño."

Castán, C., and J. R. Cayón. 1980. *Las Monedas Hispano Musulmanas y Cristianas, 711–1981*. Madrid: Artegraf, S.A.

Ceca Potosina: Catalogo de la Exposición de Numismática. 1988. Potosí: Casa Real de la Moneda.

Clausen, Carl J. 1965. *A 1715 Spanish Treasure Ship*. Contributions of the Florida State Museum, Social Sciences, No. 12. Gainesville: University of Florida.

Cockrell, Wilburn A., ed. 1981. *In the Realms of Gold: Proceedings of the Tenth Conference on Underwater Archaeology*. Fathom Eight Special Publication No. 1. San Marino, Calif.

Craig, Alan K. 1962. "Counterfeit Coins of Alto Peru," *The Numismatist* 75, no. 12: 1603–1609.

———. 1988. *Gold Coins of the 1715 Spanish Plate Fleet: A Numismatic Study of the State of Florida Collection*. Florida Archaeology, No. 4. Tallahassee: Florida Bureau of Archaeological Research.

———. 1989. "Mining Ordenanzas and Silver Production at Potosí: The Toledo Reforms." In *Precious Metals, Coinage, and the Changes in Monetary Structures in Latin America, Europe, Asia*. Proceedings of the 1985 Stockton Conference on Monetary History, ed. Eddy van Cauwenberghe, 159–183. Leuven, Belgium: Leuven University Press.

———. 1993. "The Ingenious *Ingenios:* Spanish Colonial Water Mills at Potosí." In *Culture, Form, and Place: Essays in Cultural and Historical Geography*. Edited by Kent Mathewson. Vol. 32 of *Geoscience and Man*. Baton Rouge: Geoscience Publications, 125–156.

———. 2000. *Spanish Colonial Gold Coins in the Florida Collection*. Gainesville: University Press of Florida.

———. Forthcoming. *Treasure Bars from Florida Waters*.

Craig, Alan K., and Adon A. Gordus. 1993. "Numismatic Discoveries from the Florida State Collection," *Actes de XIe Congrès International de Numismatique* 4: 129–133.

Craig, Alan K., and David Simmons. 1995. "An Atocha Coin of Great Historic Interest," *Gaceta Numismática*.

Craig, Alan K., and Robert C. West, eds. 1994. *In Quest of Mineral Wealth: Aboriginal and Colonial Mining and Metallurgy in Spanish America*. Vol. 33 of *Geoscience and Man*. Baton Rouge: Geoscience Publications.

Crespo R., Alberto. 1977. "Esclavos Negros en Bolivia." In *Bicentenario del Virreinato del Río de La Plata*, vol. 2. Buenos Aires: Academia Nacional de la Historia, 119–139.

Cunietti-Ferrando, Arnaldo J. 1971. "Ensayadores de la Ceca de Potosí de los Siglos XVII y XVIII," *Gaceta Numismática* 50: 43–47.

———. 1972. "Los Primeros Ensayadores de la Ceca de Potosí," *Cuadernos de Numismática* vol. 1 (3): 1–16.

———. 1987a. "Ensayo de Catalogación de Monedas Potosínas del Escudo Coronado: 1617 a 1652," *Cuadernos de Numismática y Ciencias Históricas* 14 (57): 41–48.

———. 1987b. "La Casa de Moneda de Potosí Hasta la Reforma de 1652," *Cuadernos de Numismática y Ciencias Históricas* 14(56): 37–45.

———. 1995. *Historia de la Real Casa de Moneda de Potosi durante la Dominación Hispanica, 1573–1652.* Buenos Aires: Imprenta Pellegrini.

Dargent Chamot, Eduardo. 1986a. "Las Cecas Peruana y las Reformas Borbónicas," *BANCA* 15–16.

———. 1986b. "Los Esclavos de la Ceca Potosína del Siglo XVII," *Humanitas* 4.

———. 1988. *La Moneda Peruana en el Siglo XVII: (Reflejo de una Crisis).* Vol. 7 of *Cuadernos de Historia.* Lima: Universidad de Lima, Facultad de Ciencias Humanas.

Davis, John L. 1977. *Treasure, People, Ships, and Dreams.* Publication No. 4. San Antonio: Texas Antiquities Committee.

de Llanos, Garcia. 1983. *Diccionario y Maneras de Hablar que se Usan en las Minas y Sus Labores en los Ingenios y Beneficios de los Metales (1609).* Serie Fuentes Primarias, No. 1. La Paz: Museo Nacional de Etnografia y Folklore.

Dym, Kurt A. 1969. "Fine Silver Content of Some Spanish-American Coins (Spanish text)," *Gaceta Numismática* 13: 37–40.

———. 1970. "Apuntes Numismáticos Relacionados a la Obra del Dr. Pedro Vicente Cañete y Domínguez," *Gaceta Numismática* 20: 25–28.

———. 1971. "Notas Históricas Relacionadas con la Casa de Moneda de Lima y Potosí y Observaciónes Referente a Acuñaciones Durante el Reinado de Felipe III," *Gaceta Numismática* 21: 30–33.

———. 1973. "Analysis of Four Spanish-American Coins of the Vice-royalty of Peru (Spanish text)," *Gaceta Numismática* 30: 24–31.

———. 1985. "Los Ensayadores Baltazar Ramos y Agustín de la Quadra de la Casa de Moneda de Potosí," *Cuadernos de Numismática* 12 (46): 21–27.

Friede, Juan. 1963. *Documentos Sobre la Fundación de la Casa de Moneda en Santa Fé de Bogotá (1614–1635) Conservados en el Archivo General de Indias, Sevilla, Transcritos y Anotados.* Bogotá: Publicaciónes del Banco de la Republica.

Gordus, Adon A., and Alan K. Craig. 1995. "Metal Content of Silver and Gold Ingots and Coins from 16th–18th Century Spanish Shipwrecks." In *Material Issues in Art and Archaeology IV, Proceedings of the Materials Research Society, Pittsburgh, Pa.*

Gordus, Adon A., and Jeanne P. Gordus. 1989. "Identification of Potosí Silver Usage in 16th–17th-Century European Coinage Through Gold-Impurity Content of Coins." In *Coinage of the Americas Conference.* New York: American Numismatic Society, 22–42.

Grunthal, Henry, and Ernesto Selschopp. 1978. *The Coinage of Peru.* Frankfurt am Main: Numismatischer Verlag P. N. Schulten.

Hahn, Emily. 1980. "Trove: The Saga of Kip Wagner, the First Modern American to Grow Rich from Ancient Spanish Treasure." In *Love of Gold,* 33–74. New York: Lippincott & Crowell.

Hamilton, Earl J. 1934. *American Treasure and the Price Revolution in Spain, 1501–1650.* New York: Octagon Books.

Hampe, Teodoro Martínez. 1986. "Relación de Salarios de los Altos Funcionarios Indianos," *Historiografía y Bibliografía Americanistas* 30 (1).

Hanke, Lewis. 1956. *The Imperial City of Potosí: An Unwritten Chapter in the History of Spanish America.* The Hague: Martinus Nijhoff.

———. 1958. "Luis Capoche and the History of Potosí, 1545–1585," *Inter-American Economic Affairs* 12 (2): 19–51.
———. 1966. *La "Historia de la Villa Imperial de Potosí" por Bartolomé Arzáns de Orsúa y Vela.* Lima: Universidad Nacional Mayor de San Marcos.
Harris, N. Neil. 1986 "Coins of the *Nuestra Señora de Atocha*," *The Numismatist* (October): 2017–2040.
Helms, Anthony Zacharia. 1806. *Travels from Buenos Ayres, by Potosi to Lima; with Notes by the Translator, Containing Topographical Descriptions of the Spanish Possessions in South America.* London: Printed for Richard Philips, Bridestreet, BlackFriars.
Hudson, Jack C. 1970. "Spanish Colonial Mints and Their Silver Coinage." Unpublished manuscript, on file with Florida Bureau of Archaeological Research, Tallahassee.
Jaimes Araujo, Beatriz L. 1995. "Las Biblioteca de la Casa Nacional de Moneda," *Boletin del Archivo Historico de Potosí* 10: 23–27.
Janson, Hector C. 1985. "El Medio Real Potosino de 1656," *Cuadernos de Numismática* 12 (47/48): 3–12.
Krause, Chester L., Clifford Mishler, and Colin R. Bruce II. 1993. *Standard Catalog of World Coins, 18th Century Edition, 1701–1800.* Iola, Wis.: Krause Publications.
———. 1996. *Standard Catalog of World Coins, 17th Century Edition, 1601–1700.* Iola, Wis.: Krause Publications.
Lane, W. H., & Son. 1974. *The Association Coin: Catalog of Rare Coins and Artifacts Recovered from the Wreck of His Majesty's Ship Association.* N.p.: W. H. Lane & Son.
Lázaro, Jose Luis. 1996. *Los Redondos de Lima, Méjico y Potosí y Otras Acuñaciones Especiales.* Madrid: Dayton S. A.
Lazo García, Carlos. 1992. *Economia Colonial y Regimen Monetario, Peru: Siglos XVI-XIX.* 3 vols. Lima: Banco Central de Reserva del Perú.
Lazo García, Carlos, José Torres Bohl, and Luís Arana Bustamante. 1990. *Las Primeras Acuñaciones de Oro en la Ceca de Lima.* Vol. 9 of *Cuadernos de Historia Numismática.* Lima: Banco Reserva del Perú.
Lost Treasure of King Philip IV, The. 1952. Nassau: The Development Board.
Lyon, Eugene. 1990. "Track of the Manila Galleons," *National Geographic* 178 (3): 5–37.
Machicado, José Vázquez. 1964. *Catálogo de Documentos Referentes a Potosí en el Archivo de Indias de Sevilla.* Potosí: Casa Nacional de Moneda, Editorial "Potosí."
Marrota, Oscar, and Miguel A. Morucci. 1995. *Catalogo de Monedas de Plata Columnarias y de Busto, Ceca de Potosí, 1767–1825.* Buenos Aires: Artes Gráficas MacGar.
Marx, Robert F. 1985. *Shipwrecks in Florida Waters: A Billion-Dollar Graveyard.* Chululota, Fla.: The Mickler House.
McLean, A. Torrey. 1992. "The Case of the Dyslexic Mint Worker," *The Numismatist* 105 (6): 778–782.
———. 1994. "Potosí Cobs: A Coinage in Transition," *The Numismatist* 107 (1): 60–68.

McNickle, A. J. S. 1962. *Spanish Colonial Coins of North America-Mexico Mint: Variations in the Coat-of-Arms as an Aid to Identification.* Mexico: Sociedad Numismática de México.

Medina, José Toribio. 1919a. *Las Monedas Obsidionales Hispano-Americanas,* Santiago de Chile: Imprenta Elzeviriana.

———. 1919b. *Las Monedas Coloniales de Chile.* Santiago de Chile: Imprenta Elzeviriana.

———. 1919c. *Las Monedas Coloniales Hispano-Americanas.* Santiago de Chile: Imprenta Elzeviriana.

Mendieta Pacheco, Wilson. 1988. *Potosí Patrimonio de la Humanidad.* Potosí: Editorial "El Siglo."

———. 1995. *Archivo Historico de Potosí: Catalogo Cajas Reales.* Potosí: Casa Nacional de Moneda, Impreso Editorial "El Siglo."

Mendoza L., Gunnar. 1954. *Guerra Civil Entre Vascongados y Otras Naciones de Potosí.* Potosí: Cuadernos de la Colección de la Cultura Boliviana, Editorial "Potosí."

Menzel, Sewall H. 1989. "La Misteriosa Casa de Moneda Colonial de Panama," *Cuadernos de Numismática* 16 (68):1–10.

———. 1995. *The Potosí Mint Scandal and Great Transition of 1652.* West Palm Beach, Fla.: EN RADA Publications.

———. 1997 "Las Monedas de Medio Real de Potosí—1652," *Gaceta Numismática* 124 (1–97, 4a época): 39–43.

Meylach, Martin, and Charles Whited. 1971. *Diving to a Flash of Gold.* Garden City, N.Y.: Doubleday.

Morris, Roger. 1992. *Atlantic Seafaring.* Auckland: David Bateman Ltd.

Muñoz, Miguel L. 1975. "Historia Numismática del Estado de México." In *Biblioteca Enciclopédica del Estado de México.* Vol. 44. México City.

Murray, Glenn S. 1986. "Potosí and Its Historic Mint," *The Numismatist* 99 (12):2472–2488.

———. 1990. "Exploring the Historic Lima Mint: A Photographic Tour and Chronology of Events," *The Numismatist* 101: 1200–1212.

———. N.d. "Project Segovia '92." Unpublished manuscript in possession of the author.

Nesmith, Robert I. 1946. "The Spanish-Colonial Coinage of Philip II—1556–1598," *Hispano-Americana* (November–December): 168–170. Part 1 (January–February 1947): 13–14; part 2 (November–December): 142–145.

———. 1950. "Castles and Lions on Spanish Colonial Coins: A Study of Details of Design as an Aid to Identification, *The American Numismatic Society Museum Notes* 4: 99–104.

Pearson, Charles E., comp. 1981. *El Nuevo Constante: Investigation of an Eighteenth-Century Spanish Shipwreck off the Louisiana Coast.* Anthropological Study Series No. 4. Baton Rouge: Division of Archaeology, Department of Culture, Recreation and Tourism, Louisiana Archaeological Survey and Antiquities Commission.

Pellicer i Bru, Josep. 1975 *Glosario de Maestros de Ceca y Ensayadores.* Barcelona: Asociación Numismática Española.

Phillips, Carla Rahn. 1986. *Six Galleons for the King of Spain*. Baltimore: Johns Hopkins University Press.

Ponterio & Associates. 1990. "The Paul Karon Potosí Cob Collection." In *Public Auction Catalog of Sale No. 42*. Santa Monica, Calif.

Pradeau, Alberto F. 1938. *Numismatic History of Mexico from the Pre-Columbian Epoch to 1823*. Whittier, Calif.: Western Printing Co.

———. 1975. "Nueva España y México: Ligaciónes Monetarias," *Gaceta Numismática* 38: 38–50.

Purser, William J. [William F. C.]. 1970. "La Plata para las Monedas del Primer Siglo del Virreinato," *Revista Numismática del Perú* 6: 6–15.

———. 1971. *Metal Mining in Peru, Past and Present*. New York: Praeger.

Quesada, Vicente G. 1950. *Crónicas Potosínas*. Potosí: Sociedad Geográfica y de Historia "Potosí."

Reed, Mort. 1962. *Cowles Complete Encyclopedia of U.S. Coins*. New York: Cowles Book Company.

Restrepo, Jorge Emilio, and Joseph R. Lasser. 1998. *Macuquinas de Colombia, 1622–1756*. Medellín: [privately printed].

Rodriguez Lorente, J. J. 1965. *Catalogo de los Reales de a Dos Españoles*. Madrid: Altamira Talleres Graficos, S.A.

Rudolph, William E. 1936. "The Lakes of Potosí," *The Geographical Review* 26 (4): 529–554.

Sebring, Thomas H. 1992. "The Silver Shoals Treasure and the Men Who Found It," *The Numismatist* 105 (5): 641–644; 708–709.

Sedwick, Frank. 1985. *The Practical Book of Cobs*. Maitland, Fla.: [privately printed].

Sedwick, Daniel, and Frank Sedwick. 1995. *The Practical Book of Cobs*. 3d ed. Winter Park, Fla.: [privately printed].

Sellschopp, E. A. 1971a. *Las Acuñaciónes de las Cecas de Lima, La Plata y Potosí*. Barcelona: Asociación Numismática Española.

———. 1971b. "Nuevos Datos para la Diferenciación de Monedas Limeñas y Potosinas bajo el Reinado de Felipe II," *Gaceta Numismática* 32: 29–35.

———. 1972a. "Clasificación de los Reales de a Ocho de la Casa Moneda de Potosí en los Años 1617–1651," *Cuadernos de Numismática*

———. 1972b. "Aplicacion de Documentos en la Numismática," *Cuadernos de Numismática* 1 (4): 1–10.

———. 1973. "El Ensayador y Su Sigla en las Monedas," *Cuadernos de Numismática* tomo 2 (6): 1–4.

———. 1974. "Los Puntos Encima del Valor en las Monedas Macuquinas de Lima, 1684–1751," *Gaceta Numismática* 34: 35–40.

Serrano Mangas, Fernando. 1991. *Naufragios y Rescates en el Trafico Indiana durante el Siglo XVII*. Lima: Seglusa Impresores, S.A.

Skowronek, Russell K. 1984. *Trade Patterns of Eighteenth-Century Frontier New Spain: The 1733 Flota and St. Augustine*. First vol. of *Volumes in Historical Archaeology*, edited by Stanley South. Columbia: University of South Carolina.

Smith, Roger C. 1990. "Marine Archaeology Comes of Age in Florida." In *Underwater Archaeology Proceedings: Society for Historical Archaeology Conference, 1989*, 110–116.

———. 1991. "Florida's Underwater Archaeological Preserves." In *Underwater Archaeology Proceedings: Society for Historical Archaeology Conference, 1991*, 43–46.

———. 1994. "The Ship at Emanuel Point: An Examination of Florida's Earliest Shipwreck." In *Underwater Archaeology Proceedings: Society for Historical Archaeology Conference, 1994*, 14–18.

Superior Galleries. 1984. *1984 Premier Sale, January 30, 31, February 1, 2, 1984.* Beverly Hills, Calif.

Swiss Bank Corporation. 1991. *Collection of Spanish Colonial and Spanish Coins, Auction 27.* Zürich.

Tandeter, Enrique. 1993. *Coercion and Market: Silver Mining in Colonial Potosí, 1692–1826.* Albuquerque: University of New Mexico Press.

Trelles Arestigui, Efrain. 1982. *Lucas Martínez Vegazo: Funcionamiento de una Encomienda Peruana Inicial.* Pontifica Universidad Catolica del Peru. Lima: Talleres Gráficas P. L. Villanueva.

Valda Martínez, Edgar Armando. 1995a. "Los Archivos en la Ciudad de Potosí," *Boletin del Archivo Historico de Potosí* 10: 41–57.

———. 1995b. *El Archivo Historico de Potosí.* Potosí: Casa Nacional de Moneda, Impresso Editorial "El Siglo."

Vargas Ugarte, Ruben. 1955. *Historia del Perú: Virreinato Siglo XVII.* Lima: Libreria Studium, S.A.

Vogt, George W. 1978. *Standard Catalog of Mexican Coins, Paper Money, and Medals.* Edited by Colin R. Bruce. Iola, Wis.: Krause Publications.

Wade, Nicolas. 1981. "Galleon Yields Gold, Silver, and Archaeology," *Science* 212: 1486–1487.

Wagner, Kip, and L. B. Taylor. 1967. *Pieces of Eight, Recovering the Riches of the Lost Spanish Treasure Fleet.* London: Longmans, Green and Co. Ltd.

Walton, Timothy R. 1994. *The Spanish Treasure Fleets.* Sarasota, Fla.: Pineapple Press.

Ward, Christopher. 1993. *Imperial Panama: Commerce and Conflict in Isthmian America, 1550–1800.* Albuquerque: University of New Mexico Press.

Webster, Edwin C. 1993. *The Defense of Porto Bello.* Canal Zone: Panama Canal Press.

Weller, Robert. 1990. *Famous Shipwrecks of the Florida Keys.* Vol. 1. Birmingham: EBSCO Media.

———. 1993. *Sunken Treasure on Florida Reefs.* West Palm Beach, Fla.: Florida Treasure Brokers.

Weller, Robert, and Ernie Richards. 1996. *Shipwrecks Near Wabasso Beach.* West Palm Beach, Fla.: EN RADA Publications.

Index

Alan K. Craig is a recently retired professor of geography at Florida Atlantic University. His specialties include numismatics, mining, geomorphology, and the paleoecology of maritime environments.